DENNIS KAVANAGH is Professor of Politics at the University of Liverpool and before then he was Professor of Politics at the University of Nottingham. He has written over twenty books on British politics and is co-author with David Butler of the Nuffield studies of British General elections since 1970.

DR ANTHONY SELDON is headmaster of Brighton College and both co-founder (with Peter Hennessy) and first director of the Institute of Contemporary British History. He is the authorised biographer of John Major and the author or editor of several books on recent history including *Conservative Century* (1994), *How Tory Governments Fall* (1996), *Inside Number Ten* (1999) and *The Foreign Office* (2000).

More from the reviews:

'Most entertaining' ROY HATTERSLEY, *Independent*

'An informative and useful guide to who does what in Number Ten'
PAUL ROUTLEDGE, *Spectator*

'Detailed and careful . . . unusual and interesting.'
GEORGE WEDD, *Contemporary Review*

'This book shows that there is nothing new about overweening Prime Ministers or their battles to subdue the Whitehall machine. Ministers and Mandarins might pick up a few tricks about the hidden influence of Number Ten on governments. They might also draw some salutary lessons from realising that neither Prime Ministers nor their political henchmen nor wily civil servants ever seem to achieve ascendancy over each other for long. *The Powers Behind the Prime Minister* is office politics writ large. By rights its accounts of the real life doings of some civil servants, some long dead, and its diagrams of who sits where in the office next to the Cabinet room should make dull reading. Yet it rattles along like some great pageant on the theme of *Yes, Minister*. Here is Lord Melbourne worrying about church appointments and crying: "Damn! Another bishop dead." There is Lloyd George building a temporary village – a veritable garden suburb – at the back of Number Ten to house his retinue of personal policy advisers. With him is his chief adviser busily leaking to the press and talking even in 1917 of "doctoring" information. Spool on and there is Edward Heath glowering at top civil servant Burke Trend who has organised a Commonwealth summit bang in the middle of the yachting season. And here comes Robert Armstrong, smoothest of the mandarins, with his elegant little joke about being economical with the truth. Right now he is ordering a car so that he can beat Harold Wilson and his entourage back to Number Ten. Wilson's political aides are plotting against him and he is stealing a march on them by being the first to greet the new Prime Minister at Downing Street. Fast forward to the 1990s and we have "Bonaparte" Blair importing over 20 political aides into Number Ten – more than ever before. A group of Cabinet Ministers complains that staff in the Number Ten policy unit are "Tony's narks in Whitehall". Mr Blair himself is busily focussing on the big picture, ignoring details. "Yes and potentially fatally so" murmurs a mandarin . . . What this book shows is that the influence of the various groups operating inside Number Ten – policy unit, press office, Prime Minister's Office – depends very much on personalities. As the people alter so the power of each section waxes or wanes. Kavanagh and Seldon must be right.'

SUE CAMERON, *Sunday Telegraph*

'The book's value lies in what it has to say about the leadership styles of different Prime Ministers. An interesting comparison is drawn, for example, between PMs who are considered "path-finders" – Heath, Thatcher, Blair – and "stabilisers" – Wilson, Callaghan, Major . . . and worthy material on the Ministerial tensions that existed during the Thatcher era which serves as a useful reminder of the way we were.'

STEPHEN MCGREGOR, *Glasgow Herald*

'A remarkable work of political analysis which gives an increased understanding of the realities of government and of democracy in practice. The authors use previously undisclosed material to paint a fascinating picture of what really has been going on within Number Ten during its occupancy by six different Prime Ministers over the past thirty years.'   MARK NICHOLLS, *Aberdeen Press & Journal*

'An important study and a valuable contribution to our knowledge of modern politics.'   DESMOND MCCARTAN, *Belfast Telegraph*

'One of the best pieces of political analysis and a must for *Yes Minister* fans and serious commentators alike, this perceptive view inside 10 Downing Street is an eye-opening look at democracy in practice.'
Eastern Daily Press

'Fascinating . . . it paints the clearest possible picture of the last six Prime Ministers.'   *Crossbow*

'A memorable, scholarly work of descriptive exposition . . . this is welcome indeed, shedding light as it does on an under-researched and important area.'   GARRETT O'BOYLE, *Sunday Business Post*

'The demystifying of Number Ten is part of the new politics aimed at opening up the way British government works. This excellent book takes us a good deal further. They chronicle and chart the occupants of Number Ten over the past century with excellent diagrams about the geographical distribution of power inside the building. Their book is to the top officials who serve the prime minister what Namier's work was to the MPs in the eighteenth-century Commons.'
DENNIS MACSHANE, *The Stateholder*

THE POWERS
BEHIND
THE PRIME MINISTER

The Hidden Influence
of Number Ten

DENNIS KAVANAGH
and
ANTHONY SELDON

HarperCollins*Publishers*

HarperCollins*Publishers*
77–85 Fulham Palace Road,
Hammersmith, London W6 8JB

www.**fire**and**water**.com

This paperback edition 2000
3 5 7 9 8 6 4

First published in Great Britain by
HarperCollins*Publishers* 1999

ISBN 0 00 653143 1

Set in PostScript Linotype Plantin Light and Photina Display by
Rowland Phototypesetting Ltd
Bury St Edmunds, Suffolk

Printed and bound in Great Britain by
Clays Ltd, St Ives plc

CONTENTS

LIST OF ILLUSTRATIONS

Margaret Thatcher (© *Hulton Getty*).

Margaret and Denis Thatcher, 1987 (© *Popperfoto*).

Mrs Thatcher poses with her Cabinet, May 1989 (© *Topham Picturepoint*).

Mrs Thatcher and Bernard Ingham (© *Rex Features*).

Margaret Thatcher in London in March 1990 with Charles Powell (© *PA News*).

Margaret Thatcher leaves Number 10 Downing Street, 28 November 1990 (© *PA News*).

John Major, 27 November 1990 (© *Topham Picturepoint*).

John Major's Cabinet, 28 July 1994 (© *PA News*).

Jonathan Hill (© *Universal*).

Sarah Hogg, Head of the Policy Unit from 1990 to 1996 (© *Gemma Levine, Camera Press*).

Judith Chaplin, Political Secretary from 1990 to 1992 (© *Universal*).

Prime Minister John Major and his wife Norma wave to crowds on the night of the 1992 election victory (© *PA News*).

The launch of Labour's 1997 Manifesto with the Shadow Cabinet team (© *Richard Open/Camera Press*).

Blair's new Cabinet meet at Number 10 for the first time, 8 May 1997 (© *PA News*).

Blair meets Clinton at the White House (© *Peter Marlow/Magnum*).

Blair in close conversation with Alastair Campbell (© *Peter Marlow/Magnum*).

PREFACE

The nature of the Prime Minister's job has not changed fundamentally since the days of Walpole (1721–42), regarded as Britain's first premier. New roles have appeared, such as leader of his political party in the mid-nineteenth century, while other roles have declined relatively, including the importance of the relations with the monarch and the patronage role. But the complexity of the job, and the speed of response demanded, *have* changed out of all recognition. In 1806–7, Lord Grenville received sixty letters a week; by 1970–74, for Edward Heath, this number had risen to three hundred in an average week; by 1999, Tony Blair received 7,500 letters a week marked 'Prime Minister' – over a thousand letters a day. In addition to this postbag, written messages, phone calls, e-mails and other electronic communications bombard Number Ten Downing Street. There are daily demands for a position or a statement from the Prime Minister on many subjects, the details of which he will often have but a hazy picture.

How does the Prime Minister manage? He has no more hours in the day or weeks in the year than Walpole had 280 years ago. How does he decide what communications he should see? Which people should he see of the many besieging Number Ten with demands for urgent meetings? How does he decide what speeches to give, how to respond to demands for decisions, how to lead the discussion in meetings and what conclusions he should arrive at, or how to respond when a visiting head of government or minister calls on him?

The simple answer is that he or she does not personally decide most of these questions at all. Forty years ago, Charles Petrie wrote a book, *The Powers Behind the Prime Ministers*, in which he showed that Prime Ministers from William Gladstone to Stanley Baldwin relied on an official who often became much more important than a mere confidential aide. The position has now changed again. No longer does the premier rely on just one or two key figures for advice: the prime ministership is now an office. In the same way that Francis Bacon in the seventeenth century might claim to have read all printed books, so Prime Ministers in the eighteenth and nineteenth centuries, up to Lord Salisbury at the start of the twentieth century, could see and read all relevant items and make up their own minds on all key matters. The First World War and Lloyd George changed all that. From then onwards – and the expansion of the Number Ten Private Office staffed by career civil servants mirrors the change – the premiership in Britain began to become a collective. Aides increasingly took decisions for the Prime Minister, deciding who and what he should see and what he should say. There was nothing sinister in all this: it was inevitable. The Second World War and the expansion in the size of the state saw further growth in the size and scope of the Number Ten Private Office, a trend heightened since the 1960s by Britain joining the EEC in 1973, Northern Ireland, and by the proliferation of the media and their demand for instant responses from the Prime Minister.

Number Ten thus resembles the studio of a great Baroque artist, say Rubens. The finished product bears the master's name, but much of the painting, especially the routine work, was not executed by him. But it is all executed in the style and the name of the master. The great trick of the modern premiership is that Number Ten has to act seamlessly as if everyone important in it *is* the Prime Minister. This lays great stress on the picking of staff, sufficiently intelligent to advise or act for the master but also sufficiently self-effacing to subdue their own distinctive preferences.

Some critics of British government complain that there is a 'hole in the middle' in Number Ten and that the Prime Minister needs a stronger system of support to provide strategic direction to the rest of Whitehall. The same 'hole' might be said of our knowledge of what goes on in the Prime Minister's office, the Number Ten village. Little is known of the people who work there, how they go about their work and how this has changed in recent years. We have written this book in an attempt to shed light on the work of this village.

We have incurred many debts in this study. First of all we are grateful to over 150 former and present staff in Number Ten who agreed to grant us interviews, some several times. Some of the interviews were off the record, but a number were not. We met only three refusals, from a Principal Private Secretary, a head of the Policy Unit and a Political Secretary to a Prime Minister. Many also kindly agreed to read early versions of our manuscript and, as usual, must remain anonymous. Vernon Bogdanor, Peter Riddell and Rod Rhodes helpfully commented on earlier versions of the manuscript. We are also grateful to Annemarie Weitzel who typed successive versions of the manuscript with her customary speed and skill. Dennis Kavanagh would like to thank Marian Hoffmann and Michelle Harvey at the University of Liverpool for secretarial help. Anthony Seldon would like to thank Mary Anne Brightwell, Lauren Heather and Josie Buckwell at Brighton College. Lewis Baston provided research support for Chapter Two. We are also grateful for help under grant L124261002 from the Economic and Research Council's *Whitehall Programme*.

PREFACE TO THE SECOND EDITION

The Constrained Premiership

In 1973, Arthur Schlesigner Jr. published the highly acclaimed *The Imperial Presidency* in which he argued that the powers of the American presidency had grown to such an extent that the office had acquired almost imperial powers. The following year came Richard Nixon's resignation in the wake of the Watergate scandal. Gerald Ford and Jimmy Carter – two relatively weak Presidents – followed before the presidency began to recover under Ronald Reagan.

In the late 1980s the political talk in Britain, with Mrs Thatcher in her prime, was of the over-powerful Premier. Had the constitution become lopsided, and did it need redressing to counter-balance an over-powerful Chief Executive? Then came Mrs Thatcher's humiliating fall and the seven years of John Major. With Tony Blair's arrival at Number Ten in May 1997, and his seemingly unstoppable sway, the debate turned to the over-powerful Presidency. Peter Hennessy, the Hercule Poirot of Whitehall studies, published *The Prime Minister* in 2000, just as Blair's apparently unassailable power was beginning to crumble. Hennessy tells a story of increasing Prime Ministerial power at the expense of Cabinet, Parliament and other key players, including ministers and other stakeholders. The burgeoning size of Number Ten has permitted this accretion of power, which Blair shares in Downing Street, to some extent, with Gordon Brown. In time, Hennessy's book may be seen as the British equivalent to *The Imperial Presidency*.

In the first edition of *The Powers Behind the Prime Minister*, we took a different line to most commentators. It was Prime Ministerial weakness that we saw, rather than Prime Ministerial power, excessive or otherwise. We argued that Prime Ministerial pro-activity was the exception rather than the rule and that the Prime Minister has been dominant only for a minority of the time. The forces bearing on him, including almost impossibly high expectations and his limited powers of command have meant that he has been the victim of events more often than their shaper. Whenever the Prime Minister has been in control, as perhaps in 1945–47, 1951–53, 1957–61, 1966–67, 1970–71, 1982–86, 1987–88, 1990–92 and 1997–2000, it has often been fragile.

Since 1945 the powers of successive Prime Ministers have probably shrunk. Britain's loss of Empire and decline in relative international standing, the government's diminished control over the economy and utilities (in the wake of privatisation) and 'the hollowing out' of the state because of the loss of powers to the EU and the Scottish parliament have reduced the standing of the Prime Minister outside the Westminster village.

The interplay of four factors have determined whether or not the Prime Minister is able to dominate: operating in the same direction as the climate of ideas; overwhelmingly favourable circumstances and the avoidance of destabilising events; support from the powerful interests of the day – media, financial, industrial, academic; and finally individuals within the Prime Minister's camp being able and collegiate and not overwhelmingly powerful outside it.

It came as no surprise, therefore, that Tony Blair, even with his great advantages of a landslide victory, overwhelmingly supportive media, a united party and favourable economy and positive economic outlook would encounter severe problems before long. Once the initiative has been lost, as Churchill found after 1953, Heath after 1971–2, and Major after 1992, it is very hard to regain it.

The book argues that even the 'collective premiership' which emerged in the post-war period, and the significant expansion in the staffing of Number Ten, were insufficient to compensate for the difficulties and shortcomings inherent in the Prime Minister's position. In spite of Blair's efforts to make his Number Ten more powerful and better resourced than it has ever been, he has expressed his impatience and frustration wih the obstacles he has found. Indeed, we argue that his 'power grabs' were 'a reaction to felt weakness, a frustration with the inability to pull effective levers'. But in contrast to most comparable heads of government, the size of the Prime Minister's Office and the Cabinet Office combined are notably small, especially for a country the size of Great Britain. Even the moving of Number Ten to modern, spacious offices (which we advocate) and a huge further increase in staffing towards the scale of the office of the Prime Minister in such Commonwealth Parliamentary systems as Canada, Australia and New Zealand would not have been sufficient in themselves to create a commanding chief executive, although it would go some way towards it. Our conclusion is thus that Britain has an under-powered, rather than an over-powerful premiership.

DAK
AS
October 2000

The Missing Link

NUMBER TEN DOWNING STREET is the most powerful office in British politics. Yet it is also the least written about of any of the great departments of state, and the least understood.[1] What goes on behind the shiny black-painted door remains a mystery to followers of politics as much as to the casual observer of the British political scene. In contrast, the literature on the power of the Prime Minister himself, and on the question of whether or not the office has become 'presidential', is both vast and inconclusive. Ferdinand Mount, an acute commentator who has had experience of working in Number Ten under Mrs Thatcher, is not alone in his complaint about our sketchy knowledge of 'how the office actually operates, what staff are at its disposal, how its commands are issued'.[2] Cabinet is known to meet at Number Ten, and most Prime Ministers have lived there. But who are the smartly-suited men and women who ply their way along Downing Street before being swallowed up behind the door? How much influence do they have? Even the policeman standing outside has an inscrutable air about him.

The operation and effectiveness of Number Ten interested both of us from earlier work. Individually, we have written books on Prime Ministers and their influence, and together we have edited books assessing the influence on policy of the governments of Margaret Thatcher and John Major. The lack of information about the office of the Prime Minister struck us increasingly; the paradox of the intensity of study into other, less influential aspects of the British body politic and the almost complete dearth of material on Number Ten is remarkable. Hence this joint effort.

Number Ten adjoins Numbers Eleven and Twelve, respectively

the residences of the Chancellor of the Exchequer and the Chief Whip. On the right as you travel up Downing Street from Whitehall is the Cabinet Office, and on the left, the Foreign and Commonwealth Office. Here, in Downing Street, is the engine room of British politics and government, crowned by Number Ten itself. From the outside, however, the building's modest appearance hardly makes it look like a seat of government; inside, it seems more like a stately home than a headquarters. Douglas Hurd noted in 1979: 'It is hard to imagine anyone governing anything substantial from Number Ten.'[3] Twenty years later a member of Tony Blair's Policy Unit thought the atmosphere was 'too genteel and peaceful, the place too compartmentalised'.[4] He had recently come from working in the open plan of the Labour Party's media centre in Millbank, a far more high-tech, sophisticated building.

This book opens the door on the hidden world of Number Ten, part museum, part powerhouse. It throws the spotlight on the men and women who work there. It examines the various units serving the Prime Minister and shows the fluidity of their roles. It takes the reader through the six premierships from Edward Heath's (1970–74) to Tony Blair's, describes how each Prime Minister liked to organise his or her work and to use his or her staff, and examines whom they relied on most, and why. It takes the reader through each important room and corridor in the building, and reveals how physical proximity to the Prime Minister usually results in enhanced influence, which in turn explains why battles are so keen over who occupies which office space.

The Powers Behind the Prime Minister tackles one core feature of the job of Prime Minister: how the incumbent is helped in carrying out his or her job. A British Prime Minister has both an official role which relates to government, and a political role which relates to his party and to elections. The staff in Number Ten who help him to carry out these tasks are either political, who come and go with the incumbent, or official, who are career civil servants.

The Prime Minister's personal support has often occasioned strong feelings. Ever since Lloyd George in 1916 created the Cabinet Secretariat and a 'Garden Suburb' of personal advisers, efforts to build up staff support, separate from the Civil Service, have met powerful opposition from colleagues, civil servants and the official opposition. Indeed the reaction to Lloyd George was so hostile that it seemed doubtful whether either body would survive his downfall in 1922; in the end the Secretariat was greatly reduced and the 'Suburb' abolished. There was controversy again over the role of Lord Cherwell's Statistical Section, which Churchill established in 1940. Labour's Foreign Secretary George Brown in 1968 and the Conservative Chancellor of the Exchequer Nigel Lawson in 1989 both resigned, claiming that they were being undermined by the Prime Minister's personal advisers. Some have argued that the influence of a 'kitchen cabinet' or an *éminence grise* undermines the role of the Cabinet and verges on the unconstitutional.

Few biographies or autobiographies of Prime Ministers give more than a dutiful and perfunctory nod in the direction of their advisers or say much about how their office operated. In his thousand-page memoir of his 1964–70 government Harold Wilson makes no mention of his Political Secretary Marcia Williams, his economic adviser Tom Balogh, or either of his Press Secretaries.[5] Ted Heath gives only two references to Sir William Armstrong, dubbed at the time 'Deputy Prime Minister' in Heath's 1974 government. Wilson's is an extreme but not atypical case. Many helpers have shared the Prime Minister's view that the place for backroom boys is in the back room – on which our book sheds some light.

To set the operations of Number Ten in context, Chapter One describes the internal geography of the place and the location and remits of the people who work there. Chapter Two provides the historical background up to 1970 by showing how Prime Ministers from W.E. Gladstone to David Lloyd George, Winston Churchill and Harold Wilson all added to Number Ten as a political office, each leaving their individual stamp. But the office has probably changed more in the thirty years since 1970 than it did in the two centuries leading up to that year. In 1970, information still arrived at Number Ten via couriers in the form of letters, telegrams or typed minutes. Now, at the end of the century much information flows to and within the building electronically. In 1970, the public could wander up to the front door. In 1999, access to the entire street is heavily restricted by iron gates and ramps, and the building has been physically strengthened to withstand armed attack.

In 1970, the building still had a calm, unhurried air. Harold Wilson had a senior staff of only ten or fewer aides, two or three of whom were political appointees. By the end of the century the building buzzed night and day with a steady flow of staff and visitors, and the building was populated by more than forty senior prime ministerial aides, over half of them political appointees.

The succeeding chapters of the book examine the transitions and performances of different Prime Ministers since 1970 and address the following questions.

- Has the Number Ten staff been sufficiently large and well-informed to allow the Prime Minister to optimise his or her potential?
- How have Number Ten officials balanced loyalty to the Prime Minister with respect for Civil Service values and traditions?
- How far have Prime Ministers been able to control the agenda, and to be proactive, in line with their initial ideas and ambitions?
- How have different Prime Ministers managed the media? Is one style more effective than others?
- Are those with most influence in Downing Street those with the 'biggest' jobs, or is influence more a question of personal relationship and chemistry?
- How has each Prime Minister organised his or her day or had it organised for him/her?
- How, and how far, does each new prime ministerial team learn about how Number Ten operated under previous incumbents?
- How has Number Ten reacted to 'new' offices, for example the Policy Unit or the CPRS?
- How have Number Ten and the Cabinet Office adapted to the changed foreign policy role of Britain between 1970 and 2000, and especially to entry into the European Community in 1973?
- Most important of all – has Number Ten mitigated, or contributed to, the fact that most premierships since 1970 have either ended in tears or been characterised by an inability to control the agenda?

The authors' answers to these questions will be found in the final chapter.

A warning. This book views the political world almost exclusively from Number Ten. It is not a comprehensive portrait of life at the apex of British government, but a view from one, neglected, part of the apex. Such a perspective has its limits – it does not discuss at length the Cabinet Office, which is an indispensable appendage of Number Ten; nor does it consider the impact in the Whitehall departments of decisions in and messages from Number Ten; and it has little on the Whip's Office or on the processes of policy formulation or policy implementation. These are areas that have been much better written about by others in many studies over the last thirty years. Our task is to take a much closer look at the missing link.

CHAPTER ONE

The Geography of Influence

THE BLACK FRONT DOOR to the house at Number Ten Downing Street, originally modelled in the 1770s with its brass letter box bearing the name 'First Lord of the Treasury', was replaced recently by a metal bomb-proof door which opens into the large tiled hall. But it is at the other end of a long, narrow corridor that power lies. Crossing through an inner hall, still part of the original building constructed by George Downing in the 1680s, one walks along an interconnecting corridor until one reaches a large internal lobby, or Cabinet Ante-Room. This is the grander seventeenth-century building joined to George Downing's building in the 1730s for the first so-called Prime Minister, Sir Robert Walpole (see diagram overleaf).

Here is the heart of power in the British state. Straight ahead lies the Cabinet Room, utterly dominated by the large coffin-shaped Cabinet table. In here, Cabinet meets every Thursday during the political year, key Cabinet committees meet, and some Prime Ministers have chosen to work (including James Callaghan periodically, and John Major for all but his first few months).

Proximity to this fount of influence is critical. The closer anyone can be to this room, the more influence he or she is likely to have. All eyes are on the Prime Minister. Even though some premiers in our period have chosen to work in the first-floor study, up the elegant staircase lined with the portraits of past premiers, they frequently cross through the lobby.

Until 1997 the inner private secretaries' room, as it was known, had been colonised, as an indication of their closeness to the centre, by the Civil Service, as had the larger rectangular-shaped outer room

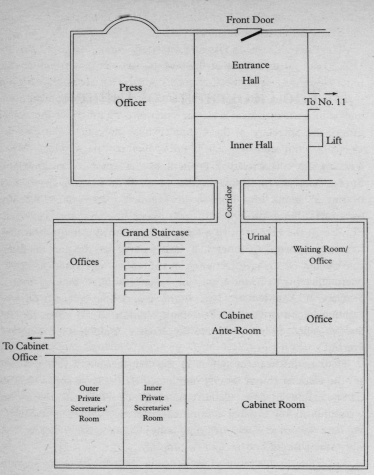

Front Door

Entrance Hall

Press Officer

To No. 11

Inner Hall

Lift

Corridor

Grand Staircase

Urinal

Offices

Waiting Room/ Office

Cabinet Ante-Room

Office

To Cabinet Office

Outer Private Secretaries' Room

Inner Private Secretaries' Room

Cabinet Room

Number Ten c.1970

that shares the same north-facing aspect. In these two rooms, the most consistently influential advisers to the premier have worked night and day, 365 days of the year. A duty clerk is present at night, and during weekends and holidays. Every day a vast range of diverse matters is brought to Number Ten's attention often by ministers and their departments either by electronic means, correspondence or telephone.

These are handled by the private secretaries, and they have to know the Prime Minister's mind.

The Prime Minister's Principal Private Secretary heads the Private Office, and sat until 1997 at the desk by the window in the smaller inner room nearest to the Cabinet Room. He (it always has been a male) is one of the 'inner circle' of guardians of the British Constitution and is in frequent touch with the other two members of that small group: the Secretary to the Cabinet whose domain is through the interconnecting door between Number Ten and the Cabinet Office, and the Queen's Private Secretary, who is based in Buckingham Palace. When a new Prime Minister enters Number Ten, the first two people he spends time with are the Principal Private Secretary and the Secretary to the Cabinet.

The Prime Minister's Principal Private Secretary might be junior in rank (he is usually promoted to Deputy Secretary while in the post) to Whitehall's other top officials, including the Permanent Under-Secretaries of the four key Civil Service departments, Treasury, Foreign and Commonwealth Office, Home Office and Defence; but through his proximity to the Prime Minister, his control of information and his awareness of the total picture, he may well have more influence on the outcome of decisions, on policy and on appointments, depending on the qualities of the particular incumbent. The position was rarely more influential than under Robert Armstrong (1970–75), Kenneth Stowe (1975–79) and Robin Butler (1982–85) or, before our period, under Jock Colville (1951–55). As one incumbent said: 'it is the best job in Whitehall'.[1] The less energetic the Prime Minister (as with Churchill, post-stroke, during 1953–55 or Harold Wilson 1974–76), or the greater the strain on the premier (as in 1973–74 or 1978–79) and the closer the personal bond, the greater will be the Principal Private Secretary's influence.

The Principal Private Secretary and the other civil servants in the Number Ten Private Office are seconded from Whitehall departments and normally serve in the office for some three years before returning to their previous departments. There is thus in Britain no especial Prime Minister's *corps*: the thinking is that they work at Number Ten for sufficient time to gain a unique perspective without becoming overly identified with the Prime Minister personally or, dread idea, politically, which could compromise their future relations with other ministers and departments in their subsequent careers. Churchill's Principal Private Secretary, John Colville, Macmillan's Philip de Zulueta (1959–64), and Thatcher's Foreign Affairs Secretary, Charles Powell (1984–90) were regarded as being 'spoiled' by too close an identification with their Prime Minister and did not return to the Civil Service on leaving Number Ten. Thus the ideals of objectivity and transience have not always been realised although the intention has always been that they should. Since 1970 the pressure has been arguably even greater on the Press Secretary, the Prime Minister's mouthpiece to the world. Not all have managed, like Donald Maitland (who served Heath), Tom McCaffrey (under Callaghan) and Gus O'Donnell and Chris Meyer (under Major), successfully to resume a Civil Service career after leaving Number Ten.

The Principal Private Secretary co-ordinates information to the Prime Minister and oversees the preparation of his boxes, which keep him constantly up-to-date (or bogged down) with paperwork. Papers go into a number of different named trays or coloured folders, entitled for much of our period 'Immediate', 'Weekend', 'Reading' and 'Signature'. Along with the Foreign Affairs Secretary, the Principal Private Secretary has the key to the 'top secret' folder, sometimes called the 'hot box' until Blair, into which goes information dealing with intelligence, security and other highly confidential matters. Honours and appointments are similarly delicate subjects which the Principal Private Secretary handles.

If the Principal Private Secretary is often seconded from the Treasury[2] (not inappropriately, given the Prime Minister's title of First Lord of the Treasury and the Treasury's responsibility for budgets and economic policy), the other most powerful department in Whitehall, the Foreign and Commonwealth Office (FCO), has its man in the second most important Private Office job at Number Ten. Thus do the two most powerful departments ensure that they have deep roots into the seat of power. The Foreign Affairs Private Secretary too had (until 1997) a desk in the inner private secretaries' room, further away from the Cabinet Room and by the wall facing the Ante-Room. Usually officials of 'Counsellor' rank or higher, the incumbents are high fliers in their early forties who can look forward to an ambassa-

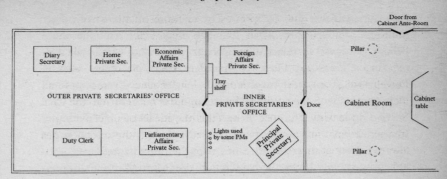

Number Ten under John Major

dor's post as their promotion after a successful tour of duty at Number Ten: several have finished their careers at the head of the FCO.[3] Their task is not just to act as the bridge to the FCO on foreign affairs but also to keep the Prime Minister informed on defence and Northern Ireland matters.

The job has expanded in scope considerably over the last thirty years, following British membership of the European Community in January 1973 and the outbreak of the troubles in Northern Ireland in the late 1960s. The job has gained considerable profile from the influence wielded by one particular and long-serving incumbent, Charles Powell (1984–91): Powell acquired executive powers and privileges, some of which were originally outside the foreign affairs desk, of which his successors were the beneficiaries. By the 1990s, indeed, the Foreign Affairs Private Secretary had become akin to the US President's key National Security Adviser, dealing directly with foreign heads of government and their senior aides rather than, to the annoyance of the FCO mandarins, conducting business through them and the ambassadors on the spot. So large did this job become that by 1994 an Assistant Foreign Affairs Secretary was appointed to help share the burden.

The door into the outer private secretaries' room is often kept open. Inside are five desks (see diagram above). The most senior of these private secretaries oversees economic affairs, a Treasury posting which gives this key economic department a further lever in Number

Ten. The job was created in 1975 by splitting off the more purely economic matters from other domestic issues (for example social policy). The post is of Assistant Secretary rank, and usually taken by a younger Treasury high flier, typically aged in his or her early to mid-thirties. In 1992, the first woman, Mary Francis, was appointed to this post. (She later became the first female to be a Private Secretary to the Queen and then moved into the private sector.) Of the other two private secretaries, one manages non-economic home policy issues and the other focuses on the Prime Minister's parliamentary role, a key responsibility being the handling of Prime Minister's Questions.

The remaining two desks are normally filled by the Diary Secretary and the Duty Clerk. The former, a junior civil servant until 1979 when Mrs Thatcher made it a political appointment, is responsible for keeping the Prime Minister's diary, dealing with the Prime Minister's correspondence, overseeing travel arrangements and the smooth running of engagements. Given the pressure on the Prime Minister's time, and the clamour for access to him or her, the post is a crucial one. While the job was conceived as clerical, in practice and particularly since the appointment became political, the Diary Secretary has come to accumulate considerable potential authority, balancing the complicated demands and pressures on the Prime Minister's time. Tony Blair's Diary Secretary, Kate Garvey, is situated close to his office, deliberately to guard his door and keep the diary running to time. The diary itself is a conventional desk diary with a separate page for each day. The Prime Minister's activities and appointments for the day are widely distributed to Number Ten staff, including security officers, police and staff who man the front door.

The final desk is filled by a duty clerk, who rotates throughout the day and night and acts as bridge to the other duty clerks in a section downstairs called 'Confidential Filing', which holds the Number Ten files. He or she is also a round-the-clock link between the outside world and the Prime Minister. One of the private secretaries will also be on site, or on call, throughout the year. If the Prime Minister is away, and the Private Secretary 'on call' has gone home, the most senior figure manning the Prime Minister's office will be a duty clerk, though the Private Secretary on duty will be just a phone call away. When a major news story comes into Number Ten at night or in a holiday period, the duty clerk has to decide, in consultation with the Private Secretary on call, whether the Prime Minister should be disturbed.

The working conditions are astonishingly cramped. But the open plan nature of the office, which might appear distracting with telephones ringing and many comings and goings, has its uses: 'it allowed us all to know what was going on in other areas. Working in Number Ten required a certain ability to work calmly, flexibly and under great pressure: a special camaraderie existed between us all.'[4] Although not everyone in the private office sees what the Principal Private Secretary sees, it is common for the private secretaries to overhear conversations and to read notes to and from their colleagues. Indeed, such a ready flow of information is important if the Private Office is to act as a co-ordinated unit serving the Prime Minister.

Tony Blair has made the most significant changes of any premier since 1970 to the working of the Private Office. Over Easter 1998 he moved his own base into the inner private secretaries' room, pushing the incumbents into the outer office, and some of the outer office incumbents out into the rest of Number Ten. More significantly, he has reorganised staffing. Jonathan Powell, a former FCO diplomat (and brother of Charles) was brought in as a political appointee with the title Chief of Staff, in effect usurping some of the traditional role of Principal Private Secretary. This latter post continued with the same name, and with the incumbent John Holmes keeping the work he had handled as Foreign Affairs Private Secretary before his promotion, while in 1998 a new Economic Private Secretary, Jeremy Heywood, was given the task of co-ordinating domestic policy submissions for the Prime Minister. Heywood became Principal Private Secretary in 1999.

Private secretaries require a mix of outstanding intellectual ability, stamina and urbanity. They represent the Prime Minister to Cabinet ministers, other senior figures in Whitehall, foreign governments and the world outside. Recruitment to these high-powered and high-prestige jobs is surprisingly informal. When a vacancy is due to arise the Principal Private Secretary writes to relevant Permanent Secretaries inviting them to submit the names of likely candidates. Those short-listed will usually be interviewed by the Principal Private Secretary (under Blair by Jonathan Powell), the incumbent and sometimes by the Prime Minister. There is no formal provision for the involvement of Number Ten's political staff (it is after all a Civil Service appointment), although those who have had dealings with a candidate in the past may offer comment. The choice of the Principal Private Secretary is more personal to the Prime Minister and he may interview or chat with candidates suggested by the Cabinet Secretary. A Prime Minister may well appoint somebody he has known or worked with before, as Chamberlain did with Arthur Rucker (1939), Wilson did with Michael Halls (1966), and Major did with Alex Allan (1992). The same personal interest is also shown in appointing the Foreign Affairs Private Secretary. John Major interviewed three candidates before appointing John Holmes in 1996, and Blair saw two before appointing John Sawers in February 1999.

The Private Office is thus the lynchpin around which Number Ten and the Prime Minister function. Several Prime Ministers have arrived suspicious of their Private Offices, such as Churchill in 1951, Harold Wilson in 1964 and Mrs Thatcher in 1979, but left office enamoured of them. The private secretaries sift all paperwork coming to the Prime Minister in their relevant areas, deciding what he should see and not see and what should be passed on to the Cabinet Office, the Political Office or the Policy Unit. They offer him advice on how to handle the material, brief him before meetings, propose whom he should see, draft his speeches and letters, lobby for his cause with the Private Offices of Cabinet ministers and other key individuals, prepare him for Parliament, Cabinet, committees, the media (in association with the Press Secretary) and overseas trips. One of them also attends nearly all the Prime Minister's meetings, taking careful note of what is said, listens in to his or her phone calls on government matters and, since Harold Macmillan (1957–63), attends all Cabinet meetings and key Cabinet committees. A Private Secretary's notes of a meeting or telephone conversation between the Prime Minister and a minister are sent to the Private Office of the other minister. These constitute a record of what was said and, if appropriate, of points for action.

The Prime Minister cannot help being aware of only a fraction of what is going on in his own government or the country at large, let alone in the world beyond Britain. The private secretaries are the key instruments filtering the world and making it manageable for him or her. To do the job well, they have to know how the Prime Minister would react to a proposal or reply to a letter; in this sense we have a collective premiership.

The private secretaries find that a strong constitution and a high sense of professionalism help them to survive the punishing hours on the job. Whitehall has its own reasons, as discussed, for rotating private secretaries but Civil Service concerns come second. One former Private Secretary told us 'My job at the end of the day was to help the Prime Minister. This could create difficulties with other departments, but that was my duty as I saw it. Of course, I had to ensure that Mrs Thatcher was aware of the department's views also.'[5] Another reason is that such a regime over too long a period is exhausting. One Private Secretary agrees, 'Of course you see little of your family. Your wife has to be understanding. You can watch or listen to the news and any item can affect your work in Number Ten the next day. The job can take over your life.'[6] The growing volume of paper to be digested, helped or not by new technology, has increased the workload. The norm is twelve or more hours a day in the week and one weekend in four on duty. Grades and titles disappear under the forces of collegiality, the need for flexibility and speedy action, and the companionship that emerges between the Prime Minister and his Private Office. As one former Private Secretary remarked, 'You have to respect the Prime Minister, otherwise you could not put in the long hours.'[7] Another affirmed, 'An organisation chart or assignment of fixed spheres of responsibility could not properly describe how we work.'[8]

From the 1920s (the decade in which the Civil Service ensured that only civil servants would staff the Private Office) the Principal Private Secretary was initially undisputed master of Number Ten.[9] But since then, he has had to share some of the influence and access to the Prime Minister with other players, none more consistently influential than the Cabinet Secretary.

There are of course many permanent staff – duty clerks and a number of other officials elsewhere in Number Ten – who are not on secondment and who commonly serve for many years in sections on honours, records and correspondence, in what is now called the Direct Communications section. There are also the 'Garden Room Girls' who are the secretariat to the Prime Minister and the Private Office and who operate on the lower ground floor room beneath the Cabinet Room. When the Prime Minister travels around Britain, he will commonly be accompanied by a Private Secretary, a Garden Room Girl and his Press Secretary or somebody from the Press Office. When he goes abroad he will take a larger but similarly composed retinue with him, all to keep him in touch with developments in Number Ten.

If one leaves the outer private secretaries' room and travels up a half flight of stairs and past a small warren of offices, one comes to a locked and, until the 1980s, green-baize door, leading to the other great source of official advice for the Prime Minister, albeit physically outside Number Ten, the Cabinet Office. To pass between the Cabinet Office and Number Ten in the past a key had to be borrowed from the Private Office or the Cabinet Secretary's office. Today the connecting door is still locked and many Number Ten staff, as well as Cabinet Office staff, possess a swipe card. The reason why so many Number Ten staff seek access is in fact prosaic – access to the Cabinet Office canteen.

The physical separation of the two offices is a symbol of the Cabinet Secretary's duty to uphold the independence of the Civil Service and of the fact that he is not a member of the Number Ten staff.

This other key co-ordinating office in Whitehall was established by David Lloyd George in 1916 to service the Cabinet, by circulating papers and agendas in advance, taking minutes (before that date, amazingly, no formalised minutes from Cabinet meetings had been taken and the only record was the Prime Minister's letter to the sovereign), and sending conclusions around to relevant Civil Service departments for action. After Lloyd George's downfall in 1922, Maurice Hankey, the Cabinet Secretary, continued in the post, survived several changes of government, and managed to establish the independence of the Cabinet Office from the Prime Minister and Number Ten. This separation reduced somewhat the influence of the Private Office and 'was a significant factor in hindering the evolution of British government in a prime ministerial direction'.[10] A certain rivalry grew up between Number Ten and the Cabinet Office, both performing vital and not always distinct roles. Both put up papers to the Prime Minister, the Cabinet Office focusing on the work of Cabinet and its committees, offering full and detailed advice on the handling of meetings, and the Private Office co-ordinating submissions from Civil Service departments and from the world outside Whitehall.

Only eight individuals have held the key position of Cabinet Secretary. Maurice Hankey (1916–38) was the first incumbent and largely defined the role, serving five Prime Ministers. Edward Bridges (1938–47) served three, Norman Brook (1947–62) served four, Burke Trend (1963–73) served four, John Hunt (1973–79) served four, Robert Armstrong (1979–87) served one, and Robin Butler (1987–97) served three. This continuity contrasts with the turnover among Cabinet ministers and Permanent Secretaries, who serve in post for an average of just over two and three years, respectively.

Since 1983 the Cabinet Secretary has also combined this task with that of Head of the Home Civil Service, and he chairs the Senior Appointments Selection Committee (SASC) which meets monthly. This committee contains other Permanent Secretaries, but they can only advise the Cabinet Secretary on promotions. He also chairs a weekly meeting of senior Permanent Secretaries. The Cabinet Secretary may expect to see the Prime Minister frequently, sits on his right at Cabinet, reports on the progress of business through Cabinet committees, and briefs him on meetings and events and more delicate matters such as Civil Service promotions and conduct, intelligence and constitutional issues. Norman Brook in 1947 began the system of providing and overseeing, 'steering', briefs for the Prime Minister on the handling of his Cabinet or Cabinet committee business, covering likely points for discussion and possible outcomes. Cabinet Secretaries overview the whole waterfront of the government.

The Cabinet Secretary has been called the Prime Minister's Permanent Secretary; in practice, the more the Prime Minister relies on his Principal Private Secretary, as Heath did on Robert Armstrong (1970–74) and Major did on Alex Allan (1992–97), the less daily influence the Cabinet Secretary has had. The Cabinet Secretary, not least through his weekly meeting with Permanent Secretaries and his overview of the progress of the Cabinet committees, has a good idea of the administrative performance of ministers. How good are they at executing their business and do they command the respect of their subordinates within their departments? The Prime Minister, with his multi-focused attention, may know less about their quality than the Cabinet Secretary, who is in touch with the Permanent Secretaries. It is no surprise, therefore, that a Prime Minister will usually consult him before government reshuffles. In planning Cabinet and Cabinet committee business for the following week, the next few weeks and again the next few months ahead, the Cabinet Secretary works with the principal chairmen of the Cabinet committees, usually non-departmental ministers such as the Lord President or Lord Privy Seal. The Cabinet Office owes a dual allegiance, to the Prime Minister and to the Cabinet as a whole; where a Cabinet Secretary becomes too close to a Prime Minister, as happened to John Hunt, who admitted to having to spend increasing time advising Prime Ministers Wilson and Callaghan rather than Cabinet as a whole, difficulties can arise.

As with the Number Ten Private Office, the Cabinet Office is staffed by high fliers seconded from other departments. Some thirty officials now people the senior echelons of the Cabinet Office, operating in five secretariats: economic and home, overseas and defence, European, central (which directly supports the Cabinet Secretary) and constitutional; and one unit, the Assessment Staff, covering security and intelligence matters. There was also a science and technology secretariat until the chief scientific adviser was transferred to the Department of Trade and Industry. The body was initially subsumed within the new Office of Science and Technology (OST) within the Office for Public Service and Science established by John Major after the 1992 election. The OST then moved to the DTI in 1995.

These secretariats are run by deputy secretaries, some of whom, such as Pat Nairne (1973–75) acquire considerable importance in their own fields. The heads of the secretariats meet weekly under the Cabinet Secretary to plan business for the immediate week and the next few weeks ahead, and also sometimes join the Cabinet Secretary for his weekly meeting with the Prime Minister to review future business.

From 1971–83 the Cabinet Office also provided the home for the Central Policy Review Staff (CPRS), a body which aimed to think 'long-term' for both Prime Minister and Cabinet. The CPRS promised much, given the seemingly pathological inability of democratic governments to think beyond winning the next general election. But in the event it delivered little after a successful first two years under its head, Lord Rothschild. It was not just that Prime Ministers have been forced by the pressure of events, and despite their best intentions, to be overly concerned with the short term. Geography played its part too: the CPRS was on the wrong side of the green baize door, and was insufficiently entwined in the 'policy loop'.

Tony Blair announced changes in the role of the Cabinet Office on 28 July 1998. These followed a review by the new Cabinet Secretary, Sir Richard Wilson. Wilson's review pointed to improvements which could be made in policy formulation and implementation and in handling cross-departmental issues. The Office of Public Services (OPS) was merged with the rest of the Cabinet Office to promote these improvements. The review also led to the creation of a Performance and Innovation Unit, which was charged with focusing on issues that crossed departmental boundaries and involved more than one public sector body, and with proposing innovative ways to improve the delivery of the government's objectives.

Much play was made, not least by the satirical writers of the 1980s television comedy series *Yes Minister* and *Yes Prime Minister*, of the rivalry between the Principal Private Secretary and the Cabinet Secretary, and also with the Cabinet Secretary's possession of the key (now card) required to unlock the interconnecting door between the Cabinet Office and Number Ten.

An easier way back to Number Ten was to walk out through the front door of the Cabinet Office into Whitehall and then turn right and right again after a few yards into Downing Street. Once back in the building, a right turn from the Number Ten front hall leads to the Press Office which came into existence in 1931, fifteen years after the Cabinet Office itself. Hitherto, the limited relations with the press (and the BBC after its foundation in 1926) had been managed comfortably by one of the Private Secretaries. But the proliferation of the media into broadcasting and the immediate catalyst of the 1931 economic crisis, demanded an office exclusively dedicated to managing press contacts. The work of the office was regularised in the 1940s, with the demands of war and postwar reconstruction requiring specialist skills, not least with the burgeoning regional and overseas media clamouring for comment 'from the top'.

The Press Office is now headed by the Prime Minister's Official

Spokesman or Chief Press Secretary, who occupies the bow-windowed ground floor room that one passes on the way to the front door of Number Ten. In adjacent rooms work up to ten subordinate press officers and secretaries. Two kinds of Press Secretary have come to fill the post: career civil servants who might or might not have specialised in information, such as Donald Maitland (1970–73) or Jonathan Haslam (1996–97), and journalists already known to the Prime Minister, such as Joe Haines (1969–70, 1974–76) or Alastair Campbell (1997–). The function of both types of Press Secretary has been the same, to link the Prime Minister with the outside world and ensure the best and most sympathetic possible coverage for what he or she is trying to do. With increasing awareness from the 1960s of the importance and possibilities of shaping the media's portrayal of the Prime Minister, the work of the office has risen up the pecking order in Downing Street. Three Press Secretaries in particular in our period – Joe Haines, Bernard Ingham (1979–90) and Alastair Campbell – reached the inner circle of advisers to the Prime Minister, and their counsel crossed the hazy boundary between advice on how to communicate one's message to advice on what the actual message should be. Again, as with private secretaries, a wide degree of leeway is given to press secretaries in deciding how to present the Prime Minister to the outside world. As with private secretaries, and others at Number Ten, they have often had to act and think as if they *were* the Prime Minister. Acting as an effective communicator for the Prime Minister has sometimes involved strains for a civil servant who was Press Secretary. Bernard Ingham was thought to have exceeded the role of a civil servant when he worked for Mrs Thatcher and he and his role became the subjects of parliamentary and public debate.

A tension existed throughout the period between the Number Ten press operation and the Whitehall information service, nominally run by the Director General of the Government Information and Communications Service (GICS). Trying to co-ordinate the release of government news stories has been a constant headache for the Number Ten Press Secretary. Ingham took over this duty in 1988 when the head of the GICS was ill and retained it when a new head was appointed a year later. His successor as Press Secretary, Gus O'Donnell (1990–94), did not combine the two posts.

A key part of the work of the Press Secretary has been to provide information to the Lobby, a distinctively British institution under which selected media outlets had been permitted to send designated journalists to twice-daily 'unattributable' briefings (11 am in Number Ten and 4 pm in the House of Commons) in which the Press Secretary puts across the Prime Minister's message and responds to questions about his, and the government's, thinking. Until recently because the briefings have been unattributable, terms like 'sources close to the Prime Minister' were often used. Under John Major the sources were identified as 'Ten Downing Street'. Thought has been given over the years to replacing the Lobby system with attributable press briefings, 'on the record'. This would make the Press Secretary the equivalent of the White House Press Spokesman, which would also have the effect of boosting his public profile if not his influence. Other voices prevailed until 1997, when Blair's Press Secretary put the Lobby on the record, but did not admit television cameras to the Lobby briefing. In March 2000, Campbell agreed that he could be named at briefings, but soon after he stepped down from taking the daily lobby sessions. Now a 1200–1500-word note on the lobby proceedings is available within two hours of the event and distributed widely across Whitehall.

The trend, nevertheless has been for the Prime Minister to make increasing numbers of press appearances himself, either to make statements like John Major's announcement in the Number Ten garden in June 1995 that he would submit himself for re-election as party leader, or question-and-answer style as Ted Heath did in 1972. With the proliferation of satellite and cable media from the 1980s, and the Internet in the 1990s, the work of the Press Office has had to adapt itself even more to new technology than any other Number Ten department.

Walking back to the main hall, and climbing up the stairs (albeit which would have until 1999 brought one to the front of the building) or taking the very slow and small lift, brings one to the Appointments Office on the first floor, concerned with senior ecclesiastical and other 'Crown' appointments such as Regius Professorships and Lord-Lieutenants. The quarters are now occupied by the Strategic Communications Unit, a body set up in 1998. The Appointments Office has been moved to the Cabinet Office, although the Appointments Secretary remains in Number Ten. Historically, this responsibility rested with the Private Office, but in 1947 it was transferred to a designated Secretary for Appointments. The work is relatively apolitical. Only five civil servants have held this post since 1970, longevity being considered valuable for the important though behind-the-scenes work on which the incumbent is engaged: advising the Prime Minister (which means, for most, except interventionist premiers like Mrs Thatcher and Tony Blair, in effect *telling* the Prime Minister) who should be appointed.

The present Appointments Secretary is John Holroyd and he heads a staff of eight, who cover both appointments and Number 10's work on honours. Some Number Ten advisers, such as Marcia Williams under Harold Wilson, resented the prime space overlooking Downing Street being given to what they considered fairly arcane work. But the Office is a reminder of the Prime Minister's other political patronage powers. Gladstone regarded the ecclesiastical appointments as among the most troublesome of his duties. A less devout predecessor, Lord Melbourne, once complained, 'Damn it. Another Bishop dead.'

The Appointments Secretary until recently also acted as a kind of domestic bursar, responsible for the fabric of Number Ten and of the Prime Minister's country house, Chequers. As the staff of Number Ten has grown, an Executive Secretary (a career civil servant) has been appointed to run the building and assume these duties. Not the least of the Appointment Secretary's jobs is to operate a number of charities, including one for literary figures who have fallen on hard times. No better illustration can be given of the extraordinarily diverse work that takes place in this small late seventeenth-century building.

Walking across to the back of the building, above the ground floor rooms, one reaches the three interconnecting state drawing rooms, remodelled in the late 1980s by Quinlan Terry (who had worked with the architect Raymond Erith in the extensive remodelling of Downing Street in the early 1960s). To the west is the White Drawing Room, one-time boudoir of Prime Ministers' wives. The room is in frequent daytime use for meetings of up to six or eight people sitting on elegant sofas and chairs, and in the evenings for entertaining guests; it is the

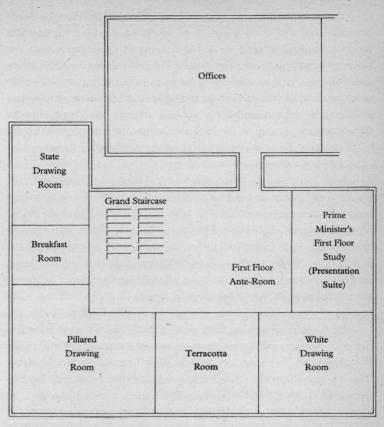

room that has commonly been used for television interviews. Next to it is the middle drawing room (the Blue Drawing Room until the 1980s, then the Green Drawing Room and now the Terracotta Room), where Prime Ministers traditionally greet reception guests by the door. Through double doors towards the east is the Pillared Room, the largest of the three, the focal point of receptions for up to two hundred guests. Back onto the landing again, facing the main staircase, one can turn left (east) to Sir John Soane's state dining room (for up to sixty-five seated guests) and small dining room, or right (west) to the Prime Minister's study, used by many of the Prime Ministers for much of the time during our period.

A further flight of stairs brings one up to the second floor self-contained flat at the back of the building, overlooking the garden. This was heavily altered for the Attlees in the late 1940s and has been little changed thereafter. Four to five bedrooms, depending on designation, a kitchen, dining room and medium-sized sitting room are the main rooms. The flat was used during the week by all premiers in our period except Harold Wilson (1974–76), who lived in his nearby Westminster flat, and Tony Blair, who lives with his family in the larger flat next door over Number Eleven. The sitting room was much used, famously by Heath for last-minute briefings before Prime Minister's Questions, and by Mrs Thatcher, shoeless and whisky in hand, for late-night political gossip with close aides. It was not until Arthur Balfour became Prime Minister in 1902 that the principle of the Prime Minister normally living in and working from Number Ten became firmly established, though some notable nineteenth-century premiers, including the Duke of Wellington, William Gladstone and Benjamin Disraeli, lived there for at least part of their time as Prime Minister. Many, however, found it insufficiently grand.

Leaving the flat and walking back across into George Downing's building, one comes to a suite of offices overlooking Downing Street, used for political and constituency work until it became the home of the Policy Unit. The Policy Unit was introduced by Harold Wilson in March 1974. In the light of his earlier experience at Number Ten (1964–70), he felt that he needed more political and policy advice to counterbalance that from officials. The Civil Service, perhaps inevitably, was suspicious of its appearance in their midst, although there had been clear antecedents, most recently the small team operating under the economist Thomas Balogh from 1964 to 1969. After some intense discussions, a 'concordat' governing the Policy Unit's *modus operandi* was drawn up, and the five or so specialist members of the Unit, including its head Bernard Donoughue (1974–79), were signed up as 'temporary' civil servants, which allowed them access to 'classified' papers and information. Wilson described its purpose as being his 'eyes and ears'.[11]

The original aim was for the Policy Unit to provide policy analysis, in both the short and medium term, primarily on domestic policy. It would work up papers for the Prime Minister, and comment upon submissions from the Cabinet Office and from departments to help ensure the Prime Minister's own political objectives and manifesto commitments were not being swallowed up in the daily administrative grind. By keeping in regular touch with Whitehall departments, and not least with political advisers to ministers, whose numbers had burgeoned since the 1960s, the Policy Unit could keep the Prime Minister abreast of what was going on in the departments. At the outset Donoughue dealt with the more pressing issues, leaving the Central Policy Review Staff (CPRS) to tackle the long-term ones. In the real world, this distinction often broke down. But, given political pressures and the narrow time horizons of ministers, the differing time dimension helped ensure that the Policy Unit had more influence than the CPRS.

The Policy Unit, however, has not always operated as originally intended. It tends to reinvent itself under each Prime Minister. Different Prime Ministers had different ideas on the Unit, and it has tended to be sucked into short-term firefighting rather than longer-term analysis, even after the demise in 1983 of the CPRS, whose *raison d'être* had been forward thinking. Mrs Thatcher began the process of bringing civil servants into the Policy Unit on short-term secondment from departments, a practice which has continued to the present day, although Blair's contains only one. The Policy Unit has survived four changes of premier and two changes of party government (its survival, in 1979, was by no means a foregone conclusion), which is in itself proof of its value. To be effective, the Unit has to establish good working relationships with the Private Office and with Whitehall departments – to ensure that it remains in the policy loop it must receive important papers, at the right time, and attend the key committees and meetings. It also has to be seen to be enjoying the Prime Minister's confidence; he has to want to use it and find it useful, and he himself has to carry authority in Whitehall. But only in limited periods has the Policy Unit played a key role, as under Donoughue (and then only between 1974 and 1976), John Redwood (1984–85) and Sarah Hogg (for her first two years only, between 1990 and 1992). The loss of John Major's authority after the forced exit from the ERM in September 1992 affected the Unit's standing with ministers and departments and forced it even more into short-term concerns.

On the top floor of Downing Street were small bedrooms for staff working overnight, and, until its transfer to the Cabinet Office in the mid-1990s, the telephone switchboard, affectionately known as 'switch'. No-one has anything but praise for the patience and skill of the telephone operators, not least in connecting the Prime Minister and an interlocutor wherever they may be in the world. In 1999 the bedrooms were converted to offices for extra staff, including those in Research and Information and assistants for the Policy Unit.

Returning by stairs or lift to the ground floor front hall one passes the interconnecting corridor to Number Eleven and Number Twelve running parallel to Downing Street. By using it, people may move to and from the Chancellor's residence at Number Eleven and the Chief Whip's office at Number Twelve away from the gaze of cameras stationed in the street outside.

Off to the left of the Cabinet Ante-Room is the room used for much of the period until 1997 by the Political Secretary, the figure who links the Prime Minister with his or her political party. (It is now occupied by the head of Blair's Policy Unit, David Miliband.) The Prime Minister faced a problem keeping in touch with his own party after civil servants alone ran the Private Office from the late 1920s. Conscious of the supposedly watertight distinction between head-of-government and party political business, the Prime Minister used a variety of people, notably the Chief Whip in Number Twelve, and leading figures from Central Office and Transport House – Conservative and Labour Party headquarters respectively – to keep him in touch with the party at large. The Prime Minister's Parliamentary Private Secretary, of whom more below, was another key bridging figure with the parliamentary party.

In 1958, Harold Macmillan brought a close friend, John Wyndham, into the Number Ten Private Office to offer political advice, but the job of Political Secretary was only formalised when in 1964 Wilson brought in his own secretary, Marcia Williams. Edward Heath, while in opposition, became convinced that this job would be a useful addition to his staff at Number Ten, and invited Douglas Hurd, a former diplomat and since 1967 head of his Private Office, to fill the post. Wyndham was wealthy enough to provide his services free of charge, Mrs Williams was at first paid by Wilson personally, but since 1970 the Political Secretary and his or her staff have been paid by the governing party. Wyndham, Hurd and Marcia Williams have all written about their experiences in Number Ten; their different perceptions reflect not only their very differing personalities, temperaments and political outlooks, but also those of the Prime Ministers they served. Indeed Heath's remit for Hurd was to be as different as possible from Mrs Williams!

Although the title changed to 'Political Adviser' for Tom McNally from 1976–79 when James Callaghan was Prime Minister, it reverted to 'Political Secretary' upon Mrs Thatcher's arrival in 1979, and the function of the job had changed little. A Political Secretary is expected to possess or quickly acquire many assets – to be a party supporter, have experience or knowledge of Whitehall, know the party, have a good political sense and enjoy good personal relations with the Prime Minister. Often he or she will already have served for spells in the party's organisation or as a special adviser in Whitehall, and can expect to see and talk with the Prime Minister several times on an average day. The Political Secretary also needs to be discreet, for he or she will attend discussions about political honours and government reshuffles, take the minutes at Political Cabinets (meetings of Cabinet ministers when the Cabinet Office withdraws and party political business is discussed), accompany the Prime Minister on party tours, supervise the handling of correspondence and listen in on his political telephone calls. Having a close political aide in Number Ten, commenting on papers, dealing with party correspondence, liaising with all the various party bodies and committees, smoothing relations with the party, and drafting political speeches, has fully justified the need for the Political Secretary. No Prime Minister since 1970, with the possible exception of James Callaghan, has enjoyed an easy relationship with his or her parliamentary party; without the Political Secretary, relations might have been much worse.

Traditionally, in this office sits also the Parliamentary Private Secretary (PPS), who also assists as a bridge between the Prime Minister and the *parliamentary* party, attending party committees and backbench meetings, consorting with MPs in corridors and tearooms, and acting as a two-way means of communication, helping to explain the one to the other. A few, not many, of these incumbents have become important figures in their own right, advising the Prime Minister on policy matters as well as on candidates for promotion to office (or for sacking). Before our period, Christopher Soames, PPS to Winston Churchill (1953–55), was an example of a conspicuously effective Parliamentary Private Secretary, while after 1970 Ian Gow (1979–83), PPS to Mrs Thatcher, also stands out as an influential figure. For the most part, however, Prime Ministers have been content to have amiable figures carrying their bags beside them who did not bring them too many uncomfortable truths. With so many hard-nosed professionals to serve them at Number Ten, they have often appreciated having a comforting companion, not least because the Parliamentary Private Secretary invariably accompanies the Prime Minister on the journey to the Commons for the ordeal of Prime Minister's Questions.

Although the distinction between political and official staff is important, the two sides have also to work together with the shared aim of serving the Prime Minister. The Prime Minister relies on the private secretaries to protect his interests in the Whitehall and parliamentary maze. The Private Office secretaries have to appreciate the political side of the Prime Minister's job, to take on board the problems he has with his party in Parliament and the challenges he may face at the forthcoming annual party conference or the need to prepare for a general election. Indeed in the last year of a Parliament or the months preceding a general election there is a general clearing of the decks and the Prime Minister devotes himself increasingly to party politics. The political staff see him more frequently and pressures on the officials decline. If a Prime Minister does not do the political job well he is unlikely to survive. The Private Office staff have an interest in his political success because if he is in trouble and lacks authority it impacts on their own work.

Number Ten is far from ideal as the head office of a large corporation. It has over one hundred individual rooms, which have been designed for various purposes in the past. Incapable of expansion upwards, downwards or externally, it is also a listed building, which imposes its own constraints on expansion. It is possible to speculate that if space had permitted the staff might have increased considerably. About 150 people work in the building in 1999. Despite this figure having grown from 64 in 1970 under Harold Wilson, 70 in 1979 and 120 on 1 May 1997, Number Ten retains the atmosphere of a small village or a large extended family. The policy-oriented members of the Private Office, Policy Unit, Political Office, Press Office, Strategic Communications Unit, Research and Information Unit totalled nearly 50 in 2000. These constitute the Prime Minister's office and his most senior aides.

A Prime Minister's entourage of advisers thus consists of members of several units centred around Ten Downing Street. But it also includes the Foreign Secretary and Chancellor of the Exchequer, other Cabinet ministers, party influentials, Political Office staff, the Policy Unit, the Press Office, leading members of the Cabinet Office and the Private Office staff. In Appendix II we have tentatively tried, for each Prime Minister, to place these actors in one of three concentric rings, according to their closeness to the respective premier. Those closest to the Prime Minister are located in the innermost ring, but influence can be fickle; it can alter within a premiership.

It is worth recalling that there is no formal job remit or list of duties for a Prime Minister. The absence of formal limits, to quote H.H. Asquith, provides opportunities for an incumbent to make of the office what he chooses and is able to make of it. Prime Ministers have some discretion in how they organise their lives in office. Much depends on their personalities, skills, goals, and the circumstances of the time. Each one may draw up his own staffing arrangements, emphasise some aspects of his role rather than others, and even decide whether he wants to live and work in Number Ten. Tony Blair has been the most radical Prime Minister in our period in doing the job in his own way.

Prime Ministers also differ in their sense of purpose. Some, notably Lloyd George and Winston Churchill in wartime, and Mrs Thatcher, have been mobilisers. They were primarily concerned with the achievement of goals, not overly bothered about opposition and the cost of disturbance. Many other Prime Ministers have been conciliators, more concerned to maintain the consensus and cohesion of a group, willing to represent and respond to diverse interests and, if necessary, sacrifice policy goals. Philip Williams has drawn a distinction similar to that of the mobiliser and reconciler when distinguishing Labour Party leaders as either *pathfinders*, who try to lead the party in a new direction, or *stabilisers*, who are primarily concerned with maintaining party unity. Hugh Gaitskell (1955–63) and Blair are examples of pathfinders: Wilson and Callaghan were primarily stabilisers.[12] The same distinction can be applied to the Conservative Prime Ministers, with Heath and Thatcher examples of pathfinders, and Major a stabiliser.

It is difficult to lay down a 'how to' statement for Prime Ministers because each one differs in what arrangements he feels comfortable with, and what works best for him. The first statutory reference to the office of Prime Minister was in the Ministers of the Crown Act (1937) and dealt only with salaries. Since 1968 the Prime Minister has always also taken the office of Minister for the Civil Service, making him head of the executive in its official as well as political guise. One shrewd student suggested that we have therefore to 'set out the practices that seem to apply in most circumstances, and to describe the repertoire of roles that a premier may undertake'.[13]

The Prime Minister has responsibilities as:

- head of the executive branch
- 'custodian' and shaper of government policy
- national leader in war and peace
- chief appointing officer, including appointing and dismissing ministers, and dispenser of patronage
- leader of the party in Parliament
- senior British representative overseas (apart from the sovereign who is head of state, with symbolic power).

The various roles in the British governmental system coincide to some extent with the administrative divisions of the Number Ten offices. Support exists for each of his duties. The fact that the support is sectionalised, although concentrated in Number Ten, may offend advocates of tidy-minded administration.

FUNCTION	SUPPORTING OFFICE
Head of the executive	Cabinet secretariat Private Office
Custodian and shaper of government policy	Strategic Communications Unit, Research and Information Unit

National leader	Private Office
Party leader	Political Secretary
	Parliamentary Private Secretary
Head appointing officer	Appointments Secretary (Crown appointments)
	Cabinet Secretary (senior Civil Service and ministers)
	Principal Private Secretary (Private Secretaries and ministers)
Leader of party in Parliament	Political Secretary
	Parliamentary Private Secretary
	Private Secretary – parliamentary affairs
Senior British representative overseas	Private Secretary – foreign affairs

Yet a Prime Minister personally has remarkably few formal powers and 'owns' few policies. Acts of Parliament assign duties and powers to Secretaries of State rather than to the Prime Minister. James Callaghan recalled that, having coped with the demands of being Chancellor of the Exchequer, Home Secretary and Foreign Secretary, he found the task of Prime Minister to be one of relative idleness.[14] This is some claim, considering that his government had to cope with the economic pressures that led to the IMF negotiations in 1976 as well as the 'winter of discontent' in 1978 and for much of the time lacked an effective majority in Parliament. Mrs Thatcher, by contrast, was a famed workaholic, making do with four hours of sleep a night, taking work on holidays, intervening frequently in departments, and constantly calling for more briefing papers.

It is sometimes suggested that the job has become too much for one person or the office, as presently constituted. Such claims need to be treated with caution, just as claims that the Prime Minister is becoming a more powerful actor also need to be treated with caution. What is undeniable is that the nature of the job, while retaining some continuity, has shifted. Examination of how Gladstone spent his time in February

1893, a year into his fourth administration, when he was eighty-three, is interesting. There were seventeen days when Gladstone spent long periods on the front bench in the Commons as Leader of the House (often eight or nine hours a day), including seven major speeches. He also chaired five meetings of the Cabinet (all lasting at least two hours) and a party meeting and wrote by hand ninety-four official letters, many of them long and technical. This was in addition to the regular interviews and deputations. Even earlier, Sir Robert Walpole and William Pitt the Younger spent most of their waking hours doing little else as Prime Minister, holidays apart. Of twentieth-century Prime Ministers Campbell Bannerman, Asquith, and Baldwin all had time for leisure. Churchill (1951–55) and Harold Wilson (1974–76) were very much part-time Prime Ministers. Abroad there have recently been numerous elderly or fragile leaders; Reagan, Mitterrand, Yeltsin and Mandela have hardly followed demanding schedules. What matters more is the temperament and ambition of the leader, rather than the nature of the office.

At the end of the twentieth century British Prime Ministers spend more time travelling at home and overseas, responding to media pressures for interviews and trying to manage the media. They probably spend less time in Cabinet and in Parliament. The new technology, particularly faxes, e-mail, pagers and mobile telephones as well as jet travel, adds to some parts of the workload and eases others.

A Prime Minister may be less confined by routine in his work day than a Cabinet minister. But he still faces predictable demands on his time. During the week there are regularly scheduled Cabinet meetings and Cabinet committees, meetings with ministers, parliamentary business managers, backbench spokesmen, the Cabinet Secretary and deputations, preparations for Parliamentary Questions and the visit to the Monarch. There will usually be weekly bilaterals with the Chancellor, the Foreign Secretary, the Chief Whip and other party 'business managers'. Throughout the year there is the regular calendar of the budget, the autumn party conference and other party gatherings, meetings of the European Union's Council of Ministers, as well as Group of Seven/Eight (G7/G8) and Commonwealth conferences. Near the end of the Parliament the Prime Minister's attention will increasingly turn to general election planning and the election manifesto. Almost daily there will be boxes from the Private and Political Offices to read and annotate, speeches to prepare, and the churn of events with which to cope. In addition there will be a stream of ad hoc meetings with businessmen and representatives of special interest groups, and an unavoidable minimum of foreign visitors passing through London who expect to see the Prime Minister. Study of a Prime Minister's diary[15] tells only the scheduled part of the story of who has access to him and what he is doing. It fails to show who is popping in regularly such as the political and private staff, or the Cabinet Secretary. A Political and a Private Secretary may discuss business, however briefly, with the Prime Minister several times a day.

A Prime Minister may intervene in any department, calling for papers and summoning its senior officials. Almost inevitably if there is a crisis – to do with foreign policy, the exchange rate, party divisions, or a scandal affecting a colleague – he will be involved. Ted Heath took office in June 1970 promising not to get drawn into such matters. He proved unable to stand aside not least when it came to dealing with industrial disputes. The passage of the Maastricht Bill in early/mid-1993 and concern over BSE (or 'mad cow disease') in 1996 dominated John Major's Number Ten, as did the IMF negotiations in 1976 for Callaghan, the Falklands War in spring 1982 for Mrs Thatcher and the Northern Ireland peace process for Tony Blair in the first half of 1998 and Kosovo and Northern Ireland in 1999.

Proposals for the reform of British government often include recommendations for a stronger centre, via the recruitment of more staff to help the Prime Minister and even the creation of a Prime Minister's Office or Department. One commentator has been particularly outspoken, referring to the '. . . grotesque inadequacy of the Number Ten machinery which is understaffed, poorly organized and badly resourced for the job it has to do'.[16] The regularity with which this topic is broached suggests that something is missing and that there is a hole in the heart of government. The question of how well, as well as how, the Prime Minister is served by Number Ten runs as a leitmotif throughout the chapters that follow.

CHAPTER TWO

The Prime Minister's Office
1868–1970

WHILE ROBERT WALPOLE was the first person who merits the name 'Prime Minister', and was also the first incumbent to live at Number Ten, little had changed in the way the Prime Minister conducted his affairs in the one hundred and fifty years leading up to William Gladstone's first premiership from 1868. It remained an essentially personal premiership, with few helpers, and with the Prime Minister, if he wished, able to see and digest for himself all the correspondence and business that came his way. The major changes began in the late nineteenth century. Britain may have been at the heart of a great worldwide empire under Gladstone and Benjamin Disraeli, but there was little evidence of Number Ten appearing to be overloaded. In comparison with 1970, Parliament sat far less often, government had far fewer responsibilities, the Prime Minister was rarely called upon to make an urgent decision, Cabinet meetings were informal occasions, and the constant grind of Cabinet committees was unknown. Only the Prime Minister took notes at Cabinet and that was largely for the purpose of giving a regular report on its proceedings to the monarch.

From the mid-Victorian age to Edward Heath's arrival at Number Ten in 1970 Number Ten burgeoned in size, specialisation and sophistication. The principal factor behind the development was the huge increase over these years in government activity, and the need for urgent responses from the Prime Minister across a broad waterfront. The premier's international role also increasingly took his attention, as Britain changed from having a foreign policy guided by Lord Salisbury's 'splendid isolation' at the end of the nineteenth century to being part of a complex web of international relationships demanding daily responses from Number Ten.

Prime Minister Gladstone was able to see all important correspondence that came to him, and he was able to command his life personally – who he should see, and how he should spend his day. He did not, however, work entirely alone. The career of Gladstone's first Private Secretary, Algernon West, appointed shortly after the Liberals won the 1868 general election, illustrates some of the changes that were taking place within the Civil Service in the third quarter of the nineteenth century. West was reputedly the last Civil Service recruit never to have taken an examination of any kind,[1] and therefore the last beneficiary of the patronage-based system that existed before the Northcote–Trevelyan reforms of 1854, which created the modern, meritocratic Civil Service, took effect.

West moved into Number Ten while Gladstone remained living in some grandeur in his house nearby, in Carlton House Terrace.[2] As West records: 'my life now became stereotyped. I moved into the little room looking to the west, and into this room I went every morning to open letters, which poured in at every hour of the day. At half-past nine breakfast was brought to me and by eleven o'clock I had succeeded in analysing the correspondence.'

West went on to assist with the writing and planning of the legislation to disestablish the Church of Ireland, a cause which he strongly supported.[3] During the legislative process he was 'brought into daily communication' with George Glyn, the Liberal Chief Whip.[4] The pressure of work for West was cyclical, with long lazy summer holidays balanced by late nights in the office and the House of Commons during the passage of major Bills.

West was succeeded in 1872 by William Gurdon, a civil servant, who had previously been Treasury Clerk, and who had served as a more junior Private Secretary since 1868. Gurdon systematised prime ministerial correspondence by producing form letters for answering various standard types of enquiry, an important stepping stone in the bureaucratisation of the premiership. His system was encoded into the 'Book of Knowledge' and used and occasionally updated by

Gladstone's later private secretaries in the 1880s, Hamilton and Seymour.[5] Gurdon, though a civil servant, had openly Liberal sympathies and was a prospective parliamentary candidate in 1884 before being obliged to withdraw. Political work was handled by Lord Frederick Cavendish.[6] Earlier, Gladstone had used his son, W.H. Gladstone, as his Parliamentary Private Secretary. The size of Gladstone's staff in his first ministry of 1868–74 never exceeded three, a figure and structure little different to that for eighteenth-century premiers.[7]

Gladstone's successor, also his predecessor, Benjamin Disraeli, appointed as his 'Principal' Private Secretary, Montagu Corry. He was one of the first to make the role more than a step on a career ladder, and had impressed Disraeli in 1865 at a party.[8] His importance was enhanced by the bouts of ill-health which dogged Disraeli during his second premiership (1874–80), and by his frequent absences from London. Corry dealt with both administrative and political work, the equivalent functions of the Private and Political Offices as they emerged in the twentieth century. In a period in which the Conservative Party was being renewed, he was deputed by Disraeli to foster new political talent. He organised groups of young Conservative figures (such as Walter Long) to meet Disraeli in Downing Street and he also appears to have been able to pull sufficient strings to ensure parliamentary nominations.[9]

Corry accompanied Disraeli to the Congress of Berlin in 1878,[10] and shared something of his unusually close relationship with Queen Victoria, apparently being offered at one stage a senior role in Buckingham Palace.[11] Disraeli's contemporary critics accused Corry of being the real Prime Minister. By 1880, according to one of Disraeli's biographers, 'Monty Corry had become more than a private secretary, he was a surrogate son. And he was nearly everything else for Disraeli, from male nurse to Minister without Portfolio.'[12]

Disraeli lived in Downing Street only from 1877 to 1880; previously he had lived at his own house in Whitehall Gardens, a short walk away. By 1877 he was too ill to walk to the office; when he moved in, a distinction was drawn between personal and government spending which persists to this day. Extensive refurbishment of the domestic accommodation, vacant for thirty years, was required –

Disraeli himself had referred to Number Ten as 'dingy and decaying' in 1868.[13] Gladstone moved into Number Ten only after the 1880 election, and he also took over Numbers Eleven and Twelve.[14]

In the mid-1870s Gladstone, according to his biographer Roy Jenkins, decided he was poor and sold his Carlton House Terrace home for one in Harley Street which he never much liked. So he occupied Number Ten for his last three periods in office, from 1880 to 1885, in 1886, and from 1892 to 1894,[15] a time which witnessed a growing sophistication if not a marked increase in size in the organisation of the premier's office. On regaining office in 1880, Gladstone appointed Arthur Godley as Principal Private Secretary, the top Civil Service post in Number Ten. In 1882 he was succeeded by Edward Hamilton, a career civil servant who had entered the Treasury during Gladstone's first government in 1870 and author of a famous diary.

One of Gladstone's aides emphasised the 'junction box' nature of the work of Private Secretary, acting as the Prime Minister's channel to the royal household, the Cabinet and more or less anyone else in public or private life.[16] Correspondence was handled at several levels of security, with some material going to junior private secretaries, some to the Principal, and some (identified by another sealed envelope within the outer envelope) straight to Gladstone personally. The pattern of three secretaries paid from public funds, one at least with Treasury experience and one with a specialism in Church affairs, seems now to have become firmly established.[17] They liaised on policy questions with the Queen's Secretary, Cabinet ministers and MPs. However, they were largely concerned with routine work and appear to have had little influence on policy matters.[18]

We owe to Hamilton a description of Gladstone's daily routine in 1880–85. He rarely slept beyond 9 am, and until the official day began at 11 am read newspapers and – if there was nothing especially urgent – literature. He would then have a meeting with the Chief Whip and deal with the day's letters and papers, which the Private Secretaries had sifted for him. In this period policy was often developed through correspondence.[19] A lunch and then a walk would follow before he went to the House of Commons, where he remained, with breaks for tea and dinner, until the end of the sitting. He would spend some seven hours a day in the Commons chamber, sitting on the Treasury bench. It was a less frenetic routine than in the early 1870s.[20]

Herbert Gladstone MP, Gladstone's son, was another aide during Gladstone's second administration, fulfilling again the Parliamentary Private Secretary's role of acting as a bridge between Prime Minister and Parliament. He appears to have spent most of his time not at Number Ten but in Westminster.[21]

The Conservative Lord Salisbury's three periods as Prime Minister saw little development of the Number Ten office. This inertia occurred because for nearly the whole period he was his own Foreign Secretary, and also because he had a minimalist view both of the functions of the Prime Minister and of how much government should be doing. As a member of the House of Lords, he could keep some distance from the heat of the fray in the House of Commons. He was the last Prime Minister not to use Number Ten as his regular office, nor did he live there.

According to Lady Gwendolen Cecil, his daughter and biographer, Salisbury saw the role of Prime Minister as fourfold – the central function being to control Cabinet, then to oversee relations with the Queen, then to dispense what forms of patronage he could not devolve onto another member of the Cabinet, and finally to lead his party.[22] Absent was a role as legislator or policy formulator: 'There is no evidence upon which he can be credited with the paternity of any measure introduced while he was Prime Minister,' wrote Lady Cecil.[23] This absence is in contrast to the detailed handling of important measures which Gladstone took upon himself personally.

Salisbury's prime ministerial staff were drawn from the Foreign Office rather than from the Treasury, Gladstone's preference. He had an unusually long-serving Principal Private Secretary in Schomberg McDonnell (1888–92, 1895–1902), who took over after his predecessor, Henry Manners (1885–86, 1886–88), was elected a Conservative MP. McDonnell had also worked as Salisbury's Private Secretary when the Tories were in opposition. Friends and relatives, including his son Robert and a nephew, performed some tasks too,[24] though the former complained that he 'really had nothing to do' because of his father's reluctance to delegate.[25]

Salisbury was Prime Minister almost in his spare time, not having the title of 'First Lord', and even his Foreign Office routine was relaxed by modern standards. Lady Cecil records that: 'he never went down to his office [Foreign Office] till after luncheon, and his afternoons there were devoted exclusively to interviews, – mainly with foreign representatives. All his paper-work, the composition and writing of the telegrams, private letters and draft despatches through which his policy was enacted, was done in the mornings and evenings in the solitude of his own room in Arlington Street or Hatfield [his country house], with the occasional assistance of his shorthand-writer, Mr. Gunton.'[26] Salisbury even dispensed with the services of Mr Gunton when he was acquainted with the person to whom he was writing. He was perhaps the last Prime Minister who was a truly all-deciding premier.

Gladstone took West back to Downing Street for his fourth and final spell as premier (1892–94); West had retired from the Civil Service, but both he and Gladstone were in favour of his taking up some sort of central role. A seat in the Commons was considered and rejected, and West was too senior to take the title of Private Secretary,[27] so he was given the title of 'Chief of Staff' in 1892. West played a large part in helping Gladstone to form his Cabinet.[28] He also took upon himself the duty of finding staff for Number Ten:

> When the Secretariat was arranged with Mr. Gladstone, I went to see George Murray at the Treasury to ask him if, in the peculiar circumstances of the case, he would consent to be Mr. Gladstone's private secretary. I explained to him my position, which he understood perfectly, and from that day to the end of Mr. Gladstone's government we never had one moment's difficulty. . . . My old friend, Spencer Lyttelton, of course, came back and specially undertook ecclesiastical and royal bounty questions, and I had the good luck to bring with me Hans Shand, who had been my secretary at the Board of Inland Revenue, and to whom I owed so much.[29]

The exact use of rooms in Number Ten during Gladstone's last ministry is unclear, but in October 1892 he held his first Cabinet of the autumn 'in his own room – the corner room on the first floor [now the "white room"] (over the old Cab room)'.[30] Gladstone's old age, and an unusually divided and fractious Cabinet, created a large space for West to take on a general role as troubleshooter within the government at large. In February 1893, for example, he was in action patching up a 'frightful row' between Morley and William Harcourt.[31]

West found time in January 1893 to write an article on 'The Prime Minister's Day', in which he described the functions of the Prime Minister as 'The Prime Minister has everything to do. The Prime Minister has nothing to do', but as First Lord of the Treasury he is dispenser of Church patronage, 'probably the only duties of office that keep [Gladstone] awake o' nights are the distribution of Cabinet seats and appointments to clerical preferments'. West then addressed the wider functions of the Prime Minister: 'though unknown to the theory of constitution, the Prime Minister looms large in the eyes of the public. This means an enormous letter-bag to deal with, which is the first task of the Prime Minister's day.' There is also the function of leader of the party, addressed mainly by a meeting with the Chief Whip at noon. As for matters of state, 'The work of the Prime Minister is, indeed, very much what he chooses to make it.' There are frequent consultations with individual ministers, Cabinet and committee meetings and meetings with officials and representatives of important interests. After Cabinet meetings there was the duty of writing a letter to the Queen. In the evenings there was the Prime Minister's role as leading parliamentarian. 'In the case of a Prime Minister over eighty', West asked, 'ought not an eight hour day suffice?'[32]

Rosebery became Liberal Prime Minister in succession to the ailing Gladstone on 3 March 1894, and met his first Cabinet in a room at the Foreign Office; on 9 March he told Edward Hamilton that 'he will eventually sit at No. 10, when Mr. G is cleared out; but this will not be for some days'.[33] He was installed at Number Ten on 12 March, although for a while he continued to live at his private house in Berkeley Square. Rosebery, however, never enjoyed being Prime Minister, suffering from insomnia, illness and a disintegrating government. His presence in Number Ten always had a provisional air, as if he were expecting to move out imminently.

George Murray continued as Private Secretary on the advice of Hamilton, and served throughout Rosebery's short tenure of office. Among his many tasks was liaising between Rosebery and his Liberal colleague and rival, Harcourt, with whom he was barely on speaking terms. Hamilton recorded on 30 September 1894 that Murray 'now suits Rosebery very well' and incidentally notes the presence of a 'domestic' Private Secretary called Waterfield.[34] After 1895 Murray went to the Treasury and eventually became Permanent Secretary, while maintaining a lifelong friendship with Rosebery: in Rosebery's declining years, long after his premiership, 'nobody was more affectionately attentive than Sir George Murray, who had become the most conspicuous pillar of the civil service, and enjoyed Rosebery's personal confidence to an extent to which no one else had attained since the death of Edward Hamilton'.[35] Sundry other figures, including friends dealing with his personal affairs, added to the Number Ten retinue. But there was little sense of its being a harmonious or particularly efficient machine.

Arthur Balfour, who had been First Lord of the Treasury and the tenant of Number Ten Downing Street since 1895, established the tradition that Prime Ministers take up residence there.[36] Balfour had gained vital experience as Leader of the Commons while his uncle, Salisbury, enjoyed the comparative tranquillity of the Lords. Throughout his term of office as Prime Minister, his Principal Private Secretary was Jack Sandars, noted by contemporaries as being one of the most powerful Private Secretaries of the age. Like those who followed him, Sandars was brought in because of his personal loyalty; he had been Balfour's personal secretary since 1892. He also had some political experience, having stood as a Conservative in the 1892 election.

Sandars' remit was wide-ranging, because Balfour was easily bored by his duties. He combined what would now be considered the jobs of a Political Secretary and a political Press Secretary, 'the eyes and ears of his "Chief" as he called Balfour, in party and press matters'.[37] He advised on reshuffles and dealt with the Chief Whip on party business. He was also Appointments Secretary, and Principal Private Secretary: 'Balfour would send him to see King Edward VII when he thought he could avoid going himself.'[38]

Sandars played a key role behind the scenes supporting Balfour's cause in Parliament, in liaison with the omnicompetent former Conservative Chief Whip and now Cabinet Minister, Aretas Akers-Douglas. But when Balfour's popularity began to wane, the control his chief aide exerted over access to the Prime Minister attracted criticism within the party, a pattern which was to be repeated under later Prime Ministers. Sandars' influence seems to have risen as the premiership wore on, and he played a key part in the decision of Balfour to resign in December 1905. There were, however, personality differences between the languid Balfour and his controlling Private Secretary. Sandars is barely mentioned in Balfour's intimate correspondence with Lady Elcho, suggesting a lack of rapport.

Henry Campbell-Bannerman's two-and-a-quarter year premiership (1905–8) saw a split in the functions once carried out by the over-mighty Sandars. Yet the power wielded by his private secretaries, especially his principal aides, was still considerable. Campbell-Bannerman's Principal Private Secretary, dealing with 'relations with the Palace and other Ministers'[39] was Arthur Ponsonby. The ideal-type of pre-1914 Private Secretary, Ponsonby came from a Civil Service background, having retired from the Foreign Office in 1902. He had political ambitions himself, contesting Taunton for radical Liberalism in 1906 and eventually serving in the first two Labour governments as a minister. His relationship with his Prime Minister was based on personal and political loyalty, almost a patron–client pattern, culminating in his succession to Campbell-Bannerman's seat in Parliament.

Campbell-Bannerman's Political Secretary was Vaughan Nash, a former journalist who had helped him in speeches, research and party work since the early 1900s. When Ponsonby retired in January 1908, Nash became Private Secretary and brought in a Foreign Office civil servant, Montgomery, as assistant.

A third Private Secretary was Henry Higgs, a Treasury official in charge of 'patronage and ecclesiastical affairs'.[40] There were also two Parliamentary Private Secretaries, but they apparently 'were never given anything to do'. Campbell-Bannerman's Private Office was perhaps the first to collect ideas from the government departments for the King's Speech and draft them into the text.[41] The seeds of a more activist Number Ten were being sown from the earliest years of the century.

On Campbell-Bannerman's resignation in 1908 Herbert Henry Asquith became Prime Minister, the last to serve without a Cabinet Secretary. Asquith had been Chancellor of the Exchequer, and retained some of his aides when he moved from Number Eleven to Number Ten. But Vaughan Nash remained *in situ* as Principal Private Secretary until 1912 when he was succeeded by Maurice Bonham Carter (who became his son-in-law in 1915). Asquith was perhaps one of the more congenial Prime Ministers for whom to work, with an easy-going temperament and the ability to work very efficiently when he put his mind to it. He hugely enjoyed gossip, socialising and drinking, and Bonham Carter inevitably became something of a crony.[42]

His future son-in-law, however, was more an emissary, buffer and sifter than a policy-making influence. During Asquith's premiership (1908–16) Number Ten staff specialised more, and the office became more bureaucratic. This was a period in which the highest diplomatic skills were required; there were delicate negotiations with Buckingham Palace and with the Irish, as well as a hung Parliament from 1910, and an uneasy Cabinet with more than its share of egos, not to mention the outbreak of war in 1914. Speechwriting was a task of growing importance, though Asquith was a skilled extempore orator when he wished. An important role for the Principal Private Secretary remained taking the political temperature, as the work of the Parliamentary Private Secretary, the Prime Minister's 'eyes and ears' in the Commons, was still ill-defined.[43]

The Asquiths occupied the whole house for their family – the two children from his marriage to Margot were only 11 and 6 when he became Prime Minister in 1908.[44] Under the influence of Margot, Number Ten acquired a social cachet and glamour that the house has never since lost. On moving in she initially considered the place poorly laid out for entertaining, the exterior 'liver coloured and squalid' and taxi drivers uncertain of its location. Margot's talents as hostess quickly overcame these obstacles and for the first time since Gladstone's government in the 1880s, it became a centre of family and social activity.[45]

*   *   *

43

The modern British prime ministership was invented by David Lloyd George. Not just did he oversee the arrival of the Cabinet Office, but his premiership also saw enhanced powers for the Prime Minister and an increase in the scale of the Downing Street machine. Lloyd George's tenure thus marks an important staging post in the evolution of the collective premiership. Before him, there had been powerful individual advisers, such as Corry with Disraeli, West in Gladstone's governments and Sandars under Balfour. But such figures were ad hoc, and depended on the ambitions of the advisers and the habits of premiers. After 1916, the system emerged of a growing number of powerful individuals with important jobs to do who the Prime Minister had no choice but to trust.

Lloyd George came to power in December 1916 with the central government machine manifestly unable to cope with the strains of Britain's first total war. The main instrument of central co-ordination he deployed was the creation of a small War Cabinet of non-departmental ministers and the provision of a secretariat to ensure that its decisions were implemented. This Cabinet Secretariat produced the agendas and papers for Cabinet meetings, and the minutes and follow-ups. Previously, Cabinet meetings had been more informal occasions and the Prime Minister's task of taking notes for a letter to be sent to the monarch had been a considerable drain on his time if Cabinet meetings were at all frequent or prolonged. The new secretariat was based in Disraeli's old home in Whitehall Gardens but also worked in offices in Number Ten.[46]

The pivotal figure in the new regime was Maurice Hankey, who had already made himself indispensable as secretary to the Committee of Imperial Defence. Under his watchful eye, the Cabinet and its committees would be attended by secretaries who took minutes, recorded decisions and circulated them to Cabinet ministers and to others whose departments were affected. Hankey was to spend twenty-two years in his post and was the undisputed father of the Cabinet Office. As well as helping to despatch business more efficiently he emerged as a confidant to a succession of Prime Ministers. Tom Jones, Hankey's deputy and a diarist, helped the Cabinet Secretariat develop its co-ordinating function across Whitehall. Lloyd George's premiership thus saw a major shift in the development of central machinery towards serving Cabinet government as a whole. At first Civil Service departments were suspicious of the new entity, eyeing it as an extension of the power of the Prime Minister. They need not have worried unduly, as the Cabinet Secretariat was created to facilitate smooth administration rather than to proffer policy advice, in as far as one can wholly separate the two.

Lloyd George did, however, set up his own separate Prime Minister's Secretariat[47] to fill the policy advice gap and to strengthen his own role in the wartime Coalition government, in part because he lacked any party organisation to back him up. The Prime Minister's Secretariat was housed in temporary accommodation in the garden shared by Number Ten and Number Eleven Downing Street (and eventually sprawled into St James's Park) and quickly became known as the 'Garden Suburb'.

The Garden Suburb was organised into four very broad groups, and was headed by Professor W.G.S. Adams and then by Philip Kerr, and briefly at the end by Edward Grigg. Its remit was vague ('to assist the Prime Minister in the discharge of the heavy responsibilities which fall upon him under the War Cabinet system') but it ended up covering most areas outside military operations.[48] Its work ranged from broad thinking about postwar collective security to preparing briefings for the Prime Minister. Initially it was envisaged that the Garden Suburb would handle routine communications between the Prime Minister and other ministers, but this role was acquired by the new Cabinet Secretariat. The Garden Suburb handled three important matters beyond policy planning: briefing and writing for the Prime Minister's speeches, contact with the press and the promotion of the work of the government through official publications in the form of the War Cabinet reports.[49] Kerr became a close adviser on many matters, and accompanied Lloyd George to the Paris Peace Conference in 1919. In his remaining three years as a peacetime premier, Lloyd George also used the Garden Suburb to deal with ministerial and other entreaties that he did not want to hear personally,[50] a clear case of the Prime Minister, even after the war, being unable to manage all the demands on him without reliance on others.

The Garden Suburb acquired a sinister reputation during the 1920s, which to some extent rubbed off on the Cabinet Office, as a nest of ideologues allegedly attached to imperialism, centralisation and social reform. This disapproval was overdone, and scholarly research tends to reject the idea of its having a collegiate line or 'policy'.[51] Its main policy impact was on thinking towards Ireland, a particular interest of Professor Adams. The distaste for Kerr and Lloyd George personally created an unfortunate precedent for Prime Ministers' political and advisory institutions that lasted even into the 1970s. In reality the Garden Suburb was little more sinister than a glorified Downing Street Policy Unit with a few more staff.

The Number Ten Private Office under Lloyd George consisted of three secretaries, including his mistress Frances Stevenson, and was housed in the room off the Cabinet Room, beyond the pillars. John T. Davies, a fellow Welshman, was Principal Private Secretary. He had previously served as Lloyd George's Private Secretary between 1912 and 1915 when Lloyd George was at the Treasury and a year later at Munitions and the War Office. William ('Bronco Bill') Sutherland (1916–18) dealt with the Garden Suburb and also the press; they worked on different levels, literally and metaphorically.[52] While Sutherland dealt with the press barons, Kerr and his allies would engage, despite professions of distaste, with leaking – what in a later day became known as 'spin doctoring'.[53] Kerr in fact used the phrase 'doctoring' the news to criticise the press barons; the concept and even part of the designation of spin doctors thus existed in 1917. The one facet of the Prime Minister's work which was comparatively neglected under Lloyd George – parliamentary duties: he never had much time for the House of Commons, and left responsibility for it to others.[54]

During Lloyd George's unusual premiership, distinctions that had been emerging over the previous fifty years between private and political staff blurred. Under earlier administrations, most private secretaries had been drawn from the Civil Service and returned to their Whitehall department after working at Number Ten. In 1921, Lloyd George recruited a civil servant, A.J. Sylvester, to his Private Office; Sylvester's fortunes thereafter were tied to Lloyd George's and a few months after the end of his government he became his Political Secretary, a post in which he remained until Lloyd George's death in 1945.

As well as the private secretaries, Lloyd George introduced a Number Ten typing pool in two basement rooms facing onto the garden, and the typists have been known ever since as the 'Garden Room Girls'. Their existence freed the private secretaries from much routine clerical work. Frances Stevenson dealt with all the most confidential matters, as the little scene witnessed by Tom Jones after the fall of the coalition in 1922 illustrates: 'I saw the PM in the Cabinet Room . . . Captain Guest came in and I withdrew to Miss Stevenson's room and found her burning masses of papers in the fireplace, and looking sadder than I have ever seen her.'[55]

Lloyd George's own domestic arrangements were shaped to some extent by his private life and his relations with Frances. He lived in Number Ten with his wife for most of his premiership, though he lived at Cobham at times early on and at the house built for him at Churt in 1922 in his last months as Prime Minister.[56]

Andrew Bonar Law, though only Prime Minister for seven months (October 1922-May 1923), left a decisive mark on the institutionalisation of the office by sorting out what of the Lloyd George revolution would stay and what would go. The Cabinet Secretariat, and Maurice Hankey, were to remain, but the Garden Suburb was scrapped and the large retinue of personal secretaries was mostly dispersed.[57] The Garden Suburb was seen as an undesirable manifestation of a presidential and personal style of leadership, deemed out of place in the British system of democratic government.

Bonar Law's Private Secretary before he became Prime Minister, J.C.C. Davidson, became in name his Parliamentary Private Secretary, although in effect he was Chief of Staff, having been instructed to oversee the abolition of the Garden Suburb and the paring down of the Cabinet Office. He was also the main channel for relations with the press.

Davidson's replacement as Bonar Law's Private Secretary set a new precedent: the establishment of the office of permanent Principal Private Secretary, who remained at Number Ten despite changes of premier or indeed government. Colonel Ronald Waterhouse was recruited by Bonar Law from the army in 1919 to cover Davidson's office during a business trip. After Davidson was elected to Parliament in 1920 he took over from him permanently, later moving across to Number Ten as Principal Private Secretary. When Bonar Law resigned in May 1923, terminally ill, Waterhouse continued in his job under the premierships of Stanley Baldwin and then under Ramsay MacDonald, the first Labour Prime Minister. Davidson wrote of Waterhouse that he 'was a subtle and somewhat sinister figure who deserved the description of an intriguer on occasions, but who had no influence on politics'.[58] In practice, however, it is hard to imagine someone in such a focal position not having any impact on policy or politics.

Other 'regulars' also began to appear at this time. Geoffrey Fry mainly 'dealt with the problems of patronage, civil and ecclesiastical'.[59] Patrick Gower had been Private Secretary to Bonar Law as Chancellor of the Exchequer (1917–19). After joining him in Number Ten in 1922 he, like Waterhouse, remained to work for Baldwin and then MacDonald. Bonar Law also appointed Edith Watson to the Private Office; she had been his Private Secretary since 1914. She also was to remain at Number Ten, until 1945, having established control over preparation for Parliamentary Questions.

Waterhouse's duties included relations between Downing Street and Buckingham Palace, and were used to striking effect when Bonar Law suddenly resigned in May 1923. Waterhouse, it has been alleged during a long-running historical dispute,[60] misrepresented Bonar Law's views on the succession to the King, in order to preserve his own position as Principal Private Secretary. Stanley Baldwin, the victor, let him continue; Lord Curzon, the vanquished, probably would not have done so.

Baldwin took no great interest in the administrative arrangements at Number Ten in any of his three periods as premier (1923–24, 1924–29, 1935–37). His Private Secretaries were relatively anonymous figures, compared with the rising stars of the past and the Civil Service high fliers of the future. As his most exhaustive biography comments: 'About Baldwin's private secretaries it is less easy to speak. If his own maxim was self-effacement, they redoubled it. He kept few papers, compared with most Prime Ministers, and no diary. They kept none. They took it as their duty to shield their Chief from the press, importunate Members and the eager public; they were discretion incarnate

... there is no way to pay tribute nor to analyse how much they affected and influenced Baldwin's life.'[61] It was the perfect epitaph to traditional Civil Service values.

Given Baldwin's consensual style as Prime Minister, his private secretaries probably had little direct political importance. His main concern was process rather than policy; he was a delegator by nature and allowed his ministers to do their jobs with a minimum of interference or central co-ordination. As Roy Jenkins wrote about his working hours, 'All subsequent Prime Ministers would, I think, regard a sixty-four hour week which closed at 5pm on Friday as a semi-holiday.'[62] He preferred to work by political and personal contacts, spending more apparently leisure time than usual for a Prime Minister in the House of Commons, and working hard on his speeches.[63] He was also the last Prime Minister to be a real leader of the House.[64]

The private secretaries, then, were left with keeping the official machine going and protecting Baldwin's time. His main personal confidant was from the Cabinet Office, Deputy Secretary Thomas Jones, who helped with speechwriting. In the December 1923 election this support even extended to party-political campaign speeches; it is noteworthy that Jones was able to maintain close relationships with Liberal Lloyd George and Tory Baldwin in turn. Baldwin was less enamoured of Maurice Hankey, although it appears that by the time of his return to power in 1924 he had thought better of politicising the Cabinet Office and kept the civil servant Hankey in place.[65] In general, Baldwin was a stolid and self-contained man, much given to musing on the essential loneliness of the office of Prime Minister.[66]

The accession of the country's Labour government in January 1924 then marked the first time that the transfer of power from one party to another had not been accompanied by a clearout of Downing Street staff. This was a significant step on the path to the establishment of a permanent and impartial official staff at Number Ten. Ramsay MacDonald retained the existing set of private secretaries, and this pattern continued in the subsequent on changeovers of power at the end of 1924 to the Conservatives and in 1929 back to Labour. Ronald Waterhouse served three Prime Ministers as Private Secretary between 1922 and 1928, two Conservative and one Labour. Over the previous half century no Private Secretary who had served a Liberal Prime Minister worked for a Conservative successor, or vice versa. The Civil Service's colonisation of Number Ten was ironic in view of MacDonald's and Labour's distrust of the Civil Service.

MacDonald was temperamentally unable to delegate and was initially so suspicious of the political affiliations of the officials that he insisted on opening all his letters personally. He 'never brought himself to make full use of the well-tried official machine which was now at his disposal', in the words of his biographer.[67] As a result, MacDonald worked far harder than he needed to have done, a factor that contributed to the personal and political exhaustion that characterised his periods in office, exacerbated by the stress of combining his first premiership in 1924 with the office of Foreign Secretary.

For the most confidential matters at Number Ten MacDonald relied on Rose Rosenberg, his Personal and Private Secretary; she had earlier been his Private Secretary as leader of the Labour Party since 1922. She was 'installed in an office leading out of the Cabinet Room' and had control over a special secret cupboard of documents to which only she and the Prime Minister had access.[68] Rosenberg also handled liaison with the press, including arrangements during the foreign tour to the USA and Canada in 1929 at the start of his second premiership, when she organised a travelling party of 'fifty to sixty' journalists on the ship and on land and fed them with regular press conferences with MacDonald.[69]

The tireless Rosenberg was also MacDonald's link with the Parliamentary Labour Party:[70] 'Rose, go and feel the pulse of the House,'[71] MacDonald would command. On top of all this work, she was the gatekeeper controlling access to the Prime Minister, and prepared his daily diary in the form of a set of cards placed on his desk.[72] When she resumed her role on MacDonald's return to power in 1929, she was helped by a political appointee in association with the Private Office, Herbert Usher, formerly a journalist and an unsuccessful Labour parliamentary candidate. Although Usher joined the Civil Service in 1935, the officials' Private Office still clearly contained a vestigial political element. The widower MacDonald also relied on his children, Malcolm and Ishbel; Ishbel was his Downing Street hostess.

MacDonald's first government in 1924 saw the introduction of the system of ministerial cars and drivers. MacDonald's finances had been severely stretched by the obligations of entertaining and giving gratuities to staff which went with the job. His predecessors were much wealthier men. The Number Ten staff, and others, thought it wrong that the Prime Minister should travel to engagements strap-hanging on a London bus, and an old friend of MacDonald's, Alexander Grant, was approached to help out.[73] The government car service was set up shortly afterwards.

MacDonald was less worried about the loyalty of his officials in the second period of Labour government after 1929. Thomas Jones was under less suspicion, and Robert Vansittart, who had fully expected to be removed from Number Ten when the Conservatives fell, was kept on as Foreign Affairs Private Secretary until he became Permanent Secretary at the Foreign Office in 1930.[74]

After the formation of the National Government in 1931, Rose Rosenberg stayed on to serve MacDonald, who remained as Prime Minister, although her role shifted to become more of a personal guardian of the ageing and increasingly isolated premier, who stayed on until Baldwin succeeded him in 1935. She is one of the more remarkable unsung figures in the early history of the Labour Party as a party of government; biographical information on her is scarce and she was renowned in her retirement for discretion. She left no published diaries or memoirs, yet she did the job of several in the 1990s.

By the time Neville Chamberlain succeeded Baldwin in May 1937 as Prime Minister at the head of the National Government, the central machinery of government had changed utterly from its composition on the outbreak of the First World War; already it had many of the main features in existence when Heath became Prime Minister in 1970. The Cabinet Secretariat and the enlarged Number Ten Private Office were in place. Within the Private Office, the jobs of Principal Private Secretary and private secretaries specialising in foreign affairs and Parliamentary Questions had been consolidated, while another of the secretaries oversaw patronage and church affairs. Number Twelve Downing Street had also settled into its groove as the centre of the government's whips operation for ensuring the smooth conduct of parliamentary business and liaison with opposition parties.[75] The

Prime Minister met regularly with the Chief Whip to review business.

The practice of introducing Prime Ministerial 'advisers' into Number Ten had also been established. On Baldwin's return to power at the general election in 1935, he brought Horace Wilson, formerly Permanent Under-Secretary at the Department of Labour, closer into the heart of government. Wilson's formal title since 1930 had been Chief Industrial Adviser. When Chamberlain succeeded Baldwin, Wilson's role expanded; he was sent as the Prime Minister's personal emissary to Berlin in September 1938 and accompanied him to the Munich conference. Though one can exaggerate Wilson's influence on Chamberlain, he was so closely associated with appeasement that his reputation was bound to suffer with the collapse of that policy; he left to become Permanent Secretary at the Treasury in 1939. Chamberlain's use of Wilson acquired such a bad reputation that Prime Ministers thereafter became wary of sending personal advisers on diplomatic missions.

Chamberlain also brought the first official press officer to Number Ten, as head of a one-man Press Office. Information officials had started to appear around Whitehall in the First World War and the system spread during the inter-war period.[76] George Steward had himself been a career civil servant in central public relations since 1931, but took a minimalist conception of his role, doing little more than handing out government statements. His single-handed Press Office was served by a 'Garden Room Girl', Sheila Minto, who was postwar head of the Garden Room until 1968. The more high-profile task of briefing the Lobby was usually handled by the Prime Minister personally.[77] Unlike Baldwin, Chamberlain was never at ease in the House of Commons, and made great use of his Parliamentary Private Secretary, Alec Dunglass, who as Alec Douglas-Home became Prime Minister from 1963 to 1964.

The Private Office was relatively stable in Chamberlain's three year office, although the Principal Private Secretary from 1939 to 1940, Arthur Rucker, also suffered from a close identification with Chamberlain and his policies. Shortly after the outbreak of war, the Private Office was strengthened by the secondment from the diplomatic service of John ('Jock') Colville, a young official, minor aristocrat and a notable diarist. The initial job description he was given by a Foreign Office official could serve as a general comment on the Private

Office: 'He said it was an interesting job, which would mean being "in the know" the whole time, but that it would entail a good deal of drudgery.'[78] The drudgery included Church patronage. One can presumably regard Colville's description of 9.30 am as 'the disgustingly early hour we start work' as ironic.[79]

Colville later reflected on the 'curious' nature of his job, in a way familiar to many private secretaries and assistants: 'sometimes, as today, I am dealing with matters of the greatest significance; at other times I have not enough to keep me occupied and am acting as little more than an office boy.'[80] We owe to Colville a vivid portrait of life at the apex of British government. Chamberlain would regularly take a walk in St James's Park at 9.30 am; would arrive in the House of Commons in plenty of time for Questions; did not require a secretary to be present in the evening; and on Friday retired to Chequers, 'where no murmur was heard', and which contained one telephone, to be used only in an emergency.[81] Not that Chamberlain himself was lazy. David Dilks, his biographer, writes 'His hours of work were at least equal to Churchill's, since Chamberlain did not have a substantial sleep in the afternoon. He would normally sleep for five and a half hours or so. He was extremely good at apportioning his time, and knew how to concentrate his attention.'[82]

Under the extreme circumstances of war and bombardment it is not surprising that Churchill and his Private Office formed a particularly strong bond; three of the private secretaries, John Martin, John Colville and Leslie Rowan, contributed to an affectionate memoir of Churchill as a boss, in *Action This Day*, written in the 1960s, in response to the published diary of Churchill's doctor, Lord Moran.[83] The main matters normally shielded from the eyes of the private secretaries were the special buff boxes which contained 'Enigma' transcription secrets, decrypted from German communications by the now famous operation at Bletchley Park.[84] By the latter stages of the war, Churchill's staff were trusted to send out letters and messages under his name even on major subjects, another key stage in the evolution of the collective premiership. Churchill's staff also stamped his signature on correspondence, another important step. Colville became personally and politically identified with Churchill, to the point of seeking the

Conservative nomination for the Chelsea constituency twice in 1945. It is therefore surprising that he served for a brief time in Attlee's Number Ten after the 1945 election.

The bombing of London, and the precarious nature and siting of the buildings in Downing Street, meant that alternative accommodation for Prime Minister and staff had to be found. A ground floor for the Number Ten Annexe and basement beneath it for the Cabinet War Rooms were established by the autumn of 1940 under the building which is now the Treasury, although Number Ten itself continued to be used and was equipped with an air-raid shelter, reinforced beams and steel shutters protecting the 'garden rooms'. The first floor sustained severe damage in a raid in 1940 and more superficial in 1944.[85]

As in the First World War there was an expansion in the staffing at Number Ten to equip the Prime Minister for war needs. This time it took the form of the Statistical Section, which Churchill brought with him in May 1940 from the Admiralty, under the control of the Oxford physicist Professor Frederick Lindemann. A close ally of Churchill, who dubbed him 'The Prof', he joined the government (as Lord Cherwell) in the office of Paymaster General in 1942. The Statistical Section had around twenty young staff, mainly economists and compilers of charts. They provided brief advisory memoranda and tables to Churchill on supply and economic matters. The unit was wound up with the Government's defeat in July 1945.[86]

Brendan Bracken, another close political ally of Churchill, presided from 1941 to 1945 over the Ministry of Information, which handled Number Ten press relations. Before that he had been Churchill's PPS, and he remained a close political adviser thereafter. His successor as PPS, Harvie-Watt, proved a more successful link than Bracken with Labour MPs, whose support to Churchill as head of a Coalition government was critical.[87]

On winning the 1945 general election, the retiring Clement Attlee realised, albeit with mixed feelings, that he needed a more substantial public presence than he had hitherto enjoyed. He thus appointed a permanent Press Secretary, who understood politics and journalism. This move was despite his comment that 'I am allergic to the press.'[88] He chose Francis Williams, a journalist who had worked for the wartime Ministry of Information, when the boundaries between the Civil Service and the outside world became more porous. His title was technically 'Adviser on Public Relations to the Prime Minister' and his access to persons and papers was considerable – a morning chat with Attlee, access to Cabinet minutes and papers, and rights of attendance at Cabinet committees.[89]

Attlee's notoriously brusque approach to those who failed him had another side – a willingness to delegate and to listen to expert advice from his staff. Williams, according to a journalist who dealt with him, 'was left alone to do the job as he saw fit. Indeed, he told me that he had to do his own lobbying of other ministers and departments, supplemented by research into Cabinet papers, to discover what was happening on current and controversial subjects.'[90] Williams left in 1947 and was replaced by Philip Jordan, another journalist.

Attlee's Parliamentary Private Secretaries, Geoffrey de Freitas and then Arthur Moyle, were important in informing him about the mood of the large Parliamentary Labour Party (initially 393 MPs) and protecting him from the plotting of leadership rivals such as Herbert Morrison. His second PPS, Arthur Moyle, was useful in consolidating his alliance with Ernest Bevin, Foreign Secretary and trade union leader. The role of the Prime Minister's PPS had gradually increased in scope since the turn of the century, taking over some linking functions between the Prime Minister and the parliamentary party from the Chief Whip and the Private Office. Not government ministers, and not bound, therefore, by the Official Secrets Act, PPSs were not supposed to be shown classified papers, a rule broken by most premiers, including Churchill.

Attlee admired the Civil Service and accepted the staff in place at Number Ten. The Private Office became the pivotal organ linking the Prime Minister with the rest of Whitehall, at the heart of the implementation of an ambitious domestic agenda. As his Principal Private Secretary, Attlee inherited Leslie Rowan from Churchill, while Laurence Helsby (who succeeded Rowan in 1947) handled economic matters. The post of Private Secretary for Parliamentary Affairs, initially held by Edith Watson, then Paul Beards, was consolidated, its main task involving assisting the Prime Minister with Parliamentary Questions and his other parliamentary utterances.[91] The post of

Private Secretary for Overseas Affairs continued initially under Colville, while the 'Appointments Private Secretary' was held by Anthony Bevir until 1947, when a separate 'Appointments Office' was set up under him,[92] combining under its aegis Church and other forms of patronage dispensed by the Prime Minister. Bevir had been appointed to the Private Office in 1940, but found the off-beat world of Appointments much more congenial. He remained until 1956, and his successors have had similarly long terms in office, some ten years on average rather than three years, the customary length for Civil Service secondments to Number Ten.

The return of Churchill in 1951 posed more of a threat to the Private Office status quo. Like Mrs Thatcher twenty-eight years later, he arrived with profound suspicions about the staff. On his first visit he glowered at the private secretaries and complained that they were 'drenched in socialism', and asked 'Is this the way you did things for Mr Attlee?' Wiser counsels eventually prevailed.

The most unusual feature of Number Ten during Churchill's peacetime government was the sharing of authority between two Principal Private Secretaries, David Pitblado and John Colville. Pitblado had been appointed under the Labour government: more important than fears of Pitblado being compromised was that he was not personally known to Churchill, nor on the same wavelength. Churchill duly tried to replace Pitblado with his wartime Principal Private Secretary Leslie Rowan, but was told that he was too senior. Very well, he would have Jock Colville, his flamboyant wartime Private Secretary. He was too junior. Churchill persisted and Colville was duly appointed. But the Civil Service high command, Colville included, were not willing to see Pitblado summarily ejected from a post he was admirably suited to fulfil, and the Joint Principal Private Secretary formula was agreed.[93] In theory, there was a division of responsibility between them, Colville taking foreign policy and Pitblado domestic, but in the informal conditions prevailing at Number Ten this was no more than a rough guideline.[94] Together with two other private secretaries, the double act persisted throughout Churchill's term. Colville was personally and politically close, while Pitblado was relegated to second fiddle.

Churchill's Number Ten was short on political input. He did not formally have a Parliamentary Private Secretary until 1953, when his son-in-law Christopher Soames, who had de facto assumed the role, was given the de jure title. As with Colville, his importance was greater than his job description. They both brought Churchill solace[95] and provided an audience for his stories and reminiscences. Churchill did not officially have a Press Secretary, although by the 1950s there was a weight of expectation that someone should speak for the Prime Minister and Lord Swinton was initially given control over government information. In 1952, Fife Clark, a journalist and the government information officer, was appointed 'Adviser on Public Relations' to the Prime Minister, in effect the Downing Street spokesman.[96]

For a period in the summer of 1953 Churchill was incapacitated by a stroke. One of the more astonishing chapters in the history of the Private Office was the way in which the official machinery was kept going in the absence of the Prime Minister without anyone finding out; Colville, Soames and to a lesser extent, Pitblado were able to make, or defer, decisions during the period, with the assistance of Cabinet Secretary Norman Brook.[97]

In the Civil Service beyond Number Ten, Churchill rescinded the departure of Norman Brook from the Cabinet Office, a move that had been announced under the Labour government. The man groomed to take over, Thomas Padmore (nicknamed 'Mr Podsnap' by Churchill), was unceremoniously stood down. Churchill's motive was again personal, not professional, he did not feel comfortable with the unknown Padmore. In the absence of a strong central direction of policy, Brook was to have considerable scope to exercise influence on the conduct of government.[98]

Churchill's Number Ten reflects how far the office had moved since 1900; for long periods during 1953–55, his last two years in power, the premiership was being run and decisions were taken not by the Prime Minister but by key Number Ten aides. He also delegated administration and policy, particularly in domestic affairs, to his ministers and rarely intervened actively. He did not need an extensive apparatus to impose his will and co-ordinate policy. His main interventions came in defence (for the first six months he was also Minister of Defence) and in foreign affairs, where Colville's – and Churchill's own – vast experience were sufficient. Neither did he take a forceful approach as party leader, nor worry unduly about the rising cacophony of protest at his remaining in power. A stable, loyal team who would protect him from disgruntled colleagues and allow him to pursue pet projects and retire with dignity in his own time were his main requirements. The team delivered their master's wishes, and he left Number Ten on 5 April 1955 having the night before entertained the young Queen Elizabeth II to dinner.

Even before the Suez crisis of 1956, the Eden administration was an unhappy ship, with rivalry between senior ministers, press criticism, and a second budget needed in 1955. William Clark, his Press Secretary, and a critical observer of proceedings, recalled that 'Eden had a very low boiling point and he found it a considerable strain to run one of the roughest offices in the world; the main duty of the private secretaries was to soothe him'.[99] Pitblado stayed on for a year as Principal Private Secretary, while Colville himself immediately departed and his foreign affairs work was undertaken by Freddie Bishop, who in turn became sole Principal Private Secretary in 1956. As expected when Churchill departed, most of his personal retinue left with him, leaving Eden to bring in a largely new team. To Burnham and Jones, Eden's arrival was 'more reminiscent of handovers in the nineteenth century'.[100] As in the 1990s, royal matters caused a heavy deployment of Private Office resources, in this case to consider the ramifications of the proposed marriage between the Queen's sister Princess Margaret and the commoner Peter Townsend.

Eden's first PPS as Prime Minister was Robert Carr, who was followed by the relatively low-profile Robert Allan. Robert Rhodes James, Eden's biographer, assessed their contribution: 'Carr and Allan were exceptionally nice young men, in whom Eden had total confidence and trust, but with all the wisdom of hindsight it might have been better to team Carr with an older and more experienced PPS, of a hardened and cynical disposition. But this was not the type of politician who had any attraction to Eden; he preferred to have close to him those whom he liked and trusted.'[101] There was little else in the way of high-level political input in Eden's Number Ten, which one might explain in part by the strategic drift and lack of policy direction that took hold after the election of May 1955. Eden found it difficult to delegate, even in speechwriting, and frequently made nervous phone calls to ministers and officials about press stories.[102]

William Clark was appointed Press Secretary with the mission to stabilise the arrangements that had persisted in press relations since 1951. Clark was a diplomatic journalist for the *Observer* and television, who had – like Francis Williams under Attlee – spent time during the war as a member of the government's information services machinery. At a meeting before his appointment Eden had told Clark 'I like people I know'.[103] His time with Eden appears to have been disillusioning for him. Eden's personal relationships with the media deteriorated[104] and Clark had to bear the brunt of Eden's bad temper and his over-sensitivity to criticism.

As the Suez crisis developed, Clark perceived increasing signs that Eden did not trust him, a feeling confirmed when he was banned by Eden from the Private Office[105] even though this step was shortly afterwards rescinded. Eden and his allies considered Clark too indiscreet, especially for a Press Secretary.[106] The military operation against Egypt disgusted Clark and he decided to resign on 5 November: 'The week just past has been the worst by far of my life. The knowledge of collusion, the deception, the hypocrisy.'[107] He offered Norman Brook, however, to postpone the announcement until the end of hostilities, and suggested to him that the next Press Secretary should be a political appointment. Clark's departure is, to date, the only resignation of a member of the Downing Street staff on a point of principle.

Charles Hill was given the task of overseeing government presentation in the wake of Suez, and set in train the selection of a new Press Secretary. The search had not been completed when Eden resigned in January 1957.[108]

Harold Macmillan's intention to draw a line under the hullabaloo of the Eden interlude was demonstrated with a little gesture: a notice on the door between the Cabinet Room and the Private Office reading 'Quiet, calm deliberation disentangles every knot'.[109] In truth, his calmness was often an act. He was happy to let it be known that he relaxed, like Gladstone, by reading and by meeting people 'with no possible interest to gain from you'. Macmillan's diaries convey his keen interest in the high political issues of the economy, the Commonwealth and international affairs. They contain few entries on social policy. Much of the domestic agenda was left to Butler and to other home ministers.

Macmillan began the repoliticisation of the Number Ten machine with the addition of John Wyndham, a close associate since the war, as a political adviser. Wyndham, an aristocrat of independent means, sidestepped the question of who would pay for his political services by remaining unpaid, although he was technically a temporary civil servant and worked alongside the official members of the Private Office.[110] In his memoirs[111] Wyndham clearly identifies with the private secretaries and says little about his political role; he is also a classic example of a court jester who lightened the tone of the place.

In the Private Office, Macmillan inherited Freddie Bishop as Principal Private Secretary until he returned to the Cabinet Office in 1959. The Civil Service machine had by this time firmly established the convention that it could move a private secretary on against the Prime Minister's wishes and even in the face of his resentment.[112] Bishop was thus prised out under Treasury pressure.[113] He was succeeded by Tim Bligh until 1964. But the Civil Service hierachy did not always prevail. Some of Macmillan's staff were felt to have become personally over-identified with the Prime Minister during his long term of office, and Harold Evans, the Press Secretary, Tim Bligh and the Foreign Affairs Private Secretary Philip de Zulueta (1956–64) all later left the Civil Service for the private sector. They all received honours in Macmillan's resignation Honours List.

Macmillan upgraded the private secretaries by changes in the Cabinet Room. As well as a new coffin-shaped table (allowing the Prime Minister to see all his ministers), a small table was installed behind the pillars for the private secretaries to sit in on meetings. He would occasionally call his Private Office his 'major-generals' and have informal discussions with them collectively before lunch and at the end of the day over a glass of sherry, to which other officials could drift in.[114] Officials were encouraged to air their views on policy.

As during 1941–45, prime ministerial and government public relations were merged – this time in the shape of the Cabinet minister Charles Hill, who had been selected as media troubleshooter by Eden. A close ally of the Prime Minister in a government post dealing with information is inevitably going to end up 'spinning' for the Prime

Minister and performing duties which in other circumstances would be performed from within Number Ten. As overall controller of government publicity, Hill was technically in charge of the Downing Street Press Secretary Harold Evans. Evans was appointed shortly after the transition. Like Francis Williams and Fife Clark, he had been a journalist and moved into Whitehall during the Second World War. The historians of government media management wrote that 'Until Mrs. Thatcher came to power no government since Mr. Macmillan's had elevated the control of information to such a high level,'[115] and the integration of prime ministerial, government and party publicity was the most complete yet.

Evans conducted Lobby briefings on a regular basis and was responsible for the 'institutionalisation'[116] of the practice. He also established regular meetings at Number Ten or at newspaper offices between himself, the Prime Minister and senior editors and managers. The practice continues, as does Evans' suspicion that the results it produces are meagre.[117] He also started to offer journalists 'on the record' interviews with the Prime Minister.[118] Purely party occasions, however, were still out of bounds, and speech writing and press briefing were undertaken by a Conservative Central Office employee, George Christ, who would also do some of the most political Lobby briefing. Eldon Griffiths later joined as a speechwriter.[119]

Macmillan's period in power saw the wholesale rebuilding of Number Ten under the direction of the architect Raymond Erith; from 1960 to 1963 the Prime Minister and his entourage were moved to Admiralty House. The foundations had 'almost disintegrated' – and the opportunity was taken to make several other alterations, such as the alteration of the private flat and the addition of extra office space and a bow window in the Press Secretary's office facing into Downing Street.[120] The work ran behind time and over budget (about double in each case)[121] but still failed to cure the State Rooms of dry rot. The building of a completely new Number Twelve at the same time increased office space for the Chief Whip's Office, but the rebuilding was most radical on the second floor, where flats were extended all the way along the roof from Ten to Twelve Downing Street;[122] some surplus space opposite the Number Ten flat was later freed up to accommodate political staff.

The institutional architecture of Number Ten in contrast remained very stable under Macmillan. There was a proposal early on to bring in a Chief of Staff, a political figure such as Enoch Powell, but the idea was rejected.[123] Perhaps more notable were the shifts in the demands made on Number Ten, the Press Office having to cope with the sudden spread of TV ownership and the abandonment by TV news in 1958–59 of restrictions on coverage of political events; and the Private Office and secretarial staff facing the increasing demands of prime ministerial foreign visits and summits.[124]

Macmillan's epic African tour in early 1960 lasted six weeks, and he took Bligh, Evans and Wyndham with him. It was fortunately a placid time in British politics, as a crisis would certainly have strained the facilities of those deputising for the Prime Minister, considering the then primitive state of communications with Africa. Aircraft, however, had begun to reduce the amount of time spent travelling to foreign destinations – Churchill would still frequently sail by ocean liner for some of his journeys in the early 1950s – even as the frequency of tours and summits increased. It was not until the 1970s, though, that routine meetings of the European Council and the G7 would be part of the prime ministerial diary.

When Macmillan retired in 1963 so too did John Wyndham, and the Private Office under Alec Douglas-Home returned to being staffed exclusively by the Civil Service. Malcolm Reid joined to fill his place, while Bligh was eventually replaced as Principal Private Secretary by Derek Mitchell from the Treasury, and Oliver Wright from the Foreign Office joined the team in the overseas post: (Wright had been Home's Private Secretary at the Foreign Office). For political advice Home retained George Christ and Eldon Griffiths, and also Nigel Lawson and John MacGregor, both later to become Cabinet ministers under Mrs Thatcher; they had worked from Central Office but at Macmillan's disposal since May 1963.[125] Here was an embryonic Political Office, in the sense that it provided Home with a group of young, ambitious political figures at his command, although their duties concentrated more on speechwriting than on relations with the party.

One little-known event illustrates the informality of Number Ten life. Derek Mitchell, Principal Private Secretary to the Chancellor of the Exchequer, Reginald Maudling, was appointed to succeed Bligh as Principal Private Secretary in Number Ten. The two men were good friends from their days in the Treasury, but Bligh adamantly refused to vacate his post at Number Ten even on promotion. He enjoyed the heady atmosphere of power and wanted to remain with Home to handle any negotiations with an incoming Labour government in 1964. The frustrated Mitchell turned to William Armstrong, Permanent Secretary at the Treasury, who advised him to find a desk in a remote part of Number Ten and bide his time. Instead, Mitchell moved into the Private Secretaries' inner room and sat at the desk opposite Bligh. While Bligh worked his way through the papers, used the telephone and responded to the Prime Minister's requests from the other side of the double door leading to the Cabinet Room, Mitchell sat opposite him and read novels. In due course Bligh caught a heavy cold and had to be away, so Mitchell moved into his desk. But Bligh came back so Mitchell returned to his former desk and carried on with his novels and sometimes visited the cinema in the afternoon. This extraordinary situation continued for nearly four months, such is the addiction of Number Ten: the episode has never been made public.

The 1964 election saw some friction between the official and political functions of Number Ten of the sort which were to recur in 1966. Derek Mitchell reported to Labour's George Wigg that 'I was under pressure to give access to No. Ten for certain people from the Conservative Central Office – three of their public relations and speech writing people' but he refused, arguing that it would be wrong before a dissolution and wrong after, because the government machine should not be touched by party politics during an election.[126]

Harold Wilson came to power on 16 October 1964, promising to modernise Britain. Six months before winning the election, Wilson stated his thoughts on Downing Street in an interview with the academic Norman Hunt. He complained that Number Ten had become too remote and amateurish and was understaffed. Shortly afterwards he pointed out to American political scientist and Presidental writer Richard Neustadt that Downing Street had only thirty-five staff.[127]

Wilson promised to be an interventionist Prime Minister and

wanted Number Ten to become the 'powerhouse' of his project to modernise Britain. The Cabinet Secretary was to play a key role in this new regime. With the air full of suspicion of an allegedly pro-Tory Whitehall 'establishment', it seemed certain that Prime Minister Wilson would go beyond the traditional Civil Service sources of advice. He certainly could not look for much advice on government from his future Cabinet colleagues; Wilson himself had been President of the Board of Trade under Attlee, but as a consequence of Labour's thirteen-year period in opposition only two other members of his shadow team, James Griffiths and Patrick Gordon Walker, had prior Cabinet experience. Wilson was acutely conscious of his role as the experienced captain with an inexperienced and possibly gullible team to command.

His most controversial appointment proved to be Marcia Williams, who had been Wilson's amanuensis since 1956 and it had been unquestioned that she would have some role within Number Ten. Her position when Labour won the election of 1964 was similar to that of those designated Private Secretary at the turn of the century. She had handled the Wilson side of the advance planning for a transition and talked with the then Number Ten Principal Private Secretary, Tim Bligh.[128] Their encounters had not gone well, and confirmed Marcia Williams in her deepening suspicion of the Civil Service. As she wrote: 'Tim Bligh made it clear during these meetings that the Civil Service considered that there was no place for me, or my office colleagues, at Number 10.' Battle lines were being drawn, and the Private Office was not considered an appropriate base for her, even with the Wyndham precedent under Macmillan. Her title caused conflict, until the cumbersome title of 'Personal and Political Secretary' was devised for her. Wilson paid her salary out of the Prime Minister's allowance.

The culture clash of the first change in party control of government since 1951 was accentuated by the different tastes and style of Wilson and his entourage in contrast with his patrician predecessors. Many writers on the Macmillan and Douglas-Home period stress the cosy, family atmosphere of Number Ten; Wilson's staff changed the atmosphere. Mrs Williams became the focus of conflict between the needs of a modern party leader and the traditional culture within Number Ten, a conflict exacerbated by her uncompromising personality and hold over Wilson. The first conflict was over the siting of her room, a comical episode straight out of *Yes Prime Minister*. She was at first assigned the room previously used by the Appointments Secretary, off the Cabinet Ante-Room. Wilson instructed Mitchell to remove the Appointments Secretary, so that Mrs Williams could move in, adding: 'Tell him he can have a stained glass window, if he moves somewhere upstairs'. In 1965 she acquired further accommodation for her Political Office upstairs – on the second floor near the Prime Minister's flat – previously used by Number Ten staff.[129] The formation of the Political Office was one of the reasons for the growth of official staff numbers during 1964–70 from forty-four to sixty-six.[130]

Mrs Williams' best access to Wilson was the time she carved out in the afternoon when he was often in his room in the Commons. She found the unwritten tradition that governs so much of Number Ten activities unreliable and irregular on matters such as who paid for Christmas cards and communications with the party headquarters, and she records 'anger that no one bothered to advise us on the possible and the impossible in order to smooth our path a little'.[131]

Williams has been portrayed as an *éminence grise* and a key member of the 'kitchen cabinet' around Wilson, and inevitably she became a target for gossip and for critics who wanted to attack Wilson indirectly. She was responsible for Wilson's personal and political correspondence and engagements, particularly linkage with party headquarters, trade unions and constituency parties, and she typed his political speeches. She was in regular contact with Labour MPs and ministers who would drop into her office for gossip. She was to the left of Wilson on many foreign policy and defence issues, and Tony Benn's diaries record that she would attend dinners for Wilson's old associates from the left. But her influence over policy has probably been exaggerated; in 1969–70 she was sometimes absent because of pregnancy.

The question of what papers Marcia Williams was entitled to see caused considerable conflict. Working on his boxes one night in June 1965 Wilson rather tetchily wrote on the back of one of his folders containing Cabinet papers 'I should like Marcia to see all these in future. I haven't had time to read these tonight (Sun).'[132] Derek Mitchell, Principal Private Secretary, and Burke Trend, Cabinet Secretary, discussed the request and offered to let her see all domestic

material except those graded 'Top Secret', including Cabinet conclusions (which Trend was reluctant to allow). Mitchell pointed out
that the file Wilson had written on contained some Joint Intelligence
Committee (JIC) material. Wilson confirmed on his copy of the memo
that 'I did not mean her to see Defence (inc JIC) Foreign or Cabinet
conclusions.'[133] The issue brought in George Wigg, who on 19
October had been appointed as Wilson's adviser on matters of intelligence, defence, and MI5 vetting; he had the right to attend Defence
Committee meetings and see its previous papers. Wigg vigorously
opposed Mrs Williams having the right to see such material.

The suspicion Mrs Williams felt for the permanent officials was
reciprocated from the start. In the first week, Mitchell wrote to her
suggesting that if they could not work together, then support for
Wilson would suffer. The two had a private talk and Marcia Williams
told Mitchell that smooth working was impossible because officials in
Number Ten, and the Civil Service at large, were determined to
frustrate the Labour government. Wilson sympathised with the problems faced by his private secretaries, but as he told one: 'when all my
supporters have fallen away, she will be the only one still totally loyal'.
Wilson usually worked in the Cabinet Room. 'At one end the Private
Office wanted to discuss government business with him, at the other
end, Marcia wanted to talk over party matters', recalled an official.

Thirty years later some private secretaries have still not got over
the experience of Mrs Williams. One recalled: 'She was ghastly to us,
but she was central to his life and had marvellous political judgment';
another said, 'I have never experienced anything like it. She made my
life difficult. She would throw tantrums to get the Prime Minister's
attention.' Her high work pressure, and suspicion of any pretenders
to her role as Wilson's closest adviser, led to Mitchell's sardonic disapproval[134] and a head-on clash with key figures amongst the normally
good-humoured Garden Room Girls. Sheila Minto, the head, became
her number one hate, followed closely by Jane Parsons a Garden
Room Girl from 1946 to 1981. On their side, many detested her, for
what they considered her bullying manner, the way she undermined
staff, and for her lack of respect for their work. Jane Parsons wrote
to Mitchell in February 1966 to complain about use of official photocopiers: 'a large amount of political work we suspect is being done'

she observed and pointed out that while a blind eye could normally be turned this was different in an election environment.[135] Mitchell was more than normally punctilious about the distinction between political and official, admitting in a note on the election campaign that 'I was regarded by my predecessor and by some Conservative ministers as unduly puritan in my approach.'[136] Indeed, Mitchell had been regarded by Home's Number Ten as 'a socialist: a John the Baptist for Wilson'. Despite no lack of personal approval for the work of the new government, his insistence on correct form ran straight into Wilson and Williams' desire to run a tougher political operation at the centre.

The boundaries between the political and official aspects of Number Ten became particularly apparent at the 1966 election. A special warning about discretion was issued, and extremely detailed guidelines went into operation in March 1966 on the separation of official and political expenses, down to separate billing of phone calls made from hotels by members of the same touring party – and of course the Downing Street photocopiers. Temporary political staff passes were rationed and they had to bring their own office furniture; Mitchell thought that 'it is wrong if the PM's office assumes the character of an alternative party headquarters'[137] – something it effectively did become in 1970 and in some late elections.

In 1966 the independent-minded Mitchell was replaced by Michael Halls as Principal Private Secretary. Halls was a Wilson personal appointment; he had been his Private Secretary at the Board of Trade during the Attlee government. It is still regarded as an exception to the succession of high fliers that the Head of the Civil Service recommends to the Prime Minister as his Principal Private Secretary. Prime Ministers have the right to turn down recommendations on, for example, grounds of clashes of personality. Senior officials, however, felt that Wilson had grown tired of the tensions surrounding Marcia Williams. She also knew Halls, and he wanted somebody she would accept and work with without argument. An intriguing interview comment from a Number Ten Private Secretary throws much light on the way the top Civil Service élite regarded themselves: 'We on the Private Secretary circuit all knew each other very well and we all reckoned that we kept government going. A quick call hither and thither and we would have everything on the road. It all depended on mutual respect and everyone being from the top drawer, all 22-carat players. But there was a feeling in the later 1960s that standards had slipped and we were being let down.'[138] Mitchell had not considered it appropriate to accompany the Prime Minister to political events, but Halls, ever anxious to fall in with Wilson's wishes, did. Later Principal Private Secretaries have tended to go with the Prime Minister to party conferences to be discreetly on hand should official business suddenly arise – a common event in the 1980s and 1990s when public spending issues were settled around the time of the party conference week.

Trevor Lloyd-Hughes was appointed Press Secretary at the start of the Wilson government. He was a former journalist and was felt by civil servants to have done a very good and professional job, and who understood the proper way to conduct government business. But Marcia Williams was unimpressed: she felt he was not confident in his role and was hesitant in dealing with other journalists and unnecessarily cautious about the political aspects of Number Ten press relations. Political public relations being important to Wilson, another person was appointed specifically to deal with it, namely Gerald Kaufman. Joe Haines, a journalist, also joined in 1969, first as deputy to Lloyd-Hughes and then as his replacement later that year; Haines was more willing to get involved in political matters.[139]

Under Wilson, the Prime Minister's 'kitchen cabinet' became a subject for debate and press comment on a previously unknown scale, as the pace of academic interest quickened. The powerful presence of Marcia Williams, and the establishment of an explicitly political arm of the Number Ten operation, were relatively new. More attention was also paid to the array of 'irregulars' – friends and advisers with varying degrees of official status. Wilson's solicitor Arnold Goodman was regarded as the most mysterious and effective 'fixer', who excelled at keeping derogatory gossip out of the newspapers. George Wigg, Paymaster General, was another key figure, though his influence waned over the 1960s. But his aides did not meet him in his kitchen and they certainly never displayed any of the powers of Cabinet ministers.

As Economic Adviser to the Cabinet, Wilson appointed the Oxford academic Thomas Balogh. He had the status of a temporary civil servant and was based in the Cabinet Office until 1966 when he was found an office in Number Ten. His small office had two junior aides, Andrew Graham and John Allan. For all the suspicion about his role as a manipulator behind the scenes, Balogh found his position frustrating, having little access to relevant Cabinet papers or to Wilson, because of his location in the Cabinet Office. Wilson had instructed Mitchell not to give Balogh an office in Number Ten: 'I do not want him popping in every few minutes.' On the key decision, taken in the first few days of the new government, not to devalue sterling (a decision opposed by Balogh) he was effectively sidelined by Burke Trend, the Cabinet Secretary, and Laurence Helsby, the Head of the Home Civil Service. Wilson was much closer to the former than the latter. Trend asserted his authority over which papers made it into the Prime Minister's boxes while Balogh had not necessarily helped his cause when, before 1964, he had written a scathing essay on the Civil Service for a volume called *The Establishment*.

The Civil Service took increasing control over Wilson's time from 1966 and the political staff gradually retreated into a defensive circle around him at just the time when relations needed to be kept up with new Labour MPs and ministerial colleagues. The divisions within the Wilson administration seeped out quickly through leaks, and were revisited in a series of memoirs and diaries for years afterward. In this breakdown of convention-codes, as well as in the crisis management style of Number Ten activities, a precedent had been set.

Wilson for the first eighteen months usually worked in the Cabinet Room, doing his boxes there and holding meetings. Then the Appointments section was moved upstairs, so freeing the study for him. It also enabled office space in Number Ten to be given to Balogh. In the evening Wilson would gravitate to the upstairs flat but would continue to wander around Number Ten. He worked and gossipped late into the night and, before retiring would read the first editions of the daily papers. He used the White Drawing Room and Dining Room regularly and entertained a good deal, hosting, for example, dinners with business people, university Vice Chancellors and even Permanent Secretaries. After dinner he might invite them to the Cabinet Room; they would come down to sit at the Cabinet table and Wilson would encourage them to talk. Burke Trend, the Cabinet Secretary, was not entirely happy about this use of the Cabinet Room and sometimes claimed that it was not Wilson's room but his.[140]

Wilson's government was defeated in June 1970, its ranks divided, and with little legislative success considering the overwhelming size of its majority after the 1966 general election. It was one of many postwar governments to have been 'blown off course'. Marcia Williams blamed the Civil Service, her worst fears confirmed. Her diagnosis is not convincing. Wilson's government ultimately failed for many of the similar reasons of successive governments, as we shall see.

By 1970 the Prime Minister's office had become both larger and more differentiated than it had been in 1870. The functions of the office during the hundred years underwent shifts in nuance rather than complete redefinition, with the party and national leadership roles becoming more prominent, and relations with Buckingham Palace and Church patronage less so. Number Ten itself became more compartmentalised, into Private, Political, Press, clerical and PPS offices, while some functions relating to the co-ordination of government business went to the Cabinet Office. The dividing line between party political and official Civil Service activity became clearer, where once it was opaque. Until Lloyd George it made little sense to talk of separate political and official institutions within Number Ten.

The Lloyd George interlude left a lasting legacy. While his philosophy of centralised government control was dampened by Baldwin and MacDonald in the 1920s and 1930s, his premiership showed the needs and benefits of a powerful centre, and the increasingly focused Civil Service was able to gain control over the Private Office, the key entity within Number Ten. With increasing pressure on the Prime Minister himself, by a series of steps Number Ten moved ineluctably towards a collective premiership, where aides took key decisions for the Prime Minister, who had no choice but to trust his or her staff.

The high point of Civil Service dominance during the century was in the 1940s and 1950s, and even here politics crept in. The loss of Colville, Bligh and de Zulueta and later Charles Powell from the Civil Service was a sign of the strains that arise when professional civil servants carry out the full range of prime ministerial activities, a problem that mounts the longer a Prime Minister stays in office. In the nineteenth century, West and Hamilton were able to combine a political and personal loyalty with Civil Service work, but the British bureaucracy did not evolve into a French-style *cabinet* system, where top ministerial aides came and went with changes of leadership. The establishment of a Political Office under Marcia Williams after 1964 was a transition to a new model with a dedicated party political presence within Number Ten, although this new model did not become entrenched until it survived the change of government in 1970.

In June 1970, therefore, Wilson handed Heath a machine which had been repaired many times over the years, but never overhauled, still less had a new engine inserted. It was even more differentiated in its functions than ever before, with an efficient and depoliticised (thanks to the double act of Williams and Mitchell) Private Office at its core, and with young private secretaries who could once again look forward to high-flying careers in the Civil Service. But, more than any other part of the British state, Number Ten is a machine that responds to the wishes of its master, and Heath was now at the controls.

CHAPTER THREE

Edward Heath
(1970–1974)

THE HEATH GOVERNMENT came to office in June 1970 as probably the best prepared of any in postwar history until Tony Blair's in 1997. Like Blair too, Ted Heath also sought to 'modernise' British government. Unlike his Labour counterpart, however, Heath had long experience at the centre of decision making. He had been Chief Whip under Anthony Eden and Harold Macmillan, part of the old 'magic circle', and handled big issues such as Europe in 1961–3 under Macmillan, and the abolition of resale price maintenance (RPM) in 1963–64 under Home. He was the first Conservative leader to be educated at a grammar school and the first, in 1965, to be elected in a competitive election. Heath had a keen interest in policy. Under Home's leadership in opposition he had chaired an ambitious policy review, and as leader after 1965 he retained the key post himself.

Like Harold Wilson, Heath spoke about the need for the modernisation of British industry. He regarded this development as essential to meet the challenge of competing with Europe. Heath also promised to run his government in conscious reaction to that of his immediate predecessor, Wilson. In his foreword to the 1970 election manifesto he criticised 'government by gimmick'. As opposition leader he insisted on shadow ministers speaking to their brief and sticking to their last, a cause of tension for Enoch Powell, who liked to range broadly. Enoch Powell's famous and fateful 'rivers of blood' speech on immigration in 1968 trespassed on the territory of the Home Office and gave Heath his opportunity to dismiss his right-wing foe from the Shadow Cabinet: had he not, four senior colleagues, Quintin Hogg (later Lord Hailsham), Edward Boyle, Lord Carrington and Iain Macleod would themselves have resigned.

Heath's government achieved Britain's entry to the European Community, the culmination of a personal crusade for the Prime Minister. But the government was challenged by industrial relations disputes, a breakdown of order in Northern Ireland which led to the imposition of direct rule on the province from London, and the bitter reaction to the introduction of far-reaching statutory controls over prices and incomes. Little of this, or the massive rise in the price of raw materials or the quadrupling of oil prices in October 1973, had been anticipated in 1970. Heath's plan to call a general election on the back of economic prosperity was in ruins. At the end of his tenure as Prime Minister, Heath was exhorting the electorate to prepare for sacrifice.

In opposition after 1964, the Conservatives reviewed most aspects of policy and administration. The machinery of government in general was subject to intensive study in 1965–70, attention being given primarily to management structures within the Whitehall departments and to the reorganisation of ministries.[1] But the body at the heart of government, Number Ten, oddly was not examined in detail.

David Howell wrote a long paper in 1970[2] for Heath's Machinery of Government Group, called 'A New Style of Government', in which principles and proposals for the reshaping of Whitehall were discussed. The only mention of Downing Street was in a proposal for an increase in the staff attached to the Prime Minister and the Cabinet, and the inclusion of a 'high powered analytical capability' at central level with a particular role in overseeing the budget. Evidence to the group from the redoubtable Whitehall figure Dame Evelyn Sharp (Permanent Secretary at the Ministry of Housing and Local Government, 1955–66) had notified it of several deficiencies in Whitehall, including the fact that 'there is a serious lack of advice available to the Prime Minister'.[3]

Occasional ruminations were heard from Heath's advisers about the establishment of something akin to a Prime Minister's Department. This would have entailed a much beefed up Number Ten, which almost certainly could not all have been fitted into Number Ten itself, an important flaw in the proposal. Similar thoughts had been expressed in the highest reaches of the Civil Service. William Armstrong, Head of the Home Civil Service (1968–74), had a dream of splitting the role of Cabinet Secretary, and taking over the prime ministerial duties of the position as the nucleus of a prime ministerial Department.[4] The context for such ideas was in the reform of the Executive Branch of the United States government leading to the establishment of the Office of Management and Budget in 1970 and the increased importance of White House advisers under President Nixon (1969–74). Interest was also high among British administrative circles in the work of the Chancellor's Secretariat in the Federal Republic of Germany.[5] But plans were stillborn.

Heath used Number Ten as an office and a town house, but also as a social base and a showcase for his tastes to a greater extent than any other Prime Minister before or since, capitalising to the full on each Prime Minister's right to decorate the house with art owned by the nation.[6] His personal space extended downstairs from the residential flat on the second floor not only into the study on the first floor but also into the adjacent 'white' drawing room where he would relax and play his piano.

Heath loved filling the houses in which he lived with objects of beauty, and the internal appearance of Number Ten changed considerably during his tenure, including extensive refurbishment of the Cabinet Room. Marcia Williams, now Lady Falkender, familiar with the house as Political Secretary to Harold Wilson in 1964–70 and again 1974–76, commented that in March 1974 'the first thing that struck me was the number of changes that had been made inside the house'.[7] The changes to the design of Number Ten were an aspect of Heath's personality and aesthetic sense as well as his personal style of command; the internal changes in the Wilson era in contrast had been minimal, not least because Wilson arrived in 1964 in the wake of the great alterations of 1960–63, and thus deemed further change inappropriate.[8]

The atmosphere in Number Ten also changed with the arrival of Heath: 'it all became a little more formal', recalled one insider. 'The fact there was no longer Wilson's golden retriever ("Paddy") nor

Siamese cat ("Nemo"), nor children, albeit grown up ones, padding around, coupled with Heath's less easy-going manner meant it felt like a different place.'[9] He was unusual in one other sense too: he was the only premier since 1945 not to be married, and thus had no partner with whom to share the building, or the trials of the job.

Heath's daily routine proved that a Prime Minister can limit the incursions of the job into normal human life. He was not obsessed by his newspaper coverage; he would read one or two first editions at 11 pm and read most newspapers over breakfast after waking up at about 7.45 am, late for a Prime Minister. He did not have the press pre-digested and edited for him, as was the practice of many incumbents. Robert Armstrong, Principal Private Secretary, Douglas Hurd, Political Secretary, and Donald Maitland, Press Secretary, would go up to the second floor flat to see him most mornings to discuss the day's business ahead. Heath wanted to listen to their firm recommendations.[10] He would then work on boxes upstairs until the first meeting of the day, normally at 10 or 10.30 am if a Cabinet or a Cabinet committee. On Tuesdays and Thursdays while preparing for Question Time he would go back up to the flat at lunchtime with Maitland, Hurd, the Private Office and Timothy Kitson, his Parliamentary Private Secretary – occasionally joined by speechwriter Michael Wolff. Until dinner time he would have meetings or work in the Cabinet Room or in his first floor study, and he would try to go swimming at about 6 or 7 pm. He tended then to go back up to his private sitting room upstairs on the second floor, listen to music on his hi-fi record player and work on his overnight boxes. He would also relax over some television, and would tend to go to bed at around midnight. 'As well as trying to organise a Government properly, I ought to organise my own life properly, and that is why I deliberately take recreation,' he told a reporter in 1972.[11] He worked hard, but compared with the workaholism of Mrs Thatcher, with her four hours sleep a night, and even of John Major, with his six to seven hours, his was a more measured lifestyle.

All non-media requests for meetings and engagements, of which there were many, went first to the Diary Secretary in the Private Office (journalist requests went first to the Press Secretary). Liaison would then take place between Heath, the Private Office and the political staff to see who would secure a meeting, and for how long. Requests from foreign dignitaries would be limited usually to visiting Heads of Government and Foreign Ministers. Heath's staff also tried to keep slots available for others, including leading businessmen, who requested time with him. Regular weekly meetings, usually on Friday morning, took place with the Cabinet Secretary, reviewing progress and planning the next week's business.[12]

Heath was keener and more successful than many premiers at relaxing during the weekend. As Robert Armstrong, his Principal Private Secretary, said, 'he would leave Number 10 on Friday afternoon either to go to Chequers or down to Cowes (on the Isle of Wight); he would not be seen again until Sunday evening'. He would not take boxes when sailing, regarding that wholly as leisure time – and because he would say he did not want to lumber the boat with additional weight. He enjoyed going to Chequers, and felt more at home there than James Callaghan or John Major, both of whom had country homes. At Chequers he would entertain and seek conversation with people who interested him, including musicians, or who he felt had something to contribute to political discussion.[13]

Perhaps curiously, for a Prime Minister who so loved the house at Number Ten, to the extent of having no other home ready for him when he was suddenly defeated in February 1974, he did not want to show off the power base to the media. He did not, for example, attempt the 'Rose Garden' strategy of inviting journalists to meet him in the back garden which Harold Wilson had followed in 1970 when the general election came. Opportunities for being interviewed and filmed in Number Ten were unexploited, to the subsequent regret of one of his publicity advisers, Geoffrey Tucker.[14]

Ted Heath was a self-sufficient person, did not make friends easily, had little need, or aptitude, for 'small talk', and few people felt that they could totally understand him. On long-term strategy he had two strong political instincts; one was to enter the European Community and the other to secure an enduring industrial peace with the trade unions. Outside these goals he had little interest in speculative long-term thinking. Heath was by nature a doer. His manner did indeed strike some as erratic, rude, and egocentric. Few penetrated beneath the surface. With his personal staff, however, he was more relaxed.

...ad learned not to worry about the long silences, they
...ing with him. His insistence on concrete recommenda-
...cause of mutual incomprehension when he encountered
...ional civil servants such as Burke Trend, the Cabinet Secre-
...1973, who relied on the Socratic method of eliciting decisions
by question and answer. Douglas Hurd, the Political Secretary,
referred to 'Heath's deadpan voice, the sardonic question, the long
quizzical silence'.

These characteristics were displayed in Heath's approach to election timing. During December 1973 and early January 1974 he listened
to the views of ministers, Central Office and regional party officials
and backbenchers. Against the background of the miners' work to
rule and threatened strike, and a three-day working week, a general
election seemed to offer a way out. Most of the advice pointed to the
advantages of calling an election on 7 February. This was reinforced
by advice from the party's private opinion pollster, who warned that
a later election might be more risky as the issue of the miners' challenge
to the government might be overtaken by other issues. Heath listened
to all this advice, without showing his hand. In the end he called the
election three weeks later, and lost.[15]

One top civil servant who did chime with Heath's style of working
was William Armstrong, the Head of the Home Civil Service, who
was closely involved in his big policy initiatives, notably the switch to
incomes policy and intervention in industry. The close detail involved
in the legislation was meat and drink to a civil servant of William
Armstrong's cast of mind.

In Number Ten were Heath's three most powerful advisers –
Robert Armstrong (no relation to William), Douglas Hurd and Donald
Maitland. The demarcation between the three was informal but
clearcut. Materials from Hurd were given to Heath in a special box,
different in colour from the regular government business. 'A very
important feature of the Heath administration was the clear division
between the government and the Conservative Party staff. Heath was
absolutely determined that this would be the case,' Maitland insisted.[16]

Among his Cabinet Heath relied heavily upon the three ministers
who successively held the office of Lord President of the Council,
William Whitelaw, Robert Carr and Jim Prior. Lord Carrington,

Defence Secretary until late in 1973 and Party Chairman from April 1972, was another Cabinet colleague close to Heath. Tony Barber, the Chancellor of the Exchequer after the tragic premature death, just weeks after the election, of Iain Macleod, was less involved over time. Heath distrusted the Treasury for its reluctance to embrace Europe, or to welcome the public spending increases and the dash for growth more enthusiastically.

When key decisions were being made Heath liked to convene a group, usually of Hurd, Tim Kitson, Maitland, Robert Armstrong, some others from the Private Office Peter Gregson or Christopher Roberts (later Robin Butler) and sometimes Michael Wolff, in the upstairs flat. He would drink many cups of coffee and as the subject and different options were tossed around 'Ted would be sitting there like a sphinx'.[17] After thirty minutes or so he would announce his own conclusion and that was it.

Heath's aloof manner was hardly calculated to improve the morale of the backbenchers, particularly in a climate of economic turbulence, political problems and frequent U-turns. He was thus greatly helped by Francis Pym, his conciliatory Chief Whip, who knew that he had few sanctions over dissident MPs (notably, the most outstanding dissident, Enoch Powell). Pym saw his task as one of winning the consent of MPs or at least assuaging their doubts. He worked hard to persuade Heath to grant a free vote on the Conservative side on the terms of entry into the EC in October 1971.

Douglas Hurd took over from Marcia Williams as Political Secretary, a very different character and outlook. Hurd was a former diplomat (from 1952–66) and a committed European who joined Edward Heath's Private Office in 1968 after a spell in the Conservative Research Department. It was assumed by all sides that he would join Number Ten in some capacity if the Conservatives won the general election, and he was peremptorily given the title Political Secretary on the day after the election. The remit of the Political Secretary, like many jobs at Number Ten, was not initially clearly defined; on taking office, Douglas Hurd admits, 'I had no idea what a Political Secretary was or what he did. Nor was there anyone I could ask.'[18] His experience perfectly answers our opening statement about the fluidity of roles in Number Ten. Marcia Williams had carved out a specific and high-profile role for herself, and part of the idea of Heath's new broom image was to avoid having a Marcia figure; 'the one point made clear to me about my new duties was that I was expected to carry them out in quite a different way to Mrs Williams'.[19] The (correct) perception in the Heath camp was of frequent turf wars between the Political Secretary and both the Press Office and the Private Office in the Wilson era and there was a determination to prevent such conflict from recurring. By all accounts this was achieved throughout 1970–74, though the credit must be due more to the diplomacy of and the friendship between Hurd, Maitland and Armstrong, and to their mutual trust, than to any diktats on the subject from Heath. Marcia Williams felt, with understandable justice, that she had had to battle with the Civil Service to have her role recognised. Hurd, to a degree, profited from her victory. He occupied her small office off the Ante-Room outside the Cabinet Room.

The job of Political Secretary under Hurd was larger and more powerful than it has been at almost any time since. Its importance during 1970–74 is partly a reflection of the personal value Heath placed on Hurd, and of Hurd's intellect and diplomacy, and partly of the fact that the Policy Unit, created by Wilson in 1974, was to take over some of the work once done by the Political Secretary. Hurd had unrestricted access, day or night, to the Prime Minister and extensive rights to information (including classified papers) and would attend many important ministerial meetings with him. Though the diplomatic calendar was not as crowded in the early 1970s as it was to become by the late 1990s, the Political Secretary played a considerable role in accompanying the Prime Minister on foreign trips: here Hurd's diplomatic experience was again at a premium.

Although Hurd did not attend Cabinet or its committee meetings, he was present when ad hoc and informal meetings involving the Prime Minister were convened, learning much as a result. His excellent relationships with the Private Office ('I spoke their language') enabled him to wander into their inner and outer office, glance at papers, gossip about developments and share information. He and members of the Private Office met up in the outer office for tea most days. Here, Hurd's fourteen (and only recently-ended) years as a public servant in the Foreign Office gave him a great advantage: he was regarded to a significant extent as a Whitehall 'insider'. Hurd benefited in particular from having a close relationship and understanding with Robert Armstrong: they had been at school together, both in College at Eton. Hurd drafted speeches for Heath, and his strategically-sited office was a clearing house for political gossip and chat for ministers going in and out of the Cabinet Room.[20]

As Political Secretary, Hurd kept the Prime Minister in touch with the party and particularly with Central Office. But, as the months passed, he became increasingly caught up in crisis management. The years 1970–74 were a turbulent period, with one apparently unrelated crisis following another. Douglas Hurd found himself skipping erratically from one issue to another:

> Suddenly an issue would take the centre of the stage for a day or two. During that short time I would know where each of the characters stood. I would go to their meetings, listen to their private talk, maybe draft a speech or notes for a broadcast. Then the issue would disappear from my sight as suddenly as it had come.[21]

The political direction provided by the Political Secretary was, reflects Hurd, 'crowded out by the sheer pressure of events',[22] while Civil Service advice outweighed it.

The structure of ministerial 'special advisers' was beginning to develop during the Heath government. Drawn from party ranks, or from business, they were short-term appointments designed to give the minister political and policy advice. The aim was to provide a counter and supplement to advice from the Civil Service. Hurd, assisted by Michael Wolff, had the task of finding these political advisers for ministers, particularly in departments such as the DTI and the DHSS; Brendon Sewill, one such adviser, had been Director of the party's Research Department and was already ensconced in the Treasury.[23] In the dying months of Heath's administration, Hurd attempted, as if in response to a perception of lack of strategic direction, to bring the developing network of special advisers together into a forum, to share problems and help impart a common purpose. But his initiative did not have the time or the propitious circumstances in which to succeed, though a regular such meeting of special advisers was to follow in later years. The same failure to bear full fruit can be said about the expansion of the Political Office with the recruitment of William Waldegrave from the CPRS in late 1973, when Hurd had been adopted as a parliamentary candidate: 'I came in quite explicitly as Douglas Hurd's successor . . . I had my own room. I was supposed to have a year's training.'[24] His remit included writing speeches and the election manifesto.

Tim Kitson, MP for Richmond in Yorkshire from 1959 to 1983, was appointed Edward Heath's Parliamentary Private Secretary after the 1970 election. This was a surprising choice; Kitson was not known as a political ally or personal friend of Heath and had roots in the centre-right of the party; in the 1965 leadership election he had voted, not for Heath, but for Reginald Maudling. But it was felt that he would be able to build bridges with the right, as well as to the parliamentary party at large.[25] After an awkward first few weeks he and Heath hit it off on a personal level and he became one of Heath's most loyal friends. Unlike most Prime Ministers' PPSs, who shared the Political Secretary's ground floor room, Kitson worked out of the office just opposite the door to the prime ministerial flat on the second floor of Number Ten. From here, Kitson shuttled frequently back and forward to the House of Commons.[26] He became a regular late-night confidant and conversation partner for Heath.

Kitson's job of justifying the ways of Edward Heath to the parliamentary party was not an easy one. Heath was in some ways not interested in 'politics' at all. He was interested in reaching the right, rational, decision. Once he had done so, he seemed to regard anyone who did not agree with him – including, perhaps especially, Conservative MPs – as obstructive. He had notoriously little time for the 'game' of day-to-day politics, being more at home in Whitehall than Westminster and having a Chief Whip's functional attitude to getting the flock through the correct division lobby. The House of Commons environment of rather superficial and transitory personal contact was one in which Heath's distinctive personality and brand of humour were not best appreciated and, as his biographer John Campbell confirms, he could seem unambiguously rude.[27] There is no doubt that Heath increasingly neglected his backbenchers, and spent insufficient time talking with them and befriending them, in the Commons Smoking Room or Tea Room. He was also niggardly ('mean' his MPs felt) in distributing political honours. Some of the government's legislation was controversial and dissent on the Conservative benches rose. In his latter years as Chief Whip between 1957 and 1959, Heath had seen Macmillan almost daily: by contrast, his own Chief Whip, Francis Pym, saw him only weekly. Mrs Thatcher was fully aware of this deficiency in her predecessor, and set out with the intention of avoiding the same mistake; later on however, she too fell victim to the same alienation from her parliamentary flock. Without Kitson's mediation, the gulf between Heath and his backbenchers would have been deeper still.

Donald Maitland, Heath's Chief Press Officer, was a civil servant, in contrast with Harold Wilson's appointment of professional journalists, first Trevor Lloyd-Hughes, then Joe Haines. Maitland was a man much to Edward Heath's taste. They had worked together on the attempt to negotiate entry to the European Economic Community in 1961–63, when Maitland had served as government spokesman, and he shared Heath's enthusiasm for Europe. Maitland had held senior Whitehall posts, having been head of the Foreign Office's News Department before serving as Principal Private Secretary to two Labour Foreign Secretaries (George Brown and Michael Stewart). A meticulous, civilised and essentially conservative mandarin of the old school, he was also deemed to have been the best Arabist scholar of his generation.

Maitland had been promoted Ambassador to Libya in 1969, so the call to Number Ten came as a surprise to him, entailing a hurried weekend evacuation from the turbulent and at times confusing world of Tripoli diplomacy. He returned to an office in Number Ten on Monday, barely a hundred hours after the polls had closed. Maitland went on to serve as Chief Press Secretary for exactly three years, departing in June 1973 to take another diplomatic post. He and Heath had always seen the office as a fixed-term three-year Civil Service posting, thereby pre-empting the risk of a Chief Press Secretary becoming over-identified with a Prime Minister as occurred under the tenure of Bernard Ingham (1979–90). Both Heath and Maitland were scrupulously correct in such matters.

Maitland, as expected, proved a crucial and most effective appointment for Heath, who had wanted to elevate the role of Press Secretary to cover European and foreign affairs, and was also in favour of making the role of Press Secretary more open and public.[28] He had been impressed by the role of State Secretary in the administration of Willy Brandt, German Chancellor, and he wanted Maitland to fill the same position.[29] According to one insider who worked in the Press Office under both Wilson and Heath, 'Maitland raised the intellectual level of Number Ten's press operation. There was much less improvisation. With Wilson you had to react to things that were happening, and had to take chances on what government policy was sometimes. We reverted under Heath to serious study, to knowing the full facts before making a commitment.'[30]

Henry James, himself later briefly to be Chief Press Secretary in 1979, was brought in with his domestic background to balance Maitland's foreign expertise. James was given the formal title of 'Press Secretary', which was traditionally reserved for a member of the Government Information Service. Maitland learned fast on the domestic side and gradually the office of Chief Press Secretary assumed its traditional, though powerful, role across the terrain of both foreign and domestic affairs.[31]

The Press Office began work early in the day, preparing for the daily 11 am briefing at Number Ten given by Maitland to the Lobby. He would supply the correspondents with an abundance of information about the Prime Minister's business. The 4 pm briefing was held in the House of Commons and would again be conducted by Maitland. Issues arising from the twice-weekly Prime Minister's Questions could be brought up at this meeting. Heath was most unusual in keeping the media at bay, retaining a lofty disdain towards them and their trade. He never enquired what had been said in Lobby briefings, and was far less concerned than most premiers – notably Wilson, Major and Blair – about bad press. He kept a strict distance from influential media figures, shrank from having press favourites, and gave no journalists honours. Heath never complained himself if he felt errors had appeared in the media: Maitland would contact the journalist concerned, but never the editor. Joe Rogaly, social affairs correspondent of the *Financial Times*, David Watt (also *Financial*

Times) and David Wood (*The Times*) were among the political journal-ists most respected at Number Ten.[32]

The guiding principle of Heath's press relations operation under Maitland was that 'comment was free but facts were key'. They would correct errors of fact but not bother too much about adverse comment in the media.[33] It was all rather a sanitised, almost austere press oper-ation, and legitimate questions can be asked about whether such dis-tance under Maitland played to Heath's best advantage. Yet Heath trusted Maitland implicitly. When Heath trusted someone, he did not ask himself too many questions. And the Lobby journalists also respected Maitland, knowing that what he said would be authoritative, and welcoming his commitment to his role as spokesman for the whole government, rather than being a party political mouthpiece.

Heath and Maitland were keen for the government's line to be communicated to the electorate directly, for them to make of it what they would, rather than being sieved by the media. This belief led to the most notable formal innovation in press policy during the Heath years – the prime ministerial press conference; two such events were staged during his years as premier. The House of Commons has traditionally cavilled at government announcements being made first elsewhere, and some government information officers across Whitehall were wary about the press conference plan. Heath believed that the House of Commons' *amour propre* would not be offended:[34] deep down, he may not have greatly cared whether it was or not. Both press conferences were held at Lancaster House – one concerning Europe, and the other the second stage of the prices and incomes policy. As well as emphasising the authority of Heath as leader of the government, they were designed to display Heath's off-the-cuff speaking abilities and skill in dealing with questions from the floor to maximum advantage.[35] In the event the press conferences caused greater dissent within the media than within the government or Parliament.

Heath felt a need to communicate with and educate the public on the great issues of the day. The early 1970s were also a time of significant transition, in which the place of television – and the neces-sary repositioning of the press in British politics – was developing rapidly. As Donald Maitland put it: 'This was a period when the written press was getting uneasy about the influence of television at their expense. We had to make use of the rise of TV without putting the press's nose out of joint.'

Other innovations for handling the media were also discussed, including on-the-record briefings after Cabinet meetings.[36] Maitland conducted a straw poll among Lobby correspondents about whether they would prefer to end the unattributable system of briefings, and have all meetings on the record and attributable. The Lobby itself voted to maintain the status quo.[37] Maitland and Henry James also tried, without success, to interest the Lobby in the idea of induction tours of and talks on government departments. They hoped to prevent common misconceptions, such as the idea that the agenda for the Cabinet was set by last night's news, from being propagated in print, but such idealistic overtures were regarded with suspicion by journalists.[38]

The way in which government publicity was organised would defeat any attempt at a neat management chart. The Prime Minister's press operation had at least three strands – speaking for the Prime Minister, speaking for the government as a whole, and making sure that departmental ministers and press officers were co-ordinated and were not contradicting each other. The third part caused particular difficulty.

Under Maitland there were a number of different information co-ordination operations. One concerned Northern Ireland and was run out of the Ministry of Defence; one was about Europe and was run by Anthony Royle at the Foreign and Commonwealth Office, and the most complex, about prices and incomes, was run from Number Ten itself. There was a multiplication of committees, including the 'Co-ordination of Government Information Committee' which met roughly weekly from 1972 on, composed, *inter alia*, of Michael Wolff, Barbara Hosking (from the Number Ten Press Office), Geoffrey Johnson-Smith MP and occasionally Nicholas Scott MP, and seemed to deal mainly with the anticipation of events and announcements on a weekly cycle. As the coal and oil crises broke in late 1973, it was proposed to set up yet another committee, to deal with energy presentation.[39]

The proliferation of mechanisms for co-ordination of publicity was a source of concern for the political staff and ministers. Jim Prior, on taking over as publicity co-ordination minister in late 1973, a similar role to Hill under Macmillan, bemoaned 'the proliferation of co-ordinating machinery'.[40] Day-to-day responsibility for information control was vaguely divided between Number Ten and the Cabinet Office team under Geoffrey Johnson-Smith, a junior minister with previous experience in BBC television. Strategic co-ordination and relations with senior media executives were under the control of Robert Carr. Emergency response, the Lobby and party matters were co-ordinated by Jim Prior as Leader of the House and a party Deputy Chairman. Prior advocated concentration in one place, 'and this in effect means the [Downing Street] Press Office'.[41]

Maitland's departure in June 1973 saw another former Head of News Department at the Foreign Office (1967–71) succeed him, Robin Haydon. Friends of Robin Haydon stress that he was 'unhappy' and even that his appointment was 'a fundamental mistake'.[42] He was persuaded to leave a job he was enjoying, High Commissioner in Malawi, for one for which he had little natural affinity. Heath wanted someone with practical experience of handling the press and overseas knowledge, and Haydon's previous job at the FCO News Department made him a natural choice. But Haydon did not have Maitland's manner with journalists, nor was he as comfortable with domestic politics, especially with the crisis of the three-day week then raging.

The deterioration of the Number Ten press machine and its relations with the media was a small contributing factor to, as well as perhaps a symptom of, the collapse of the Heath government. James Margach (of the *Sunday Times*), no friend of Heath, said that in his last few months at Number Ten, Heath made abortive attempts to get onto good terms with Fleet Street, hosting meals and phoning press proprietors.[43] The strain was telling on Heath (and others, including William Armstrong and Victor Rothschild). According to Waldegrave, 'he was dividing the world into black and white and taking pot shots at the press'.[44] February 1974, the month in which the Heath regime finally crumbled, was characterised by political and administrative disorganisation.

Robert Armstrong was the Principal Private Secretary for all but the first day of Heath's premiership. An omnicompetent individual, he was a consummate team-builder and sought to create a family atmosphere in the Private Office, and more generally in Number Ten. With his almost unrivalled experience at the top of Whitehall, he looks back to Heath's Number Ten as a time of peculiar harmony when the machine, despite the travails, always worked effectively. Below him were, at the outset, Peter Moon and, from January 1972, Tom Bridges (son of Edward Bridges, a former Head of the Home Civil Service from 1945–56, and grandson of Robert Bridges, the Poet Laureate) on Foreign Affairs; on Economic and Home Affairs, Peter Gregson 1970–72, then Christopher Roberts until 1973 and then Robin Butler; and on Parliamentary Affairs, Christopher Roberts until 1972, then Robin Butler, who joined from the CPRS, and finally Nick Stuart from 1973. The most junior figure in the Private Office was the Diary Secretary, initially Alan Simcock, then Mark Forrester, both civil servants on secondment. It was a typically high-powered unit, containing two future Cabinet Secretaries and Heads of the Home Civil Service – Robert Armstrong himself (1979–87) and Robin Butler (1988–1997).

Butler was the outstanding Private Secretary below Armstrong. Recruited from the Treasury by Armstrong, further consolidating the Number Ten-Treasury axis, Butler was very much his protégé. Armstrong's formal tasks as Principal Private Secretary consisted of general supervision of the Private Office and selection of private secretaries, oversight of the intelligence and security services, ministerial and other non-church appointments, honours, relations with Buckingham Palace, constitutional issues and the machinery of government. He was particularly involved with the EEC, and more generally with keeping up to speed with whatever was concerning Heath at any particular point in time.[45] But his importance extended far beyond his official list of duties.

Sandy Isserlis had been appointed Principal Private Secretary (by Wilson) shortly before the 1970 election after the premature death in April of the incumbent, Michael Halls. Isserlis' arrival was greeted with relief by some in Whitehall, who felt frozen out by Halls' lofty manner.[46] But Isserlis was more suited to Wilson's personality than Heath's, with whom the personal chemistry did not work, and he was not surprised that William Armstrong decided that Robert Armstrong should replace him after a few weeks. All this was understood in

Whitehall and was not regarded as a reflection on him personally. His departure, however, did not profit his subsequent career: unusually among Prime Ministers' Principal Private Secretaries, Isserlis failed subsequently to rise much higher in the Civil Service. Joe Haines, who had been Harold Wilson's Press Secretary at Number Ten, believes Isserlis was only a stop-gap after Halls' sudden death, and that Labour had no intention of keeping him on if the party had won the election in 1970,[47] an assessment not shared by other Whitehall figures.

Armstrong's Treasury background and economic expertise were of importance to Heath. Just as important in the eyes of William Armstrong, who selected him, was the fact that Robert Armstrong loved music, and so would have a head start over some others in achieving a close rapport with Heath.[48] He had been Secretary to the Board at Covent Garden since 1968 and his father, the musician Sir Thomas Armstrong, had known Heath when he was the Organ Scholar at Balliol College. Heath became devoted to Armstrong, and found him one of the most intelligent and companionable officials he ever encountered.[49]

Armstrong's importance was all the greater for two main reasons. The lack of empathy between Heath and Burke Trend, the Cabinet Secretary, meant that Heath relied correspondingly more for advice on his Principal Private Secretary. Highly sensitive issues, such as those concerned with the bank rate or the budget, and sensitive phone calls to the White House, would be handled by Armstrong. He also played a key role in speechwriting, drafting many of the speeches himself. Intelligence was an area in which he had particular expertise, and he was closely involved in the identification in 1972 of the 'fourth man' (following the other pro-Soviet British spies Burgess, Maclean and Philby). Secondly, Armstrong provided some of the social support a wife might have offered – though Heath did not shun all such responsibility – taking, for example, a close personal interest in domestic matters such as placements at formal meals, and in the appearance of the dinner table. Musical occasions were a pleasure they shared, Armstrong helping to arrange after-dinner musical events. Unsurprisingly, Armstrong came to form with Heath a bond that endured long after their time in Downing Street. Armstrong provided significant support in the production of Heath's memoirs for example, which eventually appeared in 1998, twenty-four years after he ceased to be Prime Minister.

Heath and the Private Office held each other in mutually high esteem; he took a personal interest in ensuring that the practice of recruiting the highest quality civil servants was maintained.[50] On returning to Downing Street in March 1974, Harold Wilson thought that the Private Office was 'working far better than it ever did when I was here before', and when presented with Robert Armstrong's expressed willingness to be reassigned elsewhere, invited him to stay in his post, a position he held until April 1975.[51]

The Foreign Affairs Private Secretary is traditionally, and by rank, the second most important figure in the Private Office after the Principal Private Secretary. But when Moon was there, some of his work was done by Robert Armstrong, especially the high-profile relations with Europe; his relations with the Elysée, the office of the French President, as well as with some figures in the European Commission and in the office of the UK's Permanent Representative in Brussels were especially close. Moon accepted this fact with good grace, but the FCO was keen that Moon's successor, Bridges, should claw back the lost ground. The task was facilitated by Bridges having a long-standing relationship with Armstrong, dating back to their days at Eton. Once in Number Ten, Bridges rapidly realised that Armstrong's range of contacts in Europe, and his determination to 'Europeanise' the Treasury and other departments, should not be disturbed. So while Bridges looked after most non-European foreign business for Heath, he collaborated with Armstrong on European business.[52] Relations between Number Ten and the FCO were notably good at this period, in contrast to the mid/late 1980s, facilitated by Heath's close understanding with Foreign Secretary, Douglas-Home. The relationship was also facilitated by the long-standing friendship (dating back thirty years) which Bridges and Armstrong both had with John Graham, the Foreign Secretary's Principal Private Secretary, and with his successor from 1972, Antony Acland, all of whom had been at Eton.

The Private Office was the core link between Heath and the rest of Whitehall. A great deal of responsibility rested with the private secretaries at this time, because the crucial requirement of 'knowing the Prime Minister's mind' was particularly difficult. Staff found his utterances gnomic and his written comments brief and cryptic, and they had difficulty in persuading him to have a one-to-one talk with Cabinet colleagues either in person or on the phone. Plane journeys were welcomed by the Private Office for the opportunity they offered to capture Heath for briefing sessions and for obtaining decisions.[53] 'There was a friendly competition between my little black box and the Private Office's multitude of red ones', which black usually won, according to Hurd.[54] The *pièce de resistance* of the Private Office was a box – blue with a red stripe – later to be named 'Old Stripey' by Harold Wilson. This was the invention of Robert Armstrong for especially sensitive material (mainly to do with intelligence matters and high-level appointments and personal matters) to which only he, Tom Bridges and Heath had keys. As Armstrong explained: 'Hitherto, specially sensitive material was put inside the PM's usual red boxes, but in "double covers" (two envelopes). The PM was provided with another set of double covers for him to place the material into when read, but PMs found this arrangement fussy and tedious. Hence "Old Stripey".'[55] It was often the first thing the Prime Minister went to,[56] though sometimes Hurd's 'little black box' proved the more irresistible to Heath.

Not the least of the Private Office functions was to be on call (as was the Press Office) during the night and at weekends. The private secretaries were on a duty rota: the resident clerk at Number Ten would ring them always if a crisis blew up before obtaining the go-ahead to disturb the Prime Minister.[57] As weekends saw a focus on foreign affairs business, and the entertaining of foreign leaders, Moon and then Bridges had regular and occasionally exhausting stints of weekend duty.[58] Keeping track of Heath in the holiday season was particularly difficult: if he were sailing, business had to wait until he reached port,[59] or had to be dealt with by Douglas-Home if it could not wait.[60] On one occasion Armstrong had arranged for a device to be constructed which would maintain contact between Number Ten and Heath who was to race in the Channel. When Heath was approached about this he expressed his unhappiness and asked its weight. When Armstrong replied, 'Fifty-two pounds', Heath shook his head and said that it was too heavy and that such a device would allow his rivals to know his location in the race. In the end there was a compromise and a rudimentary system of making contact was established, but when Heath was spending a weekend sailing Armstrong always took care to know where Douglas-Home could be contacted. The machine did not always work, or possibly was switched off by the crew of *Morning Cloud* as the duty private secretary discovered during a particularly tense weekend in the Cod War with Iceland.

No regular task was more pressured, or exhibited better the degree of teamwork involved, than preparation for Prime Minister's Questions. Christopher Roberts was a master of Question Time preparation and parliamentary business in general. Heath, like Thatcher, insisted on extensive briefing and, according to some staff, could be highly nervous when going to the House of Commons. Roberts prepared the questions dossier for Heath for Monday and Wednesday evenings; he would read them overnight. The following morning, outstanding questions and new developments would be chased up around Whitehall by Roberts. At 1.30 pm, the Private Office and other close aides would meet in Heath's second floor flat, mainly to discuss handling, but matters of substance would also be raised. Heath typically might say: 'How shall I handle it today? Should I be calm and statesmanlike? Or should I rough it up?' Like many Prime Ministers, he enjoyed these sessions, despite the time pressure. It was during this forum that Hurd produced the phrase 'the unacceptable face of capitalism' to describe the activities of entrepreneur 'Tiny' Rowland, founder of the company Lonrho. Heath knew that the tone for the whole event would be set by his first response to Harold Wilson.[61] There was no love lost between the two leaders.

Upstairs on the first floor overlooking Downing Street, rather tucked away from the pressurised world of the work of the Private Office, was the Appointments Secretary. In Heath's time this was the province of John Hewitt. Heath took a close interest in the appointments of archbishops and bishops. He prided himself on being a good churchman and member of the Church of England, and formerly had been news editor of the *Church Times*. In his memoirs he states that he 'cared deeply about Church affairs'. In common with most premiers in our period, however, church attendance may have been more a duty than a deep spiritual need. Blair may well be the only premier since 1970 to have derived real support from their faith. Hewitt worked directly to the Prime Minister and was not part of the Private Office.[62] He was assisted by a small staff of three or four people, recruited before such jobs were widely advertised around the Civil Service.[63]

Heath was served by two Cabinet Secretaries, Burke Trend until the autumn of 1973 and then John Hunt. Hunt and Trend were as we have seen, different personalities. Trend was the old-fashioned, quintessential mandarin, the embodiment of the traditions of the Civil Service, who had already in that capacity served three Prime Ministers before Heath: Harold Macmillan during 1963, Alec Douglas-Home (1963–64) and then Wilson, whom, despite his quirkiness, he had relished working with for six years. Like Donald Maitland, Burke Trend had an emotional attachment to the Commonwealth, but unlike Maitland he had little instinctive sympathy for the European ideal, or the sensitivity or flexibility to adapt fully to Heath as Prime Minister.

Heath certainly respected Trend, especially on highly confidential matters such as appointments and intelligence, and found his advice level-headed and invariably wise. But he found his approach to government business academic, and his personal style remote.[64] Trend saw himself as the servant of the Cabinet collectively rather than just the Prime Minister. He was sceptical about some of Heath's innovations in Whitehall, notably the Central Policy Review Staff.[65] The two men clashed on a number of issues, including over discussions with the Nixon administration. Heath wanted to ensure the British line with Washington was cleared with partners in Europe; Trend disagreed. On European questions, Pat Nairne, the head of the Cabinet Office's new European Secretariat, was particularly important to Heath, to some extent compensating for Trend's lack of zest for matters European. Nairne chaired a weekly meeting on Fridays in London, co-ordinating very effectively all government business concerning Europe.[66]

Two episodes serve to illustrate the difference in style between Heath and Trend. While Heath was at Chequers, Trend submitted a brief for a Cabinet discussion which ended with a paragraph proposing that the Cabinet ask itself a series of questions. Heath rang Trend in a fury. 'How dare you put all these questions, wasting my time. If you don't know the answers you should bloody well find out.' Trend retorted, 'No, these are perfectly fair questions that follow a logical sequence. If the Cabinet asks itself those questions in that order, it will ineluctably arrive at a conclusion.' Ted replied curtly 'That's not the sort of brief I want.'[67]

The second episode came in 1973. Trend had been negotiating the timing of the Commonwealth Heads of Government meeting in Ottawa. Heath had let it be known that mid-August (the sailing season) should be avoided. But Trend went ahead, without referring back to Number Ten, and confirmed the time bang in the middle of the period Heath had sought to avoid.[68] Consternation ensued.

Trend's retirement in 1973 was not unwelcome on either side.[69] When John Hunt arrived that autumn he sensed an 'air of defeat' hanging over the government. He did not work for Heath in the latter's prime. The two nevertheless developed an excellent rapport and Hunt found Heath good to work for, though demanding.

The job of Cabinet Secretary during the Heath government was separate from that of the Head of the Home Civil Service, as it remained until 1981. During Heath's premiership the Head of the Home Civil Service was the office that carried more weight, almost exclusively because of the powerful personality and style of its incumbent, Sir William Armstrong, a much more commanding man than Helsby before him.

William Armstrong's formal responsibilities as Head of the Home Civil Service did not fully describe his unusual role under Heath. The impression that he was embracing tasks outside the strict purview of a civil servant gathered weight after 1972, when he was seen to have played an instrumental role in the switch to incomes policy.[70] A phrase applied to him, which he came to regret bitterly – 'Deputy Prime Minister' – had been coined by Bill Kendall of the Civil Service union, the CPSA, at a press conference on 6 November 1972.[71] It came, like his namesake Robert's phrase during the Spycatcher saga in the 1980s – 'economical with the truth' – to haunt his later career.

Armstrong and Edward Heath met at a kind of crossroads, the

former a committed, active civil servant, the latter a highly pragmatic politician fascinated by the structures of government. Heath has often been described as a Permanent Secretary *manqué*, a description those who worked with him recognise as having an element of truth, though he remained a politician to his fingertips. Neither should one characterise William Armstrong as a politician *manqué*. But he did possess well-developed political antennae and became very committed to Heath and his political success – too much so, he recollected later. If Heath had been a mandarin, he would have been one in the hands-on mould of William Armstrong rather than that of the more cerebral Burke Trend. Colleagues of both men at the time speculated about what might have happened had Armstrong been Prime Minister and Heath a mandarin.

Heath and Armstrong were in some senses made for each other. Both were action men, but were also cogitators. By 1971, with the work of implementing the Fulton report on reform of the Civil Service, set up by Wilson, largely complete, Armstrong cast around for some fresh project to occupy his abilities and energies. Unlike Trend, he showed no signs of tiredness as his long official career approached its close. The first thought was that he would devote himself to dominating the macro economic struggle against inflation, but that would have meant moving into the territory of the Permanent Secretary at the Treasury, Douglas Allen, a colleague and friend. Industrial relations and incomes policy then suggested themselves as a suitable task, and one that he took on willingly. Some saw an echo here of Horace Wilson. From mid-1972, this subject was taking the greater part of his time, while he delegated his oversight of the Home Civil Service – the nub of his job – very much to his deputy, Philip Rogers.[72]

Armstrong was influential in the change of economic policy from late 1971 to reflation and intervention in industry; in the lead-up to the Industry Act, 1972, over which even some key officials from the Treasury and free-market ministers at the DTI were kept in ignorance. Armstrong was the architect of the statutory prices and incomes policy in 1972 and was also present with Heath at the July 1973 meeting with NUM leaders to talk about the third stage of the incomes policy, a meeting of which Cabinet ministers were unaware. One close insider commented of the Heath–William Armstrong relationship: 'They were so alike. William fitted in with Ted's instincts, to work with trade unions. That was what William was all about.'[73]

William Armstrong as well as Burke Trend became figures of some opprobrium to the more radical 'Heathmen' such as David Howell, who disliked the slide from the free market into statism and corporatism: 'The low point of Burke's and William's influence was the return to incomes policy,' said one.[74] Heath himself disagreed: if the policy was at fault, then the blame should not be laid at Armstrong's door. 'Armstrong's part was in dealing with the prices and incomes policy, because he acted as secretary at the meetings with the trade unions and the employers. But . . . he wasn't dictating policy at all.'[75]

As the story of the life and death of the Heath government after 1972 became increasingly one of industrial relations, Armstrong's contribution became absolutely central. In the final crisis in the winter of 1973/74, the government proposed an institutionalisation of tripartite talks, which would have increased the role of Armstrong or his successor immeasurably, but the offer was declined by the TUC. Heath's biographer, John Campbell, argues that Armstrong's uncompromising line on the crisis contributed to Heath's failure to settle matters with the miners.[76] In an atmosphere of almost impossible stress, Armstrong's physical and mental health broke down in January 1974, just weeks before the government he had tried so loyally to serve. Concerns arose about his stability. He was talking apocalyptically about the strike, the threat to national security, and complaining about Number Ten rooms being bugged. He was making wild plans to cope with the crisis. On 1 February 1974 he was taken gently out of the system and sent to a villa in Barbados owned by Victor Rothschild.

William Armstrong subsequently expressed his misgivings about his close identification with Heath. In a BBC interview a few weeks after Heath's defeat he admitted that he had exceeded his 'proper role' as Head of the Civil Service.[77] It was a sad ending to the career of one of the most brilliant and distinctive civil servants of the post-war era. He served as Chairman of the Midland Bank until his death in 1980, aged only sixty-five.

Victor Rothschild was appointed Head of the Central Policy Review Staff, the body proposed by the party's machinery of government group before the 1970 election. The CPRS belonged on the Cabinet Office side of the baize door separating Number Ten from the Cabinet Office. In its founding principles it was always made clear that it worked for the Cabinet collectively, although the Prime Minister had ministerial responsibility for its activities.[78] Its role was to overlap somewhat with that of the new Number Ten Policy Unit, created in 1974, but the collective role, and the licence to think the unthinkable given it in 1971–73, put it in theory at least beyond the more routine and tactical role of the Policy Unit after 1974. Another comparison would be with the work of the more partisan and non-government 'think tanks', which sprouted during the 1970s and 1980s, such as the Centre for Policy Studies and Demos.

The CPRS consisted of between fifteen and twenty civil servants, on leave from their departments, and high fliers recruited from outside the Civil Service (given the status of temporary civil servants). Its two main functions during Heath's government were to prepare six-monthly reviews of government strategy, and to prepare studies of particular areas, consumer policy being one such investigation. In its first task it had to work closely with the Whitehall departments, relating objectives to a coherent strategy. In its second, it might take direct assignments from the Prime Minister, as from Heath on 24 December 1973: the report of 6 February 1974 on possible reform of the Industrial Relations Act was the result, but by the time it reported the government had barely three weeks of its life left.[79]

Victor Rothschild's informal, personal role hung between the Cabinet Office and Number Ten; William Waldegrave, possibly the most political member of the CPRS in 1971–73, recalled how 'Victor Rothschild had a technique of using me as a sort of runner [to Number Ten]'.[80] Heath gave strong support to Rothschild in his official role, and listened carefully earlier on to his private advice. He was an influential voice alongside Home Secretary Maudling in favour of the switch to incomes policy in 1972.[81] But Rothschild's 'thinking of the unthinkable' tellingly did not embrace neo-liberal economics, growing in popularity on the right of the party. One such disappointed insider observed, 'Though Victor's adversaries were the same as mine, at heart he was an old style Keynesian or social democrat on economics. On some micro matters he was helpful. That was all.'[82]

Relations between Heath and Rothschild deteriorated after a notable occasion on 25 September 1973 when a sombre statistical discussion of Britain's economic future from Rothschild contradicted an upbeat speech from Heath. There were businesslike apologies and the work of the CPRS continued as before, but the personal rapport was damaged.[83] A couple of months later Waldegrave was translated into the Political Office. Rothschild offered some cynical, but economically justified, advice on how to deal with the miners and their crippling work to rule:

> Victor had various quite intelligent ways off the hook. His main contribution at that point was to suggest that the shift in oil prices meant that you should take all energy prices out of the statutory incomes and prices policy on the grounds that the whole thing was busted [because of the Middle East crisis]. But by that stage Ted wasn't in the mood to listen to advice like that.[84]

Rothschild, a noted bon viveur and free spirit, gave lunches for the Permanent Secretaries and served 'cider cup', cider discreetly but generously laced with stronger liquors to loosen tongues and overcome inhibitions and discretion. One participant recalls: 'Trend would take a sip, another one would take a glass – and talk freely – and X would be visibly the worse for wear.'

According to David Howell, the Parliamentary Secretary at the Civil Service Department and a key thinker on the emerging neo-liberal or 'new' right wing of the party, the hopes of the CPRS providing a radical alternative source of advice to government to that of the Civil Service were stymied at the start. 'The Civil Service hijacked it. William Armstrong and Burke Trend moved in round the Prime Minister early on.' He saw the spiking of the CPRS as part of a more general emasculation of his own radicalism. 'Armstrong and Trend moved in on me – lunch at the Athenaeum on the second day of the government. They said these were interesting ideas and they had also prepared a number of papers on how Whitehall could be run more effectively. And hey presto, it was all in their hands, not mine. And Ted ceased to have any time to keep the momentum moving.'[85] As it seemed to Howell, only in the 1980s did the ideas he expounded on limiting the size of government reach fruition. 'He [Heath] had wanted to have people like me around him at Number Ten. But the machine, and Cabinet colleagues, moved around him. Momentum was lost as early as the first few weeks. I was a disappointed young man.'[86]

The CPRS nevertheless, despite initial reservations from the Civil Service hierarchy, became a valuable adjunct to government in the eyes of most insiders, and they were thus critical of Mrs Thatcher's decision to abolish it in 1983. While there is no doubt that the CPRS was never more effective than it had been during 1971–73, its significance has tended to be exaggerated. Its reports on individual areas had little effect on government policy, while its long-term strategic role lapsed when Heath lost interest in it and became distracted during 1973. The CPRS, the first dedicated long-term thinking organ in Whitehall's peacetime history, ironically did nothing to prevent the government being blown off course in 1972–74.

Another unusual presence in and around Number Ten was Michael Wolff. He had served Heath closely in opposition as speechwriter and general fixer, and for a few days during the interregnum after the 1970 general election handled media relations at Number Ten. In this capacity he encountered suspicion from the civil servants in the Number Ten Press Office, perhaps because they feared that he would be a permanent appointment and the office might be lastingly politicised.[87]

Both Wolff and Heath were accustomed to the simpler arrangements of opposition but adjusted rapidly to the presence of the Civil Service machine, and Wolff's involvement with press relations duly faded. He became instead 'Special Adviser to the Government'. His salary was paid by the party and he flitted between Number Ten and Conservative Central Office with a wide if vague brief. Papers on virtually anything passed across one of his desks, although it was party and government propaganda which particularly captivated him. Wolff had a penetrating intelligence and a remarkable gift with words. He worked closely with Hurd at Number Ten as a link between him and the Conservative Party more generally, and helped Heath with many of his speeches and pronouncements, including his message to the nation about entry to the EEC.[88]

Heath abhorred sitting down to write speeches. In theory, the Private Office looked at his programme every four months or so to see which major speeches were coming up, and to decide what the focus of each should be. Then, three weeks before, the Private Office presented him with a skeleton of the speech. Heath's response was often unenthusiastic, in part because he did not wish to focus on an event still so relatively far ahead. Speechwriting often thus became a rather rushed, last minute affair. He preferred taking decisions to communicating them. In fact, officials thought that, apart from on television, he was good. One said, 'he was better when he spoke for himself, but his advisers wrote those clipped short sentences for him'.

Heath's apparent indifference to the arts of political communication was a trial to his political advisers, particularly Hurd and Wolff. In Number Ten, the young William Waldegrave was nonplussed when Heath returned a speech with the comment: 'This will not do', but no guidance as to what he wanted. Heath was widely regarded as a dry, even boring speaker. Because he would engage with the speech only at the last moment Hurd claims that the resulting draft would often contain more of the writers than it did of Heath. Before the 1970 general election a team was assembled to help him with speech-making, interviews and broadcasts. Their approach was to sit with Heath and encourage him to talk freely about policy and values, and then to go away and draft something along the lines of what he had said. Once in Number Ten, however, Heath no longer had, or was prepared to make, the time to follow even this course. Hurd claims that as a result Heath forgot all the lessons others had tried laboriously to drill into him about communications: 'Instead of speaking to people Mr Heath would too often speak at them', and 'Much of his matter was incomprehensible to the television audience'.[89] He also tried to get the Prime Minister to use everyday language, and provided him with a list of technical words to avoid; it included 'unified tax system', 'productivity', 'threshold agreement'.[90] Wolff complained that Heath had a disconcerting knack of removing the most striking or colourful phrases from drafts or speeches. James Douglas, Director of the party's Research Department, concluded: 'He always had a clear idea of what he wanted to say but somehow never knew how to say it. He expected his speechwriters to be able to communicate for him the thought that he was incapable of communicating!'[91]

Heath had several personal friends who were regular visitors at Number Ten and on whom he could rely for support and advice about matters his officials could not readily discuss. Sara Morrison, Central Office official and wife of a Tory MP, was perhaps the closest and most valued source of advice on social matters and on his personal dress and presentation. A trio of political wives, Rosemary Wolff (wife of Michael), Araminta Aldington (wife of close friend Toby) and Sally Kitson (wife of Tim, his PPS) were also helpful.[92] Barbara Hosking, a holdover from the Wilson Press Office, developed a personal friendship with Heath, based on a common interest in music.[93]

An especially close confidant was his personal physician, Brian Warren (knighted 1974), who acquired an access that can be compared with that of Lord Moran, doctor to Winston Churchill during both his spells at Number Ten (1940–45 and 1951–55). Warren had contested the Brixton division of Lambeth in the 1959 general election. While Heath was at Number Ten, Warren was a member of Westminster City Council, and was an influential figure in London local government and Conservative medical circles. Warren's importance was as a source of emotional support and comfort. Prone to mild hypochondria, Heath would call Warren in often, though, as journalist James Margach wrote, 'Edward Heath . . . was the fittest of all the Prime Ministers of the century and never had a day's illness worth mentioning'.[94] But, as with Moran on Churchill, Warren had no discernible political influence, despite the former's beliefs. A representation of the influences on Heath of Number Ten figures is given in Appendix II. The inner circle pre- and post-late 1972 consists exclusively of civil servants except for Hurd.

Heath's Number Ten was, he and others in Downing Street believed, a significant improvement on Wilson's from 1964–70. Several parts were felt by senior Whitehall figures to have worked better, notably the Private Office and Press Office, the latter at least until 1973. Relations at Number Ten were more harmonious, demarcation between government and party matters more meticulously followed, and professionalism more to the fore. The difference between Wilson and Heath as captains of Downing Street, as indeed between them as leaders of government, was, however, rather less than was hoped back in June 1970. However strong the sense of camaraderie at Number Ten and however smooth the working of the team, it did not anticipate or handle well the economic and political crisis of 1973–74.

So the central question remains of how well the admittedly rather grand pair of back-to-backs in Downing Street served in the early 1970s as the engine room for the leader of a modern industrial nation bent on modernisation, the government of which became even more complex with membership of the European Community from January 1973. Donald Maitland, on arrival, was struck by how amateurish the whole Number Ten operation was.[95] Douglas Hurd, twenty-five years on, still considers the place 'ill-equipped', and would approve of an increase in the resources available to the Prime Minister.[96] The overall number of staff employed at Number Ten did not change under Heath. In his May 1972 interview with the *Evening Standard*, he commented with equanimity that there were virtually the same number of people employed there as under Harold Wilson – sixty-three or sixty-four. Exactly the same number were employed at Number Ten by Mrs Thatcher in 1986.[97]

The prospects for the establishment of a Prime Minister's Department were perhaps at their highest in the late 1960s and early 1970s, but the option was not taken. Britain's central administration was being recast, with the establishment of the Civil Service Department in 1968 and of the jumbo departments thereafter. Management reform was in the air. Edward Heath was perhaps the most personally inclined of all the Prime Ministers since Lloyd George to experiment with Britain's central institutions. He had no compunction about upgrading his office towards presidentialism in his relations with Parliament, in creating the Central Policy Review Staff, and in acquiring such trappings of authority as the press conferences. In William Armstrong he had an eager recruit for the office of first Permanent Secretary or Chief of Staff. David Howell had proposed a Prime Minister's Department on the lines of those in Germany, the USA, Canada, France and Italy.[98] The reasons why the development did not happen are perhaps to be found less in Civil Service lack of enthusiasm than in Heath's own unwillingness to push ahead to create such a new body, as he could have done so had he wanted to. Had he been convinced, he would have risked upsetting Cabinet, Parliament, Whitehall, and arousing allegations of rampant presidentialism.

Heath's Number Ten was clearly an important stage in the development of the institutions of the Prime Minister's Office. The Central Policy Review Staff, despite its institutional survival until 1983, was not the same after the fall of Heath, and is therefore in a sense the most transitory of the changes made to the central operations of the British government in 1970–74. The office of Political Secretary survived the change of government in 1970 and has become an accepted part of the institutional scene. The burden of that office, and the collective and long-term purpose of the Central Policy Review Staff, led to an increasing realisation that there was a gap for medium-term policy advice for the Prime Minister. The logical next step was to build on the embryonic office set up under Thomas Balogh in 1964.[99]

Heath, by declining the option of a Prime Minister's Department and deciding instead to improve the existing system's effectiveness, preserved the rather ramshackle Number Ten machine. The path of cautious reform of the machinery of government, which he inherited from Wilson, was to be followed by all his successors. The Heath government still subscribed to the objectives of full employment and the accepted Keynesian techniques of managing the economy. But the world changed. The quadrupling of oil prices by OPEC countries in late 1973 and the end of the Bretton Woods system of fixed exchange rates had introduced instability and meant the end of economic growth for the time being. It does indeed seem at best unlikely whether a Prime Minister's Department could have done more to allow Heath to regain the initiative. Once he had lost it in 1972, he was to be on the back foot for the rest of his premiership, a common situation for the Prime Ministers who followed him.

CHAPTER FOUR

Harold Wilson
(1974–76)

THE ONLY TWO 'OLD LABOUR' PREMIERS during the period covered by this study were, by a strange stroke of irony, also the two most conservative incumbents at Number Ten. Neither Harold Wilson nor, from April 1976, James Callaghan, sought to introduce socialist measures, or to govern in a radical fashion. Few innovations, apart from the Policy Unit, were introduced into Whitehall, and despite the 1970s being the most politically unsettled since the Second World War.

Wilson was much changed from the bright, energetic and confident figure of 1964. He looked older than his fifty-eight years. Close aides had noted a sharp decline in his powers of concentration and application. He easily picked up colds and other illnesses and found it difficult to shake them off. In no sense was he a thrusting chief executive. His objective, as in opposition from 1970–74, was to keep the party united in pursuit of moderate policies. He prided himself on his ability to be the only man who could stop the party splitting between the right-wing followers of Roy Jenkins and those on the left who looked to Tony Benn. As party leader in opposition he had paid a heavy price for his earlier cavalier treatment of left-wing resolutions from the party's National Executive Committee and the annual conference. He would now have to live with a more assertive and suspicious NEC and conference: with trade union bloc votes and an anarchic party structure, it was to prove impossible for Wilson, as it was later for Callaghan, to dominate the party machine. Wilson had also lost much ground with commentators and colleagues as a result of his tortuous balancing act over the European Community whilst in opposition.

Wilson may have expected at best to deny the Tories victory in the general election called by Ted Heath on 28 February 1974.[1] Deep down, however, he was not certain he had the relish for a prolonged period of office. The difficult and exhausting time as Leader of the Opposition, fighting battles with the left, staving off their attempts to introduce a socialist economic policy, had taken their toll. Age – he would be sixty in 1976 – a sense of ennui, perhaps even the first effects of the Alzheimer's disease that would later afflict him, and drink, all ground him down: he confided in those closest to him that he would stay on for a limited time only. Had he won in 1970, he had planned to stay on for only two years. After the 1974 election victory his doctor told him in confidence that he should not think of staying on any longer than that two year timespan, advice he followed almost to the day.[2]

Wilson determined that, second time around, he would run the government differently from his earlier tenure as premier from 1964–70: 'I acted as captain in my first period at Number Ten, when I almost alone had experience of Cabinet,' he would say, 'but now I will act as sweeper.'[3] And so it proved, except that he did little sweeping. Vast swathes of government work passed him by, to the mounting concern of his Private Office, who found it progressively harder to make him focus on business.[4]

Of all postwar premiers, only Winston Churchill in his last two years rivalled Wilson during 1974–76 for inactivity.[5] 'When I saw him in December 1975, after a lapse of a few months, it seemed to me he'd lost all his elastic,' said one close observer.[6] 'In his last year, his work capacity was as little as he could persuade us to let him get away with,' said a Private Office aide.[7] By the autumn of 1975, indeed, the Private Office was constantly protecting him, shielding his workrate not just from the rest of Whitehall, but from his own Cabinet ministers.[8] 'On Tuesdays and Thursdays, Question Times, before going into the chamber to answer questions, he'd pour himself up to three brandies to steady his nerves. After he left the chamber, he had little left to give until the next day.'[9] Not all private secretaries agree that his decline was so stark, though many do. One wrote, 'I always found him quite eager to take official papers, particularly if it took him away from a reception or a social occasion, which he disliked, unless they were with close political buddies.'[10] Neither of his excellent biographers, Ben Pimlott and Philip Ziegler, whose books bring Wilson so vividly to life, perhaps fully conveys the full extent of his deficiencies as premier during his last months.[11]

Wilson had several reasons for feeling unhappy with his lot. One seasoned commentator wrote that the problems that met Wilson in 1974 were 'perhaps greater than those faced by any other postwar leader':[12] he was certainly in a far tighter spot than he had been in 1964. The general election in February 1974 saw Labour achieve just 37 per cent of the vote, and the party lacked a parliamentary majority. The early election caught Labour on the hop. What little forward planning had taken place had been done by the party's left, which Wilson immediately discounted. Heath's government had fallen amidst spiralling inflation, exacerbated by OPEC's quadrupling of oil prices (inflation peaking at 16 per cent during the campaign), a huge balance of payments deficit and low productivity. Trade union power was at its apex; the left of the Labour Party, with Tony Benn in the vanguard, demanded a full-scale socialist economy, while Heath's power-sharing initiative in Northern Ireland was coming under mounting strain.

Wilson, like his predecessor and his successor, struggled to cope with the crumbling of the postwar consensus based on Keynesian management of the economy and full employment. Britain was widely regarded, for the first time since 1945, as a badly governed country. The electorate, suffering from Heath's 'three-day week', from curtailed radio and television, and power cuts, were fretful about what the future would hold. Insiders in Number Ten speak of it as a frenetic, anxious time: some had doubts about their ability merely to stabilise the volatile country. In a farewell interview after losing the election in 1976, President Ford warned American voters: 'It would be tragic for this country if we went down the same path and ended up with the same problems that Great Britain has.'

Wilson's first priority once back in Number Ten was to settle the miners' strike, which he did, and then to win a working parliamentary majority for Labour; all else was to come second to positioning the party favourably for an early general election.[13] Holding the Labour movement together – even if it meant appeasement – was the order of the day. While other leading countries such as the United States and Japan deflated, government spending in Britain rose by 9 per cent in real terms over the 1974 figures. By October, the month in which Wilson called the second election that year, wage inflation reached 22 per cent and rising.[14] While Heath's Northern Ireland settlement, as expected, fell apart, and unemployment rose, there had been almost a complete dearth of policy, let alone of fresh thinking. Wilson achieved the election victory he craved, but as in 1910, the only other year in the century that saw two general elections, the government's victory was incomplete: Wilson acquired an overall majority of just three.

The result suggested caution in policy, a conclusion not unwelcome to Wilson. While keeping his own pro-EEC leanings largely to himself, he sought to remain in Europe, and utilised the referendum idea he had fallen upon in opposition as a perfect pretext for holding together his divided Cabinet and party. The close relationship with the United States was to be further entrenched with its help for Britain's modernisation of its nuclear deterrent. The election over, government spending could be tightened, Benn further emasculated after the referendum by moving him from Industry to Energy, and the left's prescriptions for the economy and social policy sidelined. By the late autumn of 1975, with the referendum pledging Britain to remain in the EEC safely over, Wilson told the Queen he would go in the coming spring.[15]

Wilson was the first Prime Minister since Lord Salisbury at the turn of the century not to live in Number Ten. He and his wife, Mary, retained their home in Lord North Street, half a mile away to the south west side of Parliament. The unexpected defeat in the 1970 general election, and the humiliating return to Downing Street to pack his belongings in the early hours of the morning, had traumatised him. He yearned for more space and privacy.[16] In addition, according to a member of the Private Office, 'Mrs Wilson had hated and resented the lack of privacy at Number Ten between 1964 and 1970, and was not prepared to put up with it again. And Wilson perhaps already knew that he would not be Prime Minister for more than two years and thought that the departure would be easier if they had not lived in Number Ten.'[16]

Informality was the chief characteristic of Wilson's style as Prime Minister from 1974–76: there was none of the correct observation of protocol and occasional hauteur of Heath or later of Callaghan.[17] 'It was marvellous: you could say what you liked to Wilson,' recalled one official, while another described the mixed blessing of how 'with Wilson, you could conduct business anywhere – in the car, in the corridor, travelling between meetings. With Callaghan, he wanted things on paper, and meetings were always pre-arranged.' Another said, 'Wilson would *never* tell anyone – unlike Callaghan – "don't be impertinent".'[18]

On Monday mornings, Wilson would arrive at Number Ten from Chequers by car after the rush hour, and on other weekdays from Lord North Street by 9 am. First port of call would be the Private Office to pick up on the latest developments before going up the main stairs to the Prime Minister's first floor office, where he would always work, and where meetings would begin at 9.30 or 10 am.[19] The Diary Secretary would see him to inform him of any changes to his daily appointments card. The boxes he had worked on overnight would then be dispersed by a duty clerk to the relevant private secretaries and elsewhere around Number Ten. Increasingly, the Private Office recommendations appended to the various papers for Wilson – for example 'the key passage in this paper is on page 7, lines 15–19. I recommend the following response' – would be found to have been endorsed wholesale by the fading premier.[20]

Chairing Cabinet and committee meetings was one of Wilson's main commitments during the week, accounting for over a fifth of his working time. Though Barbara Castle lamented in her diary that 'Cabinet government barely exists any more',[21] in his last period at Number Ten Wilson chaired just over one hundred full Cabinets, usually on Thursday mornings, and he chaired nearly 150 meetings of Cabinet standing committees and sixty meetings of ad hoc committees. The most important committees he chaired were on economic affairs (named MES, Ministerial Economic Strategy), foreign and defence policy (ODP, Oversea and Defence Policy), energy (EN), Northern Ireland (IRN) and the industry committee (IDV).[22] This sounds an impressively industrious list of chairmanships, though in the opinion of one observer 'many times what he did could hardly be called "chairing"'.[23] He came to rely heavily on his 'steering briefs'.

Among Cabinet colleagues, those with greatest influence over Wilson, in descending importance, were James Callaghan (Foreign Secretary), Denis Healey (Chancellor of the Exchequer), Michael Foot (Employment Secretary) and Harold Lever (Chancellor of the Duchy of Lancaster).[24]

Callaghan was Wilson's de facto deputy; after their split over union reform in the late 1960s, Wilson and Callaghan realised they would have to work together, and from the early 1970s they and their staffs kept in close personal touch. Healey, next door in Number Eleven, worked closely with Wilson and frequently used the ground floor interconnecting corridor to call in to see him. Foot's influence owed much to his position as broker with the party's left, as well as his chairmanship of key Cabinet committees. Lever's importance with Wilson was *ad hominem*: he performed something of the role of economic counsellor, especially on international finance, played by Thomas Balogh in Wilson's earlier government.

Well below these top four came Eric Varley and Merlyn Rees.[24] The influence wielded by Wilson's erstwhile close ally, Barbara Castle, was on the wane, while two other key figures, Roy Jenkins and Tony Crosland, although respected by Wilson, were not close to him. The former in particular he deeply mistrusted.[25] Wilson's appointments diaries confirm that he saw less of Castle, Crosland, Jenkins, Rees and Varley than of the top four.[26]

Parliamentary duties weighed heavily on Wilson. While he became increasingly aloof from socialising with MPs or listening to debates in the Commons, he still took his formal parliamentary duties seriously. He delivered some one dozen set-piece parliamentary speeches, making an important personal input to them while writing speeches to be delivered by him outside Parliament was left largely to his staff.[27]

Question Time on Tuesdays and Thursdays caused him considerable apprehension. He knew that his famed memory and ability to think quickly on his feet were waning fast. 'I lost count of the times he told me how Harold Macmillan would be physically sick before Questions,' recalled one aide.[28] The Private Secretary responsible for Parliamentary Affairs would monitor the Commons order papers each day and follow news stories, contact Whitehall departments for information, and by 12 noon on the day of PMQs would have put the file together covering each question, with a draft reply, a possible supplementary question and a range of responses, together with background briefing about the issues likely to come up. Wilson would like *all* his private secretaries to have lunch together on PMQ days, so that they could be ready to come in to see him, usually in his room in the House of Commons but occasionally at Number Ten, any time from 2 pm onwards. Joined by Head of the Number Ten Policy Unit Bernard Donoughue and by Press Secretary Joe Haines, he would go through the file of questions, asking his private secretaries to comment and feed in fresh ideas and information.[29] Fortified by his brandies, he would relax into the informal atmosphere: it was almost like being back as a college tutor in Oxford before the war, in the presence of sparkling and admiring undergraduates.

Parliament was also the location for Wilson's weekly meeting with the Labour Party. Wilson's role as leader of the Labour Party involved him also in bi-monthly meetings with senior party officers and monthly meetings with the National Executive Committee, which he detested and tried increasingly to avoid. The party's organisation subcommittee he regarded as his baby and he took pains to keep a close eye on it.[30] Although he managed to have only one regular annual party conference, in Blackpool in October 1975,[31] his time and energies were taken up disproportionately by two general election campaigns and their aftermaths, and the referendum on whether Britain should remain in the EEC, held in June 1975. As part of his party duties, Wilson also travelled to his Merseyside constituency roughly once a month on Friday afternoons, to show his face to his constituents and across the north western region generally.[32] One aspect of premiership had not paled for him. He relished his weekly audience, usually on Tuesday evenings at 6.30 pm, with the Queen.

Wilson held strongly to the belief, not followed so meticulously by his successors, that the Prime Minister should not be out of the country when the Commons was sitting. Overseas travel, in any case, he found irksome, averaging fifteen days abroad a year, while the most frequent overseas visitors to Number Ten were from Israel and the old Commonwealth, for both of which he felt a deep affinity, and from the United States.[33] Domestic visitors to see him also corresponded with his interests and political needs. Regular trade union callers included Jack Jones and Len Murray, while the businessman Harry Kissin and the lawyer Arnold Goodman were regular visitors, though the latter came far less frequently than he had done in 1964–70. Indicatively, perhaps, Goodman's relations with Marcia Williams had cooled dramatically by 1974.

Not even Goodman, his once very close friend, could prevent Wilson's mounting and disturbing illusions that he was being undermined by Britain's own security services, by BOSS, the South African intelligence operation, or by Mossad, the Israeli security service. The actual contents of 'Old Stripey', containing reports of the Joint Intelligence Committee and other matters, aroused little response from him of value amidst his own fantasies, which bordered on the paranoid.[34]

Periodic receptions and dinners would take place at Number Ten. Wilson could no longer be relied upon to be a good host, his official aides often finding such occasions tense: 'It could be a real nightmare. You'd try to ensure he was talking to the important guests and he'd be off in the corner chatting away to Joe Haines and Bernard Donoughue about Labour Party business. Meals could be even worse. He would talk to guests about esoteric subjects like tactics in parliamentary whipping, and foreigners would have no idea what he was going on about.'[35] It was a great relief to all when Callaghan became Prime Minister: both he and his wife Audrey were 'excellent hosts who knew how to look after guests'.[36]

Wilson's day often ended at Number Ten in his study. He might chat over drinks with Haines and Donoughue. The Deputy Chief Press Secretary, Janet Hewlett-Davies, also became a regular late evening visitor to the Prime Minister's study, becoming a close confidante and arousing inevitable suspicion.[37] She herself said of their relationship: 'He found me companionable. If he found someone he could relax and feel at ease with, he would like to really unwind with them. His conversation was a mix of business and gossip, with increasing doses of reminiscence. He talked and drank, and I just listened.'[38] Later, sometimes very late, he would be driven back to Lord North Street.

The relationship with the Cabinet Secretary is always crucial for a Prime Minister. Some Number Ten aides describe John Hunt, who succeeded Burke Trend in November 1973, as having a less satisfactory relationship than Trend with Wilson. Ben Pimlott, Wilson's biographer, believes that Wilson was more at ease with Trend's donnish style than with Hunt's managerialist approach.[39] Hunt's military bearing and career at the heart of government – he had served at the Treasury and the Commonwealth Office – belied a man of catholic interests, literally so in his religious faith; he was married to the sister of Basil Hume, Catholic Archbishop of Westminster. While Robert Armstrong was Principal Private Secretary, Wilson needed Hunt much less: a certain rivalry between the two mandarins, more imagined perhaps than real, informed an episode of the satirical television comedy series, *Yes Minister*.[40] In reality both Hunt and Armstrong thought similarly on most issues, were highly professional, and talked regularly in person or by phone. But they were both tenacious, hard-working, and conscious of their turf. Hunt also, made it his business to know everything that was going on in Number Ten. The last Cabinet Secretary not also to be Head of the Home Civil Service, he regretted that he lacked that extra handle on the levers of power, especially over top Civil Service appointments, on which he had firm views.

The post of Civil Service Head was held by Douglas Allen, who combined it with the job of Permanent Secretary of the Treasury. The two men met every Wednesday, Hunt officially the junior, though it was clear that on matters of policy and the management of business, Hunt was the key Whitehall figure. Although his main passion was his restless desire to get the business well done for the Prime Minister and other Cabinet ministers, he took a particular interest himself in defence, intelligence and Commonwealth issues. He went on to develop a strong working relationship with Kenneth Stowe, Robert Armstrong's successor from April 1975, who had been working in the Cabinet Office immediately before moving across to Number Ten.[41]

Because the official machine was running Wilson, especially in his last months, with little prime ministerial input, ensuring the smooth conduct of business was all the easier for Hunt. Every Thursday, Hunt would chair a meeting with the Heads of the Cabinet Office Secretariats, along with Donoughue and the PM's Principal Private Secretary, to schedule Cabinet and Cabinet committee business for the week ahead; a minute of the meeting would be put in the PM's box that evening for his perusal. On Friday mornings Wilson would meet with senior Number Ten staff, make any required alterations, and notify the Cabinet Office so that ministers could be alerted to the next week's Cabinet business before the weekend.[42]

Opinions about Hunt vary: many, notably officials, found him a superb operator and executor of business; others found him overly conventional and short-term in his outlook. One such, a political aide, commented wryly that 'the Cabinet Office's weekly schedule was little more than a list of what Whitehall was doing. It was all process, no thought. Of course, Wilson did not *want* to think strategically, but the Cabinet Office should have tried.'[43]

Nowhere was Wilson's dislike of change seen more strongly than in his retention as his Principal Private Secretary of Robert Armstrong. No incumbent of this all-important post in our period survived as long into a new party's administration as did Armstrong: the others left within weeks of a changeover – Isserlis in 1970, Stowe in 1979 and Alex Allan in 1997. Armstrong's retention is all the more puzzling considering his exceptional relationship with Heath. 'We knew how close they had been personally: we knew Armstrong had been intimately identified with policy, especially on Europe. We knew he and Heath shared a love of music. But Harold chose to keep him,' recalled Joe Haines, who quickly himself became conscious of Armstrong's merits and his benefits to them.[44]

Marcia Williams told Donoughue during the February 1974 election campaign that Armstrong would have to go, and she left Wilson in no doubt about what she expected him to do.[45] She was also suspicious of Armstrong for his close relations with the mistrusted Roy Jenkins, another ardent European.[46]

Wilson's aides had hoped to teach Armstrong a sharp lesson from day one. Armstrong travelled to the Palace with Heath when the latter was tendering his resignation to the Queen. As Wilson emerged from his interview with the Queen as the new Prime Minister, his entourage, Haines, Donoughue and Marcia Williams, jumped into the official car so that they could accompany him back to Number Ten. The object was not only to sideline Armstrong but to send a message to the Civil Service. But Armstrong had a spare waiting car and arrived back at Number Ten before Wilson and his party. He was the first person to receive Wilson in Number Ten.[47]

Armstrong himself was prepared to be told to go. So too were other members of the Private Office, which included in the key positions two Etonians, Armstrong and Bridges, and two Harrovians, Butler and Nick Stuart.[48] Worse, they were all arts graduates. 'We didn't think that would go down at all well with Wilson's requirement of "relevant" disciplines,' said one Private Secretary.[49] 'We all liked Ted Heath in the Private Office, and respected the causes he fought for . . . we were more than a little apprehensive when he lost the election . . . we were all rather weepy,' said one.[50]

After helping the incoming Prime Minister with the immediate transition and government appointments, Armstrong told Wilson that he had been in the job for three and a half years and would quite understand if Wilson wanted his own nominee in the key post. 'Stay,' said Wilson, who told him he thought that they were working well together and that the Number Ten machine was working better than when he was Prime Minister in the 1960s.[51] 'Had he been determined to have taken Britain out of Europe I'd have gone of my own accord,' Armstrong said, 'as I'd have felt I would have had no credibility in dealing with Europeans.'[52] Wilson saw the advantage of having someone who understood Heath's policies – several of which he would be annulling or overriding – as well as knowing Whitehall inside out, and how to make it jump to Number Ten's commands.[53] Besides, Wilson always had a profound respect for the Civil Service, and in Robert Armstrong he had one of the outstanding products of the Civil Service as he knew and understood it from his own wartime and postwar experience. Keeping Armstrong was the obvious choice, even if it meant annoying Marcia Williams. He relished having a Whitehall 'Rolls Royce' figure as his closest official, although they never developed the close personal affinity of interests and outlook that Armstrong had had with Heath.

By April 1975 Wilson assented to letting Armstrong depart – to become a deputy secretary and after two years Permanent Secretary of the Home Office. He was fortunate too in his successor, Ken Stowe, who was to serve three Prime Ministers as Principal Private Secretary (Wilson, Callaghan and Thatcher), in a job which he regarded, understandably, as 'the finest in the civil service'.[54] One insider observed that 'Wilson couldn't help but like the very untypical Whitehall figure of Stowe. He was at all times transparently straight, never played games, and was always utterly loyal to the Prime Minister.'[55] In his quiet, efficient manner, he covered up Wilson's growing inadequacies, and later helped induct both Callaghan and Mrs Thatcher into their premierships. Since 1945, only Churchill's Principal Private Secretary John Colville, who coped with Churchill's stroke and decline during 1953–55, had as much independent clout as Stowe under Wilson in 1975–76.

Stowe oversaw a Private Office team initially inherited from Armstrong. It consisted of Patrick Wright (who had succeeded Tom Bridges in 1974) and then, from July 1977, Bryan Cartledge as the Foreign Affairs Private Secretary, considered to be the second position in the Private Office and the sharer of the inner office with the Principal Private Secretary. Wright's appointment was almost strangled at birth by the Political Secretary, Marcia Williams. He had already established himself as an outstanding young diplomat destined to go to the top of the FCO, an ambition realised when he became Permanent Under-Secretary from 1986–91. But he was also an Arabist; Mrs Williams was a staunch pro-Israeli. Wright had passed muster at an interview in the Athenaeum Club with Robert Armstrong and Thomas Brimelow (the then Permanent Under-Secretary at the FCO). But a rearguard action had then to be fought to preserve his appointment when his credentials became known to Mrs Williams. She often attempted to get favoured Israelis into Number Ten over the heads of the Private Office, but Wilson, while happy to see a large number of Israelis, had become increasingly wary of seeing those she was promoting.[56] In the outer office the most senior incumbent was Robin Butler, then Nigel Wicks from 1975, as the Economics Secretary.

Robin Butler went on to rise as high in the Civil Service as Robert Armstrong, and was a man much in the same mould. Educated at Harrow and University College, Oxford, rather than Eton and Christ Church, Butler became the Prime Minister's Principal Private Secretary from 1982 to 1985, and later Cabinet Secretary and Head of the

Home Civil Service from 1988 to 1997. Butler's career too would, however, in all likelihood have been very different had his first experience at Number Ten ended prematurely, a fate actively sought by the predatory Mrs Williams.

Marcia Williams had served Wilson in the then new post of 'Personal and Political Secretary' at Number Ten during 1964–70 and had continued as his aide during the three and a half years of opposition. But by the time that Wilson asked her to return to Number Ten in March 1974, to the same post, she had become a pale imitation of her once formidable self. For the first year, she rarely chose to work from the Political Secretary's office preferring to operate instead from her home. For much of the relevant time she had journalists camped outside her home because of allegations about the involvement of her brother in a controversial slag-heap reclamation scheme and she preferred not to run the gauntlet any more often than she had to. She saw more of Wilson at weekends at Chequers, and would speak to him frequently on the phone. From her home, she would bombard Number Ten with requests, such as asking the Private Office to arrange for Frank Sinatra, who was passing through London Heathrow, to use the VIP suite.[57] Honours and appointments, and arranging favoured individuals to meet Wilson, or to receive invitations to Number Ten, were what seemed to fire her. That, and ensuring that no-one replaced her in influence with Wilson: anyone who she suspected was receiving his ear too much would become an enemy. Thus Stowe, as well as Press Secretary Joe Haines and Policy Unit Head Bernard Donoughue, became her foes. She only twice spoke to Stowe, on both occasions tersely. At Robert Armstrong's farewell dinner she offended several highly-placed guests, and was only prevented by Wilson's physical intervention from tearing into Stowe as well.[58] The reason for her antipathy, Stowe concluded, could only have been that Wilson had appointed him without involving her.[59] Yet her hold on Wilson remained: 'I could never understand why he tolerated it,' recalled one aide. 'It was so extraordinary. She was taller than him, and when they were together she seemed to dominate him like a stoat does a rabbit. He seemed frightened of her.'[60] 'Keeping her quiet became an intolerable strain on him,' said another senior aide, who spoke also of her 'dreadful screaming fits'.[61]

Speculation naturally arose as to why such a difficult and trouble-some aide should have been tolerated, indeed encouraged, by Wilson. Whatever the rumours about their earlier relationship, it was certainly platonic by 1974–76.[62] But the emotional grooves of their long relationship together ran deep. Many concluded that she had some kind of hold over him: Lord Goodman, the lawyer and *éminence grise* of Wilson's first premiership, confided to a private secretary that Wilson could have been a great premier but for one great flaw or lapse, and only one person, himself, knew what it was.[63]

Marcia Williams' attempt to oust Robin Butler shows the extent of her potential influence, and Wilson's weakness. The pretext was that Butler had admitted to her that he had once been to a *Private Eye* lunch – the satirical magazine was one of her pet hates.[64] The real reason was jealousy. Butler was only saved when Haines and Donoughue, briefed by him, went to see Wilson, protesting that Butler had only been to one *Private Eye* lunch, in 1968, and that occasion had been prompted by a desire to sue for a friend, Nicholas Bethell. Butler, moreover, they said, was rather good at his job. Surely that was a consideration? Wilson wavered, and Haines and Donoughue won the day. Butler remained, while all of them became even greater *bêtes noires* of Marcia Williams.

The haranguing of civil servants continued sporadically until the end. It is difficult, however, to see much influence by her on policy during 1974–76: her fervent anti-Europeanism, for example, yielded little fruit. 'He no longer valued her advice, simple,' said one close aide.[65] 'The hapless Bill Housden, Wilson's driver, would be deployed to keep her at bay,' recalled another.[66] Wilson even became reluctant, unless she pressed him, to let her again have access to secret papers.[67]

An interesting question is: who executed the role of Political Secretary, bridging the Prime Minister and the Labour movement, that she was not fulfilling? In part, no one was exercising the role, which helps explain why in his last period of office Wilson lost control of the party machine. The National Executive Committee went its own way, abolishing the 'proscribed' list which had exiled the far left, while the intraparty pressure group, the 'Campaign for Labour Party Democracy', committed itself to an extension of 'accountability' (seen as a veil for boosting the left) throughout the party. Albert Murray, a junior minister who had lost his seat in 1970, was given responsibility for the day-to-day running of the Prime Minister's office: he was, however, to be overshadowed and humiliated by Marcia Williams.[68] Little bridge-building between Number Ten and the parliamentary party was achieved by Wilson's three successive Parliamentary Private Secretaries, some of the least employed incumbents of that post in our period. Rarely had the gulf between a Labour Prime Minister and his party been wider than it was between 1974 and 1976.

Part of the role of Political Secretary was also fulfilled by that ubiquitous Number Ten figure, Press Secretary and former Lobby journalist Joe Haines. Moving into the job initially for the last eighteen months of the Wilson government of 1966–70, he had remained close to Wilson during opposition. With profound knowledge of both the press and the Labour Party, Haines was the obvious choice to succeed Heath's Press Secretary, Robin Haydon, who departed from the job without any formal handover. Haines, keen to make his own mark, prevented him, and all other former Number Ten press officers, from coming into the office after he took up his post.[69]

'I was much wiser when I came back in March 1974,' said Haines. 'I knew what I wanted.'[70] A smaller Press Office was part of it, which meant dismissing five press officers who had served under Heath. Working to improve the difficult relations between Number Ten and Transport House, Labour's headquarters, was another concern, although Haines considered the National Executive Committee beyond the pale: 'a complete disaster'.[71]

Haines, like Wilson, was suspicious of a press which, whether left or right, offered the government little understanding and still less credit, during 1974–76. He continued, grudgingly, to operate the Lobby system he inherited, taking the morning briefing at Number Ten himself, and leaving the afternoon briefing in the House of Commons to a deputy. But in June 1975 he finally secured Wilson's agreement to fulfil his long-standing wish to suspend the Lobby – which he thought, with its system of veiling the Press Secretary's identity, journalistically dishonest. 'In politics, a story often only has value *because* of the source. Without the source it is nothing.'[72] The system of trust on which the Lobby system was predicated, he felt, was also breaking down. There were to be no more twice-daily Lobby briefings as long as Wilson was Prime Minister, although in practice the bulk of the work of the Press Office continued much as before, with individual journalists phoning up requesting information and responses.[73] Haines failed, however, like Maitland before him, in his quest to have on-the-record briefings, akin to those given by the White House Press Spokesman: this, Wilson argued, would have given Haines too high a personal profile,[74] thereby incidentally sparing Haines the obloquy heaped on two of his successors seen as being too powerful in their posts – Bernard Ingham and Alastair Campbell.

Not that Haines was a prototype 'spin doctor'. Indeed, his attitude to the press verged on the contemptuous: his scorn was saved particularly for the 'lazy' end of the Lobby, who wrote up almost verbatim what he had said – a state of affairs many subsequent Number Ten Press Secretaries would have died for. The journalists Haines valued, such as Ian Aitken (*Guardian*), Harry Boyne (*Daily Telegraph*) and Terry Lancaster (*Daily Mirror*), would often stay away from the Lobby meetings, conducting their research in private.

If Haines was the most laid back Press Secretary of the period it was in part because he saw his role as much wider than that of handling the media: he was active not just in the Political Secretary's role, but also in policy advice, serving not just as an occasional member of the Policy Unit, but as one of Wilson's key policy advisers and his main speechwriter. He is an example of a Press Secretary making an explicit contribution to public policy, such as on incomes policy and on housing finance.

The Policy Unit is regarded by its first head, Bernard Donoughue, as 'the most important Whitehall institutional innovation in the last forty years'.[75] There is some justice in Donoughue's judgment; given the way that Whitehall innovations have often been disbanded, or translated out of recognition; the Policy Unit has proved itself of enduring value to successive administrations.[76]

Donoughue, an LSE political historian, political scientist and recent co-author of a 1973 biography of former Labour luminary Herbert Morrison,[77] had been invited by Wilson to help him with polling and policy advice before the February 1974 general election.

To his surprise, not least because his roots had been on the right of the party, Donoughue was then invited by Wilson to set up a Policy Unit within Number Ten. Wilson felt the need for more personal and political policy advice within Number Ten to counterbalance official advice.[78] Very likely Marcia Williams, ever suspicious of civil servants, seeded the idea in Wilson's mind: she was at that stage an admirer of Donoughue, though within six months she had decided that he too should be removed after she became a sworn enemy of the Unit.[79] Wilson also told Donoughue that he wanted him to keep in close touch with the Jenkinsite right of the party (in a way similar to his use of Michael Foot to liaise with the left).[80]

Wilson had been impressed by the embryonic Policy Unit in existence under him from 1964–69.[81] This activity centred on the maverick Hungarian economist, Thomas Balogh, appointed Economic Adviser to the Cabinet by Wilson in 1964 (itself an appointment that harks back to earlier precedents such as Churchill's use of the Oxford academic Professor Lindemann during the war and in the early 1950s). Balogh's office was located at first in the Cabinet Office, but after the March 1966 general election it moved through the green-baize door into Number Ten.[82] Never containing more than three economists, under Balogh's steely tutelage it broadened its interest and its advice to Wilson into matters far beyond economics – into defence, technology and foreign policy.

Wilson gave Donoughue little guidance on how to set up the Unit, or what it should do – but he did specify that he wanted Andrew Graham, an Oxford economist who had served in Balogh's unit and whose advice he had appreciated, to become a member.[83]

Donoughue wrote his own remit and recruited his staff. Recruitment was difficult because everybody knew that another general election was due soon, a Labour victory was not a foregone conclusion, and high-flying candidates for the Unit were understandably reluctant to commit themselves. Donoughue looked for people with relevant expertise, Labour Party sympathies (he himself was caught out as not being a paid-up party member) and an ability to work with the Civil Service. As he said: 'Expertise without *access* is no good.'[84]

In examining proposals going before the Prime Minister, Donoughue's rules were: do they fit in with the government's strategy? do they raise issues which cut across departments? how can we inject a political perspective into them? The Policy Unit largely concentrated on domestic politics – the official Civil Service machine was very keen that it should not have a foreign policy remit – although it became involved in European matters in the run-up to the 1975 referendum and during the 1976 IMF negotiations.

Donoughue met considerable Whitehall suspicion, as Balogh had in 1964,[85] and the CPRS in 1971. The growing numbers of ministerial special advisers out in government departments were already a source of concern: here the Prime Minister was demanding a group of six to eight outsiders wanting to see classified papers, and to make an input into all key decisions, with their base situated right at the very heart of British government. It was too much for some Whitehall traditionalists.

Donoughue was able to attend Cabinets and some Cabinet committees which the Prime Minister was chairing and receive relevant Cabinet and Cabinet committee papers. He did not, however, receive copies of the Cabinet Office briefs for the Prime Minister, although in practice he could wander into the Private Office and read them. Donoughue enjoyed good relations with the Private Office except for the Foreign Affairs private secretaries. He commented interestingly that they all '. . . seemed a little set apart from the rest of us in Number Ten. Perhaps . . . somehow they never ceased to be Foreign Office representatives to the Prime Minister. The other private secretaries were unreservedly the Prime Minister's men.'[86] In contrast with later developments, members of the Unit did not attend Cabinet committees or talk directly to ministers or civil servants in the departments. At that stage they did not feel sufficiently secure to be regarded as speaking on behalf of the Prime Minister. Their main contacts were with special advisers, chairmen of the Policy Committees of the parliamentary party, and with party headquarters. The Unit felt that the Treasury was particularly unimpressed by its arrival, Leo Pliatsky, the Deputy Secretary, being singled out by the Unit as especially dismissive. 'He thought the Policy Unit and special advisers were not to be taken seriously,' recalled one, who added, 'but when it came to the crunch on inflation it was the Policy Unit that was more serious and practical than the Treasury.'[87]

Donoughue was brought head-to-head with the keeper of the

British state, Cabinet Secretary John Hunt. With the Prime Minister determined to have his Number Ten unit, a will that could not be constitutionally blocked, all that could be done by the Whitehall establishment was to corral its scope. Over several discussions there emerged a 'concordat' between Hunt and Donoughue which, in the latter's words 'defined where we could go and where we could not go and what we could do'.[88] The concordat was important: it was official recognition by the Civil Service that the Policy Unit existed, and gave it important concessions, such as the right for its members to attend official Cabinet committees.[89] It was indeed a shock to the Whitehall system to have this outsider body in its midst, but as its work settled down, within months most apprehensions began to subside. There continued to be occasional spats, as when Robert Armstrong was pungently dismissive of a proposal from the Policy Unit to cap the increase in senior civil servants' pay.[90] By the autumn, however, Armstrong, initially cautious, was defending Donoughue and the Unit to Wilson, who was in danger of being turned against it by Marcia Williams.[91] Then, when Stowe with his ready and immediate acceptance of the Policy Unit, succeeded Armstrong in April 1975, its place became even more secure.[92]

Donoughue regarded establishing the Policy Unit as 'the most stressful time' of his life.[93] He placed great store on selecting able specialists in a variety of fields. Andrew Graham, who became de facto deputy until his departure, specialised in economics, and also helped in recruitment.[94] While Donoughue mainly worked closely with the politicians, knowing many of the Cabinet well from opposition days, and with the senior figures in Number Ten and the Cabinet Office, Graham concentrated on relationships with senior officials, especially in the Treasury, but also in other economics departments and in the Bank of England.[95]

Gavyn Davies, another economist, was one of Graham's selections: having obtained a first from Cambridge, he had come over to do postgraduate work under Graham's aegis at Balliol College, Oxford.[96] To Graham, Davies was simply 'one of the most brilliant economists' he had ever seen; remaining in the Unit until 1979, he later became a key economic commentator at Goldman Sachs and later still a member of the Treasury's Independent Forecasting Panel.

Another player was LSE social scientist David Piachaud, who had worked with Richard Crossman when Secretary of State at the DHSS from 1968–70, and was a regular contributor to the *New Statesman*.[97] Piachaud's field covered social policy, while other figures, in full- or part-time capacity, covered other domestic policy areas, notably environment, industry and devolution: foreign policy lacked a specialist, and when it came to the Policy Unit's attention, was covered mainly by Donoughue. He insisted on all members coming from outside the Civil Service, and thus disagreed with the later practice of having some permanent officials in the Unit, which he felt would lead to a conflict of interest as these members would understandably be conscious of having later to fit back into the orthodox Whitehall hierarchy, and so would feel bound to feel constrained in their activities for the Unit.[98]

Donoughue knew that physical proximity to the Prime Minister would be all-important in establishing the Policy Unit's position vis-à-vis the Civil Service. When Wilson went to see the Queen on Monday 4 March 1974 to be accepted as Prime Minister, Donoughue's main concern as he accompanied him on the journey was to lobby Wilson to secure the offices up the small flight of stairs between the Cabinet Ante-Room and the Cabinet Office.[99] This territory he duly achieved, though not all the Unit's staff could be accommodated in that small space: some had to work on the other side of the Cabinet Office door and had to undergo the ritual struggle to obtain the key from John Hunt's office to see their fellow Unit members.

To begin with, as one member frankly recalled, 'It sounded great to say we were the Prime Minister's special advisers, but to be honest, none of us had a clue exactly what we should be doing.'[100] By the summer of 1974 the Unit was settling down into what became a reasonably settled *modus operandi*. Cabinet and Prime Minister's papers would be received each morning; they would then be distributed to the members specialising in each particular area. Donoughue would then collate their comments and write a brief, on green paper, for the Prime Minister's box that evening.

Donoughue, to the end a shrewd political operator with excellent contacts especially on the right of the party, rather than necessarily a creative thinker, would see Wilson himself regularly: it was rare for

Wilson to see other Unit members individually.[101] Donoughue's influence with Wilson was in part *ad hominem*: he and Haines hunted together. Drawn to one another in part by a mutual antipathy for Marcia Williams, they worked together closely as a team, and were Wilson's two closest non-official advisers.

Did the Policy Unit make any difference during Wilson's last two years? The answer is undoubtedly 'yes', and that it carried far more clout under Wilson than under Callaghan: indeed, 1974–76, like 1983–85, 1990–92 and 1997–99, can be regarded as a heyday of the Unit's influence. Senior mandarins had high praise for Donoughue, not because he became 'one of them' – he did not – but because they found him collegial – in stark contrast to Balogh, and to some later Heads such as John Hoskyns (1979–82).[102] But assessing exactly the importance of any organisation, in or outside government, is always difficult, not least because one can never say whether a policy might have been introduced, or blocked, or amended, if the body had not existed. But the Policy Unit's impact was nevertheless clearly seen in some key episodes, notably the particular hybrid form of incomes policy that emerged, and the renegotiation of Britain's membership of the EEC, both in 1975.[103] The former involved alerting Wilson to what Donoughue and Haines regarded as a Treasury attempt to 'bounce' the government into introducing a statutory incomes policy, contrary to its election pledges, and drawing up a voluntary policy.[104] Tony Benn's White Paper on industry was a red rag to Wilson and the rest of the Cabinet. It was savagely rewritten in Number Ten. In a deliberate slapdown to Benn, Wilson with the Unit to the fore cut back the amount of money for the National Enterprise Board to buy into firms and made planning agreements voluntary, not compulsory.

On a day-to-day basis, the Unit helped brief Wilson for his role as chairman of Cabinet and its key committees, and assisted in the co-ordination of policy across Whitehall departments, in preparing speeches and electioneering, and in briefing the Prime Minister for parliamentary questions and debates.

The Unit also developed very radical ideas for the future of Northern Ireland, with which Wilson was personally sympathetic.[105] Selling council houses was another heterodox Policy Unit initiative, worked up from an initial idea from Joe Haines, which would have pre-empted what, after 1979, became one of Mrs Thatcher's flagship policies. But opposition from Environment Secretary Tony Crosland, who thought it would prove unpopular with Labour local authorities which would have to operate it, proved fatal.[106]

The downward turn in the CPRS's influence, originating in 1973, continued under Wilson, who even told aides during the February 1974 election campaign that he would terminate Heath's creation.[107] Why after all retain it if he was introducing his own body, the Policy Unit? The mercurial but brilliant Victor Rothschild fought his corner and remained at its head for a few months before making way for a successor, Kenneth Berrill, a much more convergent and cautious thinker. Hunt took Berrill seriously and would have long exchanges with him on core subjects of the day, such as future energy needs. But the brilliant Young Turks beneath him, of whom there were several, rapidly became restless when the high-profile outfit they thought they had joined turned out to be something more modest.[108] Even though the CPRS regained some of its former influence under Callaghan, the long-term, strategic role of the CPRS, part of its initial *raison d'être*, was lost under Wilson, never to be recovered. Wilson during 1974–76 was not very interested in the long term.[109]

Wilson enjoyed keeping the matter of the timing of his widely anticipated departure to a very tight circle – Goodman, Haines and the three most senior guardians of the British constitution, Cabinet Secretary Hunt, Principal Private Secretary Stowe and the Queen's Private Secretary, Martin Charteris. Hunt knew Stowe knew he knew, but so close was the secret regarded that they never openly talked about it.[110] The only other Private Secretary to be told was Patrick Wright, in December 1975, to prevent his making potentially embarrassing soundings about future foreign trips and visits to Number Ten.[111] Many close to the centre were surprised, not least because they had thought Wilson, as an ardent monarchist, would wait until the Queen's Silver Jubilee in June 1977.[112]

The final episode in Wilson's premiership concerned his resignation honours. The list was written by Marcia Williams in her own hand on lavender-coloured paper – hence the name 'lavender list' given to this sad affair.[113] Wilson, having spent much effort in his final premiership fending off Marcia Williams, now all but caved in to her wishes, although the odd name, such as David Frost, was removed at Haines' insistence, as he regarded such an honour as inappropriate.[114]

Mrs Williams has a rather different account of the episode. According to her, she merely copied it out neatly from a list of names which contained extensive amendments. She also wrote it on pink, not lavender, paper.[115] The honours list soured Haines' otherwise excellent and long-lasting relationship with Wilson. With the exception of Frost's name, and one other, Jarvis Astaire, the boxing promoter, the list went ahead, heaping obloquy on Wilson and ensuring that the dignity that might have been afforded him on his retirement from Number Ten after such a long spell (the longest-serving Labour premier in history) was largely denied him. But for allowing a resignation list to go ahead that smacked to many of poor judgment, and poor taste, Wilson alone must bear responsibility.

It is difficult not to conclude that the years 1974–76 were some of the most difficult in British government and in the recent history of the premiership. Wilson gave few positive signals on policy matters and his political and official staff were largely left alone. Wilson had lost interest, although he could be energised periodically over the game of politics, particularly Labour Party politics. Indeed initiatives like the timing of the referendum, the wording of the referendum resolution, the agreement to differ among Cabinet colleagues and the transfer of Benn after the referendum from Industry to Energy were all to do with internal party politics. The memoirs of most of his colleagues are damning about his almost exclusive concern with winning a second 1974 election and then with the politics of manoeuvre which followed.[116] One can only conclude also that without the loyalty and abilities of the dedicated Number Ten team around him, the full inadequacy of Wilson's last two years in power would have become evident much earlier.

CHAPTER FIVE

James Callaghan
(1976–79)

NUMBER TEN'S most experienced incomer this century (a former Chancellor, Home Secretary, Foreign Secretary, and de facto Deputy Prime Minister from 1974–76) settled into his new post in April 1976 with expected assurance. James Callaghan was sixty-four: one of Wilson's better jokes was that he had resigned 'to make way for an older man'. He knew the ways of Whitehall and had worked with a large number of senior civil servants. Callaghan took over with an economic crisis looming and a tiny parliamentary majority, one which would not last for more than a few months. He was the first Prime Minister to be elected to the post by MPs. The oldest of the six candidates who stood for the party leadership, he was chosen as a centrist figure, the one who was best able to unify the party.

After criticisms of the funding of Wilson's private staff, Callaghan was determined to be different, ensuring that his Number Ten operation would be wholly 'above board'; early on he set up a group under his first PPS, Jack Cunningham, to ensure that irregularities did not occur.[1] There was something of a pre-echo of Blair's determination after May 1997 to have a government that was 'whiter than white'. The influence of some Wilsonian figures in Number Ten, notably Marcia Williams, was considered by the new incumbent (oddly) to have been excessive and to have contributed to a 'bunker mentality' in Number Ten, and he was determined that no-one would obtain a similar position in his administration.[2] There would be no Callaghan 'kitchen cabinet'.

But in other ways, Labour's fourth Prime Minister produced little change in substance. He saw himself as a statesman, like Churchill before him and to an extent Blair after him, as being above mere party politics. As he later wrote, his belief was that the right approach to leadership was exemplified by the Welsh maxim (suggested to him by George Thomas, the Speaker) *'Byd ben: byd ont'* ('He who would lead must be a bridge').[3] Bridge-builders at a time when the gulf between the key elements to be bridged is wide, as it was for the Labour leader in the late 1970s, will have little time or energy left to strike out on original lines. And so it proved. Callaghan had neither the time nor the opportunity to innovate on a strategic scale. His creative impulse was necessarily confined to a few initiatives, notably the 'great debate' on education launched at Ruskin College, Oxford in October 1976, the 'social contract' with trade unions, tightening law and order and personal tax reform. In all these areas, Callaghan was seeking constructive and undoctrinaire ways forward.

The crushing repercussions of the IMF loan crisis during September-December 1976, the loss of Labour's parliamentary majority following two by-election defeats on 4 November 1976, and the squabbles over devolution played their parts in determining that Callaghan's ambitions as Prime Minister would be scaled down to little more than ensuring that he conducted business in orderly fashion, and to electoral survival. Domestic issues and pressures – tough public expenditure decisions, price control, wage restraint and a series of strikes, whether at Grunwick, at Ford or by the firemen – all took up much of Callaghan's personal time, and militated against him being other than reactive. It was almost as if he turned to foreign affairs with relief, international affairs being more susceptible to the stamp of the Prime Minister than home affairs.[4]

James and Audrey Callaghan would usually sleep in Number Ten's second floor flat, though occasionally they would stay in their own Kennington flat, south of the river, which they kept on throughout their three years at Number Ten. They also owned a farmhouse, Upper Clayhill Farm, at Ringmer near Lewes in Sussex (which he loved), where some weekends would be spent as an alternative to Chequers.[5] At least monthly, weekend visits would be made to his Cardiff constituency. Callaghan had a very clear demarcation in his mind between work and private time. His grandchildren and his cows in Sussex were particular sources of joy to him. He was fortunate too to benefit from the support of Audrey, his wife.

Callaghan was not a premier who welcomed visitors – early or late – up in the Number Ten flat, Ken Stowe being a very rare exception.[6] After breakfast, Callaghan would come down to the first floor study where he liked to work, though he would occasionally work from the PM's chair in the Cabinet Room, relishing the sense of history the room's ambience gave him.[7] Officials and aides would catch him early on in the study or Cabinet Room for a few minutes, but impromptu visits were not welcomed. His door was never left ajar. Even his closest advisers would usually have to book times with a private secretary to see him. Callaghan liked everything on paper, even where the answer was obvious and, unlike Wilson, detested conducting business 'on the wing'.[8]

Officials in general felt more comfortable with this more formal style of business in contrast with Wilson's easy-going manner: they knew who and what Callaghan was seeing, and could monitor how he was responding. His overnight boxes would always have been carefully dealt with: he was far more meticulous and methodical than Wilson, and officials found him to be quicker at reading and drafting than even Mrs Thatcher after him.[9]

In the afternoon he would usually go over to the House: he regarded it as essential to go to the Tea Room to visit and chat to Labour MPs, and he would often eat dinner there and work in the Prime Minister's office behind the Speaker's chair until the 10 pm vote, after which he would return to Downing Street. Even when there was an official dinner or an event outside Parliament, he would not like to return late. 'It was all very prosaic. He would call in to wish those still working "goodnight" and say "I'm going up now". There was no gossip nor chat,' recalled one aide.[10] No late-night meetings nor cabals took place up in the flat; no plotting, nor talk of plots, not least because he was under no threat from internal party challenges. He would work on the boxes until 11 pm or soon after, and then go to bed. Unlike Wilson, he would drink very rarely and then only on formal occasions, and he also needed more sleep.[11] So he went to bed and woke up with a clear head. As one close aide said: 'he told me he had a duty to be fit, just as an athlete keeps himself fit'.[12]

Callaghan enjoyed chairing Cabinet and committees. As with Wilson, such work was the biggest single call on his time. Full Cabinet was summoned on average just over once a week during the Whitehall year, and never more so than during the IMF crisis in the late autumn 1976 when thirteen hours of meetings were held. Cabinet was always chaired briskly – Callaghan prided himself on having, like Heath, the processing skills of a civil servant, despatching business as crisply as the most skilled mandarin. The key Cabinet standing committees he chaired were economic policy (EY), defence and overseas (DOP), energy (EN), Northern Ireland (IN) and devolution (DVY). He also chaired over sixty *ad hoc* Cabinet committees, known as GEN, followed by a serial number: GEN29, for example, examined possible reforms to the Official Secrets Act, of which nothing came.[13]

Callaghan had a deserved reputation for straight dealing with the Cabinet. They admired his directness, and also his personal support, not least when they ran into difficulties. As a former Secretary of State and junior minister in domestic and foreign departments, he had personal understanding of policy on a broad front. His mastery of the Cabinet, aided by his immediate dismissal of Barbara Castle in April 1976 and the departure of Roy Jenkins to the EEC Presidency that September, was complete.[14] So confident was he, that he encouraged his ministers to be innovative and independent-minded. He did not block, but neither did he particularly foster, the new monetarist thinking burgeoning at the Treasury under Healey, which found its flowering under the chancellorship of Geoffrey Howe (1979–83).

Once the protracted series of Cabinet meetings over the IMF loans was completed in late 1976, Callaghan set up a seminar, spearheaded by Harold Lever, to discuss interest rates and exchange rates. Its main purpose was to allow Callaghan to keep abreast of current financial thinking. It met on fourteen occasions in 1977–78, and included the Chancellor, Foreign Secretary, and senior representatives of the Bank of England, CPRS, Policy Unit, Cabinet Office and Private Office. Callaghan also valued the direct access it gave him to the minds of Gordon Richardson, the Governor of the Bank of England, and his deputy, Kit McMahon. If it provided a countervailing source of advice for him to that of the Treasury, so much the better.[15]

Callaghan's official biographer, Kenneth O. Morgan, described the seminar as Callaghan's most notable governmental innovation,[16] which says as much about his lack of activity in this area as about the importance of the body. Like most premiers, Callaghan was inclined to be conservative on institutional reform. Callaghan also used the Cabinet Office and Policy Unit to examine how North Sea oil revenues might be used, and to arbitrate between the different positions adopted by the Treasury and Tony Benn at Energy.[17]

Like Wilson, he attended the weekly meeting of the Parliamentary Labour Party, usually on a Thursday evening, and attended meetings of the NEC and the PLP-TUC Liaison Committee monthly. In addition to the countless informal exchanges with Labour MPs in the corridors and tea rooms, he averaged some fifty formal appointments a year in the House. Donoughue observed of these meetings: 'it could be said that Callaghan saw Labour MPs who represented something, and Wilson saw those who wanted something'.[18] Others, however, stress Callaghan's utter determination to make himself available: said one, 'it was a golden rule that Callaghan saw every Labour MP who ever wanted to see him'.[19] Meetings with Liberals and Ulster Unionists required by electoral pacts and parliamentary arithmetic also took up a disproportionate amount of his time.

Callaghan's greater interest in foreign policy than Wilson's was reflected in his receiving three times the number of overseas visitors and representatives.[20] He saw more Arabs and Western Europeans than Wilson: neither, interestingly, saw much of the Japanese, despite Japan's economic importance. Callaghan made more overseas trips than Wilson, including six to Germany, reflecting his close relationship with Chancellor Schmidt.[21] President Carter of the USA was another with whom he formed a close personal bond. His period early on as Prime Minister also coincided with a brief but particularly frenetic period of foreign commitments, including Britain's Presidency of the EEC in the first half of 1977, a Commonwealth Heads of Government meeting, a NATO summit, and an Economic Summit, all in London that same year.[22] Callaghan, like Wilson before him, had no foreign language, and they were fortunate to have Schmidt and Giscard D'Estaing as opposite numbers in Germany and France, both of whom spoke excellent English. Neither Callaghan nor Wilson especially enjoyed speaking on the telephone, even in English. Both, but

ACTIVITIES OF PRIME MINISTERS
WILSON & CALLAGHAN 1974–1979

No.	Activity
650	Cabinets and Cabinet Committee Meetings
120	Audiences with the Monarch
300	Scheduled Meetings with individual Ministers
200	Meetings with individual MPs
1000s	Meetings with Officials (Private Secretaries and Personal Advisers)
130	Meetings of the Parliamentary Labour Party
400	Parliamentary Question Times
50	Major Commons Speeches and Statements
200	Meetings with Party Committees and Officials
120	Visits to Party Constituencies and Organizations
1000	Appointments and 150 Formal Meals with British Visitors and Hosts
160	Meetings and 120 Formal Meals with Visiting Representatives of Foreign Countries
35	Official Visits Overseas (taking some 75 days)
15	Weeks of General Elections, Referenda and Party Conferences

Bernard Donoughue, 'The Prime Minister's Day: The Daily Diary of Wilson and Callaghan, 1974–79,' *Contemporary Record* 2, 2 (Summer 1988) 16.

especially Wilson, were apt to complain about speaking to some foreign leaders: 'Why do I have to talk to them?', they would say, when having to break off from important business to go to the phone.[23]

Few areas of prime ministerial life showed the benefit of Callaghan's experience more than Intelligence, not least after the eccentric oversight and interest of Wilson. As a former Home and Foreign Secretary, Callaghan knew at first hand about the work of MI5 and MI6. Unlike many Prime Ministers, he read the Joint Intelligence Committee's (JIC) weekly reports and periodic special reports with a practised eye, and made constructive comments. 'Callaghan possessed an unusually steady and mature grasp of security matters,' said one seasoned insider of the intelligence world.[24] He opposed suggestions that Parliament should scrutinise security operations on the grounds that the operations of the secret intelligence world must remain secret, and he regarded himself as the parliamentary scrutiny.

Callaghan's differing time commitments from Wilson's are explained not just by differing priorities: the times had also altered. The demands of party management as Labour moved into minority government status meant that Callaghan had to devote more energy to trade union relations, to discussions with the Liberals, and to preparing long-term policy and strategy for the general election, which involved him in a dozen meetings with the Campaign Committee.[25] He did not look forward to the monthly meetings of the NEC, with its constant criticism of government and demands for a reversal of policies. He deliberately delayed holding the Clause V meeting of the Cabinet and NEC to draw up the general election manifesto. He convened it on the eve of the 1979 general election and bluntly vetoed suggested items – such as the abolition of the House of Lords – a policy which he opposed.

Callaghan had risen in the Labour movement as a spokesman for the trade unions. In Cabinet in 1969 he had defied Wilson's plans to reform them, on the grounds that they opposed the proposed changes which would therefore split the party. As Prime Minister he invested much time in cultivating the trade union leaders, attending the TUC Labour Party Liaison Committee and meetings of NEDC, and giving dinners for them in Downing Street. He wanted the unions to acquiesce in successive stages of incomes restraint as part of the annual Social Contract. Yet all these Herculean efforts – and the incredible amount of drink consumed by ministers and union officials – came to nothing in the winter of discontent, when union members trampled on the government's 5 per cent guidelines for wage settlements. Callaghan's skill in managing the two sides of the Labour movement was extinguished, largely because the unions could not deliver the consent of their members, and perhaps because he asked too much of them.

Callaghan liked to see Number Ten as an old-fashioned railway signal box, full of levers which he, the chief signalman, could pull. The levers corresponded to the different Number Ten offices and each lever was discrete and would come into play at his behest, depending on whose particular advice he sought.[26] He came in determined to use all the levers at his disposal – Policy Unit, Private Office, CPRS, Press Office, Political Office; but the levers he gradually came to pull most were those of the regular Civil Service, both the Private and the Cabinet Office.[27] Not that the Private Office under Wilson had ever been anything less than crucial, but power within Number Ten then was more pluralistic. James Callaghan was not much interested in the machinery of government: he did not believe that Whitehall could be better configured. He thought that what was needed for a good government was a strong minister and a competent Civil Service to carry out instructions. He admired the senior civil servants and described the Treasury (in spite of the 1967 devaluation after which he resigned) and the Foreign Office – whose operations he knew well and on which he was to rely most – each as a Rolls Royce.[28]

The retention of the Policy Unit, with Donoughue at its head, was not a foregone conclusion on Callaghan's arrival in April 1976: 'not altogether expected', was how one official at Number Ten crisply put it.[29] Donoughue thought he might well be asked to go, departing along with Joe Haines and Marcia Williams, both of whom walked out of their posts without awaiting the umpire's, or signalman's, call. Donoughue received a standard dismissal notice (which went to all temporary civil servants on the resignation of a Prime Minister) but Callaghan, overcoming his reserve about academics, decided to ask him to continue. Wilson had apparently told Callaghan during the party's leadership election in the spring of 1976 how useful he had found the Policy Unit, but the advice of Tom McNally, Callaghan's incoming Political Secretary, proved decisive in the retaining of both Donoughue and the Unit.[30] Its *modus operandi* was to alter, however: 'There was a big change of atmosphere with Jim's arrival,' said Donoughue. 'It was more regular, organised and sedate, even with the deteriorating parliamentary position. Harold's frivolity, the excitement, his taste for pouring out the drinks and gossiping in the first floor study, all that was gone. Jim was much more systematic in the way that he looked at policy issues.'[31]

Callaghan used the Policy Unit for four main tasks: developing policies in which he took a personal interest, such as education (the Unit wrote much of the Ruskin speech), the IMF loan and child benefit; tracking Whitehall departments, especially those he thought were not up to scratch; preparing background papers for meetings with ministers that involved longer-term thinking and discussion; and being briefed before meetings with important outsiders – including industrialists such as Lord Weinstock or TUC general secretary Len Murray.[32]

The Policy Unit proved useful to Callaghan in providing him with fresh ideas and perspectives, and giving him leverage with his Cabinet ministers and their departments. But as Callaghan's opportunities for fresh thinking dwindled, and as the close personal relationship with Donoughue which the latter had enjoyed with Wilson failed to develop, the Unit subtly became a less vital part of Number Ten, until by the difficult final months Callaghan was scarcely heeding its advice.[33] Donoughue also advocated a tougher line with the unions than Callaghan wished to hear.[34] Fairly or unfairly, Callaghan seems to have suspected him of talking too freely to his friend Harry Evans, editor of the *Sunday Times*, who was no great supporter of either Callaghan or the government.[35] Donoughue, however, remained an ever-present figure, co-ordinating the advice of Unit members, working tirelessly behind the scenes in Whitehall to facilitate Callaghan's views, while remaining to some more conventional officials the last manifestation of a style of operator (Thomas Balogh, George Wigg, Marcia Williams) who had characterised the Wilson years in power.[36]

The Unit's membership shifted. Andrew Graham returned to Oxford to teach economics, David Piachaud went back to LSE although he remained a consultant and Gavyn Davies moved up to become one whose advice and ideas Callaghan particularly sought out and trusted.[37] David Lipsey, a former adviser to Tony Crosland but a newcomer to the Unit, became another whose advice Callaghan welcomed; his domain included environment matters and election strategy. He later moved to the Political Office to shadow McNally and then did the job of Political Secretary when McNally got a seat.[38]

The CPRS was asked by Callaghan to look at a number of longer-term problems, and he found it useful when confronted by a matrix of complex policy issues involving defence procurement decisions, which its head Kenneth Berrill helped put into context for him.[39] The CPRS's study on foreign representation was seen off by the FCO without much difficulty (though later many of its recommendations were implemented), while on day-to-day matters its influence remained negligible.[40] It contained some very able individuals, including Gordon Downey, the deputy from 1978, and Tessa Blackstone, a future minister in Blair's government. It encountered the difficulty increasingly found also by the Policy Unit: that of finding the optimal time to catch Callaghan's ear to intervene in an evolving policy discussion. It did not always choose its time wisely; at the height of the Winter of Discontent, it saw fit to offer Callaghan its considered policy on alcohol, the main feature of which was to increase taxes on spirits and beer. At other times, such as over the purchase of aircraft and aero engines, Callaghan's personal involvement upstaged any input offered by the CPRS.[41]

The Political Office in contrast recovered much of its steady influence under Callaghan. He brought in with him Tom McNally, who had been his political adviser as Foreign Secretary from 1974–76, where officials had found him an unusually skilful and indeed collegiate figure.[42] McNally had a background in student politics and as a Labour Party officer at Transport House, where he had specialised in foreign affairs. From his vantage point by Callaghan's side at the FCO he helped his master in 1976 with his campaign for the party leadership and proved to be a formidable Political Secretary in the mould of Douglas Hurd, seeing officials as agents to be worked with rather than mistrusted, as they were by his immediate predecessor. Callaghan trusted McNally's political advice, which he thought shrewd and well-informed; his advice on handling the NEC and the trade unions was particularly appreciated, as was his strategic advice on Callaghan's options.[43]

As Political Secretary McNally learned on the job. There was no 'job description' to be read; nor did he talk to Marcia Williams, who was still under a cloud because of the honours list, and he wanted too to show that there would be a change in Number Ten's atmosphere. He took over the room off the Cabinet Ante-Room, which he shared with the two parliamentary private secretaries. Next to Ken Stowe, McNally was the most influential voice for the first two years of Callaghan's period in Number Ten. In the last months of the premiership, however, when McNally was nursing a parliamentary constituency at Stockport, he found (as did Judith Chaplin after him in 1991–92) that he was often pulled away from Number Ten to his constituency. He came under heavy and conflicting pressures. His recommendations to sack Benn, to go to the country in 1978, and to try to broker deals to survive in March 1979 were all brushed aside by Callaghan.[44] Duly elected in 1979, McNally joined the SDP in 1981, to the bitterness of his former colleagues and, on losing his seat in 1983, moved into public relations before being ennobled in 1995.

For drafts of his political speeches Callaghan relied on Tom McNally and David Lipsey. McNally wrote much of Callaghan's seminal speech for the Labour Party conference in October 1976. Yet the passage that is always quoted was that dictated by his economist son-in-law, Peter Jay. 'Quite unequivocally [unemployment] is caused by paying ourselves more than the value of what we produce . . . The option of spending yourself out of a recession no longer exists . . . we must get back to fundamentals.' The speech was heard in silence by conference delegates, who proceeded to pass resolutions calling for massive increases in public expenditure. During the 1979 general election with McNally absent, Lipsey was helped with speechwriting by Roger Carroll, a journalist from the *Sun*. A number of hard-hitting speeches were prepared for attacking Mrs Thatcher, but Callaghan refused to deliver them.

The Prime Minister's Parliamentary Private Secretary was another job to find its traditional role restored under Callaghan. Initially given to Jack Cunningham, who had been Callaghan's PPS at the FCO, the position was inherited by the moderate young trade union MP, Roger Stott, when in the autumn of 1976 Cunningham was appointed a minister at Energy. Stott had a desk in the Political Secretary's office off to the left of the Cabinet Ante Room. He took his role very seriously, and also made it his job 'to be the opposite of sycophantic: I told Callaghan exactly what was going on'.[45] With such a difficult parliamentary position throughout Callaghan's premiership, Stott was to be an exceptionally busy PPS.

The most important woman in Callaghan's Number Ten (after Audrey) was Ruth Sharpe, the Constituency Secretary. She had known both him and Audrey for many years and was very much part of his inner circle. Callaghan valued her advice not just on narrow constituency matters but also on broader political subjects, especially connected with South Wales. Her style was low-key and unassuming, but she had a resolve of steel.[46]

The Chief Press Secretary was yet another job whose traditional role was rediscovered under Callaghan. Tom McCaffrey was a professional Whitehall information officer to his fingertips, who had served with Callaghan when he was Home Secretary (a particularly tough department for a chief information officer) and had then been invited across by Callaghan to become Head of the News Department at the FCO when he became Foreign Secretary. Callaghan wanted McCaffrey to join Number Ten because he knew he could trust his judgement and they had become firm friends; the appointment was all the more appropriate as McCaffrey had served as deputy press secretary in Downing Street under Donald Maitland from 1971–72 and his ambition was to be the Number Ten Press Secretary.[47] McCaffrey's was to be a pivotal relationship with Callaghan; he accompanied the Prime Minister on all his overseas trips and scarcely a day went by over the three years when he did not see him at least once.

McCaffrey was not a thrusting figure in the Bernard Ingham or Alastair Campbell mould. Nor did he aspire to being a policy adviser like Haines. But he was immensely professional and business-like, and set about regularising the work of the Number Ten media operation. His first night in Downing Street, on 5 April 1976, saw him phoning the chairman of the Lobby, saying that he would like to restart the Lobby system. This was accomplished with a glow of good will.[48] McCaffrey himself always chaired the 11 am meeting in his bow-windowed room in Number Ten, while the 4.15 pm meeting in the Lobby room in the House of Commons' Tower Room, at which he was the only speaker, was taken by the Chairman of the Lobby. McCaffrey regarded the meetings as 'very informal . . . many of the Lobby journalists were friends'.[49] How much guidance did he seek from Callaghan on what to say? Not much, apparently. 'As time went by, and our relationship developed, I just knew what Jim Callaghan's thinking was and I did not have to consult him on many matters.' Only once did Callaghan tell him he had made an error, when he had repeated but mistakenly misrepresented Callaghan's words about taking a 'personal interest' in an economic issue, which led to an irate response from Chancellor Healey about the prime ministerial intrusion on his patch.[50] Another rare slip was when McCaffrey appeared to make disparaging remarks about the departing Ambassador to the

US, Sir Peter Ramsbotham, at a sensitive point when Callaghan's son-in-law, Peter Jay, had been nominated for the succession.[51]

McCaffrey was scrupulous in observing his position as a civil servant: 'Occasionally, I would have to tell the Lobby "this is what ministers believe", but I would never attack the Liberals or Conservatives, and neither would Callaghan have allowed it.'[52] Callaghan himself, however, was no believer in the Lobby and said both in public and private that he saw no point in it, not least when Lobby journalists attacked the government. Grudgingly, he would, at McCaffrey's request, agree to talk periodically to the Lobby, but he had no relish for it, nor for the press in general. Like Heath, he would not invite editors or proprietors to Number Ten for a chat. He expressed little interest in what the press were saying. He went to bed before the first editions arrived in Downing Street. The Press Office prepared a daily summary, but it rarely aroused much of his curiosity. He kept close to some journalist associates from earlier days such as Peter Jenkins and Alan Watkins, but he evinced little interest in what others, even Labour stalwarts, were writing.[53] All the London dailies would be placed on a table in his first floor study; a shuffled order would indicate he had occasionally picked them up, only to have his worst opinions confirmed.[54] McCaffrey saw him most mornings, briefed him on any important press stories, and kept in even closer touch 'when something was happening'.[55] Those who knew Callaghan as a minister in the 1960s confirm that by the mid and late 1970s he had developed an inner self-confidence and was little concerned about the opinions of journalists and editors.[56]

McCaffrey differed from Haines too in that he took his role as de facto co-ordinator of government information much more seriously. While Henry James was the Director-General of the Central Office of Information (1974–78) and the de jure head of government information, in practice the Chief Press Secretary at Number Ten was responsible for co-ordination of government information. McCaffrey (or his deputy) met once a week with the heads of information of all the Whitehall departments, running the committee and trying to co-ordinate and synchronise the release of information, as he had seen Harold Evans do at Number Ten from 1957–64 under Harold Macmillan and then Alec Douglas-Home. Every week, he would alternate between meeting the large batch of US correspondents and the non-US foreign correspondents.[57]

The names of both McCaffrey and McNally were associated with the most notorious interview Callaghan gave. Returning from the Guadaloupe Summit in January 1979, during the 'winter of discontent', he gave a brief press interview at Heathrow. He had decided earlier not to talk to the press, but when the plane arrived back on the tarmac, being told the press were waiting, and feeling good after a successful summit, he changed his mind. At an impromptu meeting on board the plane, while McNally and Stott urged him to go ahead, McCaffrey advised him to stay clear of the press. 'Tom,' he said to his Press Secretary, 'I am telling you to go out there and set up a press conference.' None of them, however, expected him to utter remarks which were eagerly satirised by the *Sun* as 'Crisis? What Crisis?'.[58] In fact Callaghan had said, 'I don't think that other people in the world would share the view that there is mounting chaos.' But the damage had been done: the front page headline made it appear that Callaghan was living in a 'never-never land'.

The Private Office became Callaghan's closest and most important aides. The redoubtable Ken Stowe stayed throughout his premiership, adapting himself apparently effortlessly to Callaghan's very different regimen. Stowe had by 1976 become exceptionally self-confident, co-ordinating and annotating advice to Callaghan via his red boxes, liaising with the rest of the machine – chiefly with Cabinet Secretary John Hunt and to a lesser extent Head of the Home Civil Service Douglas Allen and the Queen's Private Secretary, Martin Charteris – and guiding Callaghan on tactics along the lines of: 'Okay Prime Minister, this is what you might want to do, and if so, this is how you might go about doing it.' Stowe, who had not been impressed by Wilson's workrate, suggested to Callaghan within their first month together that he involve himself more regularly and directly in the work of his departmental ministers, keeping in touch through regular reports sent into Number Ten.[59]

The almost continuous political and economic difficulties which faced the government imposed their own pressures on Stowe and his colleagues in the Private Office. Stowe was determined to keep his weekends free; he realised that he needed to take time off when he could in order to do his job effectively. He would spend the weekends with his family in Suffolk and make a point of not reading any Sunday newspapers. Late on Sunday evening he would phone the Number Ten Duty Clerk and ask, 'Has anything happened that I should know about?' Callaghan had the highest personal regard for Stowe.[60] So indispensable did he find him that he prolonged his tenure beyond the usual three-year period, which would have ended in April 1978, until after the general election, whatever the outcome.

Another official to whom Callaghan was exceptionally close was Patrick Wright, the Foreign Affairs Private Secretary. Wright was the only Number Ten figure he inherited from Wilson whom he knew at all well, Wright having been head of the Foreign Office's Middle Eastern Department when Callaghan became Foreign Secretary (they also saw each other when, at the end of 1974, Wright moved over to Number Ten). Wright was succeeded in July 1977 by Bryan Cartledge, to whom Callaghan, who could be abrupt, gave a hard time in his first few months. He grew to respect him, but it was never the warm, easy relationship he had enjoyed with Wright.[61]

Above the doorway to the outer private secretaries' room was a row of lights, one for each of the Private Secretaries: Callaghan would press a button in his first floor study when he wanted to summon one. He became heavily reliant on Nigel Wicks, the Economic and Home Affairs Private Secretary. A very single-minded public servant, he was highly efficient but not then universally popular in Whitehall: 'you couldn't help admiring him, though', was how one fellow mandarin, a critic, described him.[62] Wicks later mellowed, after his second and excoriating period at Number Ten, from 1985–88 (See p. 182–3). His successor from October 1978, Tim Lankester, found similar problems establishing his number with Callaghan to those Cartledge had experienced: 'the old boy could be very crisp and impatient with new staff, and disliked change'. Lankester was selected from a shortlist of two put up by the Treasury. 'I went in to see Callaghan in his study. He asked me what advice would I give him over a pending closure of a Hoover factory in Wales.'[63] Lankester cannot recall his answer but was relieved nevertheless to be offered the job. He rapidly established himself as a serious high flier. Like others too, he saw on closer acquaintance that Callaghan's brusqueness was rather an act.

Parliamentary Affairs Private Secretary was Philip Wood, whom Callaghan treated, uniquely in the Private Office, like a son. From October 1978 Nick Sanders joined the office, to be groomed as Wood's successor. Callaghan approached the task of Prime Minister's Questions differently from Wilson. He would see Wood the night before and examine with him all the possible angles in the dossier he had prepared, McCaffrey having alerted Wood to press stories which might be coming up. The morning itself would be devoted to other matters, notably Cabinet business on Thursdays, while Wood carried on working on the briefs. Before lunch Callaghan would be driven to the Commons, where he would have a sandwich in the tea room, frequently at the Welsh table. A twenty minute nap in the PM's Commons room would follow, before the serious preparation began at about 2.30 pm. In addition to Wood, Donoughue and McCaffrey, Ann Taylor, a junior whip, and Roger Stott would be present. Callaghan was almost invariably confident, especially when Ann Taylor had managed to ensure friendly questions from Labour MPs. Norman Tebbit and Ian Gow were the two Conservative MPs whose questioning Callaghan most feared.[64]

Callaghan's initial reservations about Cabinet Secretary John Hunt were soon forgotten. 'Their relationship became closer and closer. Hunt regarded Callaghan as the best manager of government business he had known in a premier,'[65] recalled one insider, 'though there never developed a great personal affinity.' Callaghan on his side respected Hunt for his proficiency, his 'Sherpa' work at G7 meetings and his judgement on high-level security issues.[66] Hunt was clearly a pivotal figure between 1976 and 1979. Callaghan encouraged him to be activist, including advice on his agendas with fellow ministers, and offering opinions on their qualities as chairmen, and on Cabinet making (such as on the Northern Ireland Secretary in July 1976).[67] Hunt also had a high respect for Stowe's professionalism and dedication to getting the business arranged orderly. 'A mind like quicksilver' and 'always cool as a cucumber', were two of the phrases used by insiders to describe Stowe's qualities.[68] For all Hunt's abilities and energy, and the seniority of his post, however, he never acquired the confidence or importance of Stowe with the Prime Minister.

Among Cabinet colleagues, no-one achieved the same position of closeness as Callaghan himself had enjoyed under Wilson from 1974–76. After Tony Crosland's death in February 1977, a huge blow to Callaghan, his successor as Foreign Secretary, David Owen, never achieved the same position. Michael Foot, effectively Deputy Prime Minister, was very close, especially in the latter days of Callaghan's premiership, and Callaghan always saw Denis Healey, the Chancellor, regularly and respected his advice whilst remaining wary of him. Morgan believes Foot and Healey to have been 'the two key ministers, without doubt'.[69] Merlyn Rees, Home Secretary after Roy Jenkins in September 1976, was another close ally. Roy Jenkins, however, was told by Callaghan that he had no intention of ever making him Chancellor of the Exchequer. Callaghan had not been an enthusiast for the liberal reforms made when Roy Jenkins was Home Secretary between 1965 and 1967, and like a good party manager Callaghan disapproved of the activities of the 'Jenkinsites'. He was not sorry when Jenkins departed in 1976. The Chief Whip, Michael Cocks, was always very much at Callaghan's beck and call, given the delicate state of the parliamentary balance. Cocks was not an initiator, but was totally supportive, as was Number Twelve in general. Callaghan had complete trust in them. Following the loss of its majority, and the establishment in March 1977 of the 'Lib-Lab Pact', however, it was often Stowe rather than Cocks to whom Callaghan turned, for example for talking to David Steel, the Liberal leader, over sensitive discussions. Stowe had been a key intermediary in the negotiations which set up the 'Pact'.[70]

For most of his period in office Callaghan was a shrewd and successful political operator. Although not a factional politician himself, he appreciated that the Labour Party was increasingly riven by factions and that he had to balance the conflicting interests in the party. Bernard Donoughue and Tom McNally once approached him with a list of names for a government reshuffle. He laughingly dismissed it as 'a holocaust'. Other suggestions for promotions were turned down on pragmatic grounds: 'You make an enemy of the man sacked and of the others who have not been promoted in his place.'[71] He once brought himself to the point of sacking Tony Benn: come into line tonight or you will be fired, he told his errant minister. As if to demonstrate his 'cool', he then departed for the theatre leaving a perplexed

McNally in Number Ten to handle the Benn call. Benn agreed to Callaghan's terms. The ploy had worked. Except for the last few months, Benn was mostly co-operative.[72]

Callaghan's sang-froid stemmed in part from his unrivalled experience of government but also from the fact that he never (after Wilson's appointment as leader in 1963) expected to be made Prime Minister; 1976–79 in Number Ten was thus a windfall for him. Once there, however, Callaghan wanted to win a general election and hand over in his early seventies to one of his young men who would reap the full benefits of North Sea oil.[73]

Callaghan had a natural dignity and exuded authority. His straight talking earned the respect of all around him. The atmosphere in Number Ten improved greatly on that of his predecessor. Even during the 'winter of discontent', which produced similar strains to those in Heath's final months, there was no paranoia or bunker mentality in Number Ten. Apart from some discussions with Hunt about creating a Prime Minister's department in 1977, Callaghan was broadly satisfied with the Number Ten system and indeed with the constitutional arrangements he inherited. He gently side-stepped, for example, a plan from Hunt to split up the Treasury and create a Ministry of Finance. He listened to advice and then made up his mind. His biographer correctly portrays him as the right leader and presenting the right style for the time, as well as a man who walked alone. His self-sufficiency was seen in the way that he decided on the general election date. Only at the last moment did he reveal to McNally, McCaffrey and possibly Donoughue that he would not call an election in October.[74] They and the world were sure that an election would be held then and had briefed friendly journalists accordingly. The decision came as a shock to most of the Cabinet.[75] A similar penchant for playing his cards close to his chest was seen in the fact that Healey did not know until a late stage on which side Callaghan would come down during the IMF negotiations. Several staff were again kept in the dark about the appointment of Callaghan's son-in-law, Peter Jay, as British Ambassador to the United States.

Callaghan had exceptional staff at Number Ten, and had the wisdom and experience to use them well. They respected him, and worked hard for him. Together, they ran a tight ship in exceptionally difficult circumstances, both domestically and internationally. The economy improved: the country was generally well governed, at least until the final winter. Callaghan's calm, measured style restored a measure of trust in government jeopardised by the conduct of Wilson, not least his resignation honours list. It was a conservative premiership, and a reassuring one, performing a role of similar importance to Baldwin's in another troubled decade fifty years before. His respect for the nation's traditions was seen clearly in his fondness for the Queen: he took particular pleasure from being Prime Minister during the Silver Jubilee in 1977.

But for all that, Callaghan's was not a premiership where the Prime Minister led the country, or his party, in a new direction. Labour was disunited, but so too were the opposition. The Conservatives, split after the traumas of 1974–75, were finding it difficult to adjust to a new, and female, leader. As the last 'Old Labour' Prime Minister, it must remain an open question whether, difficult economic and political circumstances notwithstanding, Callaghan could have done more to rally his party and give it a sense of greater collective purpose and direction, or whether the Labour Party needed to go through the long night of the 1980s and early/mid 1990s before it could again become a serious contender for power and the nation's trust. Had he wanted to strike out on a new line, Number Ten was ready, eager indeed, to support him. That he chose not to had nothing to do with any deficiencies in the then Downing Street machine.

Callaghan suspected that British politics was entering a new phase with the election victory of Mrs Thatcher. On Friday 4 May 1979 at 2.30 pm he took his leave of Downing Street, to allow Mrs Thatcher to succeed. Ken Stowe, his Principal Private Secretary, consoled him: 'Well you don't have to worry about all of this now, she can solve it.'[76]

CHAPTER SIX

Margaret Thatcher
(1979–83)

MARGARET THATCHER excited more speculation about how she would use Number Ten and what kind of Prime Minister she would be than most incomers to Downing Street, not least because she was the first female incumbent. Before entering office Mrs Thatcher was known for having decided political views and strong preferences regarding people. Yet of all previous postwar Prime Ministers with the exception of Wilson, she arrived with the least experience at the apex of government; most of her predecessors as Conservative leaders had already been part of an inner circle, had held a senior Cabinet post and were familiar with the working of government. She, however, had spent only three and a half years in Cabinet as Secretary of State for Education (1970–74), not a front-line department, and was neither close personally to Ted Heath nor a central player in the big policy decisions of his ill-starred government. She did not have fond memories of her civil servants or of the education world.

When she challenged and defeated Heath for the party leadership in February 1975, her candidacy was prompted in large part by the failure of more fancied figures to stand. Few regarded the party after her victory as Thatcherite; indeed, few knew clearly what it meant to be 'Thatcherite', while the term 'Thatcherism' was still some years off the coining. She became leader partly as a result of a backbench repudiation of Heath. Her Shadow Cabinet remained heavily Heathite, most of its members indeed having voted for him in the first round of the leadership election. Among her first Shadow Cabinet it was difficult to see many other than Sir Keith Joseph, Geoffrey Howe, Airey Neave, Angus Maude and John Biffen as being true believers and loyal followers. With her lower middle class social background and right-wing views, as well as her gender, she was something of an outsider.

Many senior colleagues assumed that once in government, sur-rounded by civil servants and forced to deal with the problems of the real world, Mrs Thatcher would be, as one of them put it, 'tamed'. She would realise the need, for example, to win the co-operation of trade unions if strikes were to be avoided and a workable anti-inflation policy implemented, and she would learn the limits to which public spending could be cut without hitting the quality of public services and provoking a hostile reaction among voters. Yet as Prime Minister Mrs Thatcher proved to be one of the most strong-minded incum-bents the office has seen, even if she was unclear in her first months of exactly where she was going, or how she was going to get there. She did not give way before strikes, held her nerve over the contro-versial 1981 Budget, which broke with postwar economic policy think-ing, and successfully prosecuted a medium-scale war. Although she lost some Cabinet battles, she was widely seen as a strong leader. Her public image was of a battler and a successful one.

As opposition leader, Mrs Thatcher had been suspicious of or reserved about those who could advise her on the practical business of govern-ment, and in particular on how she should organise Number Ten to work to her best advantage. She was at best guarded in her views about senior civil servants and, more unusually, about the party's Research Department under the leadership of Chris Patten (1974–79), who had been appointed to his post by Heath. But she was never particularly interested in organisation or machinery-of-government questions. If on politics she was radical, on institutions she was ortho-dox: as long as colleagues and staff endorsed her views and were competent she was not bothered about structures. Her brand of free-market Conservatism clearly differentiated her from previous party leaders, including Macmillan and Heath. Her philosophy was about reducing the range of government – by tax cuts, a preference for the market over the public sector, a reduction in state subsidies, an abandonment of prices and incomes policies and a reliance on monetarism to combat inflation, and reform of trade unions: in sum, a fundamental change of direction. Inspiration for these new ideas came from many quarters, including the Centre for Policy Studies (CPS), the free-market 'think tank' founded by Keith Joseph and herself in 1974 to explore the lessons from the social market economies of West Germany and Japan, which provided a home for many right-wing Conservatives and free-market liberals disillusioned with the Heath period. People like John Hoskyns, Norman Strauss, Alan Walters, David Young and Alfred Sherman were drawn to Joseph and, via him, to Mrs Thatcher. These were, in the title of one of the political books on the period, all *Thatcher's People*.[1]

Although Mrs Thatcher was not closely engaged personally in the exercise, some of her Shadow Cabinet ministers and party officials tried to anticipate which actions would be required early on by a new Conservative government. James Douglas, director of the Conservative Research Department (1970–74), held discussions with former Tory Cabinet ministers and senior Whitehall officials. His interval paper, *The First Few Days of Office at Number 10* (29 November 1976), is an illuminating indicator of the thinking of the time. It was presented to a small group of shadow ministers, including Howe and Joseph, who formed a Preparation For Government Group. Douglas reported to them that his advisers were divided about retaining a Policy Unit in Number Ten; some had suggested that Harold Wilson had set it up because of his difficulties with the Labour Party, difficulties which would not apply in Mrs Thatcher's relationship with the Conservative Party. Most were also against appointing a 'chief of staff' in Number Ten. The appointment of a senior figure to the post might, they argued, act as a barrier between the Prime Minister and Cabinet colleagues, and also make for a difficult relationship with the Cabinet Secretary.

On becoming Prime Minister, Mrs Thatcher moved from her Chelsea home to live with Denis in the flat upstairs in Number Ten; her children, Mark and Carol, were already living on their own. The new Prime Minister usually rose at 6 am, and would work on her boxes if she had not done them before going to sleep in the early hours of the morning. Her Diary Secretary, Caroline Stephens (since 1975), would visit her upstairs first thing in the morning and return with the completed boxes. Mrs Thatcher would descend a few minutes before her first meeting (usually at 9 am). She preferred to work in the first floor study. For the Private Office (situated on the ground floor) this had the disadvantage that they could not readily pop in, or know at all times who was with her.

Mrs Thatcher lived for her work. She eagerly read briefing papers and sometimes called for more. She enjoyed good health, took short holidays and ensured that off-the-job reading and discussion were of a serious, 'improving' kind. She was invariably punctual, well prepared and determined to test a case from officials or ministers by vigorous argument. She relaxed, after a fashion, with her husband and her children. Among Cabinet ministers, Geoffrey Howe, Keith Joseph, Cecil Parkinson and Norman Tebbit were on her personal wavelength and had ready access to her. In Downing Street she was supported by Diary secretaries, particularly Caroline Stephens (who in 1981 married her aide Richard Ryder and remained until 1986), as well as by Cynthia Crawford ('Crawfie') who was a personal secretary, a listening post and lady-in-waiting. Her close Number Ten team – including even the ever present detectives – were treated by her almost as 'family'. Within the walls, to an extent not apparent to outsiders, she was revered, even loved, by her close aides. She treated them very solicitously, taking trouble to get to know them, and not wanting to disturb even her senior team at weekends so they could spend more time with their families. The emotional and psychological support for a Prime Minister so often at odds with the outside world was fundamental to her. She did not have such a support system when she had been at Education under Heath, and she was surprised and delighted to find it when she moved to Number Ten.[2]

Mrs Thatcher was at first surprisingly innocent about the central bodies with which she would have to work closely as Prime Minister, including the Cabinet Office, the CPRS and the Number Ten Private Office she inherited from James Callaghan. The Assistant Director of the Conservative Research Department, Adam Ridley, who himself expected a senior posting to Number Ten, had therefore instructed some party researchers, including Michael Dobbs, Michael Portillo and George Cardona, to move into Number Ten to work as special advisers. Mrs Thatcher however, in a telling move, was quickly impressed with the ability and loyalty of the official Whitehall machine in her Private Office and the party lieutenants were speedily redeployed elsewhere. As one Private Office official said: 'she loved us, but she loathed civil servants at large'.[3] The political appointments declined in significance. Mrs Thatcher arrived at Number Ten with a good deal of anti-Civil Service 'baggage', as she suspected senior officials of being more interested in 'managing' in an orderly fashion Britain's decline than in ways of reversing it. From their attachment, as she saw it, to big government down to their own index-linked pensions, which insulated them from the inflationary effects of many of the policies they were urging on ministers, she eyed them with suspicion.[4] But she liked the 'can do', intellectually sure type of civil servant and her own staff. She was also impressed by those with charm, good manners and wit, such as Robin Butler and Anthony Parsons.

One can put this more strongly. The shadow of political obstruction hung across Mrs Thatcher's view of the mandarins, damaging relations in both directions in her first term of office. With her inherited generation of senior civil servants she felt that she faced intellectual snobbery, recalcitrance and at times outright opposition. Political divisions within the government probably contributed to this feeling, as some 'wet' ministers encouraged a dissenting outlook. Later, once her ascendency was assured, as it was by 1983, civil servants made their peace. But in 1980 and 1981 such an outcome was not assured.

Before the 1979 election, James Callaghan had already indicated to the Cabinet Secretary John Hunt that he would like Ken Stowe's successor as Principal Private Secretary to be drawn from a social department, rather than from the Treasury as was traditional. Mrs Thatcher had no such preconceptions. She told Hunt that she wished to see candidates for promotion in working situations – a practice to which she largely adhered. Clive Whitmore, serving in the Cabinet Office, impressed her with a presentation on nuclear weapons. Whitmore's work in the Cabinet Office had also caught Hunt's eye; the Cabinet Secretary thought his subtle, unruffled style would equip him ideally for being Principal Private Secretary at such a busy time.[5] Whitmore duly replaced Stowe as Mrs Thatcher's Principal Private

Secretary four weeks into the Parliament. Stowe's role of inducting the new Prime Minister into the job was the final achievement of a long and distinguished posting. As for his successor, 'We will both learn on the job,' she told him at their first meeting.[6] Whitmore, a grammar school boy who had gone on to Cambridge, came from a background of working in Whitehall's defence departments. Retiring rather than high profile, his appointment surprised some of the more robust minds in the Treasury, who imagined Mrs Thatcher would have gone for a more self-assured figure, not least from their own number.[7] Former Secretaries recall that he was determined to maintain a good working atmosphere and would upbraid her when she was too sharp with staff.

Whitmore was succeeded in August 1982 by Robin Butler, and the job reverted to being a Treasury secondment. Butler had earlier served in Heath's and Wilson's Private Offices and had first made an impression on Mrs Thatcher when, as Secretary of State for Education, she heard him making a presentation in 1972 as a member of the CPRS and remark that inflation was endemic and inevitable in the economy. She teased him about it thereafter: 'It was the most shocking thing I ever heard!'[8] But she had no doubt that he was the best man for the job, being more recently impressed by his work during the spending cuts of 1979–80. Butler also had the advantage of knowing the Thatcher family and in particular Denis Thatcher, who had refereed rugby at Harrow where the young Butler had been a schoolboy star at the game; later they played golf together. He was a commanding self-confident figure, a former Head Boy at Harrow. Mrs Thatcher always thought highly of Butler and appreciated his running of the Private Office and his talents in drafting memos and official speeches for her.[9] Butler also proved a source of sage advice in one of the Principal Private Secretary's least attractive duties, dealing with scandals. Butler helped to sort out the furore surrounding Mark Thatcher's alleged exploitation of his family connections to secure business deals in the Middle East, and he also had Cecil Parkinson's affair with Sara Keays land on his plate.

Initially Mrs Thatcher was wary of the private secretaries below the Principal, but she soon grew close to them, as her fondness for and trust in her close official team grew.[10] As Overseas Affairs Private

Secretary, Michael Alexander was closely involved in discussions over the independence of Zimbabwe and the EC Budget, in which she battled to reduce the British contribution. When he was due to leave in 1981, the name of Charles Powell was put forward by the FCO as one of the three candidates.[11] But she chose John Coles, an Arabist who played a key part in the Falklands War in 1982 and who went on to become Permanent Under-Secretary in 1994. Her first Economic Affairs Private Secretary was Tim Lankester, more of a free-thinker and radical than many who joined the Private Office. She became very fond of him, and of Michael Scholar who replaced him. She also inherited from Callaghan Nick Sanders as her Parliamentary Affairs Private Secretary; she found his ability to anticipate Parliamentary Questions quite uncanny. He was succeeded in 1981 by Michael Pattison, who in turn was replaced by William Rickett in June 1982. The moves followed the tradition for a new Private Secretary to do a spell on Home Affairs before moving on to Parliamentary Affairs. All were surprised, if at times disconcerted, by the close personal attention she took in their work: 'She would stand by your desk and rifle through your in-tray. "What is this?" she would say to us. She would flick through your papers and there'd be some stuff there you didn't particularly want her to see, so you'd be pretty careful what you put into your in-tray if you suspected she might drop in.'[12] But they were gratified by the trust she quickly placed in them: 'if you told her something, she'd believe it'.[13] 'Oh, the power of it', said another. 'You'd hear her quoting your points back to a Cabinet minister.'

Although Mrs Thatcher was to bruise the egos of some Permanent Secretaries,[14] many of them initially welcomed her arrival at Number Ten. There had been a sense of waiting for the election result to be over before serious policy work could be undertaken, and many had felt frustrated in the closing stages of Callaghan's government. But Mrs Thatcher wanted to change the whole culture of Whitehall, and to bring it more in line with the virtues, as she saw them, of the private sector. She took a close interest in Civil Service promotions.[15]

Early on, she hosted a Downing Street dinner for senior civil servants; it went very badly. She was heard to whisper to the Cabinet Secretary, Robert Armstrong, 'It is terrible. They are all against me.'[16] Appointing 'good' people, specifically 'can do' civil servants and those with managerial skills, was deemed the best way to change the Civil Service. She also wanted to reduce the number of civil servants and 'de-privilege' them, specifically their index-linked pensions. According to a friend, she never forgot the dinner and in 1999 still spoke of it with distaste.

She appointed Sir Derek Rayner, of Marks and Spencer, to lead an Efficiency Unit based in the Cabinet Office; the appointment was rightly seen as reflecting her view of the deficiencies of Whitehall in controlling costs and wasteful practices. Rayner waged war against excessive paper and rule books, the twin banes, he claimed, of the Civil Service. 'Scrutiny teams' were despatched into the departments, to 'root out waste'.[17] He failed, however, to persuade Mrs Thatcher to transform his small unit into a ministry, which he considered necessary if the departments were to tackle inefficiency in the long term more successfully. He left at the end of 1982.

Armstrong replaced Hunt as Cabinet Secretary in October 1979. In accepting a former Principal Private Secretary to Ted Heath and Harold Wilson, two premiers she held in contempt, Mrs Thatcher defied some expectations that she would hold this against him. Armstrong had come to her attention when, in the early 1970s, he had acted as a 'go-between' between her and Heath when she was Education Secretary. Aware of her differences with Heath, Armstrong confessed at his appointment interview in 1979 that he still regularly saw his old boss. 'Would she prefer it if he stopped seeing Heath?' Not at all. She would think the worse of him if he altered his social arrangements to accommodate her.[18] Mrs Thatcher was not without her own musical connection with Armstrong, whose father, Thomas, conducted her when she was in the Bach Choir at Oxford, but she could not rival his musical links with Heath.

Each Friday morning, Mrs Thatcher and Armstrong met to decide how Cabinet business would be handled, which matters to allocate to which Cabinet committees and subcommittees. These meetings could last from 10 am until 10.30 am or run on until even 12.45 pm, depending on how broadly across the political and government spectrum Mrs Thatcher wished to range. Between 1979 and 1981 he supervised the writing of her Cabinet briefs as well as the minutes of all the Cabinets and Cabinet committees which she chaired. Then in 1981 she virtually fired the Head of the Home Civil Service, Ian Bancroft, disbanding his Civil Service Department, a move so symbolically significant as the routing of the 'wets' in the 1981 reshuffle. She had had no time for either the person or the institution, and the loyal Armstrong's duties increased. For two years, he shared the role of Head of the Home Civil Service with Douglas Wass, Permanent Secretary of the Treasury. When Wass retired in 1983 Armstrong became the joint holder of both top jobs. He continued taking the Cabinet minutes but delegated more work to Cabinet Office deputy secretaries.

Armstrong was not as keen as Hunt had been to accrue power within the Cabinet Office. It had gained numerous responsibilities in the 1970s, notably the co-ordination of European policy. Under Armstrong, however, it did take over Civil Service recruitment when the Civil Service Department was abolished. Armstrong was effectively Mrs Thatcher's 'fixer' in Whitehall, coaxing departments to meet her wishes and trying, tactfully, to represent to Mrs Thatcher what was possible in the eyes of Whitehall. He remained throughout conscious of the need to carry his senior Permanent Secretaries with him. They also had their differences. He had some sympathy for Michael Heseltine's paper, *It Took a Riot*, which followed the 1981 inner-city riots, and tried to facilitate its progress. But neither Mrs Thatcher nor indeed the Treasury were impressed by Heseltine's calls for further injections of public money, at a time when the public finances were in a poor state. Armstrong failed to dissuade Mrs Thatcher from abolishing the CPRS after the general election in June 1983, but protected Civil Service dominance in Number Ten and did little to enlighten John Hoskyns about the memos in Mrs Thatcher's in-tray (see below).

As Cabinet Secretary Armstrong was much involved in security matters, chairing the Permanent Secretaries' steering committee which supervised the intelligence services. In 1972, while serving Heath as Principal Private Secretary, he had been closely involved in the secret identification of Anthony Blunt as the 'fourth man' in the spy ring for the Soviet Union. Mrs Thatcher allowed Blunt to continue his high-profile career as art historian, but when Blunt's secret was effectively exposed in her first year in a book by spy writer Andrew Boyle, she accepted Armstrong's advice and in a parliamentary statement openly named Blunt as a former spy.[19]

Mrs Thatcher had not given much thought to the role of the Policy Unit before she moved into Number Ten. But she certainly wished to have John Hoskyns close at hand. Hoskyns was a former captain in the Rifle Brigade who had left the army for IBM and then built up his own computer company, the Hoskyns Group, of which he became chairman and managing director. He resigned in 1975 in part to devote himself to public affairs, having become disillusioned with what he saw as the evils of the day – rampant inflation, corporatism and trade union power. Like Mrs Thatcher, he was concerned that the political establishment had shown itself willing to acquiesce in Britain's relative economic decline. He came into contact with Alfred Sherman and then Keith Joseph at the Centre for Policy Studies (CPS). Joseph welcomed Hoskyns' radical brand of thinking exhibited in his work on the 'Stepping Stones' strategy to limit trade union power – which both men regarded as the key to stabilising the public finances. This tough line met great opposition from 'wets' in the Shadow Cabinet and was only finally accepted after the 'winter of discontent' in early 1979. Though the 'Stepping Stones' was only partially followed through in government, its importance lay in bringing trade union reform back on the agenda and encouraging those who wished to curb the unions.

Hoskyns had been expecting a post if Mrs Thatcher became Prime Minister, but was not sure exactly what.[20] In February 1979 she asked him if he would come to Number Ten in the event of her winning power, and suggested that he talk to Victor Rothschild (the first head of the CPRS) about what it was like working within the upper reaches of Whitehall. His subsequent conversation with Rothschild reinforced Hoskyns's own doubts about the competence and indeed the co-operativeness of the Civil Service. The die was cast for future battle. On Monday 7 May, four days after polling day, Mrs Thatcher formally offered him the headship of the Policy Unit. She knew little about it at the time, she envisaged that he would write papers for her eyes alone. Hoskyns wrote his own terms of reference, which she approved. These stressed the importance of the government working in a more strategic way and not losing sight of its central objectives. Surprisingly, as it was only five years earlier, he was unaware of Donoughue's hard-fought-over concordat, defining the Policy Unit's *modus operandi* and establishing its privileged access.

Under Hoskyns the Unit no longer ranged over the broad waterfront of government policy; its focus narrowed to one portmanteau and highly ideological objective, the reversal of economic decline. Hoskyns asked himself 'How do we put out the fire?' At the time this meant concentrating on the issues of trade union power, state spending, inflation, public borrowing and the defeat of public sector strikes; under later Heads it was to have a broader vista.

Hoskyns hoped to keep clear of speechwriting (he failed) and he planned to work closely with the CPRS (a liaison that amounted to little). At the outset he wanted a very small Unit, because it was easier to develop a common outlook and shared focus. His first appointment was Norman Strauss, a corporate planner on a two-year leave of absence from Unilever, followed by Andrew Duguid, a middle-ranking civil servant, who took leave from the DTI. The three had some part-time help from Professor Douglas Hague, an academic economist. They were later joined by John Vereker, another civil servant, who had worked in the Number Ten Press Office.

Some detected the Civil Service establishment's hand, most particularly Armstrong's, in persuading Mrs Thatcher to 'civilise' the Policy Unit by tempering the enthusiasm of Whitehall outsiders with the experience of some permanent officials. Mrs Thatcher also felt that Hoskyns needed help, especially in formulating proposals in a manner which was likely to command support in government. While the size and shape of the Hoskyns Unit bore more resemblance to Balogh's embryonic office in the 1960s, the importation of civil servants marked a clear departure from the past, and a paradoxical one too, given Mrs Thatcher's (and Hoskyns's) residual mistrust of officials.

Hoskyns had some successes in reinforcing Treasury 'hawks' who supported ending public sector pay comparability, 'de-indexing' state benefits, and switching from volume to cash terms in public spending. He was also one of a number of advisers who were intimately concerned with shaping Geoffrey Howe's landmark 1981 Budget. Together with Mrs Thatcher's economic adviser Alan Walters and

Chief of Staff David Wolfson, he emphasised the need to take tough measures to cut the public sector borrowing requirement to below £10 billion. He attended some Cabinet meetings, but more often relied on Wolfson or Clive Whitmore to report relevant developments to him. He made a point of attending the key 'E' economic committee and reading Cabinet papers on economic issues. However, he avoided business which was not directly concerned with the government's first-term objective of stabilising public finances, the basis for 'economic turn-around' as he called it.

Hoskyns was not a party political animal. Neither he nor Strauss were members of the Conservative Party and, like Donoughue's team before them, they avoided contact with the media, which they felt would engender mistrust among ministers. Hoskyns constantly tried to reinforce Mrs Thatcher's radicalism, urging her to replace the 'wet' Jim Prior at the Department of Employment, so that tougher trade union legislation could be introduced, and he supported the departure in 1981 of the Party Chairman, Lord Thorneycroft, whose increasingly public dissent from the government's economic policy was beginning to irk. Thorneycroft was not the only one causing Hoskyns concern. He warned Mrs Thatcher in a note in the summer of 1981 about the high-handed way she behaved towards her Cabinet ministers and urged her to be more supportive; she might need there backing. She reacted badly to the advice and he regarded it as a turning point in their relationship.

Hoskyns grew increasingly frustrated in Number Ten and was furious at Mrs Thatcher's 'softening' of his draft speech for the 1981 party conference.[21] While he supported her aims and shared many of her views, he disapproved of her working style, claiming in particular that she did not think strategically. Others, including Howe, agreed; in his memoirs Howe reproduces a letter of complaint from Hoskyns written as early as February 1980:

> The conclusion I am coming to is that the way in which [Margaret Thatcher] herself operates, the way her fire is at present consumed, the lack of a methodical mode of working and the similar lack of orderly discussion and communication on key issues, means that our chance of implementing a carefully

worked out strategy – both policy and communications – is very low indeed.[22]

He informed Mrs Thatcher in late 1981 that he wished to leave Number Ten, claiming that the government had achieved its immediate economic tasks and there was a need for a second 'Stepping Stones' exercise to take the strategy forward for a second term in government. Despite their differences, she nevertheless tried to retain him and Joseph asked him to consider heading up a combined Policy Unit and CPRS. Hoskyns himself had originally wanted to expand the Unit but his request for John Redwood, a coming man of the right, to join and work on privatisation had been turned down. Encouraged by Alfred Sherman, Hoskyns now laid down precise conditions for a marriage with the CPRS, including the right to 'politicise' the CPRS (which had a high proportion of permanent officials on secondment) and to report direct to the Prime Minister rather than to the Cabinet Secretary, and support for working on a new strategy. The merger idea lapsed because Armstrong persuaded Mrs Thatcher that it would be too controversial to make a political appointee Head of the CPRS and to combine the two bodies which had different constituencies: the CPRS serving the Cabinet, the Policy Unit serving the Prime Minister. As a fallback, Mrs Thatcher then offered Hoskyns his original hope of an expanded Policy Unit, but he felt that her change of mind was a bad omen, and he decided to leave.

Mrs Thatcher increasingly found Hoskyns' lack of political sensitivity, as she saw it – or appreciation of the constraints under which she operated – an irritant. 'Hoskyns did not have much access to her,' said one senior civil servant. 'He was a systems man and would make statements like "we can't do anything until we stabilise the system". Well, she didn't understand that kind of language. She had no real idea what he was on about. Neither did others in Number Ten. Mrs Thatcher was impatient with policy recommendations which she thought were politically unacceptable or unlikely to be feasible in practice.'[23] On his side, he was aware intellectually that a political leader needs both a *comforter*, to help cope with the strains of decision-making and boost his or her self-confidence, and a *candid friend*, a person of an independent outlook whose frankness may make the leader feel uncomfortable. But the problem in reality was that Hoskyns was not really interested in the former role and lacked the forbearance to act 'merely' as an adviser.

Norman Strauss, Hoskyns' first appointment to the Policy Unit, had met Hoskyns, Joseph and Thatcher via the CPS network, and the two had worked closely together on the 'Stepping Stones' strategy. If, metaphorically, Hoskyns was the general, Strauss was a member of the SAS, with a no-holds-barred approach. To Strauss, reforming what he considered an amateurish and defeatist Civil Service ('de-privileging' it was part of the 'Stepping Stones' strategy, and well known to officials) became something of an obsession, a bigger problem even than the trade unions. He complained that Whitehall lacked competence in numeracy and in systemic and systematic thinking.[24] His stance could be caricatured: if the Civil Service is not reformed from top to bottom then nothing can be done; therefore start at the top. It could also be caricatured as naïve and simplistic. Strauss' crusade, and the forceful way he put it across, did not go down well with practical politicians, let alone civil servants, and Strauss was an early target for marginalising.

Did the Hoskyns Unit make much difference? 'Not much' is the verdict of the civil servants who were around Margaret Thatcher at the time. But important work had been done before May 1979 on tackling the power of the unions, particularly of the National Union of Mineworkers, and on how to achieve stability in government finances. Mrs Thatcher, however, was aware of a downside to Hoskyns's challenging style, sense of urgency and distrust of the official machine. She was caught between the different outlooks of her aide and the civil servants. A Private Secretary recalls a conversation: Hoskyns: 'Prime Minister, we really are in need of a strategy.' Thatcher: 'We know what our objectives are.' Hoskyns: 'That is not a strategy.' Both Hoskyns and Strauss were frustrated in their wish (supported by the CPS) to appoint more free-market-orientated special advisers across Whitehall and Number Ten.[25] They felt that Margaret Thatcher was unwilling to tackle the Civil Service head on. They also had something of a businessman's impatience with the compromises, trade-offs and concern with 'process' of politicians and civil servants. 'A politician's idea of doing something is to make a speech,' lamented

Hoskyns.[26] They were the first disillusioned radicals of her premiership: by 1981/82, amid mounting bitterness, Hoskyns, Strauss and, another zealot Sherman concluded that Mrs Thatcher was no longer interested in their views. Although some officials disparaged his style as 'gung-ho' he, in conjunction with Alan Walters and David Wolfson, succeeded in stiffening Mrs Thatcher's resolve on economic issues, particularly at the time of the 1980 budget.

There was some surprise when Hoskyns was succeeded as head of the Unit by Ferdinand Mount, the witty political editor of the *Spectator*. Out went the 'hard hat' brigade and in came an 'egg-head'. Mount thinks Alan Walters might have recommended him to Mrs Thatcher. 'Very little thought was given to my appointment: very little thought ever was to such postings under Mrs Thatcher.'[27] Mount had worked in the Conservative Research Department and had written a book, *The Subversive Family*. He was instrumental in establishing the Family Policy Group, a working party which drew on members of the Unit, the CPRS and ministers. It considered ideas for reducing social security's demands on the state's finances and strengthening family life. He presided over an expansion of the Unit's staff – he brought in Oliver Letwin and John Redwood, helped with speeches (at which he was superb) and drafted the party manifesto for the 1983 general election.

The Unit's relations with civil servants dramatically improved with Mount's arrival, assisted by the growing authority of the Prime Minister following her Cabinet reshuffle in September 1981, in which some leading 'wets' had departed, and by the Falklands success in April 1982. Robin Butler, the new Principal Private Secretary, ensured that the Policy Unit saw most of the Prime Minister's papers on a routine basis and that the larger Unit under Mount (and his successor, John Redwood) was securely in the policy loop. Mount also inaugurated the practice of the Head of the Unit having regular meetings with Mrs Thatcher, and he edited and kept short (two or three pages) the Unit papers going to the premier.

Even under Mount's expansion the Policy Unit still lacked the manpower to work up original policies, but it could claim some credit over the timing, tactics and detail of some initiatives. An unpublished internal document on the Mount Unit gives an idea of its range of activity.[28] Mount pioneered the use of seminars to question existing policy and canvass new ideas. At a health seminar the Unit urged bringing to an end the opticians' monopoly on the provision of spectacles, regularly uprating prescription charges and freezing the number of GPs. It used a seminar on agriculture to pressure the Ministry of Agriculture to save public money by eliminating the double bonus for farmers from the Common Agricultural Policy and state subsidies, and to iron out the conflicts between agriculture and conservation. Other seminars were held on housing and the environment. Mount organised his recommendations around a number of themes dear to Mrs Thatcher. These included cutting public spending by, for example, competitive tendering for defence weapons and equipment, reducing the burden of the state earnings-related pension scheme on future generations, and rewriting the transport White Paper to curtail the massive expenditure on roads. Another Mount theme was the curbing of the size of the bureaucracy via more privatisation and contracting out. The Unit also rewrote the Green Paper on Democracy and Trade Unions, to leave room for pre-strike ballots. On education it reinforced pressure for schools to opt out of local authority control and the introduction of TVEI. In much of this Mount was pushing out an opening door. Most time-consuming and ill-fated was its advocacy of the scheme for vouchers in schools, a project designed to extend parental choice.[29]

None of Mrs Thatcher's first tranche of Number Ten appointments had a more enduring importance than that of Bernard Ingham, who began work as Press Secretary in November 1979. His eleven years in the post coincided with all but the first few months of her premiership. Ingham was not an obvious choice for the post. He was a blunt Yorkshireman, had been a Labour Party supporter in the past, an industrial correspondent for the *Guardian*, and had recently served as information officer at the Department of Energy, under the left-wing Tony Benn. For the previous year he had been an Under-Secretary in that department before moving across to Number Ten, where he worked for a few months as deputy to Henry James before assuming full responsibility on 1 November.

Over the previous twenty years only Harold Wilson's two journalistic appointments – Lloyd-Hughes and Haines – had broken the run of civil servants acting as press officers for the Prime Minister. Haines' forceful, even abrasive, style had helped ensure that relations between Number Ten and the press Lobby would not be easy. Ingham was to follow this path. Until Alastair Campbell began work as Tony Blair's Press Secretary in 1997, he was Downing Street's most controversial press officer. To a greater extent than hitherto 'Downing Street sources' were clearly identified as Bernard Ingham.

'A marriage of minds' was how some insiders described the relationship between Mrs Thatcher and Ingham, although he became very close to her only from 1984. By 1979 he had clearly left Labour behind. If as her Press Secretary he was controversial, it was in part because he accurately reflected the forthright views and style of the Prime Minister. She did not appear to mind being presented as a figure apart from the Cabinet. Inevitably, Ingham's briefings for the media caused resentment among several ministers who found themselves undermined by words uttered from within the Citadel.

Ingham's particular skill in gaining a good press for Mrs Thatcher was achieved less via the twice-daily collective Lobby briefings, and more in one-to-one briefings with the political editors of such tabloids as the *Sun*, *Daily Express* and *Daily Mail* and by arranging meetings with the Prime Minister for sympathetic editors and proprietors. In presenting the overall government case, Ingham ensured that it was Mrs Thatcher's line which prevailed over that of Cabinet dissenters. A number of 'wet' ministers in her first Cabinet, including Ian Gilmour, St John Stevas, Jim Prior and Francis Pym, complained about hostile Number Ten briefing and press reports of their imminent sacking. Few of the targets doubted that Ingham accurately represented her views: that was precisely the point of their concern. Ingham himself candidly admits in his memoirs that eventually 'my thought processes were much more those of a politician than an official'.[30] This was an different role to that carried out by Maitland for Heath or McCaffrey for Callaghan.

Mrs Thatcher was too busy to do more than give a cursory glance at daily newspapers and she started her day instead listening to the *Today* programme on Radio 4. This was a cue to private secretaries to tune in early, to learn what might be on her mind later. When ministers were on the programme, they knew she would be listening intently to their words. Ingham arrived early in Downing Street to prepare a digest of the early morning newspapers for the Prime Minister. He thus became her filter on the outside world. She tried to look at his summary in particular on Tuesdays and Thursdays, before the 9 am meeting with her staff which prepared her for PMQs on those days, but her own reading of the digest declined over the years.

In his job of co-ordinating government communications, Ingham at first reported to Angus Maude, the Postmaster General and himself a former journalist. After eighteen months Maude left the government and his co-ordinating task was assigned to Francis Pym, the Leader of the House of Commons. When Pym moved to the FCO in April 1982 the job was then given to the new Leader of the House, John Biffen. These ministers would brief Ingham on that day's Cabinet. At first Maude also chaired the Monday evening meetings of Whitehall's heads of information, but after his departure, in January 1981, Ingham or, when he was absent, his deputy chaired. His predecessors as Press Secretary, Donald Maitland and Joe Haines, had not bothered with it. Ingham's taking the chair was a decisive step: he energetically applied himself to ensuring that Number Ten's line prevailed throughout Whitehall. He became a runner for, not merely the servant of, his master and in his troubleshooting role in Whitehall he had some overlap with the job as it emerged of Head of the Policy Unit.

Mrs Thatcher wanted the affluent businessman David Wolfson in her Political Office and the title 'Chief of Staff' was created for that purpose.[31] Her earlier thoughts of appointing a political heavyweight to play the role of Chief of Staff had clearly lapsed. Typically for Number Ten, Wolfson had no job description, but saw himself as 'essentially being responsible for anything that nobody else was doing'.[32] His task was not helped by his office being placed in a small room opposite the door to the Cabinet Office, away from the Prime Minister's office or the Cabinet Room. He helped to organise her diary and sought to find time to allow her to meet with other Number Ten political staff and guard against her workaholic tendency. He sat in on Cabinet meetings when he was free and saw Cabinet papers, apart from those on defence and intelligence. He arranged for John

Hoskyns and Alan Walters to attend the Prime Minister's weekly meeting with the Chancellor of the Exchequer in the run-up to the 1981 Budget. He was a sounding-board with considerable potential to affect her future; but both officials and ministers rapidly came to regard him as having no influence on policy.

It had been Wolfson's expertise as a manager of a large family retail business, Great Universal Stores, that first brought him into contact with Mrs Thatcher, when he was asked to suggest ways in which her office might deal with the inflow of 2,000 letters a week. He had also advised on a reorganisation of Conservative Central Office in 1978. Wolfson was an emollient operator, and after he moved into Downing Street he, unlike Hoskyns, experienced few 'turf' disputes with other Number Ten staff. By 1982 he thought he had achieved what he had set out to do and returned part-time to business, suggesting that there was no need to replace him. He returned to help Mrs Thatcher during the 1983 and 1987 general election campaigns and was occasionally called upon for advice. He later considered that she was becoming out of touch.[33]

As her Parliamentary Private Secretary, Mrs Thatcher appointed Ian Gow, the MP for Eastbourne. He was loyal, discreet and a candid friend. He was relentless in collecting the views of backbenchers and warning Mrs Thatcher of potential problems with the party. Some MPs nicknamed him 'supergrass'. He would come into Number Ten early in the morning, tour the committee rooms and tea-rooms in the Commons, and enjoy a late-night drink and conspiratorial chat with Mrs Thatcher. For her first two years at least she did not command a harmonious Cabinet and she was aware that the support for her tough domestic policies was probably stronger on the back benches; at a time when both unemployment and inflation were increasing, it was vital that she remained in close touch with them. Gow, firmly on the party's right wing, regularly brought supportive as well as critical MPs to her rooms at night in the House of Commons. But Gow had one issue on which he did not feel at one with his beloved leader. Mrs Thatcher reports his unhappiness with Jim Prior's White Paper on Northern Ireland and its proposed 'rolling devolution' plans for an assembly for the province.[34] Indeed he quoted her doubts about it in order to lobby backbenchers to oppose the proposals. After Gow left the post in 1983, Mrs Thatcher never again found a PPS with his mixture of loyalty and independence of mind. She also became more open to change in Ireland, notably with the Anglo-Irish Agreement of 1985, than she would have been had Gow remained at her right hand.

Richard Ryder had been Mrs Thatcher's Political Secretary as opposition leader since 1975. Ex-Radley and Magdalene College, Cambridge, he had risen to become chairman of the University Conservative Association and was still only thirty when Mrs Thatcher entered Downing Street. He remained in post until 1981, when he left to seek a seat in the Commons (he won Mid-Norfolk in 1983) and marry Caroline Stephens, the Diary Secretary. Colleagues remember him as discreet, even diffident. Having played an important part in the pre-election preparation for office, Number Ten insiders expected the young Ryder, clearly a Thatcher favourite, to play a big part in the new regime. 'She made little use of him', however, recalled one, who witnessed Mrs Thatcher humiliating him during preparation for one of her first Parliamentary Question Times.[35] In 1981 he was replaced by Derek Howe, a recruit from the press department of Conservative Central Office, who also helped for Question Time. But Gow was active in so many areas that he absorbed a good part of the Political Secretary's work.

As a woman, Caroline Stephens could be used by the Private Office to visit Mrs Thatcher and obtain a decision when she was in the bath or when she was getting dressed. One recalled: 'If we wanted a response by 8 am we would send in Caroline. She was regarded as highly intelligent, co-operative and very much part of the Private Office machine.'

Throughout her premiership Mrs Thatcher showed little interest in Conservative Central Office, apart from worrying about its efficiency as a general election approached, and left liaison with the party organisation to her political secretaries. Her happiest Central Office relationship was with Cecil Parkinson, who replaced Thorneycroft as Chairman in September 1981 and remained in the post until just after the June 1983 general election. When appointed, Parkinson was relatively unknown. Mrs Thatcher was struck by his easy manner and by his looks, and admired his presentational skills, not least on television. This was one reason which led her to make him a member of the small War Cabinet in April 1982, at the time of the Falklands conflict. On Mondays at 10 am, Mrs Thatcher held a thirty-minute 'week ahead' meeting to review political and media strategies for coming events. This was attended by the Party Chairman, the heads of the Political and Private Offices, her PPS, the Press Secretary and members of the party's Press and Research Departments.

Mrs Thatcher gradually overcame her initial hostility to political advisers. In January 1981 she recruited Alan Walters, then at Johns Hopkins University, to be her economic adviser. Walters had become disillusioned with the mixture of corporatism and Keynesianism under Heath and, almost inevitably, gravitated to the Centre for Policy Studies. The fact that he had been a monetarist economist at an early stage was a badge of respectability in Mrs Thatcher's eyes. She also felt that Walters could help Treasury officials in debating technical monetary matters with the Bank of England. Mrs Thatcher's own economic understanding was limited: she had strong instincts, but little grasp of the technicalities. She had been influenced on monetarism by city figures like Tim Congdon and John Sparrow in the 1970s and now needed Walters and others to translate her own monetarist intuition into action.

Walters' salary was paid jointly by government and the CPS and his grade was that of a second Permanent Secretary in the Civil Service. He had ready access to Mrs Thatcher, seeing and writing to her as and when he felt that he had something to say, particularly in exposing so-called 'quack cures'. She liked his irreverence and the confidence with which he challenged Treasury thinking. The tenacity with which he advocated tightening fiscal policy in the 1981 Budget, in spite of high unemployment, impressed her and lent an extra authority to those arguing similarly. Such a step flew in the face of much orthodox economic advice and would deepen the recession in the short run at least, and create political problems for Mrs Thatcher with her colleagues. In a letter to *The Times* on 30 March 1981, 364 economists, including four former chief economic advisers to the government, warned that the Conservative government's policy of decelerating the rate of growth of money supply would worsen the depression, and monetarist policy would deepen the depression, erode the industrial base of the country, and undermine social and political stability.[36] Some might have been deterred by such an unprecedented display of unity by so many leaders of an academic discipline. Buoyed by her advisers, she was not.

During Mrs Thatcher's first administration, Walters' relations with the Chancellor, Geoffrey Howe, were usually good, in stark contrast to his relationship with Nigel Lawson. Howe was aware that Walters was not always discreet and held different economic views to his own, yet asked Peter Middleton, an Under Secretary, and Terry Burns, the Treasury's chief economic adviser, to keep in touch with him and to invite him to Treasury meetings. Ian Gow, a close friend of Howe's, was an important link between the Chancellor and the Prime Minister. Michael Scholar, the Economic Affairs Private Secretary, also ensured that there were good relations between the two. Walters advised Mrs Thatcher in private memos and meetings. The Treasury for its part kept tabs on Walters via its contacts with the Number Ten Private Office. Walters returned to academic life in the US in January 1983, and thereafter his appointment at Number Ten became part time until October 1984, when he left completely. He returned full time to Number Ten, with seismic consequences, in May 1989. Despite their concerns, the official machine regarded Walters' first manifestation as providing a genuinely constructive element to policy formation; but they saw his 'second coming' as a disaster: 'he had acquired ideas way above his station', said one senior civil servant.[37]

Mrs Thatcher remained throughout suspicious of the Treasury. She regarded Douglas Wass, the Permanent Under-Secretary, as almost a crypto-socialist and was equally dismissive of William Ryrie, another key official who had been destined for the top. She was more attentive to the views of Peter Middleton and the new economic adviser, Terence Burns. The Foreign and Commonwealth Office (FCO) was another department she viewed with suspicion, especially since the 1981 EC Budget Rebate and the Falklands War, over which she felt it had been weak and indecisive. She muttered about the Permanent Under-Secretary at the FCO, Michael Palliser, but thought highly of individual diplomats such as Nico Henderson and Anthony Parsons.[38] Impressed by the value to her of the Walters appointment,

Mrs Thatcher recruited Parsons, the British representative at the United Nations at the time of the 1982 Falklands War, to be her 'foreign policy' adviser later that same year. This appointment produced a vigorous exchange of views with her new Principal Private Secretary, Robin Butler, who had succeeded Whitmore in 1982. Butler initially opposed the appointment, shared the Foreign Office concerns, and suspected that it might undermine good relations between Mrs Thatcher and her new Foreign Secretary, Francis Pym. Mrs Thatcher swept such reservations aside, and Butler came to revise his opinion of Parsons,[39] who was replaced in December 1983 by Sir Percy Cradock, another diplomat.

Roger Jackling, an official in the Ministry of Defence, was another ad hoc adviser, in his case to counsel her on military matters. Defence was a subject Mrs Thatcher had encountered only tangentially in her career, but for a Prime Minister knowledge of defence matters is essential. This appointment did not work out. The Secretary of State for Defence, Michael Heseltine, made Jackling's job virtually impossible by instructing officials not to have any contact with him. Thereafter, defence matters were re-absorbed into the remit of the Private Secretary for Foreign Affairs. It remains an open question how far Mrs Thatcher's mission was blocked, even at this stage, by senior civil servants. Certainly she and some of her entourage felt that some senior mandarins pressed their hostility to her policies way beyond the point that they should have stopped as neutral officials.[40]

Mrs Thatcher's appointment of these special advisers came in tandem with the expansion of the Policy Unit under Mount. As she began to flex her muscles as Prime Minister from 1981/82, she began to feel the need for advice which could not only enable her to scrutinise the papers and proposals from Whitehall departments but also provide her with alternative proposals. Was she, by doing so, creating an embryonic Prime Minister's Department?

In her first four years as Prime Minister, Mrs Thatcher had more impact in aborting machinery than in creating it. Both the CPRS and the Civil Service Department were casualties. The CPRS had remained a body of secondary importance since its decline under Ted Heath from 1973. The creation of the Policy Unit in 1974 further marginalised it, although in opposition the Conservatives had been

more convinced of the case for the CPRS's retention than for that of
the Policy Unit, which was, after all, a Labour creation. Mrs Thatcher
wasted no time with niceties. At her first meeting with the CPRS
head, Sir Kenneth Berrill, four days into her term, Mrs Thatcher
complained that it leaked too much, had lost sight of its original
objectives and that her government already had a clear philosophical
direction.[41] This unpromising start was followed by a damaging turnover of CPRS heads. Berrill was replaced within a year by Sir Robin
Ibbs. After two years in post he was recalled by ICI and replaced by
John Sparrow, a merchant banker, who never found his niche with
her.

In those years the CPRS worked on studies of unemployment,
alternatives to domestic rates, training, and reform of the nationalised
industries, short of privatisation. Mrs Thatcher warmed to Ibbs and
respected his background in industry. John Sparrow, at Morgan Gren-
fell, had advised her in Opposition on City issues and he continued
to write to her on financial matters when she became Prime Minister.
Sparrow was interviewed by Armstrong and Whitmore, who then
recommended him to Mrs Thatcher. Soon after his appointment he
described himself to a journalist as 'semi-detached'. An article in *The
Times* was headlined as such; some months before Bernard Ingham
had made the phrase famous when he used it about the Cabinet
Minister John Biffen. It was his misfortune to start work on 1 April
1982, the day the task force set out for Argentina, when Mrs Thatcher
had other matters on her mind. Post-Falklands, nothing happened to
rekindle her interest in Sparrow's outfit. Reflecting on the decision to
wind it up immediately after the general election in 1983, she admitted
'I never missed it'.[42]

A decisive blow followed with the leaking in September 1982 of a
Treasury-commissioned study of the policy consequences of the
recent trends in public spending in a low-growth British economy.
Here was an example of the kind of work that the CPRS was supposed
to be doing – looking to the long term and spelling out options.
The trouble was that the document was distributed around Whitehall
together with the Cabinet papers, rather than being circulated exclusively to Cabinet ministers on a more confidential basis. The wide
circulation of a controversial document which discussed massive cuts

in state provision of education and health always ran the risk of unauthorised disclosure. No-one discovered who leaked it: some close to Mrs Thatcher suspected a senior wet Cabinet minister.[43] Bitter rows followed the leak. After it hit the press, most Cabinet ministers had no wish to discuss the document and regarded many of the options as politically beyond the pale, and Mrs Thatcher and Howe were forced to abort debate of the paper. Mrs Thatcher's doubts about the CPRS were confirmed. Her decision to wind it up produced no objections from ministers, even though it had originally been set up by Heath to help the Cabinet think strategically. Only some senior civil servants proposed second thoughts.

The Civil Service Department (CSD), meanwhile, had been a product of the Fulton report into the Civil Service, which reported in 1968, and had responsibility for management and pay in the service. Again, Mrs Thatcher had it in her sights from the beginning. Her memoirs report a visit to the Department in January 1980 as 'an enlightening if not an encouraging experience'.[44] The embodiment to her of the old-style mandarin was none other than the Head of the Home Civil Service and Permanent Secretary of the CSD, Ian Bancroft. He had had a high-profile career in the Civil Service but towards the end he was not in good health, made it obvious he disapproved of much that Mrs Thatcher was trying to do to the Civil Service, and had become very defensive.[45] For her part she did not rate him highly, or indeed Lord Soames, the Cabinet minister responsible for the Civil Service, and felt that the CSD's ranks contained insufficient expertise to bring the departments up to scratch. In some respects she looked rather to Derek Rayner's Efficiency Unit to reform the Civil Service; Rayner certainly felt that the CSD was not offering what it should on management and he counselled its demise.[46] After an acidic meeting between Thatcher and Bancroft, the department was wound up in October 1981 and its functions allocated to the Treasury and the Cabinet Office; Bancroft was encouraged to take early retirement. The Treasury took over responsibility for pay and the Cabinet Office established a Manpower and Personnel Office.

We have seen that Mrs Thatcher's initial Cabinet contained few who could be considered outright supporters. One of her most widely quoted remarks before she became Prime Minister was that her Cabinet would not have time for arguments and would consist 'only of those who want to go in the direction in which the Prime Minister wants to go'.[47] That did not happen. A revolt over Howe's 1981 Budget and bitter arguments in July about public expenditure stiffened her determination to weed out Cabinet dissenters. In a September reshuffle she dismissed four of the 'wets' (St John Stevas, Soames, Gilmour and Carlisle) and she moved Jim Prior from the mainline economic Department of Employment to the comparative backwater of Northern Ireland. By autumn 1981 all major economic ministries, apart from the Treasury, had new ministers in charge. Although Mrs Thatcher was not personally close to Howe, her Chancellor, the two agreed on most policies, were at one in battling to contain the growth of public spending and at times were a beleaguered minority in the Cabinet.

She respected, but argued fiercely with, her Foreign Secretary Lord Carrington and in 1981 only reluctantly accepted his negotiated compromise over British contributions to the impasse over the EC budget, over which she had fought so hard. That episode greatly disillusioned her. When Carrington resigned as Foreign Secretary in April 1982 she judged the moment inopportune to appoint a close ally, and contented herself instead with replacing him with the patrician Francis Pym. Relations with Pym were at best cool. Mrs Thatcher was not impressed by the Foreign Office's handling of events preceding Argentina's invasion of the Falklands. Over the course of her premiership, her interest and involvement in international affairs grew, as did her disagreement with some favoured Foreign Office positions, above all on Europe. Pym was summarily dismissed after the 1983 general election.

She relied heavily on William Whitelaw, her Home Secretary, to 'square' colleagues. Although not a philosophical ally, his total loyalty to decisions which he and Mrs Thatcher agreed on in their meetings helped to undermine the 'wet' dissenters. Whitelaw was an important bridge during the tense negotiations over public spending cuts in 1980–81, persuading both her and the spending ministers to moderate their positions. He would regularly meet with her over reshuffles and difficult Cabinet issues: but despite their professional closeness, the two never became kindred or ideological spirits.

For much of her first administration Mrs Thatcher's position as premier was far from assured. Prior recalls her nerves before PMQs and fearing hostile questions over the latest rise in unemployment, while Hoskyns urged her to be more radical in policies and in her speeches ('Of course you can say it, Margaret,' he would tell her). In 1979 she was surrounded by senior figures – Whitelaw, Carrington, Pym, Prior and Soames – who were all, in her own words, on the 'wet' side of the party. By the end of the Parliament all but Whitelaw had left government or had been marginalised. To help combat this isolation she would have occasional Sunday evening chats in Number Ten with Howe, and held a Thursday morning Breakfast Group in Number Ten to anticipate the day's Cabinet agenda. The group consisted of Ian Gow and David Wolfson, among her staff, and Keith Joseph, John Nott, John Biffen and Geoffrey Howe, the holders of the main economic posts in the Cabinet.[48]

Like all Prime Ministers, Mrs Thatcher exploited her control of the Cabinet agenda and her powers to appoint members to its committees or convene ad hoc groups to produce desired decisions. She chaired the important E committee on economic policy and packed it with her supporters. There was a reduction in the number of Cabinet meetings and then of Cabinet papers, which reduced the opportunities for collective deliberation.[49] More decisions were effectively taken at bilateral meetings between Mrs Thatcher and the relevant minister or ad hoc meetings with a small group of ministers, or settled by correspondence between ministers and reported to the Cabinet Secretary. At ad hoc meetings a private secretary, not somebody from the Cabinet Secretariat, would usually take notes. The purchase of the Trident nuclear missile programme, for example, was effectively decided by a small group of ministers, outside the Cabinet, in early 1981. The decision prompted the then political editor of the *Sunday Times*, Hugo Young, to comment, with a degree of exaggeration, on 'The Death of Cabinet Government'.[50] Private secretaries sitting in on Cabinet would be amazed at how abrupt and rude she could be to some of her ministers during meetings: 'when a wet minister was speaking she would turn to us and roll her eyes in disdain'.[51] Soames, Pym, Prior and David Howell would be particularly singled out for this treatment.

Mrs Thatcher's inner ministerial circle for much of the 1979–1983

Parliament consisted of Howe and Whitelaw. In the outer ring were Joseph, Parkinson, Ridley, Nott, Carrington until his departure in April 1982, and Michael Jopling, Chief Whip throughout her first term. Also prominent in the inner circle were Gow, Walters and some of the Number Ten staff (see Appendix II).

For speeches on government matters Mrs Thatcher relied on her Private Office to exchange drafts with departments. On more political occasions suggestions came from sympathetic journalists such as Paul Johnson, Woodrow Wyatt and Bill Deedes, as well as from CPS members like Hugh Thomas and Alfred Sherman. On public relations she valued the advice of the Saatchi advertising executive Tim Bell and, on his return visits from the US, Gordon Reece, who had been the party's Communications Director before the 1979 general election.

Of all recent Prime Ministers, Mrs Thatcher seems to have had the largest group of helpers on political speeches. She usually drew on various heads of her Policy Unit (particularly Hoskyns and Mount), the Political Office, the party's Research Department, and outsiders like the playwright Ronald Millar. Staff maintained an 'ideas for speeches' file, which included old press cuttings, quotations, suggested drafts from ministers, academics, sympathetic journalists, party officials and special advisers.[52] Her speechwriting sessions demanded great stamina from the helpers, often lasting into the early hours of the morning. One later Private Secretary, Charles Powell, advised 'never put anything worthwhile in the first draft; it will be rejected'.[53] Ronnie Millar recalled that writing a Thatcher speech was hellish yet exhilarating. It emerged, like the old methods for electing a Tory leader, by 'part design, part accident and part a host of disconnected and related factors'. It was Millar who inserted many of Margaret Thatcher's memorable lines, most famously, in the 1980 conference speech, the words 'The lady's not for turning', nicely phrased, poorly delivered. 'Speechwriting for Mrs Thatcher was chaos,' said one private secretary. 'She wanted everyone to chip in, no-one knew exactly what was going on.'[54]

Mrs Thatcher was on a steep learning curve throughout her first four years as Prime Minister. A conservative organisationally, she travelled light to Downing Street in terms of staff support or preparation. Her first two top political appointees, Hoskyns and Wolfson, were businessmen who were dabbling in politics, albeit at a high level. Neither had prior experience in government or in the Conservative Party; neither was interested in learning how to play the 'Whitehall game', which they believed would substantially undermine their effectiveness. In 1982, no longer in Number Ten, Hoskyns went public with his criticisms of the 'defeatist' mandarins. In the early months criticisms from within the party and from Cabinet colleagues and attacks in the press had made her appreciate the Private Office all the more. Here was a constant source of support. In turn, private secretaries from the period still recall her mental toughness and stamina, and the coherence of her approach. 'It was an exciting time to be at the centre,' one recalled, 'She regarded us as part of her extended family.' By the end of the Parliament Mrs Thatcher had increased the number of her advisers, realised what a gem she had in her Private Office, established Ingham and Powell as her closest aides within Number Ten, and shifted the balance in the Cabinet to one more supportive of her economic policies. That was her style: if she was being blocked by a particular minister, she would change the minister rather than adopt a new bureaucratic arrangement.

Her dominance, following the successful Falklands War, the sacking of dissenting ministers, and the strengthening of her staff, prompted public discussion about the creation of a Prime Minister's Department. Certainly Hoskyns and Sherman favoured such a course, to counter their belief in a 'defeatist' Whitehall. In their view the Prime Minister, backed by a strong and like-minded Downing Street staff, would be in a position to give a lead to the departments. In 1982 Clive Whitmore prepared a paper on the creation of such a department. It would have a senior civil servant as its head and would work closely with the Cabinet Secretariat. The arrangement would have suited a Prime Minister like Mrs Thatcher as 'she liked to run things', in Whitmore's words. She found CPRS papers too lengthy and concentrated too much on the distant future to stimulate her interest. It did not help that CPRS papers went to all Cabinet ministers, rather than to her alone.

The Policy Unit under Mount also drew up a scheme in which

some policy specialists from the Cabinet Office and the CPRS would join the Policy Unit and Private Office to create a new body which would provide greater support for the Prime Minister. Senior civil servants opposed such a scheme and some were even unhappy about her appointment of a handful of special advisers. 'You have to remember the mindset at the time on the other side of the green baize door, in the Cabinet Office,' said one of Mrs Thatcher's then advisers, in 1998.[55]

After the Falklands War other concerns emerged. Mrs Thatcher had been taken aback at the strong objections made in Whitehall and by her Foreign Secretary at the appointment of a foreign affairs adviser. She did not want to broaden the front of criticism. The proposals quickly died. She was content to make ad hoc arrangements and appointments to get her own way and to use existing machinery. Portrayed at the time as a radical on machinery of government, in fact she was very conservative on organisational reform: some of her changes were even backward looking, as when she abolished the CSD in 1981, re-creating the old-style Treasury. She intervened and summoned Cabinet ministers as and when she felt concerned, and few departments were unaware of what the Downing Street line was on a particular policy. Number Ten's view was a dominant factor in Whitehall. A landslide victory in the 1983 general election, at a time of high unemployment, seemed to vindicate her style of political leadership. Anthony King noted, 'The repertory of prime ministerial styles has been extended'.[56] By mid-1983 she had established a steady platform for governing, and was in a stronger position than any Tory leader had been since Macmillan in 1959/60: the question was, how would she now use her new found authority?

CHAPTER SEVEN

Margaret Thatcher
(1983–1990)

MARGARET THATCHER continued to be the dominant personality in British politics throughout the 1980s. General election success in 1983 meant that hers was the first government to win two successive full terms of office since the Conservative victory in 1959. Another decisive election victory in 1987 made her the first leader since Lord Liverpool in the 1820s to win three elections in succession. The 1983 and 1987 majorities were the two largest of any Parliament since 1945. The Conservative Party and Mrs Thatcher were in fact favoured by the electoral system, which gave them 60 per cent of the seats on 42 per cent of the popular vote. They were also the beneficiaries of being faced with a weak and divided opposition. No other governing party this century had enjoyed such a commanding parliamentary position for so long a period.

In the years 1983 to 1990 Mrs Thatcher could point to many achievements. Her government made further big reductions in the marginal rates of income tax, from 60 to 40 per cent at the top rate and 2p off the standard rate. It continued with reforms of the trade unions and defeated the twelve-month-long miners' strike between March 1984 and March 1985. The programme of privatisation was dramatically extended to include British Airways, British Gas, British Telecommunications, British Steel, Rolls Royce, water and electricity; by 1990, only a handful of utilities still remained in the public sector. The later 1980s also saw significant reforms introduced in health and education, both of which adopted market mechanisms, as well as the short-lived and deeply unpopular community charge (poll tax, as it became generally known) reform of local government finance.

When she stepped down in November 1990 Mrs Thatcher had established her reputation as the century's most dominant and activist peacetime premier. She personified prime ministerial power, but her approach sat ill with the idea of collegial Cabinet government. It is not unusual for Prime Ministers to intervene in foreign and economic policy; the Prime Minister usually chairs the key Cabinet committees, has weekly bilaterals with the Chancellor and Foreign Secretary and often answers for economic and foreign policy at PMQs and at international summits. Mrs Thatcher had clashed with her first two Foreign Secretaries (Carrington and Pym), but her simultaneous disagreements with her Chancellor (Lawson) and Foreign Secretary (Howe) in 1988–89 were destabilising for the government. The bitter resignations of Heseltine (1986), Lawson (1989) and Howe (1990) directly arose from and raised doubts about her overbearing style of leadership.

Several other departments felt the commanding hand of Mrs Thatcher and she was a major influence on the education, health and local government reforms. The approach depended on a restless energy, an unshakeable self-confidence in her opinions, and a belief that she had embarked on an ideological crusade: the job of her colleagues was to give effect to it. Yet she did little to strengthen the premiership as an institution, in the sense of introducing procedures and mechanisms which remained in place after her departure. Her legacy was a style, an example of what could be achieved, a model to be emulated or rejected.

Robert Armstrong had an increasingly trying time as Cabinet Secretary and Head of the Home Civil Service. He did much to bring order to Mrs Thatcher's working habits – which were often reactive and instinctive – but this discipline would have been necessary in any case if the Cabinet system were to work efficiently. The paradox of Armstrong's final and most senior post is that while he clung to his predecessors' belief in the importance of civil servants assuming a low profile, Mrs Thatcher was to involve him personally in many headline-catching events – GCHQ, the Westland affair, and the *Spycatcher* book saga. His belief in the traditional Civil Service values

Ted Heath arrives at Number Ten Downing Street on his first day as Prime Minister full of ideas about creating a stronger centre of government, 19 June 1970.

OPPOSITE

Above Ted Heath with Robert
Armstrong, his powerful Principal
Private Secretary and *éminence grise*.

Below Ted Heath on his beloved yacht
Morning Cloud on the cross-channel
race, summer 1971. Heath would
refuse to carry Prime Minister's boxes
on the yacht as he said it would add to
the weight.

Above right Heath relied heavily on just
a few ministers, with William Whitelaw
to the fore.

Right Edward Heath with William
Armstrong, Head of the Home Civil
Service, who became an ever closer
personal adviser to Heath with
unfortunate consequences.

Left No other Prime Minister since
1970 found as much time to
pursue non-political interests at a
high level as Edward Heath.

Harold Wilson leaves his Westminster home in Lord North Street for Number Ten and his first full day back in office as Prime Minister, 5 March 1974. Wilson formed a close relationship with his driver, Bill Housden.

Top Wilson in the back seat of the Prime Minister's car with wife Mary (right) and Marcia Williams (left) when the latter was at the height of her influence in the 1960s.

Above Harold Wilson at the Prime Minister's seat in the Cabinet Room just after becoming Prime Minister for the first time.

Right Harold Wilson and Marcia Williams singing 'Auld Lang Syne' at Wilson's farewell party as Prime Minister in the spring of 1976.

Wilson with two of his
closest aides, Joe
Haines, Press Secretary
(left) and Bernard
Donoughue, Head of
the Policy Unit, (right),
walking down Lord
North Street.

Above Final curtain. Harold Wilson
looks out into the Horseguards from
inside Number Ten on his last day as
Prime Minister into an uncertain
future.

Left Harold Wilson with Ken Stowe,
who became his Principal Private
Secretary in 1975.

James Callaghan with his Cabinet on 12 March 1978, believed to be the first photograph of a Cabinet in session. On Callaghan's right is Cabinet Secretary John Hunt and on his left, Michael Foot.

Left Bernard Donoughue, Head of the Policy Unit from 1974 to 1979, on his way to scoring a second goal against a team of West German politicians at Crystal Palace Sports Centre, 1978.

Right James Callaghan addressing the Labour Party Conference in 1976 at the height of the IMF loan crisis.

Left James Callaghan leaving Number Ten Downing Street with his wife Audrey. Audrey Callaghan was the first wife of a Labour Prime Minister to enjoy living at Number Ten. She was a profound help to her husband.

Below James Callaghan waves as he leaves Downing Street for the last time after the Labour defeat by Margaret Thatcher in the General Election, 4 May 1979.

prompted his acute disappointment at the frequent leaks. In 1985, he issued a note of guidance on the duties and responsibilities of civil servants, reminding them that they were servants of the Crown and that, in effect, this meant of the government of the day. Armstrong had an almost impossible balancing act to perform, and it would have taxed any public servant to the limit.

Yet by the time he retired in 1987 there was a sense among senior ministers that he had allowed himself to be used by Mrs Thatcher and that the office of Cabinet Secretary had lost some of its authority under her.[1] In September 1998, one of the most senior ministers in the Thatcher Cabinets recalled: 'There are certain checks and balances in the Whitehall system. The Cabinet Secretary is one of them. Mrs Thatcher systematically weakened the office and Armstrong became a catspaw.'[2] A contrary view comes from a senior mandarin: 'Armstrong was not prepared to become an adjunct of the Private Office: under Mrs Thatcher, Number Ten talked about the Cabinet Secretary as a rival power.'[3]

Supported by Geoffrey Howe, now Foreign Secretary, Armstrong and the unions at the government signals intelligence headquarters in Cheltenham, (known after its initials as GCHQ), had arrived at an agreement that in exchange for retaining trade union membership the staff would provide guarantees of no further disruption. This compromise was rejected by Mrs Thatcher who, still enraged by a strike in 1981 when GCHQ had been called out, insisted on nothing less than the ending of union membership at the installation.[4] 'It was a great shame', said one insider, 'that she rejected the compromise, which gave her 97½ per cent of what she wanted.' He suspected it was Ingham who emboldened her not to be flexible.[5]

Armstrong also conducted the inquiry into the Westland affair in 1986. The Prime Minister and Michael Heseltine, Secretary of State for Defence, were at odds over rival rescue plans for the ailing West Country helicopter firm, Westland. As the battle raged over late Christmas and early January, Mrs Thatcher, senior ministers and officials discussed plans to issue a warning to Heseltine: he would be asked to toe the line or be dismissed. A law officer's confidential letter, prompted by Number Ten, warned Heseltine of inaccuracies in some of his statements. Once it was known that there had been a leak, the

Attorney General warned that there would have to be an inquiry into who had done it, and if it was not conducted by the Civil Service, then the police would be called in. Armstrong took up the cudgels. He, rather than Number Ten officials, such as Bernard Ingham and Charles Powell, also presented evidence to, and answered questions from the Defence Select Committee in the House of Commons. Although there was initial comment on the absence of Powell and Ingham, there was no precedent for Private Office staff from any departments being summoned before a Select Committee. Senior Whitehall officials thought that Mrs Thatcher was lucky to come through the episode unscathed, and so too were Powell and Ingham.

Even more high profile and ultimately damaging to Armstrong personally was his answering for the British government in the Australian courts when it tried to prevent publication of the *Spycatcher* memoirs of Peter Wright, a retired and embittered MI5 officer. It was an uncomfortable experience for him and under the pressure his nerves were on edge. 'She asked me to go to Australia', he later said, 'and was very supportive throughout.'[6] The government had to be represented by a member of the British establishment and she said it could not be her or a member of the security services. She felt Armstrong had considerable experience in intelligence matters and thus he was sent. Armstrong believed that publication of Wright's memoirs had to be blocked, because if he was allowed to get away with publishing details of the covert world of spies, his former security service colleagues, many of whom hated Wright, would feel entitled to publish their version of events too. Armstrong was best remembered for uttering the words in Australia 'economical with the truth': he regrets saying them, but acknowledges they have become 'quite a trademark since'.[7] The phrase (Edmund Burke's) was not a justification of lying, but rather was saying that one could tell the truth without being obliged to tell the whole truth.

More positively, he was the major player on the British side in negotiating the Anglo-Irish Agreement with Dublin in 1985. After the 1983 election victory, Mrs Thatcher began to become impatient to see progress in Northern Ireland. She felt she could trust neither the Foreign Office nor the Northern Ireland Office to act on her behalf and she asked Armstrong to be the key link with senior officials in

Dublin. Armstrong's role and enthusiasm for progress was pivotal, not least because of the authority he carried. Though she felt that the 1985 Agreement did not grant all that she would have wanted on security, she continued to believe that she had taken a step in the right direction. She was sad, but not surprised, when Ian Gow, her former PPS, resigned from the government on the issue.

It is difficult to discern Armstrong's influence on Mrs Thatcher. Some readers, for example Ferdinand Mount, of Cabinet Office briefs for Mrs Thatcher during his tenure are critical of their lack of policy analysis.[8] Cabinet Office staff reject such criticism as misguided; the purpose of the briefs is to help the chairman of the Cabinet or Cabinet committee to arrive at a decision which the Cabinet as a whole will support. They further claim that their briefs do contain policy advice, however implicit it is. Mrs Thatcher also made a point of discussing ministerial appointments with Armstrong.[9]

From early on in her premiership Mrs Thatcher had shown a close interest in the appointment of senior civil servants. In the Senior Appointments Selection Committee (SASC) which Armstrong chaired the recommendations to Mrs Thatcher were his. Claims that she had politicised the service were not substantiated in 1987 by the independent Royal Institute of Public Administration, a conclusion which did not satisfy those who thought that the definition of the 'politicisation' being investigated was too narrow. In drawing up his list of names Armstrong probably took account of Mrs Thatcher's likes and dislikes. But one insider reckoned that 85 per cent of top appointments would have been the same had James Callaghan still been in office, and only 5 per cent entirely different. The appointment in 1982 of Peter Middleton as Permanent Secretary in the Treasury is often cited as a case when the joint advice of Armstrong and Wass was rebuffed; the two had proposed another Treasury official.[10]

Projects like the Financial Management Initiative and the 'Next Steps' (1988) programme for transferring many civil servants to executive agencies further helped to transform the culture under Armstrong's successor, Robin Butler. The bowler-hatted and rolled umbrella image of the pinstriped civil servant, aloof from business and modern management techniques, went for ever. To be effective advisers and operators, civil servants require political antennae. A successful civil servant quickly learns the new policy parameters which follow a change of government or a change of minister in a department. Under Mrs Thatcher, proposals from departments which involved more government intervention in the economy or unrecoverable increases in public spending no longer fitted the intellectual framework.

Robin Butler was Mrs Thatcher's first choice as Armstrong's successor as Cabinet Secretary, even though the latter had recommended Whitmore. Butler had unrivalled experience of the Treasury and had worked in different capacities under three Prime Ministers at Number Ten. He took the Head of the Civil Service aspect of his job seriously. He spent more time than some predecessors attending to these responsibilities and made a point of getting out of Whitehall to visit government offices in different parts of the country. Much of his time was also taken presiding over the continuing managerial revolution in Whitehall as the creation of agencies speeded up. He had private reservations about the number of prime ministerial meetings that the Cabinet Secretary no longer attended, and at the rise in the influence of the Private Office and of Charles Powell in particular. At one point he had to insist to the Prime Minister that he attend her meeting with President Reagan, on the grounds that he would have little credibility with the Americans on intelligence matters unless he did so.[11] Later he worked closely with Howe when the latter had been 'demoted' to Deputy Prime Minister and Lord President of the Council. Howe chaired a large number of Cabinet committees and it was important that Butler liaised with him to make the Cabinet system work efficiently.

Butler had from 1982–85 been Whitmore's successor as Principal Private Secretary. Under him were Andrew Turnbull and Charles Powell. This was a powerful group; the former served later as Mrs Thatcher's Principal Private Secretary, while Powell, who had succeeded John Coles as Foreign Affairs Private Secretary in 1984, gradually became the dominant official. Having not chosen him for the post in the early 1980s, Mrs Thatcher now had to be persuaded to take Powell from a list of three: the Powells and Butlers had been neighbours in South London's Dulwich in the 1970s, and Butler regarded Powell as a friend as well as a high-flier. Butler was puzzled at the resistance she put up to Powell's appointment.[12]

Some Number Ten insiders regard Butler's Private Office as the one that operated best for Mrs Thatcher. She was also at the peak of her powers and Butler had to boost recruits to her office.[13] Butler advised one candidate, before his interview with her, that she would spend the whole time talking, and that he should just wait for a pause and then plunge in. Said one official: 'She was the worst interviewer in the world. She had no idea how to draw anyone out.'[14] Tim Flesher, another who had Mrs Thatcher's confidence, worked on parliamentary business. Butler carried out the usual tasks of co-ordinating, speechwriting, attending to honours and appointments, and generally adopted the policy of 'mobile reinforcement', intervening where he felt the pressure on his staff was most severe. He was at her side in the early hours, dealing with papers, just before the IRA bomb exploded in their Brighton hotel during the party conference in October 1984. The bomb came at a traumatic time domestically: officials in the Private Office remember 1984 as being dominated by the year-long miners' strike. 'The whole issue went one way then the other . . . the progress of the strike was completely in our minds the whole time, as we watched the figures of how many miners returned to work . . . she was inclined to be reckless but was pulled back by Walker, especially, but also Tebbit.'[15]

As foreign affairs – notably the EC, the Soviet Union and Eastern Europe, US relations and also Ireland – loomed larger in Mrs Thatcher's concerns from mid-decade, and as her doubts about various FCO stances grew, she turned more to Powell. The key Foreign Affairs and Economic Affairs secretaries are well placed to represent their home departments' thinking to the Prime Minister and to act as a bridge between both. It was drummed into Turnbull early on that he was not, however, there as the Treasury Private Secretary but was there to work with the other economic departments around Whitehall also.[16] Where, however, there are clear differences between the departments and Number Ten, the private secretaries can be caught in the middle, and this was the case for Powell within a year of his taking up post. Within another year it was clear he was no longer in the middle, but moving towards the Number Ten side.

Charles Powell quickly understood Mrs Thatcher's thinking, was able to articulate it and was very close to her. She liked his omnicompetent style, his elegant manners and his smooth charm. She also admired his memos and found that his speech drafts often expressed her views exactly and eloquently. His memos in reply to some proposal from a department could be written without direct referral to Mrs Thatcher, using such ambiguous terms as 'I have reason to believe . . .'. More than any other member of the Private Office he visited Chequers at weekends to help the Prime Minister with speeches and entertain foreign political leaders. There was a remarkable chemistry between them. In private he would argue vigorously with her and sometimes she would concede. 'But she would not admit it. She always had to be right and you just went along with it.'[17]

On a number of issues, particularly Europe, Powell came to reinforce Mrs Thatcher's views against those of the Foreign Office. According to one Number Ten adviser, 'Charles and Mrs Thatcher had their own foreign policy and sometimes the Foreign Office felt out of it. The latter detested him.'[18] Powell maintains that he always kept the Foreign Office informed of what he was doing, speaking to relevant officials nine or ten times a day. Tensions came to a head over Mrs Thatcher's Bruges speech in September 1988, when a Powell draft was heavily rewritten by the Foreign Office. In spite of negotiations over successive drafts Howe found the final version 'deeply dismaying'.[19] One of her seminal statements on Europe, it restated Mrs Thatcher's belief in a European free market, and in the importance of maintaining good relations with the USA, and repudiated any project for a single European state.

The atmosphere in the Private Office changed in the final years of Mrs Thatcher's premiership from the camaraderie of the first six years. A turning point was the departure of Robin Butler, who returned to the Treasury, in August 1985. Butler had throughout his three years been the commanding figure, not on titular grounds alone. He also had the force of personality to keep Charles Powell in check. In the months it took his successor, Nigel Wicks, to settle in, Powell's ability, energy and sheer usefulness to Mrs Thatcher put him in an indispensable position. Said one insider 'She regarded Wicks as too pro-European for her taste: with Charles, she felt she had an ally, fighting for her on Europe.'[20] Powell duly began to act on Mrs Thatcher's behalf in a variety of matters, hitherto the preserve of the

Principal Private Secretary. His views were sought on the highest political and official appointments. At meetings in the White House it was Powell who took the minutes. Powell's Italian wife Carla became a close friend of Mrs Thatcher and advised her on her choice of clothing and other personal matters. 'With Carla, the whole Powell package deeply impressed the Thatchers', observed another insider. 'Mrs Wicks was never remotely in on the same net. They were just very different kinds of people.'[21]

The Foreign Secretary felt slighted, particularly on Anglo-American relations, when Mrs Thatcher often preferred to have Powell close at hand. The ultra-secure 'hotline' to the White House was situated on Powell's desk and key communications effectively went through him and not the FCO. Brent Scowcroft, National Security Adviser to the President, developed a particularly close bond with Powell, and treated him as his opposite number.[22] The egalitarianism and collegiality, so often found among Number Ten officials in the Private Office, waned. By 1985/6, Powell's experience and closeness to Mrs Thatcher had made him the dominant figure in the Private Office. Powell began to rival the influence on her of one other key Number Ten figure, Bernard Ingham. The fact that Powell and Ingham remained well beyond their expected terms of duty also put both on a different footing to other officials. Indeed, articles in the press sometimes mistakenly referred to Powell as the Principal Private Secretary, rather than Nigel Wicks (1985–88) and then Andrew Turnbull (1988–92), or as her adviser on foreign policy, rather than Percy Cradock.

Wicks was a respected and hard-working Principal Private Secretary. Mrs Thatcher, however, blamed Wicks (most unfairly) for, arranging what she regarded as the infamous meeting in November 1985 to discuss Britain's joining the ERM. She thought she had been embroiled in a Treasury plot to convert her to the ERM when she found herself in a small minority facing Howe, Lawson and Tebbit, the last at this time a pro-European. Wicks, like David Pitblado before him (1951–55) had the uncomfortable experience of playing second fiddle, as humiliating for him as it was confusing for others. Media reports appeared of growing divisions between the two 'top dogs' Bernard Ingham and Powell, as the former resented Powell's habit of briefing the media on foreign affairs.[23] In fact the two worked well enough together, despite occasional spats. What concerned Whitehall and party figures was that both officials were more high profile than many Cabinet ministers.

It is too easy, however, to blame Charles Powell entirely for the bad blood between Mrs Thatcher and her Foreign Secretary. Mrs Thatcher was suspicious even before 1983 of the Foreign Office line on the Middle East, the European Community and South Africa, and the differences on Europe and the US Strategic Defence Initiative widened over time.[24] There was also a personal element to the deteriorating relationship; she became increasingly irritated by what she perceived as Howe's hesitancy and indecisiveness, and often showed him little respect in front of others. Many civil servants and ministers speak glowingly of Powell's ability to negotiate with other Whitehall departments, draft papers to Mrs Thatcher's satisfaction and advise her on policy. But his high profile and Mrs Thatcher's all too obvious dependence upon him aroused suspicion and concern, not least in the highest echelons of the Civil Service. By 1987, he had served the customary three years and Armstrong and the Foreign Office pressed for him to leave Number Ten; he was offered a posting as Ambassador to Berne. His departure was planned to coincide with Armstrong's on 31 December. Mrs Thatcher, however, rejected the appointment as too junior. Butler then negotiated a grander posting, as Ambassador to Madrid, but there was a whole series of delays before the scheme fell through. In the summer of 1989, Mrs Thatcher declared he would not be moving.[25]

Attempts by senior FCO officials to 'remind' Powell of his duties to his department of origin were not well received. He saw his loyalty as being to the Prime Minister; he was adamant: he was not the FCO's man in Number Ten.[26] The more she was pressed to let him go, the more essential to her work she claimed to find him. He began to accept that he would never be offered a suitable FCO posting, and by 1990 he became reconciled to a non-Whitehall career after Mrs Thatcher stepped down. He had become too close to power ever to be happy again with an appointment away from the front line: he may also have felt too many relationships had been soured. The same path had been followed by Churchill's and Macmillan's Private Secretaries on Foreign Affairs, Jock Colville and Philip de Zulueta. After Mrs Thatcher's bloody departure, Powell stayed on for four months to work for John Major, above all to see through the Gulf War, before heading, as expected, for the private sector.

Many senior civil servants indeed still speak critically of Powell. They felt that the experience reinforces strongly the case for a turnover after three years of officials seconded to the Number Ten Private Office. It showed that too strong an identification with the Prime Minister undermines good relations between the Prime Minister and departments, and that the collegiality in the Private Office inevitably suffers if any one official becomes over dominant.

On intelligence matters, Mrs Thatcher received each Friday a weekly five- or six-page summary from her foreign policy adviser, Percy Cradock, who also chaired the Joint Intelligence Committee, known as JIC. Cradock had earlier been Ambassador to Peking between 1978 and 1984, when he helped negotiate the Hong Kong Joint Declaration. Cradock reports that Mrs Thatcher had 'a keen appetite' for intelligence.[27] Following the Falklands campaign in 1982, the Franks report into the hostilities recommended that the chairman of the JIC be made more independent of the departments and moved from the Cabinet Office to the Foreign Office. The chairman would now be appointed by the Prime Minister and have direct access to her, and would also report directly to the Prime Minister and not to the Chiefs of Staff. The JIC normally met each Thursday morning, at the same time as the Cabinet. It consisted of the heads of the three intelligence branches (MI5, MI6 and GCHQ) and senior officials from the Foreign Office, Ministry of Defence and Treasury. Cradock's weekly summary for the Prime Minister (Digest of Intelligence) was prepared after this meeting. Every six months or so she would meet the heads of MI6, MI5 and GCHQ. Charles Powell and Cradock attended these meetings and the former would take minutes if he judged it necessary. Although Geoffrey Howe was not privy to the written and oral advice which Cradock gave to the Prime Minister, the two largely agreed on the key issues and had regular one-to-one meetings.[28]

The Private Office position stabilised somewhat when Turnbull succeeded Wicks as Principal Private Secretary in 1988 (following the course of the earlier appointments to the top job of Butler and Wicks, both of whom had had earlier stints in the Private Office). Turnbull talked with Wicks about how to handle the 'Powell factor', but realised that Mrs Thatcher was determined to retain him. Turnbull found a dual-track system operating from 1988 to 1990: the Number Ten Private Office, which was loyal but not always centre stage, and a French-style *cabinet* alongside it, with two members only, Powell and Ingham. Was there anything more that could have been done to rectify the position? 'Given Mrs Thatcher was utterly determined to hang on to both, there was nothing short of a quiet nuclear revolution that could have got rid of them,' said one senior official.[29]

Mrs Thatcher appointed thirty-seven-year-old Stephen Sherbourne as her Political Secretary on the Monday after polling day in 1983. Sherbourne had spent the 1970–75 period in the Conservative Research Department. After some time with Gallaher Tobacco he returned to politics in 1982 to work as a special adviser to Patrick Jenkin at the Department of Industry. Sherbourne had impressed Mrs Thatcher with his pre-press conference briefings for her during the 1983 election campaign; he had earlier come to her attention as a researcher in Heath's office as opposition leader from 1974 to 1975. An admirer of Mrs Thatcher, he did not, however, form a close bond with her.

Under Sherbourne the Political Office regained some of the influence it had enjoyed under Tom McNally (1976–79). The departure of David Wolfson also left a gap, albeit a small one, for Sherbourne to fill. He ran his job in much the same way as had Mrs Thatcher's first Political Secretary, Richard Ryder, a Conservative MP since 1983. At an early stage he formed a clear view of matters with which he did not want to be involved: 'You can be sucked into so many areas that you do not get anything done.'[30] He steered clear of long-term policy and left media relations wholly to Bernard Ingham. His focus was the House of Commons, Prime Minister's Questions, links with the party machine and Central Office, speechwriting, political management and 'fixing'. He did not have regular meetings with the Policy Unit but would talk over issues with the party-political members, including David Willetts, John Redwood or Oliver Letwin. He also developed the growing practice of convening regular meetings of 'special advisers' to

Cabinet ministers. Like his successor from 1988, John Whittingdale, he attended her meetings with the Party Chairman and Parliamentary Private Secretary to discuss party matters and political honours.[31]

The Prime Minister's PPS also changed at the 1983 general election, the new incumbent, Michael Alison, taking a more limited view of his role as the Prime Minister's PPS than Ian Gow, although he started the trend for the PPS to attend Cabinet meetings.

For government reshuffles Mrs Thatcher continued to consult the Deputy Prime Minister, Whitelaw, the Cabinet Secretary, Butler, the Chief Whip and her PPS; during some of the deliberations, the Political Secretary would also be present. While considering them, like other Prime Ministers, she would also muse aloud in front of confidants – Ingham, Powell, Sherbourne and perhaps a Diary Secretary. Sherbourne's interventions on these occasions were designed more to stop sackings than to suggest new appointments. He successfully advised against the dropping of the Leader of the House of Commons, John Biffen, in 1986. 'Prime Ministers occasionally need to be told about avoiding trouble. I did not want to complicate her life. I was a candid friend,' he said.[32]

On 1 November 1990 John Whittingdale, Sherbourne's successor, and Robin Harris, a member of the Policy Unit, reacted to the news of Geoffrey Howe's resignation from the government by presenting Mrs Thatcher with a reshuffle plan which was designed to strengthen her support in the Cabinet. Norman Tebbit would be invited to return as Education Secretary; if he refused, then Michael Portillo would be appointed. Mrs Thatcher agreed and, crucially, the Chief Whip, Tim Renton, was kept in the dark. The next morning Tebbit was contacted and declined, feeling obliged to spend more time with his wife, who had been partly paralysed since the 1984 Brighton bomb. Before Portillo could be contacted, however, Renton arrived on the scene, and persuaded Mrs Thatcher to promote William Waldegrave to the Cabinet.[33]

On speechwriting, Mrs Thatcher was as involved as ever and the sessions remained time-consuming and stressful for the helpers. Sherbourne found that he had to earmark many hours of the diary for preparations. Mrs Thatcher had the disconcerting habit of dictating passages to him because she would not allow a secretary to be present when she was thinking out loud. Although speech suggestions came from various quarters, there was a recognisable core speechwriting team in these mid and later years. It consisted of the Political Secretary of the day, Ronnie Millar, the journalist John O'Sullivan, until his departure for the US in 1988, and Robin Harris, from 1988. O'Sullivan and Harris were soul-mates politically. The two men rapidly developed a contempt for Major as Prime Minister, while Millar went on to become one of his core speechwriters. This group worked on the political speeches, but also provided an input into official speeches. For a party conference speech Mrs Thatcher liked to lay out different sections on the table and then move them around until she felt that it flowed in the right order.

Her political correspondence was written by a recruit from the Conservative Research Department, at first Chris Butler (who went on to become an MP) and then Nigel Hawkins. The flow of correspondence was particularly heavy at times of crisis such as Westland or following an election victory. The Political Office was also involved in manifesto drafting for 1987, along with Brian Griffiths, who had succeeded Redwood as head of the Policy Unit, and Robin Harris of the Research Department. Griffiths and Harris were prominent amongst those who pressed Mrs Thatcher to appoint a senior Cabinet minister in early 1987 to inject urgency into manifesto preparations. She, however, was reluctant to award the prize to any ministers. ('She was always jealous of having a rival,' said one of them.) Late in the day she appointed John MacGregor.

The Number Ten–Central Office link became more intense in the twelve months or so before the likely general election date. Mrs Thatcher regularly met the Party Chairman and parliamentary business managers on Monday morning to review the events for the week ahead. On Mrs Thatcher's behalf, the Political Secretary also attended a Wednesday meeting at Central Office, the party Westminster headquarters, with the Chairman, the Central Office director and the Chief Whips from the House of Commons and the House of Lords. He was also the progress-chaser for the Strategy Group, or 'A Team', of senior Cabinet ministers, established in June 1986. A good example of Sherbourne's 'fixing' occurred in late summer 1986. Relations between Mrs Thatcher and the Party Chairman, Norman Tebbit, had deteriorated sharply. Tebbit had objected to the decision by a small group of ministers (excluding himself) to allow American planes to set off on bombing raids on Libya from British bases. He was also angry at press stories reporting Mrs Thatcher's lack of confidence in his administration of Central Office. Sherbourne established a regular meeting between the two which may have contained the tensions somewhat – until the final days of the election campaign.

In January 1988 Sherbourne was succeeded as Political Secretary by John Whittingdale, aged 29. Whittingdale had served short spells in the Research Department and as a special adviser to Conservative Cabinet ministers, and accompanied Mrs Thatcher on the battle bus during the 1983 election campaign. He was approached about the post by Sherbourne in September 1987; this led to a chat ('not an interview') with Mrs Thatcher in which she typically sounded off about what was on her mind. Whittingdale had been recruited in a very similar way to be Norman Tebbit's special adviser in 1985, when Michael Dobbs, Tebbit's adviser, offered him the chance to succeed him.

Whittingdale largely followed Sherbourne's routine. However, he was more willing to talk to the press about political matters, and Bernard Ingham would hand over to him when he felt that questions from the Lobby journalists were moving from government to party matters. He also attended the weekly meeting of the Policy Unit on Thursday morning to hear brief reports of their work from each member and to inform them of the Prime Minister's future engagements. He also attended Cabinet committees with Mrs Thatcher on the poll tax, and the working party to review the National Health Service. Before taking over he had begun to attend the periodic lunches held for ministerial special advisers; as Political Secretary he continued the practice but left the organisation and chairmanship to Douglas Hurd's special adviser, David Lidington, and later Andrew Lansley, director of the party's Research Department.

Mrs Thatcher also chaired monthly lunches in Downing Street for major figures in the world of industry and commerce, organised by Alistair McAlpine, the Party Treasurer, and a close friend. Mrs Thatcher would ask her guests to talk about developments in their company or sector and she would explain what action the government was taking. Although money was never mentioned as a topic, the guests knew that raising funds for the party was the point of the occasion.

Bernard Ingham's effectiveness in presenting Mrs Thatcher's views was helped by his ready access to her, her total confidence in his ability and loyalty, and the willingness of sections of the press to retail his accounts faithfully. These presented her as the source of decisive action and popular measures, and the scourge of erring or unpopular ministers, and gave rise to such tabloid front page headlines as 'MAGGIE ACTS' and 'THATCHER STEPS IN'.[34] The result was that Mrs Thatcher was often presented as a figure apart from the Cabinet or as a leader imposing herself on it. At times this was of course true, for example in her delaying entry into the ERM from 1985 until she was beaten into submission in October 1990, or in negating the Treasury's wish to abolish mortgage tax relief. Ingham accompanied Mrs Thatcher on many of her overseas tours and this gave him the opportunity to talk to her on a one-to-one basis.

In 1988 Ingham was made acting head of the Government Information Service and co-ordinated the press and information service provided for the departments. So commanding a figure was he, and so long had he been in post as Press Secretary, that he had influenced the appointment of information officers in many government departments. Each Monday evening he chaired meetings of the officers to co-ordinate government communications. He attended the Tuesday and Thursday morning briefing sessions for Question Time. He also liaised on Thursdays with the senior minister responsible for the co-ordination of government presentation, who would brief him about the morning's Cabinet. At first this was the Lord President, Lord Whitelaw (1983–88), and then Secretary of State for Energy John Wakeham.

Ingham was so assertive and influential on the Prime Minister's behalf that it was almost inevitable that he provoked resentment among some Cabinet ministers. Howe in particular, first as Foreign Secretary and then from July 1989 as Deputy Prime Minister, felt ill-used by what he described as 'a Number Ten publicity machine'. Nigel Lawson complained of Mrs Thatcher's 'excessive and increasing reliance on Bernard Ingham'[35] and accused Ingham of promoting a caricature of Mrs Thatcher which she tried to live up to. The core problem between Howe and Mrs Thatcher was that they increasingly disagreed on the future direction of British policy towards Europe; she attached priority to the relationship with the US, while Howe emphasised that with the European Community. Lawson, like Howe, favoured a more positive stance on the ERM, and deliberately defied her wishes on exchange rate policy. Crucially, Ingham worked for the Prime Minister. Although he spent less time with her than Gus O'Donnell later did with Major or Alastair Campbell did with Blair, he knew her mind. A fair assessment would be that if Ingham undermined the sense of collegiality among the Cabinet, he was only reflecting Mrs Thatcher in doing so.

Several incidents involving Ingham were controversial. His briefing for Mrs Thatcher's Bruges speech was much more anti-EC than the main speechwriter (Charles Powell) had intended or the contents justified.[36] His briefings about some less favoured colleagues, for example the Leader of the House of Commons, John Biffen ('semi-detached') in 1986, and his dismissal of the significance of the appointment as Deputy Prime Minister of Geoffrey Howe in 1989 produced collective resentment. In his memoirs he reveals that he knew of the intention to leak the letter from the Attorney General, Patrick Mayhew, over Westland, but did not inform Mrs Thatcher and claims therefore that he did not authorise the leak by a DTI press officer. The Westland episode, including the leak, caused great political damage to Mrs Thatcher and to his own standing as an impartial civil servant. Both Cabinet Secretaries, Armstrong and Butler, tried and failed to move Ingham from Number Ten.

Ingham had close relations with some newspaper editors and political editors, but *The Scotsman*, *The Independent* and *The Guardian* for a time broke ranks with the Lobby system. They cited 'Downing Street sources' as Ingham speaking and were not prepared to regard Lobby briefings as off the record. After an uneasy period they later rejoined the Lobby. Mrs Thatcher could rely on her Press Secretary or Tim Bell and Gordon Reece, friends in the PR world, to cultivate a sympathetic press. Nicholas Lloyd (*Daily Express*), John Junor (*Sunday Express*), Bill Deedes (*Daily Telegraph*), Kelvin MacKenzie (*Sun*) and David English (*Daily Mail*) were among her favourites. Most received peerages or knighthoods. But it was Ingham who was Mrs Thatcher's true press hero. He doggedly fought for her interest in and outside Number Ten, saved her from overreacting and was an indomitable force when she was down. He was conspicuously more successful in promoting his boss's interest than Major's press secretaries were to prove. Probably no other single figure was so important to her during her premiership.

The Policy Unit under Ferdinand Mount gained some Civil Service staff from the disbanded CPRS in June 1983. Between 1983 and 1990 the Unit usually operated with seven to nine staff and three secretaries. Mount was keen to send one of his staff to each Cabinet committee, to find out what was going on, and regarded eight as the ideal minimum to cover the ministerial waterfront. Some of his team, including David Willetts, John Redwood, Oliver Letwin and Hartley Booth, went on to become Conservative MPs, and Norman Blackwell later returned to Number Ten to become John Major's head of the Policy Unit from 1995 to 1997. When Alan Walters moved from full- to part-time status as an adviser in 1983, the Unit reclaimed some influence over economic advice, via Mount's successor, Redwood, and then Brian Griffiths. However, the Chancellor, Nigel Lawson, was effectively his own man until near the end. Norman Blackwell tried in the later 1980s to include Europe in his remit, on the grounds that it was linked to much domestic and economic policy, but Charles Powell successfully resisted this incursion. Powell also took over agriculture and defence procurement, both of which had strong European Community connections.

Some members thought that Robert Armstrong was unsympathetic to the Policy Unit. 'He took the view that the Civil Service should be the advisers for ministers,' said one member.[37] There was some truth in this view, though Armstrong was happy, anxious indeed, to see civil servants seconded to the Unit, especially after the demise of the CPRS. Robin Butler, both as Private and later Cabinet Secretary, however, was regarded as supportive of the Policy Unit. But by the mid/late 1980s, most senior civil servants came to regard the Unit as an integral part of the Number Ten machine.

After the 1983 general election victory, Mount became increasingly bored with the job. He tried to secure Peter Lilley as his successor, who was unavailable, and then recommended John Redwood, despite doubts from Jock Bruce-Gardyne that he was too abrasive.[38] Redwood, originally from the merchant bank N.M. Rothschild, had joined the Policy Unit in November 1983. He succeeded Mount as head in January 1984, a position he held until September 1985, when he in turn was succeeded by Professor Brian Griffiths, an academic economist of monetarist persuasion at London's City University. Redwood also tried to keep membership balanced between seconded outsiders and civil servants. It was in this period that the Policy Unit evolved into the pattern of work which it has largely retained since. It met collectively twice a week, on Mondays and Thursdays, to discuss the immediate programme of work facing the Prime Minister. Members were encouraged to spend a day a week outside Whitehall, testing the reality of the policies on the ground.[39] Under Hoskyns the staff had been too small to look at much of the paperwork going to the Prime Minister, and was effectively out of the policy loop in any case. Now most of the papers, except for those dealing with defence and security, came to the Policy Unit as a matter of course. At Redwood's request, Mrs Thatcher intervened with the Treasury to give him access to Budget papers. He was allowed to study them, but only in Robin Butler's private office. A hard-pressed Private Office was glad to off-load some of the paperwork. The head also held a regular Friday morning meeting with the Prime Minister to review progress.

Where Mount's main interest had been in social policy, Redwood was a pace-setter on privatisation and was instrumental in persuading Mrs Thatcher of the case for further initiatives. This thinking led to the appointment of John Moore as Minister for Privatisation, based in the Treasury. As well as privatisation, Redwood's interests were in welfare reform and he developed ideas on pensions which paved the way for the expansion of personal pensions. Though the Private Office, and others in Whitehall, found Redwood's style abrasive, the Unit was never more effective under Mrs Thatcher than it was under him. Had she not been so close to Lawson throughout Redwood's spell as head, she would have depended upon him all the more.[40]

Under Griffiths' leadership from 1985, staff were closely involved in health and education reforms. Individual members maintained links with outside groups and with such free-market think tanks as the Adam

Smith Institute, the Institute of Economic Affairs and the Centre for Policy Studies. But Griffiths' tenure also saw the Unit decline significantly in influence; it was progressively sidelined as Mrs Thatcher relied more on her Private Office, while for the crucial areas of economic policy and foreign policy she turned to Walters and Powell respectively. As the political pressures on her increased, Mrs Thatcher had need of different kinds of advice. At least one party-political member of the Unit thought that the group was too bureaucratic and lacked political drive. Robin Harris had resigned as Director of the Conservative Research Department in 1988 to join the Policy Unit and was involved in speechwriting for Mrs Thatcher as well as working on home affairs. He said, 'She was my life. If she failed I was out of a job. I could see the looming problems over inflation and the community charge and how the politics were weakening her. Others in Number Ten were too complacent, the place was too bureaucratic.'[41] Griffiths himself became an increasingly marginal figure in her life, not least because the agenda had moved on to other matters like Europe and the poll tax, on which he made little or no input. On economics, as long as Walters was in the wings, she preferred to listen to him rather than to Griffiths.[42]

The importance of Mrs Thatcher's Policy Unit depended on its ability to provide useful information and perspectives on what bothered her at any particular time. It could never rival her Private Office and, inevitably perhaps, its membership was regarded by civil servants as of very mixed competence. Hoskyns left in some frustration, Mount because he was getting bored and Redwood to pursue a political career.

Alan Walters returned from the United States to be a half-time adviser in May 1989 and quickly had an explosive impact on life in Number Ten and on national politics. He had continued to tender unofficial advice, by letter or phone, and on occasional visits. It was clear that he talked too freely at City lunches, and that his words were then carried in the media, not least about his influence on Mrs Thatcher and about how she attended to him more than to her Chancellor Nigel Lawson. The effect of his influence was to reinforce Mrs Thatcher's doubts about her Chancellor. Both opposed Lawson's proposal to create an independent Bank of England, his support for

British entry to the ERM, his policy of shadowing the D-mark by adjusting interest rates, and his regime of high interest rates to squeeze inflation out of the economy – although she acquiesced in a rise to 15 per cent in October 1989. Walters could not help the fact that his sceptical views concerning the ERM, which he described as 'half-baked', had been stated in an academic journal, the *American Economist*, some months before his return to Downing Street and not yet published. The trouble was that he persisted in rubbishing the scheme, even though it was the declared objective of the government to join when the conditions were right.

With growing disappointment in ministers and her advisers, Mrs Thatcher found herself trusting Walters' advice and enjoying his company all the more. In her memoirs she instances his wisdom about the need to keep the nuclear power stations out of the electricity privatisation in 1989, his warnings against joining the ERM, his resistance to interest rate rises in 1989 and his fears about the Hong Kong currency in 1983.[43] Mrs Thatcher's view is that he 'was, in short, doing precisely what a Prime Minister's adviser should. He also had the merit of being right.'[44]

However, his role was advertising divisions at the heart of government. Eventually Lawson's patience snapped, and when in October 1989 he demanded that Mrs Thatcher set a date for the withdrawal of Walters as her adviser and she refused, he resigned. Within hours Walters had also resigned. In her account of this episode Mrs Thatcher voices a suspicion that Nigel Lawson might have been seeking a pretext to escape from an increasingly difficult position.[45] Twelve months later she acquiesced in the recommendation of her new Chancellor, John Major, and Britain entered the ERM in October 1990. Walters was no longer regularly available to stiffen her resolve in the face of political pressure in Cabinet and from much of the economic establishment. Brian Griffiths also favoured entry; even Charles Powell recognised that she had been outmanoeuvred and helped her to accept the status quo.[46]

It is to Mrs Thatcher's credit that she was always willing to step outside the formal network of advisers and seek advice from academics and experts, both to inform herself and to arm herself with alternative views to those coming from the departments. She convened seminars in Downing Street or at Chequers on a variety of subjects, including science, the economy, schools, the film industry, health, training, church and state relations and broadcasting, as well as the famous, or infamous, one on the German national character.

This last group met at Chequers in March 1990 and was convened to discuss the context of German reunification. Charles Powell and Percy Cradock invited a number of distinguished historians, including Norman Stone, George Urban, Gordon Craig, Hugh Trevor-Roper and Fritz Stern. The encounter backfired badly when the contents of one of the discussions were leaked, leading to a worsening of her already uneasy relationship with Chancellor Kohl of Germany and to complaints by some of the participants that Powell's summary of the discussion misrepresented their position. They said that the thrust of the discussion was not to her or Powell's liking, because it did not oppose German reunification.[47] She rejected advice from the Foreign Office and from Cradock, who described her opposition to reunification as '. . . the single most spectacular misjudgment' in foreign affairs during her premiership.[48]

The Parliamentary Private Secretary post (PPS) is unpaid and under Mrs Thatcher it was confined to affluent MPs. It has rarely been a springboard to higher political office, though all her PPSs served as Ministers of State, before or after their Number Ten post. Ian Gow's four successors after his departure were all wealthy old Etonians – Michael Alison, Archie Hamilton, Mark Lennox-Boyd and Peter Morrison. It is often alleged that Mrs Thatcher lost touch with her MPs in the later 1980s and that this was reflected in the poor leadership campaign she waged in 1990. Peter Morrison, her final PPS, conducted a half-hearted canvass of MPs and overestimated the strength of her support.[49] It was somehow appropriate that she was in Paris at the Conference on Security and Cooperation on the day the result of the first ballot of the leadership contest was announced. She dismissed Morrison from the job of running her campaign for the second ballot, but by then it was too late to rally support.

Some of her staff did their best to ensure that Tory MPs had access to the Prime Minister. She met MPs for a drink if she was in the House for a late-night vote. But she had never been a regular habituée of the House of Commons Tea Room or bars, and more pressing calls inevitably commanded her attention. She also had little aptitude for small talk – one trait she shared with Heath. Attempts by her PPS to counter this trend by guided tours of the tables in the Tea Room were often strained and embarrassing for all concerned. There were other causes of dissatisfaction among Tory backbenchers, which culminated in her failure to gain outright victory in the leadership election in 1990. They included the high inflation, the unpopular poll tax, disagreements over Europe and, above all, backbenchers' fear for their seats, prompted by the above in a fast-approaching general election. No massaging of egos could counter the perception among many MPs that she was an electoral liability.

There was growing resentment among the many MPs sacked from office or not promoted. More than once Mrs Thatcher was told by her supporters in the '92 Group, and by No Turning Back MPs that they were not receiving their fair share of government posts. The critics targeted the whips, particularly Tristan Garel-Jones, her Chief Whip John Wakeham (1983–87) and her last Chief Whip, Tim Renton, to whom she left the main decisions on junior posts. Her indifference to or innocence about the political leanings of many of her junior appointments is confirmed by a Chief Whip and a Political Secretary.[50] Mrs Thatcher in her memoirs notes that she often gave Cabinet posts to Conservatives 'who did not share my philosophy'. To the extent that she did this, it was a reflection of the pool of talent at her disposal. 'Competence is what mattered to her and to me,' said John Wakeham.[51]

Mrs Thatcher began the 1983 Parliament with a Cabinet much more to her liking than her post-1979 election Cabinet. It included Lord Young, Nigel Lawson, Cecil Parkinson (until October 1983), Norman Tebbit, Nick Ridley and Leon Brittan, all of whom owed their promotions to her. Jim Prior had been marginalised from the centre of political debate by being given the Northern Ireland post in September 1981.

By 1990 the Cabinet membership had undergone several changes. Interestingly, most ministers still did not share her clearcut views on Europe or her opposition to joining the ERM. Her final Cabinet included Christopher Patten, Ken Clarke, Douglas Hurd, Malcolm Rifkind and William Waldegrave, all clearly non-Thatcherites. Most of her supporters had left: Lord Whitelaw withdrew after a stroke in December 1987, to her lasting loss; Keith Joseph left in May 1986, while Nicholas Ridley felt he had to resign after his hostile comments about Germans in an interview in the *Spectator* in the summer of 1990. Mrs Thatcher was all too conscious of the diminishing number of Cabinet ministers who were of her persuasion.

As a non-departmental minister, Lord Whitelaw had chaired many Cabinet committees, he had ready access to Mrs Thatcher and ministers regularly tested the water with him. After 1983 divisions between 'wet' and 'dry' factions in the Cabinet were muted, partly because of the removal of many dissenting ministers and partly because of lower inflation, falling unemployment and economic recovery. Over time Mrs Thatcher herself became more dominant. Whitelaw was careful not to disagree with her in Cabinet or indeed in any other public forum. When he retired, nobody replaced him in his role as troubleshooter.

In the wake of the Westland affair, John Wakeham, Chief Whip (1983–87) with the support of Whitelaw, persuaded Mrs Thatcher to set up a Strategy Group, soon dubbed the 'A Team'. Wakeham felt that there was a need to demonstrate to backbenchers that the government had a grip and that senior ministers were at one with the Prime Minister. Number Ten insiders generally welcomed the initiative: 'Cabinet meets only weekly, rarely discusses politics and it is too large.'[52] But who would be a member? Mrs Thatcher appointed the holders of the three great offices of state – Foreign Secretary, Home Secretary and Chancellor of the Exchequer – as well as the Party Chairman, the Chief Whip and the Deputy Prime Minister. Selecting people by office enabled her to exclude some ministers who were not on her wavelength (for example Peter Walker).[53] The group met on Monday mornings with Mrs Thatcher in the chair. Sherbourne was progress-chaser and the Research Department director, Robin Harris, acted as secretary. Its broad remit was to prepare for the next general election and to look at forthcoming events with a view to co-ordinating responses and effective presentation in the media. The group also commissioned policy papers from Cabinet ministers. Few members think that it was more than a symbolic success: 'Too often ministers raised whatever was on their mind that day,' said Sherbourne.[54] Another said it was 'useless, ministers are hopeless on strategy'.[55] Mrs Thatcher was not a good chairman, often sounding off with her own views. The plan to meet weekly slipped to fortnightly, then monthly, and then the Strategy Group expired. The record of the 'A Team' is surely a comment on the difficulty of obtaining political cohesion and a sense of direction at the heart of British government, as Major was later to find.

Relationships with key ministers remained a continuing source of tension for Mrs Thatcher after 1983. Conflicts with Michael Heseltine over Westland and with Nigel Lawson over exchange rate policy were two of the worst cases. At meetings of senior ministers and officials in September and November 1985, the Chancellor and Foreign Secretary spoke for the majority in favouring sterling's early entry into the European exchange rate mechanism (ERM).[56] Mrs Thatcher was almost alone in opposing this course of action and warned that entry would be accomplished 'without me'.[57] Her relations with Lawson and Howe were never the same after their 1985 disagreement. Lawson, frustrated in his ERM wish, unilaterally decided to shadow the German mark during 1987–88. She was furious when she found what Lawson had been doing, which she regarded as unconstitutional and politically improper. She later had regrets about not sacking him at that point: her authority was gravely damaged and her trust in Lawson, and other Cabinet colleagues, fatally weakened. It was a major turning point in her premiership.[58] She also resisted the attempts of Howe and Lawson to strike a more positive stance about the ERM beyond the line of 'when the time is right'. Tensions rose during 1988–89: staff tried and usually failed to get her to make conciliatory remarks about him, while Labour had a field day exploiting the obvious differences between them. Mrs Thatcher was not prepared to surrender control over the country's monetary policy and interest rates and blamed Lawson's exchange rate policy for the rise in inflation in 1989.

Relations continued to plummet. When Howe and Lawson sought a meeting in June 1989 with Mrs Thatcher, before the Madrid European Council summit, her reaction was negative. According to Lawson: 'Margaret's reaction was extraordinary. I could not imagine any other Prime Minister considering it in any way objectionable to have a meeting with her Foreign Secretary and Chancellor before embarking on international politico-economic negotiations of the first importance.'[59] She grudgingly agreed to hold a meeting on 20 June and received a minute from the two ministers. This urged that the government set a date for entry provided that certain conditions were met and made a joint threat of resignation unless she agreed to a timetable for entry. On the night before the meeting, Mrs Thatcher asked Charles Powell to draft a set of new conditions (including convergence of inflation rates and completion of the single market) and pointedly refused to set a date.[60] On the flight to Madrid she sat apart from Howe and did not speak to him.

Howe had not been her first choice as Foreign Secretary for the 1983 Parliament – that had been Cecil Parkinson, until the latter informed her on polling day of his affair with Sarah Keays. Howe's differences with her extended far beyond Europe, and grew as Mrs Thatcher became more involved in international diplomacy. Howe's frequent absences abroad meant that weekly bilaterals between the Prime Minister and Foreign Secretary often did not take place. At international summits Mrs Thatcher often dealt personally with leaders of other states. Howe was irritated by the way in which she invoked the wisdom of 'my people' in Number Ten (often shorthand for Powell) to challenge Foreign Office advice, without allowing the Foreign Office to test the claims of her own sources.[61] In a reshuffle in July 1989 she moved a disenchanted Howe from the Foreign Office.

Relations with Norman Tebbit, Party Chairman between 1986 and 1987, were far from comfortable. Mrs Thatcher felt that Tebbit, an ambitious man, had positioned himself for the succession during the tense Westland affair in 1986. They had earlier fallen out over Tebbit's (all too easily overlooked) support for ERM entry at the November 1985 meeting, and also disagreed over her support for the USA's bombing of Libya.[62] On his side, he felt undermined by press reports of Mrs Thatcher's lack of confidence in his administration at Smith Square. On the eve of the election campaign she and her advisers felt that he was not giving her a sufficiently high profile or an appropriate role. She also complained about his exclusion of Tim Bell, her trusted media adviser, from the campaign. She therefore appointed Lord Young to join Central Office to act on her behalf. Near the end of the campaign there was a notorious clash between Young and Tebbit over the selection of election posters, when Young, acting on her behalf, instructed Tebbit to make changes.

The Chief Whip John Wakeham made a point of popping into the Number Ten Private Office early in the day to sense the atmosphere, gossip with Bernard Ingham and share political intelligence gained from his fellow whips. As Chief Whip he had regular Monday lunches with Mrs Thatcher and the parliamentary business managers. His reservations about her tactics were always expressed in private and prefaced by an assurance that he would support her, whatever she decided.[63] He warned Mrs Thatcher of the strong backbench opposition to proposals for imposing tuition charges on students in higher education in 1985 and that she would lose the Shops Bill in 1986; the bill was duly defeated on second reading. He also convinced Cabinet that the party would not support the sale of Austin Rover to General Motors in 1986. He (and his deputy, Tristan Garel-Jones) were frequently criticised by right-wingers who had been passed over for Cabinet promotions. Wakeham was succeeded as Chief Whip in the 1987 Parliament by David Waddington and then by Tim Renton. Renton and Mrs Thatcher were never comfortable. He kept the Whips' Office studiously neutral in the 1990 leadership contest. He also had the daunting task of informing her that her support was eroding fast after she had failed to win outright on the first ballot against Michael Heseltine.

Like most strong Prime Ministers, Mrs Thatcher is often portrayed as a destroyer of Cabinet government. The critics point to the declining number of Cabinet meetings and papers distributed to it; her dismissal of so many ministers; her preference for working through small groups of hand-picked ministers, bilateral meetings with ministers, ad hoc groups and the Cabinet committees EA and ODC, which she chaired, her interventions in departments and her interest in convening ad hoc seminars and discussion groups on issues, and her practice of recruiting her own advisers. When faced with a problem Mrs Thatcher was more likely to call people in than to set up a Cabinet Committee. A civil servant recalled: 'Politicians are not machine people. They are concerned with tackling problems by talking to all the main players and then the machine comes along and sets up a structure to deal with it'. In this respect Mrs Thatcher was a precursor of Tony Blair.

The picture can be exaggerated. Much of the above well describes Tony Blair's use of Cabinet committees and bilaterals and there is nothing new in a Prime Minister doing any of this. Indeed, every strong Prime Minister from Gladstone onwards has been accused of being 'dictatorial' or 'presidential'. The idea of the modern Cabinet as a seminar of dispassionate and well-informed decision-makers is a nonsense, as a reading of the published diaries of many former ministers shows. Most Cabinet ministers are overburdened and barely have time to read their papers. A sense of overall direction has to come from the Prime Minister and their most senior colleagues. It is now widely accepted that a decision of a Cabinet committee has the same authority as one of the full Cabinet. Harold Wilson during 1964–67 kept discussion of devaluation from the Cabinet, Ted Heath changed industrial policy in 1972 without informing many of his colleagues, and James Callaghan's 'economic seminar' bypassed Cabinet. Sheer pressure of work means that Cabinet is increasingly registering decisions which have been made elsewhere, although ministers can still raise points under broad agenda headings. Most Prime Ministers are careful to conciliate (or 'square') a key minister before a Cabinet meeting and to keep contentious issues from Cabinet until they have support for their preferred solutions. This applied to Mrs Thatcher as much as to John Major. One much quoted example of a Number Ten decision, the poll tax, was in fact fully discussed by the Cabinet ministers. More than most, it was a Cabinet policy.[64]

These qualifications are not to deny that Mrs Thatcher was interventionist – that she used all the above tactics to try to achieve her goals, and that she used them more systematically over the years. She was certainly forceful, often expressing her views at the outset of a discussion, putting pressure on a responsible minister who was about to argue a contrary case. She was also relentless in chasing a department about an initiative, 'like a dog after a bone', said Ferdinand Mount.[65]

Mrs Thatcher's working methods did not change much. She sought alternative sources of advice, she thrived on exhaustive briefing meetings, and welcomed paperwork. According to David Willetts in the Policy Unit: 'The way to get through to her was to write papers. At 2 am in the morning over a whisky and soda she would come across your paper in the box. The Principal Private Secretary was less of a gatekeeper to information because she read so much paper.'[66] Private Office staff detected little slackening of her energy even at the end. 'You could put something in the box at 10 pm and it would come back with comments at 9 am the next day.'[67]

From 1983 on Cabinet was never as argumentative as it had been in the first two years of Mrs Thatcher's premiership. But this does not mean that she always got her own way. Her position was weakened for a time after the Westland resignations of Heseltine and Brittan and she failed to persuade Cabinet to allow Ford and General Motors to purchase parts of British Leyland in 1986. Robert Armstrong has recalled that after Westland there was a reaction among colleagues against her ad hoc groups. Those who had been excluded were resentful or suspected that they might be bounced.[68] Conscious that she was in a small minority in opposing Britain's membership of the ERM, she kept the issue from the Cabinet. She knew that she could not afford a joint resignation of her Chancellor and Foreign Secretary in June 1989; far better to pick off Howe in a reshuffle soon after. Her position was weak again following the resignation of Nigel Lawson in October, and in October 1990 she felt that she had no choice but to agree to John Major's proposal that Britain enter the ERM. In the end Mrs Thatcher paid a political price for her brusque treatment of Cabinet colleagues. It was their advice that she would not win the second ballot of the leadership contest that persuaded her to stand down.

Mrs Thatcher's inner circle moved through two stages, 1982–88 and post-1988 (see figs. 7.1 and 7.2). For much of the first period, Keith Joseph, Norman Tebbit and Nigel Lawson were on the inside along with Howe and Whitelaw. She became disillusioned with Lawson (and with Howe) over the ERM issue from late 1985, and to aides described Lawson's decision to shadow the Deutschmark as 'dastardly'. In her final two years, the only minister to join Charles Powell and Bernard Ingham in the inner ring was Nick Ridley, until his resignation. After he departed, not a single politician was in her inner net.[69] Those few she was close to were to be found in the next ring, and included Kenneth Baker, Cecil Parkinson and John Major.

Mrs Thatcher's strong personality and will, backed by large parliamentary majorities and the weakened state of the opposition for much of her premiership, enabled her to dominate the political scene. She was also helped by the length of her tenure and the resulting experience she gained, and by the departure of so many senior colleagues. By October 1990 she had prepared for over 700 Prime Minister's Questions and the elaborate briefings beforehand had given her a great knowledge of the work in departments. Her confidence in her own judgement was probably increased by the adulatory receptions she regularly received in the USA and Japan and her icon-like status in much of Eastern Europe.

By 1982 she had increased the number of advisers and then boosted the size of the Policy Unit, essentially to equip her in her dealings with other departments and to forward her own policies in relation to them. But she did not take this further. Although the Private Office became more powerful in Downing Street in the early/mid 1980s, she made no permanent or influential change to the premiership. There was no Prime Minister's Department. As long as she had what she regarded as the right people in place, she was confident that the machine would respond. She had some impact on the civil service, as a result of the Rayner 'scrutinies', the 'Next Steps' programme, FMI, the abolition of the Civil Service Department, and her appointments of senior officials, but there was no politicisation on the lines advocated by Hoskyns or Sherman.

As her system of advice became an issue, however, it cost her political support. Powell and Ingham, defying the Civil Service norm of serving three-year terms, remained with Mrs Thatcher to the end, serving seven and eleven years respectively. Their continuing presence provoked great resentment as we have seen among Cabinet ministers[70] and her friends from time to time advised her to dispense with the services of one or both.[71] Indeed, when Gordon Reece phoned her to proffer her this confidential advice, both men were listening in on the conversation![72] Their influence and the length of time that they served in Number Ten could only have increased her distance from her Cabinet and some colleagues were quick to see in Westland a symptom of this. Howe admits that the loneliness of leadership makes for a kitchen 'cabinet' but suggests that this 'can all too easily become a reinforcement of mutual error'.[73] A disillusioned Francis Pym accused Mrs Thatcher and her advisers of trying to run 'a government within

a government'.[74] Lawson thought that Number Ten became a 'bunker'
and that Ingham and Powell provided a 'court'.[75] Some top mandarins
even blame Powell for her downfall: 'The over-dependence on Charles
was what eventually brought her down, because it cut her off . . . it
can't be right to have a Prime Minister so isolated as Charles let her
become from her own Foreign Secretary and Chancellor.'[76] On the
other hand, William Waldegrave, not a Thatcherite, sympathised:
'Both Powell and Ingham were outstanding and she was entitled to
have staff of her own choosing.'[77] A Cabinet Secretary spoke of Powell
giving her 'a Rolls-Royce service, exactly what she wanted'.[78] The last
word may remain with a long-serving adviser: 'In the end she went
over the top. There were many reasons – longevity, winning three
elections, being proved right a lot, and lack of senior figures like
Whitelaw who had known her before she became leader.'[79]

Mrs Thatcher's stance on the poll tax and on the ERM can certainly be defended on policy grounds. But politics was important in
undermining her. Many backbenchers became convinced that she was
an electoral liability and that with her as leader they would lose their
seats. Her uncompromising stance on the European Community did
not unify the Cabinet and contributed to an image of a government
that was both arrogant and divided. Her challenger Michael Heseltine
promised that if he won he would restore Cabinet, or more collegial,
government. She had strained the powers of the office to the limit,
and there was a reaction. Her style of premiership had become an
issue and any successor would have had to offer a different approach.

Ultimately, the Thatcher premiership is inconclusive about
Number Ten. It shows that, albeit in an unorthodox manner, it could
support a strong premier. On the other hand, Mrs Thatcher was
battling for the first two and last two years of office, and was not
consistently on top even during her heyday, 1981–88, when her strategic thinking was often lacking. A strengthened Number Ten or
indeed better use of existing apparatus might have helped her to
perform better, made her less reactive and allowed her to have been
a more measured and consistent Prime Minister. Growing disillusionment with the press, not least its fascination with Labour 'spin doctors'
led both Blair and Campbell to co-operate with separate BBC docu-
mentaries about themselves in 2000.

CHAPTER EIGHT

John Major
(1990–97)

FEW COULD HAVE ANTICIPATED John Major's abrupt arrival on the portals of 10 Downing Street on 28 November 1990. Aged only 47, the youngest Prime Minister in the century up to that point, he had been just eleven years in Parliament and three and a half years in Cabinet. Both periods were almost indecently brief as an apprenticeship for the role of Prime Minister. Barely three months in the Foreign Office and twelve months in the Treasury was too short a time for him to make much mark. Both promotions had a whiff of crisis about them, Major first replacing Geoffrey Howe at the Foreign Office in July 1989 and then in October of the same year succeeding Nigel Lawson at the Treasury, on the latter's abrupt resignation. Mrs Thatcher is explicit that she was still grooming her young protégé for high office.[1] In spite of this rushed preparation, Major's continuous tenure of the premiership has been exceeded in the twentieth century only by Asquith, Macmillan and Thatcher.

In contrast with all premiers post-1964, except Callaghan, John Major had no prior experience as leader of his party before becoming Prime Minister. Leading a party in opposition, of course, bears only a passing resemblance to leading a government. But at least it provides the experience of appointing and chairing a Shadow Cabinet, taking part in PMQs, recruiting a team of personal and political aides, running a leader's office, being grilled by the media and operating under the harsh glare of constant attention: in short, acting as a Prime Minister in waiting. Tony Blair was the beneficiary of this background and

John Major came to wish that he too had had such prior experience.

John Major possessed several qualities that recommended him for the party leadership in November 1990. Because he had remained above faction he was a more obvious unifier of a fractured party than any of the other available candidates. He was neither obviously of the left nor of the right, neither Europhile nor Eurosceptic: he may have made Mrs Thatcher believe he was 'one of us', but she rapidly believed she had allowed herself to be taken in by her favourite. He was an excellent negotiator, a good chairman, skilled in teasing out a position acceptable to people of different viewpoints. As Prime Minister he had to cope with acutely difficult circumstances, particularly after 'Black Wednesday' in September 1992, when Britain was forced out of the ERM and the credibility of the government's economic policy was destroyed. There were accomplishments, like replacing Mrs Thatcher's hated 'poll tax' or community charge by the council tax in 1991, introducing the Citizen's Charter the same year, leading the party to victory in the 1992 general election, and accruing a good economic record in the years following Britain's exit from the ERM. But for much of his period in office Major was handicapped by the lack of a parliamentary majority; the consequences of this shaped perceptions of him as a reactive premier.

Major travelled light in terms of political ideology and dogma. He was instead a man of deeply-held value, believing for example in the need to treat people fairly and decently, as reflected in his Citizen's Charter. He was a Prime Minister for harmony, for whom the leadership was an opportunity to find the common ground rather than strike out on a strong line of his own. At one low moment in Downing Street he was heard to express a wish that he could lead a national government rather than a party one.[2] His lack of ideological moorings may have contributed to the perception even among some of his own staff that he was primarily a tactician and lacked a sense of overall strategy. He seemed to thrive on challenges, becoming energised for the general election in 1992 or the leadership contest in 1995, when he faced an uphill struggle. But once he had achieved these victories, some of his staff complained that he lapsed back into what one called 'spectator mode'. The victory was won. But what to do with it? He had no burning desire to lead his followers into a promised land. More sympathetic staff, particularly officials, believe that he never really had the freedom to do what he wanted.

It is a testimony to the impact of Mrs Thatcher that commentators have asked whether her successors had a vision or ideology; have they merited an 'ism' being attached to their surnames? John Major showed little interest in such an exercise before or after he became Prime Minister.[3] He disapproved of the term 'Majorism' and ordered it to be dropped soon after entering Ten Downing Street.[4] This was done not merely to avoid annoying Mrs Thatcher – over time he did not care much about that – it was simply not his idea of what politics was about. He thought it was more important to engage in incremental problem-solving, with a view above all to making life better for ordinary people. He was, in his own words, 'a practical politician'.[5]

Until Mrs Thatcher stepped down, Major had not prepared for his promotion to Number Ten and did nothing to organise potential supporters, not least because this would have opened him to the charge of disloyalty. Her support on the second ballot of the leadership contest in November 1990 was indeed crucial in gaining him the support of centre-right MPs.

A new Prime Minister learns largely on the job. Even after some months in office, Major was still conscious of the immense pressures and challenges. He told an aide: 'Nothing prepares you for Number Ten. The gap between being a senior Cabinet Minister and Prime Minister is much bigger than being in the Cabinet and not being in the Cabinet.'[6] On staffing, Major's wishes were for a stronger Political Office and Policy Unit and a less combative Press Office than had operated at the end of his predecessor's rule. He was not quick with his paper work in the early days, often writing 'please refer' on items which dealt with subjects with which he was not familiar. He depended much on his Private Office and on established Cabinet ministers for advice. Much of the Whitehall machine remained in place, but only three key figures at Number Ten stayed on – the Principal Private Secretary, Andrew Turnbull, the Foreign Affairs Private Secretary, Charles Powell, the latter for three months, and Percy Cradock, the foreign policy adviser. In the first few days, the only senior figure in Number Ten he personally appointed was Mrs Sarah Hogg, to head the Policy Unit, although he also brought Judith Chaplin and Gus

Right Margaret Thatcher illustrates that even when relaxing over a cup of tea, Prime Ministers have to watch their backs.

Below Denis Thatcher was an all-important power behind the Prime Minister. Often ridiculed during the time, his steadying influence is only now beginning to be appreciated.

Mrs Thatcher poses with her Cabinet in the Pillared Drawing Room at Number Ten Downing Street, May 1989. Robin Butler, Cabinet Secretary, is second row on the extreme right.

Above Mrs Thatcher drinks a glass of water while absorbing the advice of Press Secretary Bernard Ingham, who became, with Charles Powell, her most trusted aide.

Right Margaret Thatcher in London in March 1990 with Charles Powell, her all-powerful Private Secretary, over her right shoulder. Powell appears calm and debonair as always.

Margaret Thatcher leaves Number Ten Downing Street for Buckingham Palace on her last day as Prime Minister, 28 November 1990.

Right John Major on the day before he became Prime Minister with Graham Bright, his future Parliamentary Private Secretary at Number Ten, in the background, 27 November 1990.

Below John Major's Cabinets were, early on at least, much more relaxed affairs than Mrs Thatcher's. On John Major's right, facing the camera, is Cabinet Secretary Robin Butler; bottom right is his final Party Chairman, Brian Mawhinney. Photograph taken 28 July 1994.

Above Jonathan Hill, a key Major aide from 1990 to 1995.

Above Sarah Hogg, Head of the Policy Unit from 1990 to 1995 and a powerful influence on Major.

Left Judith Chaplin, Political Secretary from 1990 to 1992, who died tragically young in 1993.

Prime Minister John Major and his wife Norma wave to crowds from a window in Conservative Central Office on the night of the 1992 election victory.

All the (future) Prime Minister's men. The launch of Labour's 1997
Manifesto with the Shadow Cabinet team.

Below Blair's new Cabinet meet at Number Ten for the first time, 8 May
1997. Robin Butler, on Blair's right, was shortly to be succeeded as Cabinet
Secretary by Richard Wilson.

Above Blair meets Clinton at the White House before he becomes Prime Minister. From left to right in the foreground are Alastair Campbell and Anji Hunter, two of Blair's closest aides from the moment he became Labour leader. Over his right shoulder is John Kerr, then British ambassador to the US, who Blair brought back to London as Head of the Foreign Office and Diplomatic Service.

Right Blair in conversation with Alastair Campbell, his closest aide.

O'Donnell from the Treasury. Compared with most new Prime Ministers, he knew relatively few people who were 'insiders'.

Some Prime Ministers start out with a clear idea how they wish to organise their time. John Major rapidly learned that there simply were not enough hours in his day for him to meet all the people and do all the things that he wished to. He did not always help himself, allowing visitors to stay beyond their allotted time as his natural courtesy got the better of him. This did not prevent him from complaining afterwards: 'Why do I have to see all these people?'[7] He usually rose at 6.30 am and the first people to see him in the bedroom in the flat upstairs would be his Principal Private Secretary, Parliamentary Private Secretary and Press Secretary,[8] respectively Andrew Turnbull, Graham Bright and Gus O'Donnell. After informal meetings with other staff in his flat he would start his working day in the Cabinet Room at 9 am (he moved downstairs after the first few months, abandoning the Prime Minister's first floor study). Typically, there would then follow the relentless procession of meetings, Cabinet committees, meetings with colleagues, outsiders and foreign visitors, preparations for Parliamentary Questions, attendances in Parliament and at receptions that mark the modern Prime Minister's day. He would then work on his boxes in the late evening, following a reception and perhaps a vote in the Commons.

Over his seventy-eight months in Downing Street Major held nearly 1,000 meetings with Cabinet colleagues, senior party figures and ambassadors. Each of these was preceded by detailed briefing and preparation. There were also nearly 2,000 occasions, an average of one a day, when he hosted receptions for British and overseas visitors.[9] On Monday mornings there were regular meetings with the Party Chairman and Deputy Prime Minister, the parliamentary business managers and then the Cabinet Secretary. Major also spent an average of between six and seven weeks annually overseas, attending conferences and meetings. Again, each of these was preceded by wide-ranging briefing.

Few Prime Ministers find time during the day to work on their papers. Major, like other Prime Ministers, worked through his boxes in the evening, taking on board the attached comments from his Private Office, Political Office and Policy Unit. He had less appetite for lengthy policy papers than his predecessor, not least when it came to

JOHN MAJOR'S DAY 1990–1997
1 December 1990–31 March 1997

	1990	1991	1992	1993	1994	1995	1996	1997	Total
Cabinet	2	37	43	45	44	44	45	11	271
Cabinet Committees	7	60	30	26	22	16	25	3	189
Meetings: individual Ministers	8	143	121	137	151	184	143	24	911
Meetings: individual MPs	7	90	82	121	112	102	84	11	609
British visitors/hosts *[meetings & formal meals]*	18	177	220	271	215	252	176	30	1359
Foreign visitors *[meetings & formal meals]*	14	115	140	99	104	90	81	19	662
Official overseas visits*	2	20	18	14	14	14	11	3	96
Days spent overseas*	6	49	48	42	34	39	25	8	251
House: Questions	–	–	–	–	–	–	–	–	334
Statements/speeches/tributes	–	–	–	–	–	–	–	–	71
HM The Queen:									
Audiences	3	21	17	22	16	18	19	5	
Windsor	–	2	1	1	1	1	1	–	138
Balmoral	–	1	1	1	1	1	1	–	
Overseas	–	1	1	1	–	1	–	–	

The above figures do not include Personal, Party or Constituency engagements   *excluding holidays

reading in the early hours of the morning. David Willetts, who worked in the Policy Unit under Mrs Thatcher and ten years later in the Cabinet Office under Major, noted a change. 'I was struck at how much less paper was going to the Prime Minister compared to earlier, when Mrs Thatcher was in office. With John Major the important thing was to get in and see him. If a Prime Minister wants papers the system will supply them.'[10]

John Major, like many Prime Ministers, gave strict instructions not to arrange more meetings, but when personally confronted by an

importunate individual often said 'Yes, of course', for fear of offend-
ing. His staff thought that he was the main culprit for his diary being
over-loaded. One Cabinet minister sought a private meeting with the
Prime Minister only to be told by a Private Secretary that it would
not be possible within the next two months. When the minister raised
this with Major, the latter expressed surprise and invited the minister
round for dinner that evening.[11] In their book *Too Close to Call* his
political aides Sarah Hogg and Jonathan Hill expressed the familiar
impatience of the political staff at the amount of time he spent meeting
with ambassadors, usually at the urging of the Private Office.[12] They
could see no political benefit arising from these meetings.

Major tried to keep his weekends free for visits to Chequers or,
more often, to his family home, 'The Finings' at Great Stukeley, near
his Huntingdon constituency. His constituents mattered to him, and
he spent more time with them than did most Prime Ministers. He
visited Huntingdon about one Friday in five, the frequency declining
over time, and also attended many constituency party events. Mrs
Thatcher spent most weekends at Chequers, Major about one in five.
He spent part of the Christmas and Easter holidays there and used it
for entertaining foreign visitors. It was never as much a part of his
life as it was for Margaret Thatcher or Tony Blair. One aide reflected
that going home for him seemed to be a way of escaping from the
trappings of office. If he was not abroad he would also try to keep
Fridays free for visits to the regions. This became more important in
the twelve months before the 1992 and 1997 general elections.

Major instinctively appreciated virtually all of the civil servants who
worked in his Private Office. He inherited Andrew Turnbull as his
Principal Private Secretary. Stephen Wall, who had been with Major
at the FCO, followed by Roderic Lyne and then John Holmes who
were the Foreign Affairs Private Secretaries after Charles Powell left
in early 1991 for a post in the City. Major relied heavily on Turnbull
and Wall in his first months. Turnbull returned to the Treasury after
the general election in April 1992.

Alex Allan succeeded Turnbull as Principal Private Secretary and
remained in post for five years. He had already worked with Major
at the Treasury. Major was close to Allan, finding him emollient and

patient, and he had personally appointed him to the post. Allan was also more willing to accompany Major to formal engagements, which both often found trying, and generally act as a morale-booster. Allan's father Robert had been a Tory MP and acted as Parliamentary Private Secretary to Prime Ministers Eden and Macmillan (see p. 58).

One change came about because the Foreign Secretary, Douglas Hurd, grew concerned about the growing workload on Roderic Lyne. In addition to routine foreign affairs matters, Maastricht, Yugoslavia and, above all, Northern Ireland were imposing great strains, and there was the legacy of the work accumulated by Powell. Hurd's suggestion of appointing an extra Foreign Affairs Private Secretary (also advocated by Lyne's predecessor, Stephen Wall) was rebuffed for several months by Major and the Cabinet Secretary, but finally agreed in 1994. The retirement of Sir Rodric Braithwaite as Major's foreign affairs adviser provided a suitable opportunity to strengthen this part of the Private Office.

Mary Francis (and then Moira Wallace), the Economic Affairs Private Secretary, William Chapman (then Mark Adams), Parliamentary Affairs Private Secretary and Rachael Reynolds (then Angus Lapsley), Private Secretary for Home Affairs, as well as the Diary Secretary and the Duty Clerk, completed the office. Francis had the tricky task of liaising with the Treasury when relations between Norman Lamont and John Major deteriorated after the ERM exit.

The work of the Private Office was taken up with the flow of papers coming to John Major, and with his meetings. But it was also concerned with issues that were not specifically the remit of any one department, issues on which John Major did not fully trust the department concerned, or those which were in the headlines at the time. In conjunction with the Cabinet Office it was the engine room for many European issues and the Northern Ireland peace process. It also handled constitutional matters, such as the question of taxation of the monarchy and Ian Lang's White Paper on Scotland. Alex Allan started off dealing with the Citizen's Charter and national heritage issues, but over time became heavily involved with issues of political propriety and constitutional sensitivity, such as the government's evidence to the Scott Inquiry on the Churchill–Matrix affair, the Nolan Committee on Standards in public life, and the divorce of the Prince and Princess of Wales. He was effectively a Chief of Staff. Major probably had more discussions with Allan over the 1995 ministerial reshuffle than with any other individual; it was Allan's task to keep notes on Major's various musings and conversations. The involvement irritated some of Major's campaign team in the leadership election, notably Robert Cramborne, who was furious about Heseltine's promotion to Deputy Prime Minister.[13] Allan remonstrated with John Redwood's Private Office at the Welsh Office when the right-wing Welsh Secretary failed to clear in advance speeches on Europe and 'Back to Basics'.

At the start of Major's premiership relations were far from smooth between different units within Number Ten. Partly it was a question of adjusting to a new Prime Minister, partly of rivalry for his attention, and partly of the Policy Unit becoming more assertive than it had been in the last few years under Mrs Thatcher. The first eighteen months or so were marred by the so-called 'battle of the memos'. It was not unusual for the Prime Minister to find in his box at the end of the day separate memos from the Private Office and Policy Unit on the same topic, not infrequently giving different advice. On occasion the Cabinet Office would also provide a separate memo, often a 'handling brief' for a Cabinet committee Major was chairing. It was understandable that Sarah Hogg should wish to assert the view of the Policy Unit from the start. But, according to one Private Secretary, 'A Prime Minister has enough reading to do. Adding to it is bad and to be giving conflicting advice makes it even worse.' In due course the Principal Private Secretary and the Head of the Policy Unit would meet to decide which office would write any given memo and sometimes staff in the two offices would write joint memos, incorporating different emphases.

Major was not as interested as Mrs Thatcher in seeking advice outside the Private Office and Mrs Hogg. He inherited Percy Cradock not just as his foreign policy adviser but also as Chairman of the Joint Intelligence Committee, the body which met weekly and overviewed the work of MI5, MI6 and GCHQ. At the beginning of the 1992 Parliament Cradock stepped down and the two tasks passed to Rodric Braithwaite, another former diplomat. Where Cradock, because of his background, spoke with authority on China and Hong Kong, Braithwaite did so on Russia. He was more inclined to liaise with the Foreign Office than Cradock. When Braithwaite retired in early 1994, the post of foreign policy adviser lapsed and has not been re-created since. Braithwaite himself advised against the appointment of a successor.[14] The original appointment, of Anthony Parsons, had been inspired by Mrs Thatcher's distrust of the Foreign Office. Neither John Major nor his Private Office were interested in second-guessing Douglas Hurd, who Major regarded as a firm personal friend. The chairmanship of the JIC returned to the Cabinet Office, to be filled by a Deputy Secretary in the Cabinet Secretariat.

Both Mrs Thatcher and Edward Heath had strategies of a kind for coping with a bad press. They simply did not read it, would dismiss what they read or, in the case of Mrs Thatcher, would sometimes look at summaries prepared by her Press Secretary. Unfortunately Major read the newspapers himself. For much of his premiership they were damning and this affected his mood;[15] the more this was known the more his critics, particularly in the Conservative press, attacked his stewardship. As with hounds scenting a wounded fox, his sensitivity heightened their determination to achieve a kill. Staff commented, resignedly, that Major failed to acquire the extra layer of skin which could make press comment tolerable. His morbid fascination with scrutinising the press to detect which Cabinet ministers, or their aides, were leaking against him was hardly calculated to improve his disposition. The Conservative and Eurosceptic press, which had been generally favourable for the first two years, largely gave up on Major after the exit from the ERM in the autumn of 1992. 'Black Wednesday', Michael Heseltine's announcement in October 1992 of the programme of coal pit closures, scandals about 'sleaze' and sexual misconduct affecting Conservative ministers and MPs, reversals of stance as over the QMV (qualified majority voting) row in March 1994, and the handling of BSE or mad cow disease during 1996 also brought forth press ire. The heavy-duty pounding had a cost – Major's bounce, hitherto a personal trademark as he rose up the greasy pole, his positive self-image and winning charm gave way to a darker side, more suspicious, less assured.

Many newspapers gave full rein to Conservative Eurosceptics or members of the Thatcher entourage who attacked Major for weakness or allegedly betraying her legacy. Attempts, pressed on him by aides, to court the proprietors and editors of these papers were rarely successful.[16] He regarded the exercise as beneath his dignity, having little respect for most of them, and indulged it reluctantly and infrequently. He made a point at weekends of phoning media sympathisers, notably Bruce Anderson (political editor of the *Spectator*), Sue Tinson (an *ITN* executive), Nick Lloyd (*Daily Express*) and Matthew Parris (*The Times*). When he stood for the leadership of the party in 1995 only the *Daily Express* supported him, a marked contrast to the press line-up at the 1992 general election.

As part of a changed approach to leadership from his predecessor, Major immediately appointed his former Treasury Press Secretary, Gus O'Donnell, as his Number Ten Press Secretary. This fitted in with the preference of the Cabinet Secretary, Robin Butler, who thought that the personality of Bernard Ingham had loomed too large for a civil servant. Major and O'Donnell had similar social backgrounds, shared an interest in sport and worked harmoniously together. But O'Donnell's qualities of frankness and lack of bite were not an advantage when the press became difficult in the 1992 Parliament. The forceful qualities of Ingham, the former journalist, might have been more useful, particularly with the tabloids. The decision not to invite journalists from some of the more adversarial tabloids to O'Donnell's farewell dinner in Downing Street in early 1994 did nothing to improve relations.

When O'Donnell left Number Ten to return to the Treasury in January 1994 he was replaced by Christopher Meyer, who served for two years and was then succeeded by his deputy, Jonathan Haslam (January 1996-May 1997). Meyer was an aggressive and high-flying FCO diplomat, who, however, rapidly realised that he had little taste for handling the media or Number Ten power politics. Neither he nor Haslam was as close to Major or as influential on tactics as O'Donnell. One of Major's political aides said: 'Gus had a natural empathy, but Christopher was not the sort of person to sit into the small hours of the morning, listening as John Major poured out his soul. By the end, relations were not good between them.'[17]

Number Ten and Conservative Central Office personnel met daily, first through the Number Twelve Committee and then the Cabinet Committee on Coordination and Presentation of Government Policy

(EDCP), to co-ordinate government announcements and attract favourable coverage. They largely failed in this and were regularly upstaged by Labour's more professional operation. Tony Blair's press spokesman, Alastair Campbell, was unimpressed by the Number Ten efforts and intended to improve on them if he got the chance. Indeed, in late 1995 Number Ten was discussing the recruitment of Charles Lewington, the political editor of the *Sunday Express*, to the post of Press Secretary. Unfortunately, the idea was killed when Michael Heseltine broadcast an attack on the idea of Alastair Campbell, a partisan journalist, playing such a role in government. In December 1995 Lewington moved instead to Central Office as the party's Director of Communications.

Major, in contrast to Mrs Thatcher, had no media or intellectual entourage; there was no Tim Bell or Gordon Reece or Woodrow Wyatt who could persuade the press to his point of view.[18] Early on in his premiership he gave Friday breakfasts for editors and political commentators. These occasions gradually became less productive, in part because of what editors regarded as his hypersensitivity to criticisms. As Major's grip weakened so hostile leaking from departments, or ministers' aides, increased, not only from those he dismissed – in one discussion in July 1993 that he did not realise was being recorded – as 'bastards' on the Eurosceptic right but also from the Treasury under Kenneth Clarke and Education under Gillian Shephard.[19] Towards the end it was very hard for Major to know who his loyal friends were.

The Tory press by now had little time for Major and in their eagerness to do him down helped to trigger the leadership contest in July 1995. He was so determined not to endure the speculation about challengers and stalking-horses in the run-up to the start of the autumn session of Parliament (when the party rules allowed a challenge) that he took the bold step of resigning as leader, so as to trigger a contest. Party critics (largely Eurosceptics) of his compromise position on the single currency, with their ready access to the media, made it impossible for the Conservatives to present the united face which Blair was imposing on the Labour Party. Government-inspired stories were driven off the front pages by reports of dissent, rumours about challenges to Major for the party leadership, stories about sleaze and scandals affecting Conservative MPs and, of course, Labour initiatives. After 1996 frustrated members of the Cabinet committee on presentation of policy asked why the government was failing to co-ordinate its message, as Labour was doing. The answer, Michael Heseltine told them, was simple. They could copy Labour and allow the Prime Minister and his Press Secretary to instruct Cabinet Ministers and their aides on the line to adopt. The statement was met with wry smiles, and an implicit realisation that this would not happen: Blair's credit in the bank was piled high; Major's had been all but fully spent.

Much of a Conservative Political Secretary's job defines itself – helping with or overseeing party political speeches, attending and giving briefings, generally co-ordinating the work of the Number Ten units, and encouraging the Prime Minister while keeping Central Office in the picture. The Political Secretary was also involved in preparations for Prime Minister's Questions and overseeing party correspondence.

As his first Political Secretary John Major brought in his Treasury special adviser, Judith Chaplin, who served until March 1992. The appointment was not a success. Soon into 1991, Judith Chaplin was selected as prospective Conservative candidate for the Newbury constituency and the association expected her to be visible in the constituency. The result was that she worked only a three-day week in Downing Street. As a greater burden fell on the Policy Unit, tensions, latent already under the surface between two ambitious women, Judith Chaplin and Sarah Hogg, the Policy Unit head steadily increased. Jonathan Hill (who had been special adviser to Kenneth Clarke when he had been a health minister but had recently joined the Unit) filled part of the vacuum. He was appointed the Political Secretary on the day the 1992 election was called. An exhausting and demanding thirty months in Downing Street ensued – coping with the ERM exit, difficult party conferences and the difficult and uncertain passage of the Maastricht Bill through Parliament. Hill was also heavily involved in speechwriting and tactics and worked closely with Mrs Hogg.

When Hill informed Major in autumn 1994 that he wished to leave Number Ten (his wife was expecting a third child), Major asked him to seek a successor. Major wanted someone older than Hill and who would be in post until the next general election. Various names mentioned by Hill did not elicit a positive reaction. In October 1994 he approached Howell James. James was working at the BBC and had previously been Director of Corporate Affairs under Lord Young, chairman of the telecommunications giant Cable and Wireless. James had also been a special adviser to Lord Young when the latter was a member of Mrs Thatcher's Cabinet and had worked with Norman Blackwell, who was to succeed Mrs Hogg as head of the Policy Unit.

In contrast to Hill, James did not sit in on John Major's bilateral meetings with Cabinet ministers and was less involved in speechwriting and policy. His strength was in strategy and presentation. He was minute-taker at political Cabinets, and regarded his central task as preparing for the next general election, whenever it was held. He described himself essentially as a 'fixer' and spent much time liaising with Central Office, the Press Secretary and Norman Blackwell, Mrs Hogg's successor in the Policy Unit. He and Blackwell represented Number Ten at the now daily EDCP meeting. James calculated that he spent some 60 per cent of his time liaising with Central Office and supporting the media operation, 20 per cent on PMQs and 20 per cent on Major's correspondence.[20]

George Bridges was recruited from Central Office in January 1994 at the age of 24 to be James's assistant in the Political Office. An old Etonian with gifts as a wordsmith, he proved especially effective in preparing for PMQs and in speechwriting. Bridges had strong family connections with Number Ten. His grandfather, Edward, had been Cabinet Secretary during the Second World War and his uncle, Tom, had worked in the Private Office under Heath.

John Major's Parliamentary Private Secretary from 1990 to 1994 was Graham Bright, the MP for Luton South. Bright was, like John Major, one of the 1979 intake, of modest social background, and member for a constituency a little to the north of London. They had been members together of the 'Guy Fawkes' dining club before Major was upgraded to the more prestigious 'Blue Chip' club. Bright was criticised by MPs for his lack of sharpness and his unwillingness to expose Major to the full force of criticism in the Commons; he was more of a personal comforter than a political emissary. But in this role he was a reassuring and steadying presence in the storms Major suffered. A chartered accountant, he continued to help Major with personal and financial matters after 1994.

In July 1994, after government setbacks in the House of Lords, Major decided that he needed an additional PPS, to take care of the Upper House. He appointed Lord McColl, a medical practitioner and Professor of Surgery at Guy's Hospital. McColl also took charge of links between Number Ten and the Conservative MEPs. In the Commons, meanwhile, Bright was replaced by John Ward, a choice that surprised many observers. Ward, aged 69, had been MP for Poole since 1979 and had already announced his retirement at the next election. He was well-liked and without factional allegiance, but more diffident than forceful.

The Policy Unit, as noted already, had become marginalised in the latter stages of Mrs Thatcher's premiership. Major, however, was determined to make use of it. Sarah Hogg was a recruit from economic journalism (having been economics editor successively on *The Times*, *Independent* and *Daily Telegraph*), already known to him as a sympathetic commentator from his time at the Treasury. She quickly made herself indispensable. She was forceful, and was helped by being present from the beginning of Major's premiership and therefore able to define the role not only for herself but also for her team. To quote one Cabinet minister at the time, 'Sarah is very territorial and she has a lot of territory to defend.'[21] She was close to John Major throughout her spell in Downing Street, but her peak of influence was probably in the first two years – until the end of 1992. In the prolonged period up until the spring of 1992, she and her colleagues were helped by the imminence of a general election and the discipline which preparing the manifesto imposed on ministers. She was in charge of the manifesto and ministerial contributions were addressed to her.

As expected, members of Mrs Thatcher's Unit resigned with her. Sarah Hogg asked the two civil servants, John Mills and Carolyn Sinclair, to remain and also retained an outside financier from the City, Howell Harris Hughes. John Major specifically suggested that Hogg recruit Nick True, who had been a special adviser to Norman Fowler at Social Security when Major had been a junior minister in the department. Jonathan Hill also joined, having written to Hogg asking if there was an opening. By the New Year of 1991, Sarah Hogg had assembled a staff of seven, including herself. The initial team, with its responsibilities, was:

- Sarah Hogg – Treasury, general policy oversight, specific issues (e.g. poll tax, Maastricht and GATT negotiations)
- Nick True – Social Security, Education, Citizen's Charter
- John Mills – Education, Local Government
- Carolyn Sinclair – Health, Home Office
- Alan Rosling – Defence, Energy, Scotland
- Howell Harris Hughes – Trade and Industry, Employment, Wales
- Jonathan Hill – Transport, Housing, Inner Cities, Citizen's Charter, presentations and launches.

The scope of the Unit's work in the first eighteen months expanded, partly because of Judith Chaplin's inability to act as a full-time Political Secretary and also because of Sarah Hogg's economic expertise and determination to keep the Unit at the centre of things. The Unit (except for its Civil Service members) became more involved in election preparations, political speeches and PMQs.

Sarah Hogg met the Prime Minister more regularly and spent more private time with him than any other Policy Unit head since Donoughue with Harold Wilson. She sat in on many of his sessions with Cabinet colleagues, including his bilateral sessions with Norman Lamont (Chancellor, 1990–93), to the latter's annoyance.[22] This was useful for putting the Unit in the picture about policy and helping her to understand Major's thinking and priorities. She also attended key Cabinet committees, including 'EDX', which dealt with unresolved disputes between the Chancellor and Cabinet ministers over departmental spending totals. Under Mrs Thatcher, Charles Powell had made European Community matters his own province. After his departure the Policy Unit gradually acquired a voice on Europe, but it was nowhere near as important as that of the Private Office or Cabinet Office. John Major's March 1991 speech, promising to place Britain at 'the very heart of Europe', was made in spite of Powell's cautionary advice, a case of the pro-European Douglas Hurd, Chris Patten and Sarah Hogg winning out over the sceptical Powell. The speech also powerfully disillusioned Mrs Thatcher, who was rapidly reaching the conclusion that Major was not a clone of herself.

The Unit played a key role in developing the new council tax to replace the poll tax. Hogg also contributed significantly to the party's strategy and manifesto for the 1992 election and co-ordinating work for the 1991 Maastricht and on going GATT negotiations. Nick True was Major's main speechwriter and he and Jonathan Hill took the initiative on the 1991 Citizen's Charter, and in developing a post-Thatcher agenda.[23] Together with Sarah Hogg, they formed an inner triumvirate, whose influence easily eclipsed that of all others in the Unit.

After leaving Number Ten, Sarah Hogg described the role of the Policy Unit as 'to act as a sounding board for Ministers so that they do not suffer embarrassment or rebuff by the Prime Minister'.[24] This was part of its role. She might also have added that it sought to develop and promote the Prime Minister's agenda in Whitehall. Major regarded the improvement of public services and making them more responsive to consumers – parents, patients, passengers etc. – as a priority. It was the Unit which developed the Citizen's Charter for public services – with its league tables, value for money requirements and market testing. After the 1992 general election, and particularly after the ERM exit on 16 September, she and her colleagues were drawn increasingly into day-to-day matters and crisis management. Sarah Hogg personally played a large and decisive part in the reconstruction of economic policy following 'Black Wednesday'.

As the government's popularity collapsed in the autumn of 1992, so the Prime Minister's staff were criticised, undoubtedly as a lightning rod for attacks on Major himself. One scholarly Cabinet minister compared Sarah Hogg, in this role, to Aspasia, the mistress of the Greek statesman Pericles: critics attacked the former when their intended target was the latter. Some Cabinet ministers expressed resentment at Mrs Hogg's whispering and passing notes to the Prime Minister during meetings.[25] The decline of Major's own authority also undermined the Unit's influence in Whitehall.

Sarah Hogg left Downing Street in January 1995. She remained in touch with Major, was consulted over his decision to resign the leadership in 1995 and continued to make suggestions for speeches and strategy. Finding a successor to Sarah Hogg was not easy. Ex-Conservative MPs Francis Maude and Michael Fallon were briefly considered as Hogg's successor, but both were keen to return to Parliament. Andrew Tyrie (who had been a special adviser to John Major and Nigel Lawson when they were Chancellors) was a more serious runner, but he also was seeking a parliamentary seat. Norman Blackwell, a management consultant with McKinsey, was appointed and served until the end of Major's premiership in May 1997. He had worked on energy in the Policy Unit under Mrs Thatcher and also worked with Howell James (Political Secretary, 1994–97) on the renewal of the BBC charter when the latter was at the BBC. He retained existing working arrangements, including the Monday lunchtime sessions at which staff would report on their work, and the six-monthly 'Away Days' for staff with John Major at Chequers. He was something of a technocrat, interested in strategic planning, more organised than Mrs Hogg but less political. He was influential, but in a different way, and not as personally close to Major as she had been.

At an early meeting with John Major, Blackwell proposed five themes which Major readily accepted as his agenda for the second half of the Parliament. The themes covered enterprise, opportunity, law and order, public services and the nation.[26] These were elaborated in a Major speech to the party's Central Council in March 1995, in an *Evening Standard* article when he stood for the leadership in June 1995, and were eventually published by the Conservative Political Centre in 1997 as *Our Nation's Future*.

Blackwell also organised seminars around these themes for Cabinet ministers. The seminars were usually chaired by Michael Heseltine or Tony Newton, and one on the constitution was chaired by Major. In all, a dozen were held between spring 1995 and December 1996. Blackwell made a point of getting ministers away from their civil servants and of distributing papers only a day or two in advance of the meeting, in order to reduce the chance for civil servants to brief ministers. Robin Butler was initially ambivalent about the exercise, expressing concern about whether it breached the line between party-political and governmental concerns. In the end he agreed to provide a secretary from the Cabinet Office to take minutes. Blackwell, or a member of the Policy Unit in whose remit the issue fell, would attend these seminars along with nine or ten invited ministers.[27] The sessions produced some outputs, including the estates renewal fund, a green paper on long-term care of the elderly, and proposals for an injection of private capital into social housing. But, according to one participant:

> It was difficult to get ministers to think long term. They were thinking of the next election and they did not think they could win. Some ministers were defensive and too often the sessions degenerated into talk about presentation, such as the need for a leaflet that would advertise the good work they were doing.[28]

The sessions also took up a good deal of ministerial time. One Cabinet minister recalled: 'There was a three line whip. We were pretty cynical, not least because we did not think we would be in government after the next general election.'[29]

Blackwell, along with David Willetts, also drafted the manifesto for the 1997 election and played a key part in preparing election strategy. But, like his predecessor, he was increasingly drawn into managing short-term crises, notably the 'mad cow disease' or BSE during 1996. Blackwell brought immense industry and intellectual depth to the Policy Unit, but in the fevered political climate of 1995–97 he was something of an innocent abroad, suffering from the disillusionment with Major of many Cabinet ministers and right-wing commentators, and doomed in the eyes of many as merely rearranging the deck chairs of the *Titanic*.

The Cabinet system under Major continued much as before, meeting weekly when Parliament was sitting. It started at 10 or 10.30 am and typically lasted for about 90 minutes. Major chaired the same seven standing committees as Mrs Thatcher had done, including the important ODP on overseas affairs, EDP on the economy and NI on Northern Ireland, all of which met frequently. After 1994, however, he reduced this to four or five committees. Where Mrs Thatcher was inclined to appoint colleagues with direct ministerial responsibility to chair committees, he more often chose non-departmental ministers, like the Lord Privy Seal and Leader of the Lords (John Wakeham), the Chancellor of the Duchy of Lancaster (David Hunt), or, after Hunt, the Deputy Prime Minister (Michael Heseltine). He met the

Cabinet Secretary, Robin Butler, weekly to discuss future Cabinet business one and three weeks ahead and also to discuss political issues.

There were, however, differences in the styles of the two Prime Ministers. John Major held fewer ad hoc committees than Mrs Thatcher, preferring rather to use sub-committees of Cabinet standing committees. He readily allowed colleagues the opportunity to bring up matters under the four broad agenda headings Parliamentary, Home, Overseas and Europe. The atmosphere, particularly for his first two years, was collegial and Cabinet ministers and officials commented positively that 'discussion is back on the agenda', although the meetings miraculously did not last any longer than under Mrs Thatcher. The Cabinet Secretary compared Major's early Cabinets to the 'Prisoners' Chorus' from Beethoven's *Fidelio*, as ministers, revelling in a new-found freedom, spoke up on a range of matters.[30] One official said that the minutes and range of issues considered were not different from Thatcher to Major, but that the spirit was very different.

Cabinet had increasingly over the years become a reporting body, giving approval to decisions made elsewhere, usually in subordinate Cabinet committees. But John Major was a good listener and clearly regarded discussion as an opportunity to bind Cabinet ministers to final decisions, as over the negotiations at Maastricht in December 1991, the EU's change to the qualified majority voting (QMV) rule in March 1994, or the sending of British troops to Bosnia. On these decisions Major sought the views of each member of the Cabinet; in spite of reservations by Eurosceptic ministers on the second issue, which raised the blocking minority on EU issues from 23 to 27 votes, he declared the decision unanimous. Unlike his predecessor, he did not rush to give his own views of the issue. Indeed on QMV, although he canvassed the view of each minister, he did not reveal his own preference. He was under great pressure from Eurosceptics to resist the proposal but also knew of the opposing views of Hurd, Heseltine and Clarke. One exception to the consultative style was the decision in November 1994 to withdraw the whip from the eight Tory rebels who did not support the government in the confidence vote on the EU finance bill. This was decided by notes being passed between Major and the Party Chairman at a Chequers Away Day. General support was claimed for the decision, but sceptical ministers had not been consulted and lost no time in making their dissent known to the media.

Major's consultative style of Cabinet management was initially a consequence of his temperament and his lack of preconceived ideological stances on many issues, and later also the product of his reduced power base in the 1992 Parliament. He liked to 'square' potential opponents of a decision beforehand, and if trouble was brewing he would postpone taking it to Cabinet. 'Too sensitive for Cabinet', was a phrase heard in Number Ten. Supporters called this subtlety, critics weakness. Some of the latter complained of an 'air of unreality' in discussions as Cabinet deliberately steered clear of contentious EU issues; they had different ideas from his about handling a divided party and the rapidly disappearing majority in the Commons. Major deserves credit for getting political agreement on policy developments in Bosnia, Northern Ireland and Europe, when on all three initially he felt that he lacked a majority. But there were occasions when he lost in Cabinet, notably on education spending in March 1995 when a count was taken.

Cabinet, particularly after the ERM exit, gradually ceased to be a collection of 'chums' (Kenneth Clarke's phrase in 1991). Mischievous leaks increased; many were inspired by divisions on Europe, the core issue splitting his government, some by a wish to undermine John Major, and some to advance the prospects of would-be successors. By early 1993, the Eurosceptic press (*The Times* and the *Telegraph* group, as well as the *Mail* and *Sun*) seemed intent on replacing him; he complained increasingly of the 'poison' emanating from Cabinet 'bastards'. The leaks were also evidence of the decline in his authority following Black Wednesday and an agonisingly difficult 1992 party conference. Political and official staff in Number Ten recall the deference with which Cabinet ministers and civil servants approached them before the 1992 general election to learn of Major's thinking and the marked decline in such respect from late 1992. In 1994, the Cabinet Secretary was heard to complain: 'There is an expectation that anything controversial said in Cabinet will be in the *Evening Standard* on Thursday afternoon.'[31] Ministers were inevitably less inclined to speak freely in Cabinet and John Major had come to distrust its ability to treat important business in confidence. Who was doing the leaking? No-one was sure. Accusations flew around as the air of mistrust grew. The two Chancellors of the Exchequer complained that Number Ten was spinning stories designed to weaken their position in the government.[32] By 1996–97, the 'Cabinet of chums' had become the 'Cabinet of vipers'.

Major's staff and his dwindling number of ministerial supporters urged him to use the authority of his office to call dissenters to heel, 'to bang the table', in the words of a senior colleague. He did do so, on several occasions, but never liked cracking the whip, largely because, according to the same minister, 'He said that it's not his style. But you have to, sometimes'.

John Major held political Cabinets more regularly than Mrs Thatcher, once a month during 'peace-time' politics and more often during the approach of the general elections and party conferences. For these meetings civil servants withdrew and the political staff (the head of the Policy Unit and the Political Secretary) would be present. The verdict on the political Cabinets was mixed. Interviewed in 1994, William Waldegrave thought that they were valuable and would have had more. Jonathan Hill echoed Stephen Sherbourne's complaints under Mrs Thatcher that they were largely a waste of time – 'far worse than ordinary Cabinet, a place for show-offs and creeps'.[33] Some participants claimed that John Major failed to give a lead, simply introducing speakers and providing no summary.

There was much discussion in political Cabinets during 1996 about the line the party should take about Tony Blair's impact on the Labour Party. Advisers, including Tim Bell, Norman Blackwell and Maurice Saatchi, made presentations. Danny Finkelstein, the party's Research Director, successfully argued for a strategy of warning voters of 'New Labour New Danger'. He had complained in January 1996 that ministers had made several different, sometimes contradictory, criticisms of Tony Blair's recent speech in Singapore on stakeholding. Conservative warnings that Blair still led an old-style Labour Party were not believed by voters; the party had to make voters aware of the new dangers posed by the new Labour Party. But ministers were only slightly more inclined to stick to the new message and in this respect Major proved to be a leading offender.[34] When aides remonstrated with him in early 1997 about 'going off message', he replied, 'I am the message.'

*   *   *

As Cabinet Secretary, Robin Butler played a key role in smoothing the Thatcher–Major transition. In 1992 Major and Butler took significant steps to open up government by publishing the list of Cabinet committees, including their members and chairmen, and *Questions on Procedure for Ministers*, the rule book for the conduct of Cabinet government. Like Robert Armstrong before him, Butler was drawn into the political arena as a result of government difficulties. He found himself ruling on the right of the Treasury to fund part of Lamont's legal costs in removing a tenant from his private flat, questioning the former Conservative Cabinet minister Jonathan Aitken about the payment of his Paris hotel bill, and then examining charges by Mohamed Al-Fayed that Conservative MPs had taken money for asking parliamentary questions. More time-consuming was his need to defend the Civil Service against allegations raised by the Scott report into arms sales to Iraq, and his work with Major on the search for peace in Northern Ireland.

Butler worked closely with the Lord President and Lord Privy Seal, who chaired many Cabinet committees, and the Prime Minister and Chief Whip over the handling and substance of Cabinet committees. Even before the exit from the ERM some ministers were unhappy about the lack of a clear and consistent direction from Number Ten, and argued that more groundwork should be done before issues reached Cabinet committees. Some ministers complained that Sarah Hogg was committing the Prime Minister too quickly to courses of action (for example, publishing the minutes of discussions between the Chancellor and the Governor of the Bank of England), which then produced rows. Some ministers grumbled that they had agreed a line with Major, only to see it overturned in committee by powerful ministers. This was apparently the case with Lamont (on Post Office privatisation) and then his successor as Chancellor, Clarke (on road tolls and the mobility allowance for the disabled). 'The problem is that ministers are not frightened of John Major,' said one Cabinet minister, 'and this slows up the work of Cabinet committees.' That lack of authority affected the ability of Major's 'fixers' – Newton, Hunt and Wakeham – to deliver.[35] In turn, Major himself was sometimes unhappy with what emerged or did not emerge from committees. Most of those involved agreed that there had to be a clearer 'steer' from Number Ten.

Butler took the initiative in 1993 to follow a Monday morning meeting of Major and the parliamentary business managers with a meeting with the Cabinet Deputy Secretaries to report on the progress of the Cabinet committees. Major, Hogg and Allan met over dinner at Butler's home to discuss ways in which the Cabinet Office might do more to help facilitate the smooth conduct of business. One result was to reduce the flow of competing memos from the Cabinet Office, Policy Unit and Private Office. Another was the creation of the 'Presentation' Cabinet committee in early 1995 under David Hunt, to improve co-ordination between the Cabinet Office and Number Ten. After May 1997, some officials who noted Tony Blair's encouragement of the activism of Richard Wilson (see pp. 269–71) thought that Major could have made more use of Butler.

The disloyalty and personal attacks from fellow Conservatives in the period 1992–97 hurt John Major deeply. In public he was stoical, but he sometimes unburdened himself to trusted staff in Number Ten.

Major's closest ally was Chris Patten, who was Party Chairman until shortly after the 1992 general election, at which he lost his seat. Major considered him a personal friend and appreciated his strategic advice. Patten was also Chancellor of the Duchy of Lancaster and had scope as a non-departmental Cabinet minister to act as a troubleshooter or 'fixer' for Major, coaxing ministers to an agreed line. In Cabinet, his interventions could turn the direction or tone of a discussion and invariably helped Major. Without a seat or a department he carried on with the role briefly during the 1992 Parliament, before departing to become Governor of Hong Kong. Even before Patten left, Major was having regrets about losing him; they continued for the rest of his premiership.

Once Patten had left, Major began a long-term search for a replacement. At first, he looked to Lord Waddington to play the troubleshooting role, then Lord Wakeham, Leader of the House of Lords and Lord Privy Seal. Wakeham chaired many Cabinet committees but did not develop a close relationship with Major. There was some support in summer 1993 for the idea of inviting John Kerr (the UK Permanent Representative to the EU, known as 'Machiavelli' for his brilliance at resolving issues) to be a troubleshooter-cum-*chef de cabinet* but Whitehall frowned on the idea and it was not taken further.[36] In 1994, an approach was made to Douglas Hurd, who turned it down (he was already planning to leave the government), and Major put out feelers to Patten – exaggerated by the press and Patten's biographer Jonathan Dimbleby – about returning from Hong Kong. After winning the leadership contest in July 1995, Major turned to Michael Heseltine, the Deputy Prime Minister. Heseltine's control of the new EDCP committee and chairmanship of many Cabinet committees put him in a powerful position to exercise a strong co-ordinating role. For the most part, Heseltine took the opportunity. He had had a wary relationship with Major for the previous five years, and Number Ten staff were never sure whether he was scheming for his own advancement. But once given his new role in the summer of 1995, he proved scrupulously loyal in public and became the Prime Minister's closest Cabinet ally in his last two years in office. Hurd had been Major's closest ally from the 1992 general election until he himself departed in July 1995. That said, throughout much of his second administration Major lacked a figure who would play the role often attributed to Whitelaw under Mrs Thatcher.

In some respects Major did not have the best of luck with his Chancellors of the Exchequer. The appointment of Norman Lamont as Chancellor in November 1990 seemed a good choice at the time. He had Treasury experience, had worked with Major as Chancellor, was a Thatcherite, and had been Major's campaign manager during the 1990 leadership election. But their relationship soon became strained and there were differences over the 1991 Budget.[37] Lamont was too sceptical during the Maastricht negotiations for Major's liking and his forecast of economic recovery in time for a 1992 general election proved to be ill-founded. He was also thought by senior Cabinet figures (and by Major) to have performed poorly against Labour's John Smith in the 1992 general election campaign. There was a gradual cooling in their relations and Lamont showed little awareness that his standing inside the government had virtually collapsed. Major pressed the case for economic growth and rejected Lamont's proposal to make the Bank of England independent. Immediately before and after the ERM exit, Lamont refused to give media interviews and Ken Clarke spoke on the economy for the government. Colleagues complained of Lamont 'sulking' and storming out of meetings and slamming doors. The relationship was so strained that it put later reports of the tension between Blair and Brown into perspective.

By the end, some Number Ten political aides had come to loathe Lamont, and called him 'Lamontable' in private. During one tense bilateral meeting with the Prime Minister prior to the 1993 Budget, he abruptly collected his papers and stomped out. 'We could not have gone on like that. The Chancellor is a key player on so many committees and Lamont was not doing the job,' said one Cabinet minister in June 1994.[38] The failure of the ERM policy was largely visited, however unfairly, on Lamont. The fact that it was John Major (and Mrs Thatcher) who had been responsible for the terms of entry into the ERM in October 1990 embittered him further. His friends claimed that the misplaced economic optimism he expressed in 1991 had been at Major's behest. He rejected the offer of a move from the Treasury in 1993 and resigned, a bitter and disappointed man. He never forgave Major.

Major's dealings with Ken Clarke as Chancellor started off well but became strained over European issues, particularly the single currency. Major was a good listener but believed more in the political and economic case for tax cuts than Ken Clarke. There were few other differences over economic management but on the politics of the single currency they drifted apart. Major wanted to pursue a line that would keep both the pro-Europeans and sceptics on board, hence the position of 'wait and see', or negotiate and then decide. Clarke was a supporter of British membership and regarded Major's wait and see line as just about acceptable. Major's staff felt that Clarke rose too readily to attacks from the sceptics, and thereby advertised party disunity and increased his problems of party management. In turn Clarke thought that Major was giving too much ground to the sceptics and that this only tempted them to push for more. He reluctantly accepted the suggestion of holding a referendum before entry to the single currency but that was his line in the sand. He went out of his way to let it be known that he would not remain in a Eurosceptic Cabinet.

If Major complained that Clarke's aides leaked to the media damaging stories about his 'weakness' in standing up to the sceptics, Clarke also felt aggrieved at the briefing from Number Ten and Central Office that the government was on the brink of ruling out membership of the single currency and on that he was the single obstacle to the change.[39] Some PMQs sessions were a trial for Major when news would arrive at the last moment of some 'off-message' remarks of Clarke. Number Ten's Private Secretary on Economic Affairs, Moira Wallace, was often in the dark about the latest nuance of single currency policy.[40] Norma Major, a growing influence on her husband during his premiership, became increasingly critical of Clarke, whom she regarded as perverse and obstructive.[41] Some of this irritation emerges in John Major's memoirs, *John Major: An Autobiography*, published two years after he left office.

Major had good relations with Douglas Hurd at the Foreign Office. The two men worked closely together during Major's twelve month spell at the Treasury when Hurd was Foreign Secretary, breakfasting regularly and keeping in close contact over European matters. Hurd had spent over three years at Number Ten under Heath, and both realised the importance of good personal relationships as well as agreement between the Prime Minister and Foreign Secretary. Hurd wrote the manifesto for the 1994 Euro elections, and apart from some differences of emphasis over the role of British troops in Bosnia and on qualified majority voting in the EU the two men agreed in public on all essential issues. Hurd kept private his occasional doubts about John Major's leadership style.[42] Hurd was also aware that Major was not only becoming more sceptical about membership of the single currency but was also under immense party pressure to reject British membership. Hurd canvassed the idea of a referendum on the single currency at an early stage as a device to keep the party together and his decision to step down was inspired in part by a wish to make life easier for John Major.

Like most Prime Ministers, Major was concerned to co-ordinate the work of government departments and attract a favourable media. In June 1990 John Wakeham had resurrected for Mrs Thatcher the old Liaison Committee of Number Ten and Central Office staff which had earlier operated under Lord Whitelaw. Under Major this task was at first given to a 'Number Twelve Committee', so called because it convened at the Chief Whip's office in Twelve Downing Street. It met at 8.15 daily to plan the themes for the day and the week ahead, and consisted of key Number Ten staff (Chaplin and Hogg), staff from Central Office, the Leaders of the House of Commons and House of Lords (John MacGregor and Lord Waddington), Chris Patten and John Wakeham, and Gus O'Donnell for items which were clearly governmental. This body continued after the 1992 election but over time the Number Twelve Committee became too large and overlapped with EDCP, a committee which was established in February 1995 and chaired by David Hunt, Chancellor of the Duchy of Lancaster, to co-ordinate policy and presentation. Hunt, on his own admission, lacked authority to pull rank with heavyweights like Heseltine and Clarke, and personally advocated the appointment of a more senior figure to the post. John Major had already decided that he wanted a Deputy Prime Minister to bring politics and presentation together – and the obvious candidate was Michael Heseltine.

Immediately after the 1995 leadership contest a new EDCP was established which effectively merged the two bodies. Michael Heseltine, newly appointed as Deputy Prime Minister, took the chair and it met daily, Monday to Thursday. It consisted of the Chief Whip and Leaders of the Commons and the Lords as well as key Number Ten and Central Office staff. The Cabinet Office provided the secretaries for government business; when the agenda turned to party matters they made a point of downing their pencils! Despite the new structure, and the presence of the 'biggest hitter' in the Cabinet, the body failed to promote sufficient 'good news' stories, particularly about the economy, in part because of successful Labour initiatives and in part because there were so many 'own goals' resulting from party divisions on Europe and scandals affecting Conservative MPs.[43] Labour and Conservative rebels, not the government, controlled the media agenda during the 1992–97 Parliament.

In view of the many troubles besetting the government it is not surprising that John Major had difficulty in pulling rank with colleagues. Even in 1991, attempts by the Policy Unit to draw up a White Paper on the Citizen's Charter struggled against the reluctance of departments to suggest ideas.[44] But at least the scheme took off. In a radio discussion in September 1998, Jonathan Hill, a former Political Secretary, may have exaggerated a little when he said that in the last two years of the Major administration messages from Number Ten to departments would form the basis for a discussion rather than an instruction for action.[45] Compared with the Citizen's Charter, 'Back to Basics' and Norman Blackwell's five themes had little impact.

John Major's circle of influentials is traced in three different figures in the Appendix, covering three phases of his leadership. Apart from Chris Patten in the first period and Heseltine at the end it is remarkable how much he relied upon his Number Ten officials and political staff (see Appendix II).

The time most recent Prime Ministers have spent in the House of Commons has been a casualty of the growing pressure of other demands on their diaries. Both Heath and Mrs Thatcher eventually lost touch with backbenchers – there were complaints about the lack of invitations to Downing Street or the little time that they spent in the House of Commons Tea Room – although it is true that divisions over policy and massive electoral unpopularity were more important in sowing the seeds of disaffection with both. Similar complaints were made about John Major. But in the 1992 Parliament he faced a problem which had not bothered Mrs Thatcher and indeed would not bother his successor: the lack of an assured majority, particularly on European legislation. As a result he had to make plans to head off possible defeats.

Major spent lengthy periods with parliamentary business managers trying to get the Maastricht Treaty approved without making too many concessions to party rebels. The ERM exit and then the announcement of pit closures a month later encouraged dissent early in the 1992 Parliament and it continued later. The fragile parliamentary position meant that Major's relations with the Whips' Office and the Chief Whip were important, all the more so as the majority was whittled away and because of Major's own whippish background and instincts.

Richard Ryder was appointed Chief Whip after he had helped John Major in his successful leadership campaign in 1990. The two had a good relationship until late 1992 when, like so much else, it deteriorated under the strain of a worsening political and parliamentary situation. The Whips' Office was unhappy about the hostages to fortune in Major's 'Back to Basics' speech at the 1993 conference. The difficulties of passing the Maastricht Bill had already taken their toll and Ryder was engaged for the rest of his time as Chief Whip in crisis management of scandals and trying to avoid defeats in Parliament. In late 1994 his warning that there was no parliamentary majority for the privatisation of the Post Office effectively killed off the plan. Ryder was originally not a hawk for removing the whip from the eight persistent rebels who defied a three line whip in November 1994. Over time, however, he and his fellow whips had hardened their attitudes because of the havoc the rebels caused; he was only prepared to restore the whip if they gave clear pledges of loyalty in future. Major, however, wanted them back and an unhappy Ryder sent a perfunctory letter to the rebels on 24 April 1995 informing them that they were back in the fold. The whipless eight then held a crowing press conference showing no signs of repentance. Parliamentary management was unheroically about avoiding occasions when the government would lose a vote and was often at the mercy of a handful of discontented backbenchers.

Major made more parliamentary statements than Margaret Thatcher, largely because he was reporting on more international summits. He also spoke in debates more frequently, but again this was partly dictated by circumstances – the Gulf War, debates on Europe, Northern Ireland, and BSE. He made only a handful of interventions in debates and no closing speeches after becoming Prime Minister.

A time-consuming routine was the preparation for the 15-minute sessions of Prime Minister's Questions on Tuesday and Thursday afternoons. The Private Secretary and Jonathan Hill (until the end of 1994) or George Bridges (Assistant Political Secretary from 1994) would start work on likely questions and responses the previous evening and put a note into Major's overnight box. This would be followed by a meeting between 9 and 9.30 am on the Tuesday and Thursday with the Private Secretaries, the Political Secretary (Jonathan Hill, then Howell James), the head of the Policy Unit and the PPS. Major usually began the meeting by saying: 'We must get through this quickly.' He would then go through the notes and the press digest. According to Howell James in 1996: 'He knows Blair very well and 99 per cent is correct about what Blair will go on. Blair's main concern is the media; he wants to get on the news bulletins on Tuesdays and Thursdays.' Hill or Bridges and the Private Secretary would then retire and draw up a list of responses. The PPS would also talk to Conservative MPs who had put down questions and other staff would try to anticipate the supplementary questions which Labour MPs would ask. Major would be presented with the Red Book of questions and answers to work on over lunch, which he would take with Hill or Bridges and the Parliamentary Private Secretary. He and his team would leave Downing Street for the Commons at 3.05 pm. After the fifteen-minute session the team would adjourn to the Prime Minister's room and review what had worked well and what had not. Then the Press Secretary would come from the Press Gallery and suggest what follow-up steps should be taken as a result of the exchanges. By about 4 pm the team would head back to Downing Street.

In retrospect, the staff felt that the demands on their time were disproportionate to any possible benefits from PMQs, even though most of the work was done in the departments and often consisted of updating information. For each session, they had to prepare around sixty briefs so that Major could cope with most eventualities. In early 1993 serious consideration was given to reducing PMQs to one weekly thirty minute session. In the end, Major was persuaded that the status quo provided a twice-weekly platform to rally his MPs. Mrs Thatcher had also rejected a similar suggestion.

On Europe the mood of the party changed after the 1992 election. A number of sceptics had suppressed their distaste for Maastricht in 1991 out of loyalty to Major and the need for unity before the general election. After the general election and the influx of new Conservative members, many of them 'Thatcher's children' on the Eurosceptic right of the party, the whips had a battle on their hands. The Danish rejection of Maastricht in a referendum in June 1992 only emboldened the critics. It encouraged over a hundred Conservative MPs to sign an Early Day Motion calling for a sceptic's 'fresh start' in the EU. The treaty had originally been sold to the party as a negotiating success that reversed the 'centralising logic' (Hurd) of the EU, with the treaty opt-outs and references to subsidiarity as safeguards of national independence. Critics now pointed to the Danish example and warned of the integrationist thrust of the treaty. Philip Stephens' justified conclusion was that 'Each hour of the Maastricht debate sapped the authority of John Major's administration.'[46]

After the Danish referendum Major, on the whips' advice, decided to delay trying to pass the Bill. Both Hurd and he knew that failure to pass it would involve their resignations. The eventual passage in the spring and summer of 1993 was time-consuming, often humiliating, as the rebels held out for concessions, and gained the government little credit. The popular tide, encouraged by the Eurosceptic press, had turned: the EU was unpopular with voters or it left them cold.

Troubles with the party in Parliament increased over the government's acceptance of the recommendations of the Nolan Committee on Standards in Public Life in 1995 to curb MPs receiving cash for speaking and asking questions in the Commons on behalf of outside interests. The restriction on such activities and the requirement that payments be disclosed infuriated a number of Major's MPs. Heseltine was forced to abandon the proposed privatisation of the Post Office when it was clear that party rebels would deny it a majority. Continued heavy losses in all tests of electoral opinion – local elections, by-elections, European elections, opinion polls – further depressed party morale and weakened Major's position. His PPSs, Graham Bright and then John Ward, were criticised in the Commons for not reflecting MPs' disillusion with Major, and in Number Ten for not defending Major in the Tea Rooms with more authority and for not having a wide enough range of contacts. It was hard to know *whom* to blame: but on one point, everyone agreed. They were in a deep hole.

John Major resembled Clement Attlee and Alec Douglas-Home in representing an anti-rhetorical style of public speaking. His aides commented in the early months that he wanted to lower the 'noise level' compared to Mrs Thatcher; his tone in public speaking was not triumphalist but almost conversational. Speechwriting sessions were briefer and more orderly than they had been under his predecessor. For the run of election and party conference speeches Nick True from the Policy Unit was the key draftsman until his departure in 1995, and then the role was played by George Bridges. They worked with Sarah Hogg and Jonathan Hill and, from the 1991 party conference onwards, the playwright Ronald Millar. In the Private Office, the Economic Affairs Private Secretary, Moira Wallace, was a main speechwriter. The statements on summits and foreign affairs were drafted (with input from the FCO) by Major's successive Foreign Affairs Private Secretaries, Powell, Wall, Lyne, then Holmes.

Major liked to insert anecdotes in his speeches, based on his own experience, and was at his best as an off-the-cuff speaker. Perhaps his most remarkable public performance was an unscripted address defending his 'wait and see' policy on the European single currency at a press conference on 16 April during the 1997 general election. Ronnie Millar, who had worked as a speechwriter for Heath and Thatcher, regarded Major not only as the easiest to work with but also as the most natural speaker of the three.

John Major possessed a highly developed sense of his own style and of how a British Prime Minister should present himself. For this reason he often rejected speech drafts which contained what he regarded as excessively colourful phrases or personal attacks on political opponents. He also regularly turned down hard-hitting political advertisements and posters from the party's advertising agency, M. and C. Saatchi, in the 1997 election campaign. To the despair – usually tinged with respect – of his staff, he found many modern public relations and presentational devices distasteful in politics.

By the end of his premiership it is difficult to think of any senior politician, apart from Tony Newton, with whom John Major enjoyed a close working relationship, certainly none as good as with Patten or Hurd. Over time he came to despair of his Cabinet, he was fed up with much of his parliamentary party and the press was largely dismissive. The sense of being under siege in Downing Street was similar to the mood in the last weeks of the Heath and Callaghan governments. During a meeting in Number Ten, to discuss the forthcoming 1994 Euro-elections, he asked: 'Will we ever get out of the trenches?'

Major was more at ease with his private and political staff than with the party in Parliament. ('I love the party in the country but I do not love the parliamentary party,' he said to one aide near the end.)[47] There was an inner circle of Hogg, Hill, O'Donnell, Allan, Bright, True and Wall in the period 1991 to 1994 and thereafter Allan, James, Ward, Lyne, Holmes and Blackwell. It was to these, early in the morning or late at night, that he would sound off about the disloyalty of Cabinet and parliamentary colleagues, the backbiting from Mrs

Thatcher and her entourage, and the unfairness of the press. One rather laid-back Cabinet minister, exposed to one of these sessions, complained to an aide about 'John's emotional vampiricism'.[48] Colleagues and aides were expected on these occasions to empathise with and lift John Major's spirits.

Major appointed an extra ('Assistant') Political Secretary and a PPS to liaise with Conservative peers and MEPs. There was also discussion in Number Ten about reducing PMQs to a weekly session, holding question and answer sessions with the public and increasing the Cabinet Office's 'enforcing' role in Whitehall. Nothing came of them. Blair took such steps early on in government. One lesson seems to be that such steps are best taken when a Prime Minister is strong. When his authority has been weakened, such steps will not compensate. Few of Major's staff had any sense of his Number Ten being a powerhouse and it is difficult to think of any staffing or institutional arrangements which could have compensated for the loss of political authority.

The current perception of Major as a Prime Minister is that for much of the time he was a victim of circumstances, unlucky, often on the back foot. In spite of Cabinet reshuffles, reorganisations in Number Ten and policy relaunches, short-term crises usually took over. The first sixteen months of office were dominated by the Gulf War, the Maastricht Treaty, replacing the hated poll tax and contesting the 1992 general election. All were opportunities but also potential pitfalls. It is to Major's credit that he succeeded in all of them. But the 1992 election victory and the personal mandate proved broken-backed. Not only did it soon emerge that he lacked an assured majority for the Parliament, but he had to cope with pressing difficulties. His government never recovered from the circumstances of the British exit from the ERM and the long-running divisions over Maastricht. His Eurosceptic critics in the party and the press felt vindicated by the ERM experience. The passage of the Maastricht Treaty during 1993 proved humiliating, as the government had to make concessions to rebels and on one occasion to stake its life to pass the bill. In 1995 Major took the unprecedented step of resigning the party leadership and challenging his MPs to back him or sack him. But victory in the contest did little to buttress his authority. By-elections and local elections continued to be disastrous and the party's standings in opinion polls were at an all-time low. The handling of BSE or 'mad cow disease' and the revelations of government incompetence dominated 1996. Throughout the Parliament and during the 1997 election campaign there was the steady drip-drip effect of financial and sex scandals affecting Conservative MPs.

Europe divided the party irreconcilably. Some of the Eurosceptic and right wing of the party were impervious to appeals for party unity. Much of the Conservative-supporting press wanted John Major replaced. His positioning on European issues and the single currency was designed to prevent an outright party split, but it only diminished him in the eyes of both sides.

By the time John Major called a general election in 1997 he was leading a divided and dispirited party and his own authority was in tatters. The party suffered its worst election defeat of the century. The lesson was not lost on his successor in Number Ten. Tony Blair understood some of the constraints on Major, although many of his political aides were dismissive of Major's conduct of the premiership and of the way Number Ten had performed. He was determined not only to achieve but to demonstrate his mastery of his own party and his grip over government from Number Ten.

It is doubtful that a reconfigured Number Ten or a new Prime Minister's Department could have done more to help John Major in his travails. To take one illustration, in Norman Blackwell, head of the Policy Unit between 1995 and 1997, Major had one of the most experienced planners and strategic thinkers to hold that job in our period. Yet his work bore little fruit because other factors combined to undermine his long-term thinking to keep Major on course.

CHAPTER NINE

Tony Blair: Preparations

AN ASSESSMENT OF Tony Blair's premiership in his first forty months must necessarily be an interim one. He and his aides have frequently stated that the intention is to serve at least two full terms, to implement a planned programme, and the first year or two as Prime Minister is not always a good prediction of what follows, as Harold Wilson, Ted Heath, Mrs Thatcher and John Major discovered. Already, however, Blair has shown that his premiership is distinctive in substantially increasing the size of his political staff, adopting a proactive approach to communications, and creating structures which are designed to facilitate greater co-ordination of policy from the centre. This chapter considers Blair's preparations for office, in which reforming the Labour Party and using the mass media were crucial. Indeed, his leadership of the party in opposition provides the blueprint for much of the Blair style of operating in government. This has had strengths and weaknesses.

When he entered Number Ten as Prime Minister on 2 May 1997 Tony Blair was the first incumbent since his Labour predecessor Ramsay MacDonald in 1924 not to have had any prior government experience. Indeed, only one of Blair's ministers (John Morris) had served in a Cabinet before. The reason for the personal and collective inexperience was that Labour had been in opposition for the previous eighteen years. Since entering the Commons in 1983, Blair and many colleagues had known only the life of opposition.

But Blair also began with some advantages. A new Prime Minister, particularly following a general election success, usually starts out in a strong position. The scale of Labour's election victory in May 1997 was historic, and was seen by many commentators and colleagues as a personal endorsement of the leader. Surveys pointed to a 'Blair effect', the extra voting support which the party gained from having him as leader. Labour's general election campaign concentrated on him, his opinion poll ratings were remarkably high and much of the media treated him favourably as a figure apart from his party and Shadow Cabinet.[1]

Three factors, all apparent in his leadership in opposition, have shaped Blair's approach to the premiership. One is his view of political leadership. Since being elected party leader in July 1994 in succession to John Smith, he talked much about the need for a government which would make 'tough choices' and the clear direction which he would provide. This view resonated with many voters, tired of the internal party divisions and weaknesses of John Major's government. A second is his 'project' of so-called modernisation, first of the Labour Party and then, once in power, of the constitution and public services. Forging a 'new' Labour Party, reforming it from top to bottom, was the key, first stage of the Blair 'project'.[2] A third is his confidence in the approach which had brought him success as a party leader and national figure; in opposition he had found a style with which he was comfortable and which worked and impressed the voters.

Beyond wanting to import his own trusted aides to Downing Street and concentrating on a few clear policy objectives, Blair seems to have given little thought to the precise organisation of Number Ten. Unlike Ted Heath he was not very interested in changing the machinery of government and, unlike Harold Wilson (pre-1964), he did not talk much in advance about how he would operate in Downing Street. Journalists and party figures who raised queries about future arrangements in Number Ten were impatiently referred to his chief of staff, Jonathan Powell, who had done a great deal more forward planning than was public knowledge. (As a former diplomat, Powell, unlike many close aides to incoming premiers, had some knowledge of the inner structures of Whitehall, gleaned not least from his brother, Charles, Mrs Thatcher's *éminence grise*.) Blair, not wanting to tempt fate, did not get involved in planning too closely. But, like Wilson over thirty years earlier, he wanted to make his Number Ten 'a power-house' so that he could make his impression on government. As leader of the party in opposition he had got his own way on virtually all issues and debates and had successfully marginalised most of his party critics. As Prime Minister he wanted no less.

In opposition, Blair had sat in the Shadow Cabinets of Neil Kinnock (shadowing Energy, then Employment) and John Smith (shadowing the Home Office). The experience seems to have taught him how not to run a political operation, let alone a government. His own Shadow Cabinet was not a decision-making forum. It included people he had not selected and would not if the choice had been his. He did not want to listen to the views of people who knew little about the matter under discussion. Colleagues had no doubt that in government he would emphasise his personal leadership above ideas of collegiality, but they did not quite know how – though there was more than a hint that he would follow Mrs Thatcher's pre-premiership dictum that she would not 'waste time' on internal debates. As a would-be Prime Minister he appreciated the advice and perspective of Roy Jenkins, a former Labour Chancellor of the Exchequer and Home Secretary and until late 1997 Liberal Democrat leader in the Lords. He also had discussions on foreign policy with retired Whitehall mandarins, including Michael Butler (former Ambassador to the EC), David Hannay (former Ambassador to the UN), Robin Renwick (former Ambassador to Washington), and on other matters with the Cabinet Secretary, Robin Butler, who was determined to make a success of any transition in government.

It is important to realise how far politicians' styles of leadership are reactive, despite their claims to be drawing primarily on their own personal beliefs and life experience as the key shapers of their thinking. To Mrs Thatcher, for example, both Ted Heath and Harold Wilson were, in their different ways, negative models. John Major was a contrast to Mrs Thatcher and widely applauded at first for being so. Later criticism of him as weak and indecisive, unable or unwilling to give a clear lead on European issues because of party divisions, provided an additional incentive for Blair to be as unlike Major as possible. It is true that Major was hampered throughout by the attacks from Mrs Thatcher and her acolytes, as well as by large sections of the Conservative press, and the open disdain with which he was treated by party rebels. Although Major could not help his lack of an assured majority in the 1992 Parliament, Blair regarded him as a Prime Minister who lacked authority, in large part because he failed to give leadership. In a parliamentary exchange on 24 April 1995, about Major's decision to restore the party whip to persistent rebels, he boasted: 'There is one big difference. I lead my party. He follows his.' He wanted to be seen as a man who led from the front – successfully appealing to party members to revise the party's Clause IV, distancing the party from the trade union leaders, and slapping down party critics (usually those on the left). In contrast to the massive media coverage afforded to Conservative rebels, Labour dissenters were often marginalised by an aggressive and effective Labour media-management operation. For Blair, being seen to be in charge was as important as actually being in charge. He knew that the authority and public standing of previous Labour leaders had been undermined by internal dissent and damaging leaks by party critics.

Blair also reacted against features of 'old' Labour which he thought weakened the party leader. His project of modernising Labour involved fundamental reform of the party's policies, institutions and ethos to take account of social, economic and political changes in the country. Building on Kinnock's party reforms, the role of Conference, the NEC and constituency parties were altered to make Labour more disciplined and streamlined, and to facilitate Blair's personal leadership. Under him, the party gave presentation and media management a higher priority in order to respond to the opportunities and threats posed by the media's continuous political coverage. Operating in a culture of inner-party democracy, most previous Labour Party leaders had had to possess consensus-building skills, taking account of what the annual party conference or the trade unions would accept. The result had often been fudged policies and Cabinet appointments balanced between left and right factions – all executed in the interests of party unity. Blair, however, regarded the appeasement of activists and bargaining with the NEC and trade union leaders as incompatible with his idea of decisive leadership and having a clear 'message'. The party should say what it meant and mean what it said. Blair's impatience with the NEC and Shadow Cabinet meant that he relied heavily on his personal aides and some supportive shadow ministers who were committed to the modernising project. They knew his mind and shared his ideas of what needed to be done. Those who were not 'on message' were ruthlessly sidelined. This style prompted early charges within the party of Blair's 'control freakery', charges which grew steadily over time'.

Labour's policy commitments were presented as Blair's pledges to the electorate. The successful ballots of party members to reform Clause IV of the party constitution in April 1995 and approval of the draft manifesto in October 1996 were his initiatives and effectively by-passed the Conference and party activists, always more to the left than mainstream party supporters. It was a plebiscitary style of leadership, in which the leader directly sought approval from party members, without the mediation of union leaders or party institutions. Reforming Clause IV, a classic symbol of 'old' Labour, was also a fundamental statement of Blair's seriousness about changing the party. In 1995, Blair decided to appoint Donald Dewar as Chief Whip, breaking with the tradition of leaving it to election by Labour MPs. Complaints from PLP or Shadow Cabinet members about the influence of Blair's advisers and speed at which decisions were made by Blair and Brown – with associated lack of consultation – were swept aside. Some compared the style to that of a 'Leninist vanguard' which operated by *fait accompli*. He exploited to the hilt Labour's hunger for election victory and perceptions that he was the party's main electoral asset.

Blair also used 'special events' like press conferences, major speeches, policy launches and seminars to promote new policies, gain media coverage and put his own impress on the party. The idea that there was a 'New Labour' party was advanced relentlessly in major speeches at party conferences, in his 'Mais' lecture on the party's commitment to a 'sound' economic policy in May 1995, in an address to News International executives in June 1995, and in a 'stakeholder' speech in Singapore in January 1966. The approach would be carried over to his premiership.

By the time of the general election in 1997, Labour's image had been transformed. In contrast with 1992, voters now saw it as much more united, trustworthy, economically competent and representative of Britain as a whole than the Conservative Party. Surveys showed that Blair was viewed as a strong leader. His authority in the party and his self-confidence were further enhanced as general election endorsement came from traditionally Conservative newspapers and even from right-wing commentators such as Paul Johnson.

*   *   *

Blair attracted fellow reformers who also wished to modernise the party. Power increasingly rested with the leader's office and associates in whom he invested authority. Significantly, many of these were neither members of the NEC nor, with a few exceptions – notably Gordon Brown – in the Shadow Cabinet. The 'inner core elite', whose influence derived from their proximity and loyalty to the leader in the late 1980s, naturally aroused envy in others.[3]

One of his staff spoke privately in December 1997 about Blair having executed a 'coup d'état' over the party in 1994 and about how he would run a centralised government to achieve his objectives: 'There was never any intention of having collective Cabinet government if Tony was to have the policies he wanted. As in opposition, he would have a centralised operation. It was as simple as that.'[4]

A key figure to Blair was the Shadow Chancellor, Gordon Brown, a long-standing ally and fellow moderniser. Brown was the more senior of the two and had been widely regarded as a likely future successor to John Smith as party leader. When Smith suddenly died of a heart attack in May 1994, however, Blair had become the frontrunner. Brown's decision not to contest the leadership and allow Blair a clear run as the 'moderniser' candidate, may have left the latter in his debt.[5] The two continued to work closely together on policy and party reform and election preparations, and Brown's announcements in early 1997 that a future Labour government would not increase marginal rates of income tax and would accept Conservative spending plans for the first two years in the next Parliament, proved crucial to overturning views that Labour was still a 'tax and spend' party, the charge that had damaged it so badly in 1992.

The recall of Peter Mandelson was an important statement of how Blair intended to lead the party and of the kind of party he wanted. Mandelson had been the party's Director of Communications between 1985 and 1990 and a Labour MP since 1992. He had been closely involved in Kinnock's policy changes and party reforms in the 1980s, and was the main force behind the party's adoption of modern media techniques of campaigning. When Kinnock departed after the 1992 election defeat, Mandelson was relegated to the sidelines under Smith. Although disliked by many Labour MPs and Shadow ministers – but equally liked and admired by others, including Blair – he re-emerged to become a key member in Blair's team, advising on presentation and strategy. His decision to back Blair's bid for the party leadership in 1994 earned him the lasting enmity of Gordon Brown who regarded it as an act of treachery. In early 1996 he was appointed to the pivotal job of head of Labour's general election planning team.[6]

Another moderniser to be recalled from exile after John Smith's death was Philip Gould, a campaign strategist who had also been closely involved in the 1987 and 1992 general elections. He was given charge of opinion polling, conducted 'focus groups' for the party and advised Blair on political strategy and 'positioning'. The leak of his strategy memo, *The Unfinished Revolution*, to Blair in September 1995 confirmed critics' complaints that Blair was a centraliser, bent on transforming the party. Gould's advice chimed strongly with Blair's own convictions, that the party should have a single chain of command, with authority leading directly to the leader, central control of party communications and should distance itself from the trade unions whose influence in the party should lessen. As part of what he termed a 'unitary command' party Gould urged that Blair should be the ultimate source of campaign authority and make a major statement of his 'New Labour' vision. In spite of attacks on Gould (and Mandelson) from those who did not want to see their beloved Labour Party 'modernised', Blair did not dissent in public or in private from Gould's leaked memo. In fact it accurately anticipated much of the structure and style of New Labour.[7] Gould was also a strong advocate of Blair declaring outright that Labour had changed. He reasoned that if Labour was to convince key voters that it was new, then the changes should be proclaimed boldly and not achieved by stealth.

Gould had worked on and been influenced by Clinton's victory in the 1992 US presidential election, so reversing a series of Democratic presidential election defeats. Clinton had used professional communication techniques to project a 'new' Democratic party, had stood apart from some of the party's traditional pressure groups, and presented the party as 'new'. The Democrats had experienced many of Labour's electoral problems. They were perceived as a party for the poor and the disadvantaged, not of the successful or those who wanted to get ahead. Blair and Brown had also learnt lessons from Clinton's success. Labour had to accept that the working class was now a minority and that more people thought in terms of themselves and their families. The party should therefore reassure the target 'working middle class' voters that it would not threaten their living standards by having 'tax and spend' policies, take steps to show that it had transformed itself, and use modern communication techniques to project its new identity.

Blair appointed as his Press Secretary Alastair Campbell, political editor of the *Today* newspaper and before that of the *Daily Mirror*. A close friend, he drafted some of Blair's early speeches as leader, including the one introducing the 'New Labour' theme at the 1994 party conference. He was also crucial in cultivating the Murdoch-owned tabloids and weaning them off their traditional support for the Conservative Party. His mission was considerably eased by much of the press's disillusion with, and even contempt for, Major and their wish to push the Conservative government into pursuing a more robustly Eurosceptical line.

The New Labour project relied heavily on a highly professional approach to political communications. Policy initiatives were closely linked with presentation: the latter was not an 'add-on'. Communications were carefully targeted at key voters via selected media outlets (particularly national papers), controlled and co-ordinated by the leader's office. Success in this operation required elaborate preparation and co-ordination, deciding on the appropriate publicity format and media outlets, pre- and post-event 'spinning' to reporters, to ensure that the story was prominently covered and interpreted in a preferred manner. The objective was to get the media to report Labour's agenda on Labour's terms and to put party critics and the opposition on the back foot. It also involved 'rubbishing' or marginalising internal party critics who were, in a telling phrase, 'off-message'.[8] More positively, Philip Gould has explained:

> . . . you must always seek to gain and keep momentum, or it will pass immediately to your opponent. Gaining momentum means dominating the news agenda, entering the news cycle at the earliest possible time, and repeatedly re-entering it, with stories and initiatives so that subsequent news coverage is set on your terms.[9]

In January 1995, Jonathan Powell resigned his post as a diplomat at the British Embassy in Washington to head Blair's office. As Chief of Staff, his responsibility was to ensure that decisions taken informally or by committees were actually implemented, and to supervise the arrangements for the transition to government. Another key, if more junior, figure to join was David Miliband, recently secretary of a left-of-centre Commission on Social Justice, who became Blair's policy adviser and helper with speeches. Son of the far-left academic and writer Ralph Miliband, he had built up a formidable range of links with centre-left academics and intellectuals. Miliband and Powell also convened a so-called Policy Group of sympathetic intellectuals and policy specialists to discuss themes and policies close to the New Labour project.

Sally Morgan moved from her post as Campaigns Director in party headquarters under John Smith to become head of party liaison in Blair's office. Although a moderniser, she constantly urged the impatient leader to take time to consult and carry the party. She regularly talked to or, according to others, 'fixed', trade unionist members on the NEC, key union leaders, and the party General Secretary, Tom Sawyer, on Blair's behalf. Anji Hunter, a friend since their schooldays, was Blair's long-serving executive secretary, who arranged his diary and organised the arrangements for his political events and tours. She is credited with shrewd political instincts, speaks frankly to Blair in private, and is described as 'Tony's line to middle England'. Kate Garvey acted as secretary to a diary meeting convened on Fridays by Powell, to plan the leader's schedule. Other regular attenders were Campbell, Hunter and Miliband.

These were 'Blair's people'. They were young (an average age of under 40) and strong-minded. They shared his commitment to New Labour, they had worked closely together in opposition, and they would move from Millbank Tower (the election campaign headquarters) with Blair into Number Ten Downing Street. They co-operated well but the feuds and tensions between Brown and Mandelson were carried in the press and, later, in their biographies. Blair regularly discussed key issues individually with Brown, Mandelson and Campbell. He wanted to make up his own mind and not be presented with 'pre-cooked' recommendations. The last two and Gould joined the leader every Monday and Thursday for collective discussions on strategy.[10] Blair's private office was, for a British party leader in opposition, large. It consisted of over twenty staff, five of whom were responsible for media liaison under Campbell,[11] and they had a dismissive attitude to Major's performance as Prime Minister. Most also knew that their careers were closely linked to the leader's fortunes. They were determined to be strategic, to shape events, to be proactive in dealing with the media, and to create a strong machine in Number Ten. In the three years up to and including the 1997 general election campaign they demonstrated a mastery of modern communications, to target voters, focus on themes and issues, and stay 'on message'. Achieving this had required discipline and acceptance in the party of the authority of Blair and his staff. But would this 'Millbank model' and its heavy emphasis on presentation, including the reliance on disciplined and repeated spinning of a core message and rapid rebuttal of any Conservative claims, be successfully transplanted to Whitehall and Westminster when it had responsibilities for government?

Before 1 May 1997 contacts between Blair's office in opposition and Whitehall about a transition to government had been the most advanced since the existing conventions were originally drawn up in 1963 (they were named, after the Prime Minister from 1963 to 1964, the 'Douglas-Home conventions'). As a rule, contacts between the opposition party and the senior Civil Service are held in what is expected to be the last year of the Parliament. Neil Kinnock had been so impressed with the Labour/Civil Service contacts before the 1992 general election, that he had asked that discussions should start sooner next time. Major agreed to the request.

In the British Embassy in Washington, Jonathan Powell had learned much from observing at first hand the shortcomings of President Clinton's first few months in the White House. Assuming responsibility for arranging Blair's transition to Downing Street, he convened a small group of sympathisers to plan staffing and machinery of government issues. This included Lady (Tessa) Blackstone (a Labour peer and Principal of Birkbeck College), Lady (Liz) Symons (General Secretary of the senior civil servants' First Division Association), Charles Clarke (who had headed Neil Kinnock's office and liaised with Robin Butler over the transitional arrangements in 1992), William Plowden (an authority on Whitehall), and two retired mandarins, Geoffrey Holland and Nick Monck. In January 1997, Powell began substantive discussions about Number Ten staffing, room allocation, titles and arrangements (for example, the switch to weekly rather than biweekly PMQs and an

Order in Council to recognise his political role. A 1979 Order in Council had limited advisors to giving advice to civil servants. The new Order removed this restriction for Powell and Campbell; the implication was that they could give instructions, as well as wider questions on machinery of government with Robin Butler, the Cabinet Secretary, and Alex Allan, the Principal Private Secretary. When matters could not be resolved between Butler and Powell, then Tony Blair was called in. These discussions were confidential and remain the only talks that a Cabinet Secretary and Principal Private Secretary can hold which they do not report to the Prime Minister. Blair's office also organised training weekends for Shadow ministers at Templeton College, Oxford, and opportunities to talk with ex-civil servants. However, none of the so-called 'Big Four' – Blair, Brown, Cook and Prescott – attended these sessions. Some Shadow Ministers held discussions with senior officials with whom they might work in the future but others, to Blair's regret, did not. Both Robin Butler and Tony Blair kept a tight rein on what was discussed and all policy decisions of the Shadow Minister had to be checked with Blair's office in advance.

Blair's performance in opposition gave clues to the kind of prime ministership he would run. Political strategy had been decided in his office, working closely with his aides and with Gordon Brown. Policy had not been evolved through the Shadow Cabinet or party committees but through his office and his bilateral sessions with Shadow ministers. Party unity was a major and continuing consideration because internal divisions were a gift for an adversarial media. Party discipline and central control of communications were regarded as essential if presentation was to be effective. More than any Prime Minister in our period Blair and his senior aides would enter office with a very clear idea of what they wanted to do in Number Ten.

Just as the party institutions had been squared in opposition, so Blair expected Whitehall departments to respond to his initiatives. The mood of much of the senior Civil Service before 1 May 1997 was similar to that at the end of the Conservative government in 1964 and of the Labour government in 1979. They had become tired and frustrated with the internal divisions in the government party and the lack of an assured majority in the Commons. They looked forward to the election of a government with a clear majority and, on balance, they wanted a change.

CHAPTER TEN

Tony Blair
(May 1997–)

FEW OF LABOUR'S new appointees had been inside Number Ten before 2 May, while Blair had been in the building only once – in November 1996 to attend an official dinner for President Clinton. 'We were strangers in the building. There was no point in asking anybody else where I should go, for they were as ignorant as I was,' said one adviser.[1] Another spoke of 'a collective view that we only wanted to enter Number Ten in our own right'.[2] Advice from staff who had worked in Number Ten for Callaghan was of limited value because over the preceding two decades Whitehall had changed much, under the impact of Thatcher's challenges to the Civil Service culture, the privatisation measures and the 'Next Steps' programme. And Blair's party was very different from that of Wilson and Callaghan; it was New Labour.

Changes of government in Britain are accomplished with brutal speed. Typically, of the key Number Ten advisers only a handful, including the Principal Private Secretary, remain from one Prime Minister to the next. Alex Allan moved in the course of a few hours from being John Major's Principal Private Secretary to being Tony Blair's, and provided much of the guidance to newcomers on the building's facilities and on how the government machine worked. Robin Butler briefed Blair on the matters requiring prompt government action. Senior staff who remained from John Major's premiership welcomed the speedy decision to reduce PMQs to one weekly session and Alastair Campbell's statement that the government's communications would be co-ordinated from the centre – in fact, this was a restatement of practice more sought after than achieved.

Blair gave key positions to those who had served him loyally as Shadow ministers when party leader, were well-known to him, and shared his vision of New Labour and ideas of how to get things done. Inevitably there were charges of 'cronyism', not least from those who felt excluded from the inner circle. The twenty-plus aides introduced in the first ten days into Downing Street were the largest number imported by any Prime Minister in history. The two most senior appointments in Number Ten were predictably given to Jonathan Powell as Chief of Staff and Alastair Campbell as Chief Press Secretary. Within days an Order in Council announced that both men could play a political role and give instructions to civil servants. The Order actually permitted up to three staff to have this right; it was assumed that it would also apply to the head of the Policy Unit, when appointed. The title of Chief of Staff was last held in Number Ten by David Wolfson under Mrs Thatcher. Wolfson's was the more limited role, over just one section of Number Ten, and even then was one of which he made little. Powell's title in contrast, redolent of the White House, reflected a new and powerful position. His remit was wide, and included duties to integrate the different units in the building, assume part of the Principal Private Secretary's role, and help Blair in his dealings with other Cabinet ministers and the party.

But where should Powell be based? David Wolfson in 1979 had had a small room to himself and had formally been part of Mrs Thatcher's Political Office. Powell agreed with Alex Allan that he needed to be close enough to know who the Prime Minister was seeing and what papers were going into his tray and that he should therefore be in the Private Office. If Powell had gone elsewhere, say to the Political Office, the Private Office might have been marginalised. It was reported in the press at the time that he would soon succeed Alex Allan as Principal Private Secretary, when the latter was transferred to be High Commissioner in Australia in the summer. This issue had been raised, and apparently resolved, before the election in private discussions between Powell, Blair and Robin Butler, but continued to be a source of concern for senior Whitehall figures during the first months of the new government. Powell remained as Chief of Staff, and Allan's title was assumed on his departure by the Private Secretary for Foreign Affairs, John Holmes, then the most senior member of the Private Office. When Holmes departed in February 1999 he was replaced by Jeremy Heywood, from within the Private Office. The Principal Private Secretary has remained responsible for relations with the Palace, for personnel and other administrative functions not appropriate for a political appointee, and for liaison with the opposition political parties in the run-up to a general election. In 1999 Pat McFadden moved from the Policy Unit to become Deputy Chief of Staff in the Private Office. In Spring 2000 he transferred to the party headquarters at Millbank Tower to help with election campaign preparations.

As Labour's election campaign supremo, Peter Mandelson had been close to Tony Blair and was given much credit for the election victory. In *The Blair Revolution*, co-authored with Roger Liddle, Mandelson had written a chapter on how Number Ten might be organised under Labour.[3] This advocated a stronger Cabinet Office, a Department of the Prime Minister and Cabinet, the creation of a body that would establish clear links between policy and presentation, and the appointment of a Number Ten Chief of Staff who would carry forward the implementation of cross-departmental policies. Some regarded the last proposal as a job remit for himself. Once in government, Mandelson was indeed made Minister Without Portfolio, based in the Cabinet Office, and given responsibility for the co-ordination and presentation of policy. Mandelson had a clear view of the role of the Cabinet Office – it was '. . . to support the Prime Minister at the centre of government' (speech, 16 September 1997). Significantly, he was not answerable to David Clark, the Cabinet minister responsible for the Cabinet Office.

Mandelson received copies of relevant Policy Unit and Cabinet Office papers and was an active member of nearly half of the Cabinet committees. More important than any of the above, however, was his closeness to Blair. He had ready access to him and his views were listened to. When he moved to the DTI in July 1998 his duties were shared between Jack Cunningham at Cabinet level who had the media-endowed title of 'enforcer', and Lord (Charlie) Falconer. The former was the public face, but his 'enforcer' title was regarded with derision in Whitehall. Falconer had been a friend of Blair's since they were young lawyers together and has emerged as a considerable figure. He is heavily involved behind the scenes in strategy, Cabinet and ad hoc committee work, PMQs, and in acting as Blair's 'fixer' between ministers.

Before becoming Chief Press Secretary Alastair Campbell had discussed the job with two of his Labour predecessors in Number Ten, Joe Haines and Tom McCaffrey. He continued his speechwriting and political advisory duties for Blair as well as carrying out the traditional Press Office role – briefing Lobby journalists twice daily and, for a time, co-ordinating the work of departmental press officers at the weekly Monday meetings. He also maintained his interest in cultivating the tabloids and arranging for ministers to place articles in the press.

Alastair Campbell, as well as some Labour ministers, complained that the Whitehall Government Information Service (GIS) was insufficiently proactive, that it failed to harmonise policy with effective presentation and that it swamped the overall strategy of the government in the flood of departmental communications. Indeed, by early 2000 all senior press officers had been replaced since May 1997. Few information officers could pass Campbell's alleged test of their competence at the job: did they know the lead stories in tomorrow's papers? In their turn, officers claimed that Campbell failed to appreciate the difference in constraints operating between opposition and government, and, more important, that the GIS's formal duty as an impartial arm of government was to supply neutral information, not politically biased statements. By the end of 1997 a number of GIS officers had resigned or were leaving, some following personality clashes with ministers. To allay Number Ten's dissatisfaction, Robin Butler agreed in September 1997 to establish a working group on the GIS under Robin Mountfield, the Cabinet Office Permanent Secretary. Its remit was to suggest ways to promote greater integration of policy and its presentation and improve the strategic coherence and co-ordination of the government's messages.

One outcome of the report was that the service was renamed 'Government Information and Communications Service'. Another development after the Mountfield report was the creation in January 1998 of the Strategic Communications Unit (SCU), accountable to the Prime Minister through the Chief Press Secretary.[4] The new body consists of eight staff, including two special advisers, both Labour sympathising journalists, and extra staff on the Number Ten website. It has introduced a new computer system, 'Agenda', which acts as a Whitehall-wide electronic diary and briefing service. The SCU tries to replicate the type of communications service Blair's people had grown used to in Millbank – co-ordination from a strong centre, the incorporation of 'key government messages' throughout all departmental communications and special events, and the planned use of a wide range of media outlets. Wednesday lunchtime is set aside for a 'grid' meeting chaired by Jonathan Powell until July 2000, when he was replaced by Lord Falconer, and attended by the main communications personnel, as well as Anji Hunter, Sally Morgan and Jeremy Heywood. It plans the 'grid' for the timing and content of all government announcements and thus tries to ensure that they reinforce the government's overall message. SCU staff liaise with the private offices and the information officers of departments about how departments can insert themselves into Number Ten's news agenda. 'We operate as a scheduling controller, giving take off and landing slots to departments,' according to one member of SCU. In a typical day the Unit will distribute some 500 pages of briefing to around 140 people across Whitehall. An example of the grid is shown on the next page. Each evening the Unit supplies an electronic fax to all ministers (about 100). It covers the line to take for the following day's political agenda and lobby note. It is also responsible for the government's 'Annual Report', another Blair innovation, launched to a mixed press in the summer of 1998. The two journalists recruited to the SCU, Philip Bassett from *The Times* and David Bradshaw from the *Daily Mirror*, help with writing ministerial speeches, press articles for ministers and white and green papers. The large number of press articles, not least by Blair himself, is a new trend, part of the government's attempt to go 'direct' to the people, unmediated by editors (see p. 282). Each department, moreover, has set up a Strategic Planning Unit, charged with handling long-term communications, as opposed to the day-to-day concerns of its press office.

RESTRICTED

15–21 May	Mon 15	Tues 16
Main News	**Disarmament team in Northern Ireland** **w/c NI Police Bill (tbc)** **Chx: speech to CPAG (1010)**	**PM: speech to CBI Annual Dinner (1930)** **Straw speech to Probation Council (1200) inc sentencing review (1530)**
Statistics	Econ Trends: CBI SME trends (Apr)	Consumer prices (Apr) ONS survey on elderly
Other Government News	00.01 Cooper: schemes to tackle teenage pregs w/c ESRC rept on racism in schools (tbc) Meacher: repts on UK climate change effects Raynsford: urban design good practice guidance Bassam/Battle/Hoey: help for fans abroad Straw: drug testing orders roll-out Met Police anti-mugging campaign Denham: £10m for heart care G8 conf on cyber-crime Boateng: On Track youth crime projects Chris Smith: library min standards plan	NHS non-med staff 00.01 Lord Rogers urban task force CSR priorities TUC High Court bid re parental leave cut-off Johnson speech to Fed of Sub-Postmasters Straw: £24m to speed up extra 5000 police OECD education rept Myners con doc on institutional investment Blackstone: dance & drama awards Howells: counterfeit roadshow (football strips) ECHR case on Heathrow night flights ECJ ruling on NHS sex discrim re pensions
Europe	Hoon/Vaz: WEU Ministerial; EP plenary (to 19)	EP: poss vote on 1998 Budget discharge; Culture Coun; Agriculture Coun (16–17)
Parliament	HoC: DSS PQs; Fur Farming Bill 2ndR HoL: Welfare Bill ctte	HoC: FCO PQs; Con debates on manufacturing & on education
Political	Beckett: reply to Liaison Ctte re select cttes (tbc)	HoL: E Comms Bill rept & Terrorism Bill ctte
General	1st Paddington inq hearing with witnesses New CRE chair Nat Fed of Sub-Postmasters conf (15–17)	Police Fed annual conf, Brighton (16–18) Tribunal decision on R18 videos rejected by BBFC US Fed Open Mkts Ctte

Weds 17	Thurs 18	Fri 19	Sat–Sun 20/1
Unemployment & av earnings (Apr) **Straw: speech to Police Fed (1200) inc complaints review & training & recruitment (1530)**	**Milburn: speech to RCS inc (tbc) medical school expansion** **Morton: SRA goals for rail franchise negotiations (tbc)**	**Milburn: action on security at special hospitals** **MCA: consultation on morning-after pill without prescription**	**UUP Council mtg (20)** **FA Cup Final (20)**
NHS in-patient & outpatient waits (Q4)	Retail sales (Apr)	Pub sec finances (Apr) CML Mortgage Survey (Apr), lending/monetary (Apr)	
Darling: national listening event re elderly, QEII Blackstone: degree benchmarks Blunkett: reduced fares for New Dealers Estelle Morris: approved consultants list Howells: counterfeit roadshow (design labels) Granatt before Public Admin Ctte re GCIS HSE: repts on stress at work & guidance to employers ETRA Ctte rept on rural affairs Stock Exchange before TSC	00.01 NAO rept on MOD property fraud Hoon: statement on major projects (poss) Locke: Criminal Defence Service plans (tbc) Prison Service performance indicators Armstrong/Falconer: Dome future shortlist (tbc) Irvine: review of tribunals (tbc) Pub Sec Prod Panel rept on NHS land sales PM: UK/South Africa Forum (18–19) Blunkett speech on under 5s Howells: counterfeit roadshow (CDs, tapes)	00.01 BMJ on MOD multiple vaccinations MOD: repts on Gulf War illness HO: figures on re-offending on curfews (tbc) Chris Smith: grants for small museums & galleries PM webcast DPM: launch trans-pennine express	00.011 IRA Ctte rept re Environment Agency (20)
Cook: to Russia inc open new embassy Development Coun (17–18); EU inflation stats	Industry Coun		EBRD, Riga (20–23)
HoC: NI PQs & PMQs Parks Bill remg stgs HoL: Tebbit debate on law & order	HoC: HMT PQs Care Bill 2ndR HoL: FS&M Bill 3rdR	HoC: Private Members' Bills inc Census	
Labour NEC ballot closes Pensions lobby	Hague speech to Police Fed annual conf (1100)	HSE: con doc on Railtrack indep safety company plan (tbc)	
UEFA Cup Final: Arsenal v. Galatasaray Ashford nurse killing/rape trail ends (or later in week)	ITC mtg re News at Ten FDA Annual Conf Zimbabwe v. England 1st Test, Lords (18–22)	Hungerford Bridge murder sentencing	Italian referendum on PR (21)

In 2000 Alistair Campbell's public role altered. He significantly scaled down his participation in the twice daily lobby meetings, leaving them to his career civil servant deputy, Godric Smith. Campbell, although a former journalist, was no admirer of the lobby and what he regarded as the trivial questions and sloppy journalism of many of its members. Tony Blair became increasingly concerned that Campbell was caught up in fighting daily battles with the press and needed to retreat from the front line so as to plan longer-term media strategy and help in election planning. In fact, Campbell was still heavily involved in day-to-day matters, though usually more in a backstairs capacity. Following the bitter personal attacks on Blair in summer 2000 from the novelist and Labour supporter Ken Follett, Campbell wrote a lengthy riposte in the *Daily Mirror*. His change of role only added to demands that, because he was playing such a public and partisan role, he should be paid by the party and not out of public funds.

Within the Number Ten Press Office, the original four Civil Service appointees, each shadowing a cluster of departments, were joined by two special advisers, Hillary Coffman, from Labour's press office, and Tim Allen, who had worked for Blair since his time as Shadow Home Secretary just before he became leader in 1994. Allen left in June 1998 and was replaced by Lance Price, recruited from the BBC. Coffman and Price briefed the media on government policy but, in contrast to the civil servants, were able to place it in a fully partisan political context. Godric Smith was appointed as deputy Press Secretary in May 1998: a civil servant, he hands over to a special adviser when questions turn to more party political topics. Some civil servants welcomed the introduction of the special advisers because it helped them to draw a sharper line between items which were party political and those which were governmental. While some of those departmental press officers who departed complained of hectoring and political pressure to 'spin' pro-government stories, others who remained welcomed the change to a more proactive media operation.

Campbell also decided, following Mountfield, to place all of his Lobby briefings on the record and to be cited by journalists as 'the Prime Minister's official spokesman', the first was an innovation previous regimes had considered. Campbell has a close relationship with the Prime Minister, even closer than that between Thatcher and Ingham, which was largely professional. 'Tony trusts Alastair's political judgment, more than anybody else's', said one insider. In fact Campbell came late to the Labour Party but his earthy and blunt style of speaking combined with his 'man in the street' views are regarded by Blair as a good guide to public opinion. Blair makes few important decisions about policy or presentation without discussing them with Campbell,[7] who has rights of attendance at virtually all Blair's meetings, including Cabinet and bilaterals with Cabinet ministers. 'Everything, after all, has a communication angle', he has been heard to remark. He was present at the final meetings between Blair and Brown on the comprehensive spending review, discussions on the July 1998 and 1999 Cabinet reshuffles, and at discussions with leaders of other parties, including Paddy Ashdown (Liberal Democrat leader until autumn 1999) and Lord Cranborne (Conservative Leader in the Lords until December 1998). Increasingly, senior media spokespeople have become involved in or present at policy decisions, in order to publicise and defend the announcements and thinking behind them.

The traditional weekly Monday 17.00 meeting of the Chief Press Secretary with the GICS officers has been abandoned and replaced by a Thursday 17.30 meeting to prepare for events and likely stories for the weekend and following week. Campbell also chairs strategy meetings to appraise overall policy direction and the progress in meeting government communication objectives. There is nothing new in the Press Secretary insisting that departmental announcements and statements and ministerial interviews be cleared in advance with Number Ten, or that communications are a crucial part of the policy process. What is new is the emphasis on central co-ordination and the particular steps taken by Campbell to achieve this. But for all the complaints from the media and politicians of 'control' by the centre, off the record briefings by ministers and their special advisers have continued. The greater the difficulty the government runs into, and no doubt the longer it serves, the higher the propensity for such briefings to burgeon. In 2000 there were a number of highly damaging leaks of memos from Number Ten. It was not clear whether these were deliberate leaks by aides or a result of computer hacking. The breakdown of discipline at the heart of government was embarrassingly revealed in Andrew Rawnsley's book *Servants of the People* in September 2000. Senior Number Ten figures, including Blair himself, had talked about tensions between the Prime Minister and the Chancellor and infuriated the latter. The press had a field day revealing and deploring the bitchiness at the heart of the government.

When communications are effectively co-ordinated from Number Ten the Press Office has considerable scope to decide the priority for coverage of stories (and the ministers used to promote them). At the Treasury, however, Gordon Brown refused to allow his special adviser on the media, Charlie Whelan, to be subordinate to Number Ten, or even to dismiss him, in spite of urgings from the same quarter. Whelan was a high-profile figure and the zeal with which he promoted the Chancellor was to be a source of instability and frustration for Number Ten and all too often a news story for journalists. There were cases of rival 'spinning' operations from the Treasury and Number Ten, not least in October 1997 over Britain's attitude to joining the European single currency. That the situation was tolerated for so long reflected Blair's respect for Brown and his right to appoint his own staff, as well as Brown's determination to have his own power base. But the multiplicity of off-the-record briefings by ministers and their spokesmen undermined Campbell's attempts to co-ordinate communication in the first years. Co-ordination in government was more difficult than in opposition. The ministerial infighting and rival spinning in government was 'unwashed' in great detail in late 1998 and early 1999 in media coverage of the events which led to the resignations of Mandelson and the Treasury minister Geoffrey Robinson and Whelan himself. In February 1999, in a Fabian lecture, Campbell denounced broadcasters (particularly the BBC) for accepting the agenda set by broadsheets. In a shift in media strategy, he announced an intention to target women's magazines, regional papers, ethnic minority press, overseas media and daytime live television – which duly happened.

Mandelson, until his promotion to the DTI in July 1998, chaired a 9 am daily meeting (8.30 on Monday and Wednesday) in the Cabinet Office on policy and presentation. Like the EDCP under Michael Heseltine (see p. 232) its task is to integrate the two, and it is now chaired by Campbell or Smith. This large group is attended by the

Policy Unit head and Price from Number Ten, and officials and press officers or special advisers from the Cabinet Office, the Chief Whip's office, the SCU, the Treasury, the Foreign Office, the Deputy Prime Minister's office and the Labour Party. In 2000, as Campbell was embroiled in controversy, it was Whelan's turn to claim that Campbell was now the story and should resign.

In the Private Office the already hectic pace of work increased after May 1997 partly because there was a new government and partly because the private secretaries had to familiarise themselves with new people and Labour policy documents drawn up in opposition. The luxury of a large parliamentary majority, and a biddable party, also meant that more could be accomplished on the legislative front and less time devoted to crisis management à la Major. Above all, the Private Office faced pressures from a rush of immediate tasks coming together – Britain's assumption of the EU Presidency, new legislation, a Budget, preparing the Hong Kong handover, the G8 summit at Denver, and meetings of the NATO general council and the European Council, to say nothing of Northern Ireland – all to take place in the first few weeks. Alex Allan and John Holmes, who remained from Major's Private Office, managed to read Blair's mind quite quickly and once they had secured his agreement to a decision, were often left to fill in the details. On occasions, private secretaries had to approach members of the Policy Unit, the Press or the Political Office for guidance on policy or on Blair's views. One Private Secretary commented: 'When I worked in the Private Office of other ministers I understood their minds and people in the department would come to me for guidance. Under Blair the position is more informal and pluralistic and you turn to a number of people for advice.'[8]

For three months, Alex Allan continued to serve as Principal Private Secretary. He and Powell carried out their respective roles agreed before the election. Allan retained non-political honours and dealings with the Palace. Despite the antipathy the new regime felt to Major, there was an immediate trust established with Allan, which is all the more remarkable given Allan's unusually long association with Major (five rather than the usual three years) and the admiration he felt for his former boss. Robin Butler discussed with the Private Secretaries and other senior civil servants the constitutional implications if Powell were to succeed Allan as Principal Private Secretary. Butler was aware of fears among senior officials that any politicisation of the post might be seen as a first step on a slippery slope: they wanted a clear separation of political and Civil Service functions in all areas. They voiced concern about the constitutional proprieties if Powell assumed the title and traditional duties of Principal Private Secretary, who (along with the Cabinet Secretary and to a lesser degree the Queen's Private Secretary) plays a key role in advising the Palace in the event of a hung Parliament and acting as a broker with the opposition during the run-up to a general election. Butler wanted to keep the title and the duties in the hands of the Civil Service, not least as an insurance for when Powell left. The key actors therefore agreed a clear division of roles and the Private Office, although not politicised, contains a political element. Powell chairs general Number Ten staff meetings, including the weekly diary meeting and until recently the weekly 'grid' meeting of SCU, and takes a leading role in the project to improve the physical structure and operations of the building.

Once Allan left in the summer of 1997, John Holmes, the Foreign Affairs Private Secretary, the longest-serving and most senior member of the Private Office, was appointed Principal Private Secretary. The appointment was unusual because the Foreign Affairs Private Secretary has traditionally been regarded as being too specialised to warrant promotion to Principal Private Secretary. Under John Major, the Principal Private Secretary emerged further as a combination of firefighter, policy adviser and Chief of Staff. The new arrangements allowed Holmes over time to concentrate on foreign policy, defence and Northern Ireland and, compared with his predecessor, to keep clear of domestic policy. Blair quickly came to appreciate Holmes's judgment, particularly on Northern Ireland. Holmes worked closely with the European and the Overseas and Defence secretariats in the Cabinet Office, and selected from intelligence reports the material which he thought would interest Blair. Powell also takes a close interest in foreign affairs and Northern Ireland. For nearly two years the two top figures in Number Ten, uniquely in history, were both FCO men, one former (Powell), one current (Holmes).

Mark Adams, who had been responsible for parliamentary affairs,

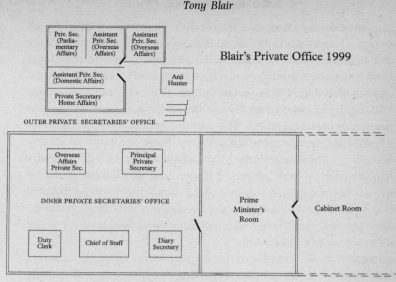

Blair's Private Office 1999

left the Private Office in late 1997, having already decided before the election to seek a career outside Whitehall. Normally, the Home Affairs Private Secretary would progress to handle parliamentary affairs as the job is given to somebody who is already working with and known to the Prime Minister. But because Angus Lapsley, the likely candidate, was already heavily burdened and reluctant to assume the new duties, Rob Read was recruited from the DFEE. Some of Read's portfolio was reduced as a consequence of Prime Minister's Questions being cut to one weekly session and he took over DETR affairs. The Economic Affairs Private Secretary, Moira Wallace, failed to break into the Blair-Brown relationship and was excluded from their bilaterals. Essentially, she (like senior Treasury officials) was a casualty of Brown's insistence on meeting Blair without officials present, a privilege not extended to any other minister. This was a legacy from their style of operating in opposition. Complaints to Blair about the informality of the arrangement from senior civil servants in and beyond the Treasury had little effect. There was frustration at the lack of communication from the meetings and the lack of opportunities which officials had to test or question the decisions.

In November 1997, Jeremy Heywood moved from the Treasury

to take over the Economic Affairs desk in the office from Moira Wallace, who became head of the Social Exclusion Unit. Blair accepted that if Heywood were to be effective he should attend and make notes of relevant Brown-Blair meetings and telephone conversations. Moreover, Blair now insisted on the change and Brown grew to accept it and Heywood. Part of the restoration was due to good relations between Heywood, Miliband and Ed Balls, Gordon Brown's Chief Economic Adviser in the Treasury. Heywood came in with the reputation of being one of the most brilliant young men the Treasury had groomed in years. He had shone not least as Lamont's Principal Private Secretary in the early 1990s, conducted the Fundamental Expenditure Review which led to a major reorganisation of the Tresury, and was credited with being the brain behind many of the Chancellor's best decisions.

Heywood was also given a role as co-ordinator of domestic affairs; this is a new departure, the thinking being that Blair wanted somebody to play a role on the domestic side similar to that played by Holmes (and after his departure in early 1999, John Sawyer) on foreign affairs and defence. The amount of work generated by the domestic departments is so large, however, that Heywood's role could only loosely be described as co-ordination. Essentially, he oversaw the work of the other three domestic affairs Private Secretaries, liaised with David Miliband (and other members of the Policy Unit) and also attended 'Away Days' of the Policy Unit at Chequers. He worked closely with Miliband and Ed Balls on the comprehensive spending review and on other issues of interest to the Treasury.

After a year in Number Ten, working in the small office off the Cabinet Ante-Room traditonally allocated to the Political Secretary, Blair decided to move to the inner private office occupied by his senior Private Secretaries. As a result Powell, Holmes and Heywood moved to the outer office with the Diary Secretary and a Duty Clerk. The other private secretaries were dispersed to offices close by. Although the most senior members of the Private Office continue to work in quarters just as cramped as before, they are at least next door to the Prime Minister and know who he is meeting and can easily catch him for a quick word.

The Private Office under Blair has been as influential as ever. The top team (Blair, Campbell, Powell) are demanding, and expect staff to be first class (and loyal). In his first year when he was heavily engaged with Northern Ireland Blair worked closely with Holmes and Powell. During the final stages, in June and July 1998, and again in 2000, of the comprehensive spending review (CSR), which linked extra funding to policy objectives, Heywood was a key figure. He attended all of Blair's key sessions with ministers and the meetings at which agreements on funding and policy 'modernisation' were reached. In February 1999, he succeeded Holmes as Principal Private Secretary. He continues to be responsible for Economic Affairs and welfare reform and oversees domestic policies. In addition, he handles EU economic issues, including questions of monetary union and tax harmonisation, and acts as 'sherpa' at G8 international conferences attended by the Prime Minister. Heywood also holds regular breakfasts with David Miliband, Ed Balls and Tom Scholar, a Treasury official, to ensure that Number Ten and the Treasury are working on the same lines.

By tradition, recruiting staff for the Policy Unit has largely been left to its head, with some suggestions from the Prime Minister. Blair's Unit has been distinctive in two respects. Until David Miliband's promotion in May 1998 it operated without a formal head throughout its entire first year. This deficiency made little difference to operations, for Miliband was de facto head and was regarded as such in Whitehall. Second, Blair and Miliband already had a good idea of who they would appoint, based on their contacts when Labour was in opposition. Former Blair aides, Millbank staff and a few outsiders were those chosen. All were known to Blair, most already knew each other, were New Labour, and constituted the largest ever Policy Unit. Past heads at times have found it difficult to recruit staff who had the desired mix of expertise and sound political outlook. After 1 May the reverse was the problem, as many staff were no longer required at Millbank and a number of outsiders lobbied to join the Unit. Blair's Number Ten was where the action was, and people wanted to be a part of it.

1997 was only the second changeover in party control in the Unit's twenty-five year history. The first had been in 1979 when John

Hoskyns came in with a tiny staff and struggled with civil servants for recognition, staff, and access to papers and to Mrs Thatcher. Things had changed a great deal since then.

Blair's advisers had preconceived ideas about how the Policy Unit had sometimes operated in the past. They thought that there had been too much rivalry between the Unit and the Private Office – 'the battle over who would write the last memo' – neglect of issues which crossed departmental boundaries, and a failure to think about the longer term. Blair's Unit would correct these faults. In fact, the charges often simplified the truth, and understated the degree of co-operation within Number Ten, not least in the last half of Major's tenure. Against a background of such criticisms of Number Ten, some senior civil servants, aware of the new mood, set to thinking of ways to promote greater interdepartmental co-operation, not least as a means of countering calls for a beefed-up Prime Minister's Department.

At an early Cabinet, Blair asked colleagues to involve the Policy Unit in their policy thinking; the implication was that they would lose standing with him if they did not. Some ministers were heard to remark about the Unit's staff being, 'Tony's narks in Whitehall'. The narks, however, have mostly come to be accepted – if not always welcomed – in departments as an authoritative voice for the Prime Minister. The Unit combines the roles of being a think tank (working up policy and seeking ideas outside from policy specialists) and a French-style *cabinet* (reinforcing the political direction of the Prime Minister). Most staff soon developed strong links to ministers and special advisers in the departments they shadowed; for instance, a Unit member sat on each of the departmental review teams set up under the 1998 and 2000 spending reviews and attended Blair's meeting with the minister to agree the terms of the department's final allocation.

In his first year Miliband had responsibility for education, speeches and, more generally, the Blair 'message'. The staff and their responsibilities, on 1 September 2000, were:

- Andrew Adonis (education, after Miliband's promotion, and cross-cutting 'opportunity' issues, and freedom of information)
- Liz Lloyd (home affairs, environment, agriculture, food safety)

- James Purnell (culture, media, sport, public services and life-long learning)
- Jim Gallagher (constitutional issues, particularly Scotland and Northern Ireland)
- Carey Oppenheim (welfare, social security)
- Geoff Norris (DTI and transport issues)
- Geoff Mulgan (social exclusion, family and welfare)
- Ed Richards (strategy)
- Roger Liddle (defence and Europe)
- Derek Scott (economy) and
- Robert Hill (local government and health).[9]

In addition, Peter Hyman has a distinctive role, working with both Miliband and Campbell on special projects and on Blair's speeches. Each member oversees one or more departments, some tackle cross-departmental issues (e.g. Mulgan on social exclusion) and many are also skilled communicators – although, as a rule, they leave media briefing to the Press Office.

Of the early eleven political appointees, McFadden had worked for John Smith, Mulgan had worked for Gordon Brown before setting up the Demos think tank, Roger Liddle had been a policy consultant and co-authored *The Blair Revolution* (with Mandelson), and Adonis joined from the *Observer* in May 1998, when Miliband was made head. According to one Unit member the other seven members are all very clearly 'Tony's people':[10] all had been advising or working for Blair or the party before the general election. At the outset all were new to 10 Downing Street, except for the civil servant, Jonathan Rees, who remained from John Major's Unit for three months until he was replaced by Sharon White, seconded from the Treasury. Although an additional civil servant joined in 1999, the Civil Service presence in the Policy Unit is at its lowest level since 1979. Offsetting the newness of Unit members to government was the fact that most of them already knew each other and many ministers and special advisers, a feature that distinguished it from all previous Units.

Blair has followed the Major practice of convening 'Away Days' at Chequers for the Unit every six months or so. At these sessions staff make presentations on current policy, future developments and possible initiatives for the second term. This device has echoes of the earlier CPRS strategy sessions for the Cabinet under Ted Heath. Esprit de corps is high, discussions at the sessions are vigorous and frank, first names are used on such occasions and the meetings reinforce the members' corporate sense that they are working for Blair. Jeremy Heywood, Jonathan Powell, Sally Morgan, and Mandelson when he was Minister Without Portfolio, also attend, but no Cabinet minister. Michael Stephenson, a member of the Political Office, chairs a fortnightly lunch meeting of special advisers, at which there may be presentations on polling, a policy issue or the current political scene.

At first, members of the Unit turned to the established Rees and the Private Office for guidance on how Whitehall operates. Two weeks into the Parliament, socialisation was further advanced with a weekend of seminars at the Civil Service College at Sunningdale. Some members, ironically, at first found the transition from Millbank to government a step-down. In opposition they had enjoyed fairly direct contact with Blair but in Downing Street the Private Office staff were physically closer to him and had more frequent access. The facilities in Number Ten also provided a culture-shock. Blair's staff had been used to pagers and mobile phones and speaking authoritatively to Shadow ministers. Downing Street, however, was behind the times in terms of information technology – e-mail had only just started and many staff lacked personal telephone lines. Moreover, ministers now have some protection from Number Ten because they have their own press officer and special advisers, and Policy Unit advice about, say, a departmental press release might just be ignored. Number Ten has invested heavily in advanced IT and the position over the past three years has been transformed. Many of the internal communications from SCU and the Press Office would not have been possible without these developments.

Blair's Policy Unit works closely with the Private Office on the domestic side, although staff are party-political, more media-savvy and are Blair's main source of advice and comment on specific policy issues, whereas the Private Office is responsible for the progression of business in Whitehall. Staff from both groups have found themselves redrafting papers from departments. Indeed, the dozen or so White

Papers produced in the first two years were a major preoccupation for the Unit staff. They had particular problems with early drafts of John Prescott's White Paper on Transport and Margaret Beckett's *Fairness at Work*. Discussions on the last were protracted and taxed Blair's patience. At one stage Beckett would not accept redrafting suggestions from the Policy Unit unless they were made in Blair's own handwriting. Mandelson was deputed to inform her Private Office that it could assume that such revisions from Number Ten carried Blair's authority.[11] Relevant members of the Unit were also closely involved in the CSR and attended the final meetings which Brown and Blair held with each Secretary of State. A senior civil servant thought that John Major's Policy Unit waited for things to come into Number Ten, but Blair's regularly suggests lines and initiatives to departments.

A member of the Unit may in a typical day communicate by phone or e-mail with officials, ministers and special advisers in the relevant department. As a rule the more frequent contact for the Unit member has been with the most 'Blairite' person in the department. Ideally, if the input is made early enough in the drafting process, the minister reads a departmental paper incorporating Number Ten's views. Frequent interaction may reflect the current salience of an issue, the Prime Minister's interest in it or his concern about how the minister is handling it. The influence of a Unit member *vis à vis* the department is likely to increase where Blair's interest in a policy handled by the department is high. Unlike the practice with some other Units, each member may go direct to Blair; he or she does not have to communicate with the Prime Minister through David Miliband. Typically, in the course of a week a member of the Unit will send a couple of memos to Blair, suggesting a policy 'steer'. During the spending reviews the perspectives of the Unit and the Private Office were blended in joint notes for Blair. This is a new emphasis in Number Ten – notes that seek to integrate the party and Whitehall perspectives, although under John Major, Alex Allan too had tried to limit the number of different memos on a topic being submitted to the Prime Minister.

Blair decided in late 1999 to increase further the resources of his Policy Unit and each member is now supported by a civil servant researcher. The civil servants are based on the top floor of a refurbished

Number Ten. It is typical of Blair that he has meshed political and official appointments.

Sally Morgan heads the Political Office. Her job involves liaison with the whips, the trade unions, the NEC and the party machine in Millbank. She is assisted by Faz Hakim, Michael Stephenson and Jon Cruddas, who are responsible for relations with the constituency parties and with the trade unions. Her job, like that of the party's General Secretary, Margaret McDonagh, is to warn about likely party reactions to government initiatives and to promote acceptance of the latter among the party at large. The partial overlap in duties creates the potential for tension. Making appointments to government posts for nearly a quarter of Labour MPs raises issues of party management as well as executive leadership. Sally Morgan was one of a handful with whom Blair discussed his first set of promotions in May 1997 and his reshuffles in July 1998 and 1999.

Anji Hunter assumed the US sounding title of 'Special Assistant to the Prime Minister'. She arranges Blair's itinerary and events once he is out of Downing Street. This covers his domestic visits, so-called 'roadshows' to promote policies, and meetings with the public and with party members. She attends the weekly diary meetings and arranges many of Blair's sessions with political editors, academics and other non-Civil Service figures, and breakfasts with business leaders. She occasionally calls journalists with an invitation: 'Isn't it about time you talked to Tony?' There was certainly no doubt about Hunter's closeness to Blair: she has known him well for more than half his life. Philip Bassett in the SCU also makes a point of contacting opinion-forming media commentators.

As Blair's PPS, Bruce Grocott keeps in touch with Labour backbenchers and helps in preparation for PMQs on Wednesdays. He had played a similar role under Neil Kinnock. Like previous PPSs he liaises with Labour MPs who are planning to ask questions at PMQs. First elected to the Commons in 1974, Grocott is enough 'old' Labour to build bridges with senior backbenchers.

Blair attends the party's bimonthly NEC sessions but rarely stays for the entire meeting, has a scheduled weekly meeting with the party's General Secretary (at first Tom Sawyer and now Margaret

McDonagh based in Millbank) and receives delegations from the TUC approximately every three months or so (the same frequency with which he meets the CBI). Most of the day-to-day briefing with the party machine is done through Sally Morgan and Margaret McDonagh.

After the election, Philip Gould created a strategic consultancy, GCGNOP, in co-operation with Stanley Greenberg and James Carville, former pollsters for Bill Clinton. The group took over responsibility for the party's opinion polling and focus groups. Gould, drawing on his analysis of polls and focus groups, continues to write frequent strategy memos for Blair, attends the Monday morning 'office' meetings (see below) and takes part in discussions with Miliband and Hyman on the electoral problems and opportunities posed by the party's position in government. Blair is the first Prime Minister to have regular weekly sessions with a pollster or political strategist and from early 2000 attended Alistair Campbell's daily 8.30 am media meeting, as well as key meetings to prepare for the next general election campaign.

In 1999 and 2000, Gould was more frequently in touch with Blair and Campbell, supplying regular reports based on his focus groups and private polling. Some idea of his frankness in reporting to Blair was provided by a memo leaked to the press in June 2000. This reported that middle Britain saw Blair as being out of touch and failing to deliver on his promises. It added 'TB is not believed to be real. He lacks conviction, he is all spin and presentation, he just says things to please people, not because he believes them'. Blair and some of his close aides increasingly blamed a critical press and unrealistic expectations among the public for the decline in his popularity.

Another central figure whose influence has carried over from opposition to the early days of government is the Lord Chancellor, Lord Irvine of Lairg, a long-standing friend of the Blairs (indeed he had introduced Blair to his future wife when both worked in his chambers). He has chaired a number of important Cabinet committees, including those on devolution, reform of the House of Lords and freedom of information: in effect, Blair delegated much of the constitutional reform agenda to him.

* * *

Robin Butler, the initial Cabinet Secretary and Head of the Civil Service, had joined the Civil Service in 1961, when Whitehall still reflected many of the Northcote-Trevelyan values of a century earlier. He had already worked at close quarters with five former Prime Ministers either as a Private Secretary, Principal Private Secretary, or a member of the CPRS, or as Cabinet Secretary. On 2 May 1997, he was coming to the end of a distinguished career while Tony Blair was starting what might be a long term as Prime Minister. Butler had already seen significant changes in Whitehall and, to a lesser extent, in Number Ten, and Blair intended to make more. Blair appreciated the experience and balance that lay behind Butler's judgments and the two were in close and frequent touch in the first few days, with Butler advising on what pressing matters should be tackled and how. But both men knew that there would be no long-term relationship.

Robin Butler sought to advise Blair and Cabinet ministers in the ways of government, pointing out how it differed from campaigning in opposition. In particular, he canvassed the case for consulting more widely among Cabinet colleagues and Cabinet committees. This was not the style which Blair had operated in opposition.

Blair's staff quickly prepared for a post-Butler Number Ten. Some of them regarded Butler as co-operative but not an innovator. They may not have appreciated his position as Head of the Home Civil Service and his duty to uphold what he and other senior civil servants regarded as constitutional proprieties. Whitehall was concerned over the large number of special adviser appointments and the fact that Treasury officials were kept in the dark about the Blair-Brown talks in the first months. Butler was aware from his soundings with Powell and reading of Mandelson's chapter in *The Blair Revolution* (see p. 253) that the new Prime Minister wanted a stronger Number Ten and a Cabinet Office that carried more clout in Whitehall. He proposed a scheme by which the departments would state their programme priorities to the Cabinet Office and the latter would then periodically evaluate the amount of progress a department had made. This would be conducted under Peter Mandelson, an early version of the role later given to Jack Cunningham. In fact, Blair and Mandelson diverted their energies elsewhere and little came of Butler's proposal. He carried on with traditional duties, such as the half-hour session with the Prime Minister on Mondays to review the progress of business through the Cabinet system, the preparation of handling or 'chairing' briefs for Blair at Cabinet and Cabinet committees and other business matters. But a major revamp of the role of the Cabinet Office would be a task for his successor.

Richard Wilson, Permanent Secretary at the Home Office, succeeded Butler as Cabinet Secretary on 1 January 1998. Something of an activist, he appreciated the importance to Blair of the implementation of policy, and the need for departments to work together and deliver overall policy outcomes. At the Home Office he had gained the trust of both Michael Howard and Jack Straw and acquired the reputation of being the kind of civil servant who would say, in a meeting, 'I'll sort it.' With Blair's agreement, Wilson set himself the task of reviewing the role and organisation of the Cabinet Office and suggesting ways in which Number Ten and the Cabinet Office might achieve better co-ordination. This remit reflected concerns which long predated the arrival of Tony Blair in Downing Street; Robin Butler and John Major had been the most recent to recognise a similar problem three years earlier. Significantly, the idea of a Prime Minister's Department was no longer a serious runner. 'It was still around in a vague way, but nobody had thought through what it involved,' said one senior official, 'but it was agreed that the Cabinet Office should build itself around the Prime Minister more and support him.'[12] But Blair's staff were determined to exercise greater control from Number Ten over the departments, to move from 'a feudal system to a Napoleonic one', to quote one.

Wilson's report, drawn up in close consultation with Powell, Miliband and Heywood, was circulated within Number Ten by mid-April, and read and informally approved by Blair during his Easter break in 1998. It was, however, only finally announced to Parliament in late July. The delay in announcing the changes was explained in part by the need to wait for the completion of the CSR and the Cabinet reshuffle, particularly the planned departure of David Clark, the Chancellor of the Duchy of Lancaster, based in the Cabinet Office. There were initial suspicions about the proposals from the Treasury, which as usual feared the emergence of a rival and perhaps the mooted appointment of Peter Mandelson as the minister for the Cabinet

Office; personal relations between Mandelson and Gordon Brown were poor. In the event, neither Mandelson nor Sir Terry Burns, the Treasury Permanent Secretary originally suggested to head the Unit, was appointed. But the main reason for delay was pressure on Blair's time between April and July 1998 – his preoccupations with Northern Ireland and then the assembly elections for the province, the Middle East, the spending review and then the Cabinet reshuffle.

Wilson proposed changes in the Cabinet Office to improve the handling of cross-departmental issues and service delivery. A new Performance and Innovation Unit was established in the Cabinet Office, designed to 'complement the Treasury's role in monitoring departmental progress' and the Office of Public Service was merged with the Cabinet Office to improve formulation, co-ordination and delivery and evaluation of policy. Jack Cunningham, the new Chancellor of the Duchy of Lancaster, had the working title 'Minister for the Cabinet Office' and a brief to encourage departments to work together in delivering agreed policy outcomes. The changes were designed to 'meet the corporate objectives of the Government as a whole, rather than the objectives of individual departments'. The unit commissions studies and form policy groups from civil servants and outsiders. Early projects have dealt with the government's presence in cities and regions, e-commerce and on ways in which the elderly can become more involved in the community. A steering group is chaired by David Miliband and has a strong Number Ten and Treasury membership.

The move builds on the trend since 1970 for the Cabinet Office to gain additional remits and capacities and on the perceived success of the Social Exclusion Unit based in it. This task-oriented group, tackling linked and cross-departmental topics (e.g. homelessness, crime, school exclusions and run-down estates) and making recommendations is regarded as a model for future initiatives. It remains to be seen how the Cabinet Office's traditional role as an 'honest broker' between departments will be squared with pressures from the centre for Wilson to be something of Blair's 'Chief Whip in Whitehall', in the words of one of Blair's staff.

Wilson also writes Blair a weekly note on issues of current concern or interest and is regularly in touch – on Civil Service promotions, intelligence and the progress of government business in Whitehall. Wilson was heavily engaged in conducting the investigations into the circumstances which led to the resignation of the Welsh Secretary of State Ron Davies, the claims about cash for access made by *The Observer* in July 1998 against Roger Liddle and whether the loan to Peter Mandelson from Geoffrey Robinson had placed him in a conflict of interest because of the DTI's investigation into Robinson. As well as his weekly meeting with Permanent Secretaries, Wilson regularly meets with a handful of senior officials to consider Blair's views. Unlike the weekly meeting, this one contains members of Blair's office. From his contacts with the Cabinet Secretariat and weekly meetings with Permanent Secretaries, Wilson gleans impressions of the competence of ministers and has learnt to cope with Blair's inquiries about how he rates them. Some of Blair's political staff were surprised that he was one of the very few people with whom Blair discussed his first Cabinet reshuffle in July 1998 but such discussions are not unusual.

Blair is the first Prime Minister since Asquith in 1908 to have young children at Number Ten. Because the second floor flat at the top of Number Ten was deemed too small, Blair and his family decided to live in a flat above the Chancellor of the Exchequer's house in Number Eleven, specially converted to accommodate them. He usually rises early, between 6 and 6.30 am, perhaps to finish work on his boxes from the previous night, make phone calls, be joined by Campbell and Powell, take a bath, and then come across to Number Ten a few minutes before his first meeting, normally at 9 am. Blair follows what is now a well-established prime ministerial routine in Number Ten, subject to variations imposed by the particular personal preferences and the pressure of events. Tuesdays and Thursdays are good days for his few Cabinet committees and other meetings, and Fridays may be reserved for visits to the regions, or his Sedgefield constituency or early weekends at Chequers. But there have been innovations.

For example, on Mondays Blair begins at 9 am with an hour-long 'office meeting' with his political staff and advisers to review the week ahead. As of summer 2000 it consisted of Powell, Campbell, Hunter, Miliband, Morgan and Heywood from the Private Office. Mandelson was a regular member until his promotion to the DTI in July 1998 and an occasional one thereafter. Blair begins the meeting with a list of his latest ideas and concerns, often about the progress and media coverage of government initiatives. Powell makes a page of action points arising and distributes it to members of the group and the Private Office. At 9.45 there is another meeting at which Campbell and Hunter are joined by Gould, Bassett and Falconer. Those attending regard it as the opportunity to set a tone for the rest of the week and for getting Blair's views on the major issues of the day.

This meeting is followed by a half-hour session with the Cabinet Secretary, again in Blair's office, to review matters of interest to Wilson. Powell and Heywood from the Private Office also attend. Blair and Richard Wilson then adjourn to the Cabinet Room to meet the Deputy Secretaries who head the different sections of the Cabinet Secretariat. This is a Blair innovation and provides him with an opportunity to question the staff on their work and the progress of cross-departmental business. This meeting also includes Mo Mowlam and Charles Falconer, the Chief Whip, Miliband and the Private Office staff.

For PMQs on Wednesday afternoon, Blair initially followed John Major's approach. A brief 9 am preparatory meeting on Wednesday was attended by the entire Private Office, the two PPSs, the Political Secretary, the head of the Policy Unit, and Liz Lloyd, who had helped him in opposition. By July 2000 it consisted of Campbell, Grocott, the relevant Private Secretary, Bill Bush and David Bradshaw and David Bassett (of the SCU). It has a strong input from people with a background in the media. The longer, now weekly half-hour sessions of PMQs mean that a broader range of questions may be raised than in the traditional fifteen-minute session and Blair is usually armed with about a hundred briefs for each PMQ, compared with the sixty or so that Major had for each of his shorter sessions. During the first 38 months in office, Blair answered 7504 substantive oral questions (i.e. excluding those which asked about his engagements), compared to John Major's 2257 over his first 38 months. He attended 105 PMQ sessions (30 minutes) compared to Major's 165 (15 minutes) over the same period.

There is no designated office in the building for the Prime Minister, who works where he or she feels comfortable. John Major had worked in the Cabinet Room and Mrs Thatcher in the study on the first floor.

As noted on p. 264, Tony Blair worked for his first year in the small office off the Cabinet Ante-Room. Here he sat on the couch and made many of his phone calls, met colleagues, read papers and gave media interviews. Some staff explain: 'He is not a desk man', although he disputes the characterisation now pointedly as a computer on a desk. Unless a meeting was in progress his door remained open and he was easily accessible to key political and official staff. Over time he was persuaded that the room was too small and inappropriate for a Prime Minister to meet foreign leaders, and the Private Office was unhappy at being excluded from the traditional gate-keeping role. Blair eventually decided to move to the office formerly occupied by the senior private secretaries, next to the Cabinet Room. The couch followed him, but the door is now closed. Blair likes brief meetings and short papers from the Policy Unit and Private Office which raise the substantive issues and make recommendations. He has regular pre-meeting sessions with relevant Policy Unit, Political Office and Private Office staff to focus on the objectives of the forthcoming meeting – 'what he wants to come out of it', according to an aide.

Although Blair has invited leading figures in the arts, science, crime prevention and education to seminars in Number Ten, with the respective departmental ministers in attendance, he has held far fewer of these than Major. Such sessions last for about three hours. He has hosted a discussion on the 'Third Way' for academics, commentators and special advisers and breakfast meetings with businessmen. He has also embarked on a rolling programme of visits to Whitehall departments to address staff on the government's strategy and how the department's work relates to it. These visits last three or four hours and in 1998 covered the Home Office, Trade and Industry, and Education and Employment.

Blair's Cabinet meetings are too brief (usually less than an hour) to be effective decision-making forums. This feature has been part of a long-term trend, since 1979 at least, but it has speeded up under Blair. Mrs Thatcher was not unique in sometimes deliberately prolonging a Cabinet if it was heading for a speedy conclusion, on the grounds that a short meeting would create a bad impression among the ever-watchful media outside. John Major's Cabinets usually lasted long enough to keep colleagues informed on the big issues, although meetings were discursive rather than decisive. Only on a few occasions has Blair allowed sufficient time for Cabinet even to be discursive; apart from receiving regular reports from the Foreign Secretary and Leader of the Commons, he tries to focus on strategic issues. Blair has discontinued the practice of 'political Cabinets': in the words of one of his staff 'all the Cabinets are political'. The agenda has changed under Blair. It starts with Parliamentary business, but is then followed by a new item, Current Events, in which Mo Mowlam reports on policy announcements for the following week. There follows the traditional Foreign Affairs slot, and then if appropriate, the distribution of papers. There are also political or strategy meetings at occasional 'Away Days' for the Cabinet, and no minutes are taken. Another member of his staff said: 'Blair the policy maker and governmentalist must not be separated from Blair the politician . . . he is not going to allow the politics to be stripped out by administration.'

Blair also chairs very few Cabinet committees himself. Defence and Overseas meets infrequently as do most of his committees on Northern Ireland, Intelligence Services, Welfare to Work (which he created and which of all committees has most engaged his energy), and the Constitutional Reform Committee, which by July 1998 had met once. He also chairs the Joint Cabinet Committee, on which Liberal Democrats sit. Lord Irvine chairs five committees, including those on freedom of information and the incorporation of the European Convention on Human Rights, and Blair frequently talks to him about the progress of business. Blair's government does not score high on Cabinet collegiality. Neither the comprehensive spending reviews nor Brown's pre-Budget statements, for example, were discussed in Cabinet although they were reported to it.

Blair's preferred method of work, as in opposition, is to hold one-to-one meetings with colleagues or to convene small ad hoc groups to tackle strategic issues. He holds bimonthly *stocktaking* bilaterals with Secretaries of State and their top officials in his key areas of education, health, crime and, more recently, transport. The systematic way in which Blair seeks to ensure that there is joint responsibility for implementing the government's strategy at official as well as at political levels is innovative; he wants ministers and Permanent Secretaries to reflect his concerns and priorities. Blair and his aides are not sympathetic to the committee style of policy-making. According to one adviser, 'we find the discussion is stripped of politics and lacks drive'. Hence the interest in project work, as in the Social Exclusion Unit. Both the bilaterals and the project approach are a carry-over from Blair's time in opposition and his impatience with the Shadow Cabinet. Table 10.1 shows that over his first 25 months in office Blair held a total of 783 meetings with individual ministers; over the same period, Major held 272 such sessions.

On the economy he has frequent meetings with Gordon Brown, on other issues he and his advisers work with the minister responsible. But he also likes to hold some meetings without the responsible minister, discussing the issue with Number Ten and Cabinet Office staff. This has applied in particular to Europe, health, education and welfare reform. In many of these discussions the Treasury is also involved. But, for the first two years, the most time-consuming issue for him, as for John Major, was Northern Ireland. Indeed Blair's involvement with the province and Kosovo in the first half of 1999 led to complaints that he was neglecting the domestic agenda. The Secretary of State for Northern Ireland, Mo Mowlam, trailed only Gordon Brown and John Prescott in the frequency of meetings with Blair in the first two years. The second most pressing demand on Blair's time in the second half of 1998 was welfare reform. The welfare reform Cabinet committee, which he chairs, has produced plans for pensioners, the disabled and widows. Some bilaterals are held with no official present, some with a member of both the Policy Unit and the Private Office in attendance, and some with just one of them present, depending on whether the focus is primarily political or governmental.

Time and foreign visits permitting, weekly bilateral meetings are held with Robin Cook, Gordon Brown and John Prescott, usually with a Private Secretary present to take notes. Additional meetings with Gordon Brown are arranged mostly at short notice and the two also speak regularly by telephone. Press reports in summer 1998 that there are regular 8 am meetings with the Chancellor were inaccurate and appear to have been Treasury-led 'spin'. Blair held many bilaterals with ministers discussing funding and policy goals as part of the CSR. The exercise has now provided a pretext for the Treasury and Number

Ten to intervene in departments, and when Blair informed spending ministers of their CSR allocations he was always accompanied by Brown. In addition every fortnight or so he invites groups of ministers to dinner in his Number Eleven living quarters.

The Blair, Brown, Prescott and Cook meeting, as a so-called 'Big Four' that existed in opposition, fell away in government. It started as a Cabinet pre-meeting, but the last two were often abroad (Prescott often deputised on overseas visits for Blair). Blair and Brown conferred regularly, often without officials being present in the first months. As noted, they have a close relationship, dating back to the time when they first entered the House of Commons together in 1983. They worked out Labour's key policies in opposition and have continued to do so in government. It is difficult to think of any recent Prime Minister and Chancellor (except Thatcher and Lawson, and then only during 1983–85) having such a close working relationship and a shared outlook on so many issues. The good personal relationship did not, however, extend to some members of the respective 'tribes' in Number Ten and the Treasury and different views were eagerly fanned by the media. There were claims that Brown still resented not being leader and that the two men had agreed that, if Labour gained power, then Brown would be granted effective power over economic and much of social policy.[13] This is what happened.

Whitehall recognises how pivotal the Brown–Blair relationship is. In his memoirs Nigel Lawson commented that the Chancellor has 'his finger in pretty well every pie in government'.[14] Brown is keenly interested in many domestic policies, notably welfare to work, social security, training and education and industrial competitiveness. The Treasury controls the total spending of departments, has more policy manpower than Number Ten, not least because of its Spending Directorate which monitors departments' spending, and is heavily involved in the comprehensive spending reviews for each department, regardless of the preferences of departmental ministers. Moreover, Brown was given the Chairmanship of the key Cabinet EA and PSX committees; the latter monitors the progress of departments in delivering 'modernising policies' in return for extra funding. Treasury claims that ministers would be personally answerable for policy delivery to Gordon Brown led an irate David Blunkett, at Employment and Education, to state publicly that he reported to the Prime Minister and not to Gordon Brown. Brown also succeeded in appointing his own key people in the Treasury, including the Paymaster General, Geoffrey Robinson, Charlie Whelan and Chief Economic Adviser, Ed Balls. The media presented them as constituting an alternative 'court'. Some reports in summer 1998 (thought to be Treasury-inspired) claimed that the two men operate a 'dual premiership', with Brown as Prime Minister and Blair as President. Brown, it was claimed, operated as managing director on domestic policy and Blair as a non-executive chairman, concentrating on strategy and Northern Ireland and overseas issues. This was resented in Number Ten.

Yet the Brown–Blair relationship, for all its closeness, has presented problems in government. Within the Treasury Brown liked to work with a very small group, excluding nearly all officials. His insistence on a one-to-one relation with the Prime Minister meant that in the first months of the government senior officials in the Treasury and the Number Ten Private Office were in the dark about many of the decisions in their discussions. Early meetings on the spending review between the two men were held without Treasury briefing papers, as Brown gave oral reports to Blair. When taxed by senior officials about this lack of transparency Blair expressed surprise at the reaction. Within twelve months, Sir Terry Burns, the Treasury Permanent Secretary, decided to retire early. The situation improved from late 1997 and a Private Secretary now attends nearly all their meetings and records their conclusions. There is no gainsaying the difficulties caused by the unusual nature of the Brown-Blair relationship, notably Brown's suspicion of staff who are not directly beholden to him. One Number Ten official spoke with concern of Brown's 'charmed circle of self-reinforcing admirers', but the two principals work well together. Rawnsley's *Servants of the People* reveals some of the resentment which Blair's aides felt towards the Treasury, and the extent to which other ministers felt excluded.

Indeed, now that the Treasury has handed control of interest rates to the Bank of England, set departmental spending allocations for the remainder of Parliament and acknowledges the limits to which it can shape macro-economic policy, a Chancellor may wish to look elsewhere to keep himself fully occupied.

In spite of all the talk of Blair's influence and his strengthening of Number Ten, it remains the case that the significant policy work is still done in the departments, which have the information, expertise, legislative time, staff and clients. Blair, like any Prime Minister or indeed any minister, is limited by time, and can concentrate on only one or two policy areas at a time. For much of April, May and June 1998, for example, he was virtually a foreign affairs and Northern Ireland Prime Minister. Working through John Holmes and with Secretary of State Mo Mowlam and Paul Murphy (Minister for Political Development in the province) as his executives, he almost ran Northern Ireland. In the first months of his premiership, the Presidency of the EU also took much time, including tours of each member state. This degree of concentration on an issue can be achieved only at the expense of neglecting other policy areas. To achieve his policy ends Blair, like other Prime Ministers, has either to persuade the minister concerned or appoint a new one.[15]

More than any recent Prime Minister, Blair is aware of the importance of presentation to promote policy and himself. Like Presidents Reagan and Clinton, he is prepared to 'go public', using various media outlets for interviews, press articles under his name, radio phone-ins and personal appearances to carry his case directly to voters.[16] His first formal public speech as Prime Minister was on social exclusion and other early speeches were used to promote his interests on welfare reform, education, the Millennium Dome and the CSR. Question and answer 'roadshows' and meetings with the public are also used to promote his New Labour agenda. Blair's remarkable standing with the public – his opinion poll-ratings remained at a record high after two years in office – is sustained by a strong media profile and associations with prominent figures like sport stars, film celebrities and the late Princess Diana. Blair's regular 'meet the people' sessions mirror Clinton's so-called 'town hall meetings'. In his first twelve months in office (2 May 1997 to 28 April 1998) Blair made over eighty public speeches, gave sixty-six press conferences and media interviews, and held twenty-three 'doorstep' interviews. In a conscious attempt to go direct to the public and avoid hostile editorialising, he has also made much use of the national and regional press to provide signed articles on issues of the day. In his first two years an estimated total of 150 articles for national newspapers plus additional pieces for overseas papers appeared under his name. The most popular outlets are the tabloids – the *Sun* and *Mirror*. An index of the heightened interest in Blair is that he received twice the total number of letters from the public in his first twelve months as did Major in his final twelve months.

Also in keeping with the strategy of appealing to relatively apolitical people Blair has tended to prefer relaxed encounters with David Frost, Des O'Connor, or Richard Madeley and Judy Finnegan on television and avoided the traditional heavyweight political programmes, such as *Newsnight* or *Panorama*. Interviewed for a television portrait of Blair on 30 January 2000, Campbell explained: 'We have to try and dominate the agenda, because good government demands it. We have to stay ahead of the media, finding new and creative ways of getting our message to the public.'

British Prime Ministers do not (yet) have a designated speechwriting unit; indeed, compared with the staff of fifteen at President Clinton's disposal, a Prime Minister does not have anybody. Officials, colleagues, journalists or friends with a talent for words are expected to help out. Blair takes the communications function of political leadership seriously; after all, he owed much of his success in projecting New Labour to it and the relevant skills of Campbell, Mandelson and Gould made them important members of his entourage. In government he has less time to devote to speeches and articles than he had in opposition, but still writes the important speeches himself. He also has strong speechwriting support in Number Ten with Campbell, Miliband, Hyman, Bassett and McFadden. Pressures of work have limited Campbell's role to an editorial one on all but the very big speeches; his chief contribution is to highlight a passage that will make a front page headline and to sharpen the opening paragraphs. Drafts of party speeches are mostly written by Campbell and Hyman, and policy speeches drafted by the relevant policy specialist in the Policy Unit. Government speeches and statements are often written by Campbell, Hyman and Miliband. Foreign affairs and Northern Ireland speeches are largely the work of the Private Office.

Because it is televised live and receives intensive media analysis, the annual party conference speech still takes more time than any other address. Over summer, Miliband seeks suggestions from departments and Policy Unit colleagues about suitable new policy statements or policies that can be restated freshly. Campbell and Hyman suggest themes and key phrases ('A Young Country' and 'An Age of Achievement') for the speech. Blair often writes important speeches and a good part of his newspaper articles himself.

In speechwriting sessions, Blair moves paragraphs around, complains of lack of colour, and never says of a draft, 'This will do.' As with most Prime Ministers, his political speeches are often completed at the last minute. That on Scotland in Glasgow in November 1998 was still being rewritten as the plane touched down. More than all of his recent predecessors, Blair enjoys speechwriting.

Backed by a majority of 179 in the House of Commons, Blair has had little need to worry about the passage of legislation through the Commons. Greater control over candidate selection and a new party code of discipline have encouraged Labour MPs to support, or at least curb their public criticisms of, the leadership. Party management is left to the whips and the large majority has meant that the Chief Whip has been a less frequent visitor to Number Ten than his hard-pressed predecessors in the periods 1974–79 and 1992–97. Blair meets Labour's Parliamentary Committee each Wednesday afternoon and following PMQs he is available in his room in the Commons between 3.30 and 4.30 pm. The committee session is chaired by Clive Soley, chairman of the PLP, and he and his six backbench colleagues voice the concerns of Labour MPs. They complained about the cuts to benefits for lone parents, reports of plans to cut disability payments, rival 'spinning' over the single currency by Number Ten and the Treasury, and the feuding between ministers that accompanied the resignations of Peter Mandelson and Geoffrey Robinson in December 1998. Blair also regularly invites small groups of Labour MPs to meet him in the Cabinet Room, aiming to meet every MP annually. These sessions are chaired by Clive Soley or by Bruce Grocott. He also holds meetings with small groups of junior ministers and bilaterals with Cabinet ministers which focus on political strategy.

But these meetings have failed to stifle traditional complaints that the leader is remote from MPs. In contrast with Wilson (pre-1970), Callaghan, and reputedly Mrs Thatcher in her first years, he rarely visits the Tea-Room to mingle with MPs. In his first nine months in office Blair spoke in only one debate and voted in only 5 per cent of House of Commons divisions; the figures were similar for the rest of his first term, a figure much lower than for his predecessors. Parliament is hardly the centre of Blair's political life. He has never been a bar/tea-room man, has little small talk and was determined to find time for his wife and young children as well as for thinking about policy. When problems in the party arise, critics predictably complain about inadequate consultation and a centralist style of leadership.[17]

During 2000 party critics complained of the leadership's obsession with spinning, intolerance of internal debate, neglect of the concerns of Labour's heartlands and deference to middle England. Even Tom Sawyer, the first Labour General Secretary under Blair, complained that the leader was losing touch. The ranks of the disillusioned supporters grew to include Peter Kilfoyle and Frank Field, both former ministers, and Ken Follet, a contributor to Labour funds, all of whom made outspoken attacks on Number Ten's style of operations.

In the postwar period, Prime Ministers have made fewer speeches and interventions in the Commons than before 1940. This reflects the decline of Parliament as a centre of political debate and information compared with the mass media, and the extra-parliamentary pressures on the Prime Minister's time.[18] On average he or she now makes six statements and participates in six debates a year. Like Thatcher and Major, Blair has followed the practice of making statements to the Commons after each major international summit. By July 2000 he had made 33 statements in the Commons, covering topics such as Northern Ireland, Iraq, E.U. and other international meetings, and the NHS.

Of recent Prime Ministers Blair most resembles Thatcher in his focus on policy goals. Blair's vacations and foreign trips are usually followed by memos to Powell (for circulation to his 'office' group and to private secretaries) about his latest concerns, ideas, and queries about progress on his policy objectives. One senior civil servant in Number Ten was impressed by Blair's sense of political strategy and tactics: 'He is not interested in simply the formation of individual government policies but what the New Labour message is and how a particular policy fits into it.'[19] Some of Blair's staff talk of him as

The Powers Behind the Prime Minister

TONY BLAIR'S DAY 1997–1999
(2 May 1997–31 May 1999)

	1997	1998	1999	TOTAL
Cabinet	25	43	18	86
Cabinet Committees (including stocktakes)	57	98	23	178
Meetings: individual Ministers	236	412	135	783
Meetings: individual MPs	92	185	87	364
British visitors/hosts [meetings & formal meals]	96	152	54	302
Foreign visitors [meetings & formal meals]	57	78	38	173
Official overseas Visits★	14	35	14	63
Days spent overseas★	20	38	26	84
House: Questions				Total to date = 66
Statements/speeches				Total to date = 20
HM The Queen: Audiences	13	20	8	41
Windsor	0	0	0	0
Balmoral	1	1		2
Overseas/other	1	0		1

★Excluding holidays.

The above figures do not include Personal or Constituency Engagements being 'a big picture man', less interested in the details. 'If it is not on his agenda or in his big picture, then he cuts it out', said a Private Secretary.[20] 'Yes, and potentially fatally so,' added a Cabinet Office official.[21] A member of the Policy Unit who had known Blair for several years was impressed at his interest in the long term. 'He does think and talk about ten or fifteen years ahead – about the constitution, Europe and the prospects for the political centre left.'[22]

Political advisers under some previous premiers have complained about the Private Office demands and the overload on the Prime Minister's diary.[23] Jonathan Powell chairs the weekly diary meetings and Hunter and Morgan guard against what they originally regarded as excessive Private Office demands on the Prime Minister's time; there were some tense exchanges in the early days. Others in regular attendance are a Private Secretary, Bassett, Philip Barton (Private Office), Heywood, Miliband and Kate Garvey, the Diary Secretary. All will have a list of the bids for demands on Blair's time. They seek to find time for Blair to think about policy – and sometimes manage to free him for weekend visits to Chequers, beginning Thursday night. Blair also insists on spending some evenings with his young family. For much of his first four years John Major lived alone in the upstairs flat in Number Ten and was more willing to attend evening dinners and receptions. Scheduled meetings with staff, ministers and visitors last fifteen or thirty minutes, as a rule. Outside the weekly diary meetings, Kate Garvey circulates a memo to key staff, requesting a simple 'yes' or 'no' response to a request for an appointment.

It goes without saying that the allocation of a Prime Minister's time is one of the most crucial decisions he and his staff can make. 'Everybody wants a word with the Prime Minister. He can't move without being grabbed. Out battle is to protect his quality time,' said the official. Both Heath and Callaghan took weekends off from their boxes and refused to have their diaries overloaded. Harold Wilson spent much time gossiping late into the night with political aides. Major complained of an overloaded diary, not least of the time taken in meeting foreign dignitaries. Blair has set out with a clear idea of what he wants to concentrate on and which activities he is prepared to cut back. The diary will have 'KF' pencilled in for periods – 'Keep

Free'. Compared with his immediate predecessors, he has reallocated his time by reducing PMQs to a weekly session, a step considered and rejected by his two predecessors (see p. 235). This single step has saved political and official staff time and energy in preparation and briefing and also freed the Parliamentary Affairs Private Secretary to handle other policy areas. He has pruned the number of official dinners, again a step welcomed by officials. 'The only essential one is the Lord Mayor's Banquet', Blair was advised at the outset by a Private Secretary. 'We are quite tough with requests from the Foreign Office', said one of the political staff, about bids for Blair to meet visiting diplomats.

In his first twenty-five months he held 173 meetings and formal dinners with foreign leaders and visitors, in comparison with John Major's 209 over the same period. The number of meetings with British visitors or formal meals hosted was 302 compared with 415 for John Major. He has cut the number of meetings with party officials and trade union leaders. If the first two changes mark a difference with Thatcher and Major, this third marks a contrast with the Wilson and Callaghan premierships. The party's structure and culture in their time meant that the leader had to cultivate the major trade unions, both for managing the party's NEC and conference and for operating the government's income policies. Reforms of the party under Kinnock and Blair have reduced the problems posed by the unions, conference and NEC. On the other hand, Blair makes a point of holding regular question and answer meetings with party members at Millbank or on his visits to the regions. Blair's visits to the Queen are far from weekly, as the table on page 286 shows. On these trips he is accompanied by either Jonathon Powell or the Principal Private Secretary. He has continued the recent trend of Prime Ministers to spend less time in the House of Commons. This has been facilitated in part by his large parliamentary majority and by halving the number of PMQs. Over the century, the larger and more professional office in Number Ten is where the Prime Minister works and takes decisions.

We have seen that over its short period Tony Blair's premiership has already been distinctive. On the official side, relations were affected by Blair's emphasis on a strong political direction in Number Ten and the importation of so many tried and trusted political aides from his time in opposition. By January 2000 there were twice as many special advisers in Whitehall as under John Major (seventy-eight to thirty-eight) and the figure in Number Ten had doubled. Political appointments are located as follows in early 2000 – Policy Unit (11), Private Office (2), Press Office (3), Political Office (6), Strategic Communications (2). The last, established in Summer 1999, is headed by Bill Bush, a researcher from the BBC, and collects data, some of which is employed by Blair in preparing for Prime Minister's Questiontime.

Blair has encouraged efforts, which have been partly successful, to change the culture in Number Ten. They include the increased resources, in the form of the strengthened Press Office and the new SCU, devoted to communications and presentation and attempts to link policy with presentation and to achieve more integration between the Private Office and Policy Unit. Also relevant has been the appointment of the Executive Secretary and the creation of a Management Board to modernise Number Ten and make it more efficient.

Moreover, there has been institutional change, for example the creation of task forces, the Drugs Unit, Surestart, the Social Exclusion Unit and the Performance and Innovation Unit, the last two based in the Cabinet Office. These changes, as Martin Burch points out, 'do not mark a break with the past but are the latest stage in the accretive development of the Centre'.[24] They are designed to promote joint departmental approaches to problems.

Almost inevitably, there have been charges of politicisation and of a blurring of the lines between political and Civil Service appointments and between serving party and government interests. Similar complaints were made of initiatives under Wilson, Heath and Mrs Thatcher. Much of the concern then and now has been overblown. There has long been a strong case for increasing the number of political aides to support the Prime Minister and for the Government Information Service to adapt to the changes in the mass media and their demands on the head of government. Defence of the status quo ante easily slides into a defence of Civil Service dominance. Indeed, the criticisms were a reminder of just how limited are the staffing powers of a British Prime Minister.[25] It is only since 1928 that the

Principal Private Secretary has been a Civil Service appointment. Before then the Private Office often consisted of a mix of political and official staff (see Chapter 2). Even later did the Number Ten Press Officer come to be regarded as a career civil servant – although Attlee, Eden and Wilson recruited sympathetic professional journalists to the post. The post-May 1997 developments therefore represent something of a return to old patterns of staffing, although with a stronger political imprint.[26] The increase in political appointments has the advantage that the Civil Service is able to offload activities which it regards as partisan to the political appointments. What has not been created is a Prime Minister's Department.

It is interesting to note that some of John Major's former staff have expressed approval of the steps. 'I always thought that John Major's Downing Street was light on the political side. He needed more people with clout who could make departments take notice,' said a former Private Secretary who had worked with and admired Major.[27] 'I agree with the extra political appointments, cutting back PMQs, and the stronger Number Ten control of communications. But there should be proper accountability and Parliament must be kept in the picture. In the right hands I would say "yes" to these measures, in the wrong hands, "no",' said George Bridges, assistant Political Secretary to John Major.[28] William Waldegrave, a Cabinet minister under Thatcher and Major and briefly a Political Secretary to Ted Heath in Downing Street, also agreed: 'I approve of steps to structure the diary so that Blair has more time for thinking, to strengthen the Cabinet Office and to make more political appointments in Downing Street.'[29]

Many features of the Blair style of operations in government are a carry-over from opposition. These include a belief that political leadership is a stock of capital that can be replenished by personal integrity, good communications, and the achievement of visible objectives (e.g. the 1997 election manifesto pledges) that are effectively within the leader's and government's control; a willingness to change established structures and patterns to enable him to work effectively and achieve his objectives. Radical changes to the Labour Party's constitution to speed decisions and achieve objectives have been followed by reforms at the centre of government to do the same;

an acknowledgment of the need for good presentation and rapid rebuttal of criticisms from the media, the opposition or party dissenters; a preference for making decisions in small ad hoc groups of people whose advice he values and on project teams, rather than formal meetings, such as the Cabinet; a practice of relying on known and trusted aides to occupy key positions in Number Ten. There was something akin to a US presidency in the importation of his own staff. It is significant that he starts his working week on Monday mornings with a meeting of his inner group.

Some of the following comments give an indication of the impression that Blair has made on the people who work for him. 'You can't sit around. He wants results,' says a member of the Policy Unit. Another comments 'This is a very media-oriented operation.' Another Blair adviser remarks, 'He is a Maoist, he is always dissatisfied and wants things done better. At times I wonder if he believes in permanent revolution . . . Cabinet died years ago. It hardly works anywhere else in the world today. It is now a matter of strong leadership at the centre and creating structures and having people to do it. I suppose we want to replace the departmental barons with a Bonapartist system.'

'I expected him to be more hands-on, more involved in details. He is a big picture man. If it does not fit into his framework he cuts it out,' says an official.

'It is more informal than in a government department or probably than under previous Prime Ministers. In a department the Private Secretary can control the minister's day. Here, it is more pluralistic and different people are providing an input,' says an official. 'It's a Tony operation. There are Tony's people and party people. The former have more regular access.' says a Labour official. 'Tony has a mission. He is impatient to achieve things on Northern Ireland, sorting out health, education and welfare and improving relations with Europe. Early on, he said to me "If I can do those, then I won't have done so badly",' says an adviser.

Talk of creating a stronger centre and promoting greater co-ordination and more strategic oversight are usually code words for combating departmentalism in Whitehall. In opposition, Blair had got his own way on policy and looked to carry on in this vein. Early on in his premiership he told a member of his Private Office that he was aware that the Civil Service provided a Rolls-Royce machine but 'He wanted to do more than to see it. He wanted to get in and drive it,' said the official.[30] After just over two years in office, ministers and officials were commenting wryly on the confident 'Tony wants' message from Number Ten. It is possible to point to at least three initiatives which Blair has taken to combat departmentalism and enhance the centre. To encourage the broad view, the projects conducted by the Policy and Innovation Unit are sponsored by a minister who is not from the major department involved. Blair's regular stocktaking sessions with ministers and senior officials in departments responsible for the core public services concentrate on meeting the government's objectives and monitoring progress towards the public service agreements. Finally, Richard Wilson has begun to convene regular meetings with a small group of Permanent Secretaries and included Miliband and Heywood, from Blair's office, to ensure that Whitehall is fully attuned to Blair's thinking. 'The Prime Minister wants Whitehall to deliver on his manifesto promises', said one Permanent Secretary. This was also a response to the concern which Blair's aides felt about their exclusion from the Cabinet Secretary's weekly meeting with the Permanent Secretaries.

Worldly-wise Whitehall watchers, however, wonder how far Blair has been able to replicate the Millbank model in government – strong central co-ordination by the leader's entourage of policy and communications. Shadow ministers become more powerful once they are installed in their departments; they control their own budgets and are supported by their own team of senior civil servants, junior ministers and special advisers. It is in this sense that some departmental ministers are 'barons', with their own 'fiefdoms'. Over time, departments usually wear down the interventionist centre, which always has other matters to deal with. According to one official, 'Blair is still trying to run the operation from Number Ten, but is gradually realising its impossibility.'

The Treasury has been an ally of Number Ten in its attack on departmentalism and provides some co-ordination through its control of spending. But the war on departmentalism has its own dangers. Ministers have as one of their functions the duty to speak for the interests and concerns which their departments deal with. British politics is littered with examples of ministers who neglected this role to comply with a Treasury or Number Ten strategy and succeeded only in damaging themselves and sometimes the government in the process.

It is always dangerous to generalise about trends in the premiership on the basis of a sample of one. Blair has been the beneficiary of a remarkable conjunction of favourable political circumstances – including the 179-seat majority, a divided and weak opposition, his own remarkable public popularity, the least ideologically fractious and factional Labour Party in memory, and a more favourable economic legacy than most new governments have inherited. These are unlikely to last. The styles of innovative or bold Prime Ministers, like Lloyd George or Margaret Thatcher, have usually provoked a negative reaction by the time they fall and Cabinet has reasserted a more collective leadership. Already, by early 1999, colleagues were speculating that Blair would have to be more collegial and involve the Cabinet more, in the wake of Peter Mandelson's resignation and graphic media reports of feuds between ministers. This was echoed by many senior commentators. They argued that the Blair style of decision making, namely bilateralism and the close partnership with Gordon Brown, reduced the sense of 'ownership' of policy among colleagues and that he might need the support of the Cabinet when he encountered difficulties. Indeed, there was some greater discussion of policy after a revolt among Labour MPs over benefit cuts in December 1997 and after the hostile reaction to the 75p increase in the basic state pension.[31] It is worth noticing that the resentment of many ministers was directed at the Chancellor Gordon Brown.

Blair entered office determined to exercise a grip from Number Ten and has made appointments and created and reformed institutions to suit that purpose. A conventional listing of the Prime Minister's functions includes choosing and dismissing ministers, appointing top civil servants, chairing Cabinet and important Cabinet committees, attending the House of Commons to answer questions, acting as head of government in international meetings of heads of government, and deciding on the date of general elections.[32] These responsibilities are unique to the Prime Minister. But they fail to do justice to Blair's emphasis on setting and overseeing strategy, communicating the ideas of New Labour to the public, and creating a stronger centre.

Blair's longer-term impact on the premiership largely depends on how successful he is. To what extent will initiatives like the SCU and the Performance and Innovation Unit in the Cabinet Office succeed in breaking down departmentalism? Will the introduction of a stronger political element, in the form of a political Chief of Staff in the Private Office make Number Ten work more effectively and set a precedent? Some features, like the enhanced capacity of the Cabinet Office at the centre and the downgrading of the Prime Minister's role in Parliament and in Cabinet management, appear to be part of a longer-term tend.

By 1999 Blair was showing impatience at the slowness with which departments were making improvements in core public services. Indeed, in a much reported speech in July he complained that it was more rooted than the private sector to the concept 'it has always been done this way'. Civil servants as well as ministers were reminded of their duty to deliver and some of the former reportedly complained of scapegoating.[33] Ministers retaliated with their own complaints of the Prime Minister's office; about decisions and documents being slowed up in an overworked Number Ten[34] and about Number Ten's negative briefing (John Prescott complained about 'faceless wonders' and 'teeny boppers') over some departments and over the Cabinet reshuffle in July 1999. The last turned out to be minor, although ministers who were targeted for moves have been unsettled over the summer. There was nothing unusual in any of the above. But when added to Blair's style of management, particularly his reliance on his office staff and neglect of the Cabinet, some friendly observers wondered if he was in danger of becoming isolated from his senior colleagues. These criticisms increased when the government was caught unawares by the backlash over the 75p pension increase and the protests over the rising cost of petrol in September 2000.

A more forceful critique of Blair's 'command premiership' is offered by Professor Peter Hennessy, a long-term observer of Whitehall and Downing Street[35]. He suggests that Blair may have over-reached himself, as many of the traditional checks and balances from the Labour party, Cabinet colleagues and Parliament have all declined. Hennessy's view is echoed by senior civil servants who have worked inside Number Ten and later became Permanent Secretaries. One commented: 'There used to be something called Cabinet Government. It was declining when I was there, in the 1980s, but now it seems almost to have died'. Another, who was a Private Secretary under Ted Heath as Prime Minister, gave Blair 'high marks for dealing with long-term strategy, presentation and getting the right mix of politics and administration, which are essential jobs for the Prime Minister.' He added, however, 'Weekly Cabinet is crucial for reminding ministers of the collective ownership of policies and Blair will be foolish to ignore it'.

A senior civil servant close to Blair and sympathetic to his attempts to modernise Whitehall complained that his handling of colleagues and the party reflected his memories of the 1980s, when Labour was so divided and un-electable. 'He is fighting the last war,' said the civil servant. The press eagerly seized on an aide's analogy between Blair and Napoleon. When taxed about this by *Guardian* interviewers at Chequers on 24 September 1999, Blair replied: 'You have got to run an efficient government and you have got to run an effective centre . . . I want to make sure that for this programme we have got we are driving it through. I just think you live with this. You are either a strong Prime Minister in which case you are a control freak, or you are a weak Prime Minister in which case you are weak really and I think I know in the end which I would like to be accused of.'

There is a tendency for Prime Ministers to react against their immediate predecessors. As noted, Tony Blair reacted against John Major as Prime Minister and against his two Labour predecessors as Prime Minister, Harold Wilson and James Callaghan. But after three years in office some of the gloss had been removed from Blair's premiership. Assets such as skilled presentation, central control and sure sense of direction were no longer so evident. Communications and presentation were marred by excessive self praise, triple counting allocations of public spending and repeat announcements designed to create the impression that new money was being allocated. The result was public cynicism about government spin. The strong centre was increasingly seen as control-freakery, witnessed in the intolerance of internal dissent, the botched intervention to manage the exclusion of Ken Livingstone as Labour candidate for London mayor and the lack of collegiality in Cabinet. A Blair memo, written to his office staff on 29 April 2000 and leaked to *The Times* and *Sun* on 17 July, contradicted his claims of indifference to image and spin. The memo reflected his worries over perceptions on his government on law and order issues. It called for: 'something tough with immediate bite which sends a message through the system', headline-catching initiatives on a number of fronts, and repeated that 'I should be personally associated with as much of this as possible.' Even normally sympathetic commentators fastened on the memo's concern with image and demands for immediate initiatives.

Perhaps the pendulum will swing back again, post-Blair, to a more collegiate Cabinet, strong departments and a rejection of proactive media management. It is more likely, however, that future Prime Ministers will retain a large Policy Unit to monitor departments and promote strategic oversight from the centre. It also provides them with additional opportunities for patronage and opportunities to increase their own political support. A political Chief of Staff, probably but not necessarily based in the Private Office, is also probably established. It relieves the Private Secretaries of some duties which might challenge the line between political and official duties. Interestingly, William Hague has a Chief of Staff, Lord (Sebastian) Coe. It is also likely that a future Prime Minister, particularly when coming direct from opposition, will bring in his own Chief Press Secretary and retain a body like the SCU. A strong communications presence is a necessary response, given the growing importance of the media. Prime Ministers have also long wanted the Cabinet Office to move beyond its traditional remit of acting as an honest broker and ensuring that the Cabinet system works smoothly, and it is unlikely that the steps to encourage policy innovation, joined-up policy and better implementation will be reversed. Indeed, if they are judged to have failed, the result is likely to be further demands for a stronger centre.

CHAPTER ELEVEN

Conclusion

NUMBER TEN'S OPERATIONS changed as much between 1970 and 2000 as they had done in the hundred years before 1970. Of the six Prime Ministers from Ted Heath to Tony Blair, three of them were Labour and three Conservative. They differed not only in the circumstances under which they operated, but also in their approaches and goals.

The government of Ted Heath was the first to face the problems involved in Britain's joining the European Economic Community while simultaneously having to cope with a breakdown of law and order in Northern Ireland. These twin burdens bore down on every succeeding government. The years of Labour rule from 1974 to 1979 (under Harold Wilson and James Callaghan) were also spent trying to tackle the effects of a severe economic recession without an assured parliamentary majority. This challenge inevitably made a deep impression on the way the two premierships were conducted. Under all these strains, the thesis that Britain had become 'ungovernable' in the 1970s began to be widely discussed, and affected perceptions, and even the exercise, of prime ministerial authority in and beyond Whitehall.

Mrs Thatcher, in contrast, enjoyed a series of commanding parliamentary majorities and was also the most ideological and policy-engaged of all postwar Prime Ministers. In the 1980s, commentators duly changed their tune from talk of the impossible strains on the Prime Minister to arguments about the strength of British government and the overbearing power of the Prime Minister. Yet no sooner had the image of an overpowerful premiership received widespread currency than the coin turned again. Major after 1992 suffered from some of the Wilson and Callaghan problems, notably the lack of an assured parliamentary majority, an economic recession, a divided political party and a hostile press. New questions began to be asked: were Major's difficulties due to the weakness of the office, as much as events or his own personal inadequacies as a leader?

No Prime Minister in our period started out in such favourable circumstances as Tony Blair in May 1997. He was backed by a huge parliamentary majority, good will from the media, a united party (at least on the surface), a relatively sound economy and an enfeebled opposition. Blair saw the Major years and drew lessons: he became a radical figure in increasing the number of his appointments and reorganising structures in Number Ten so that he could do the job the way he wished and impose his own priorities. To him, and many of his aides, the structural weaknesses of the office as well as the personality of the incumbent explain some of John Major's problems.

Heath, party leader since 1965, had given much thought before-hand to the government machine and how he should operate as Prime Minister. He is perhaps the nearest in this period to a Prime Minister schooled in techniques of business management. Wilson was the only one in these years, and only the second since 1945 (the other was Winston Churchill in 1951), to return to Number Ten after a spell as opposition leader. Wilson devoted more of his time than any other Prime Minister except Major to problems of party management, partly reflecting his interests and partly reflecting the problems in the party. But one can exaggerate the degree of Wilson's activity in party man-agement: by 1974 he was no longer an energetic figure. Both Heath and Wilson were innovators and changed institutions in Downing Street, although only Wilson's Policy Unit still survives.

If Heath's staff was perhaps the most harmonious, Wilson's was the most divided, largely because of the behaviour of Marcia Williams and the torpor of the leader, particularly in his last term. Mrs Thatcher was not much interested in creating new organisations; indeed she was more inclined to run down existing machinery or reform it. Con-scious of the need to cut the size of the government sector, she was also reluctant to expand her staff. It took four years for her Policy Unit to be restored to the size it had been under Wilson and Callaghan and in 1987 she still had fewer staff in it than Labour had in 1979. Her government also reduced the number of special advisers throughout

Whitehall to just seven in 1979; Tony Blair's government in January 2000 had nearly eighty. Although Number Ten certainly gained influence during Mrs Thatcher's premiership and she made substantial changes to the Civil Service structure and culture, she left no institutional legacy in Downing Street. Her approach relied more on getting what she called 'the right people' in key positions. Like Churchill and Blair, she was people-centred, as well as goal-oriented.

Major, like Callaghan before him, was remarkably comfortable with the people and institutions he found in Number Ten, and for the most part was willing to use them and to work through the Whitehall departments rather than build up a power centre in Number Ten. Major did spend some time, however, looking in vain for a 'fixer', who would bring ministers to order and improve co-ordination between departments, but he only seriously began this quest after it became clear that his authority was slipping after September 1992. Blair's institutional radicalism can be seen not only in his adding so many political appointments in Number Ten and creating new units, but also in his downgrading of what he regarded as the less essential features of the job, including the twice-weekly ordeal of Parliamentary Questions. He is more interested in the quality of people and their remits than in structure. If Mrs Thatcher strengthened the centre by dint of personal willpower and energy, Blair in his own way took advantage of the Prime Minister's scope to bolster staffing and organisation.

Prime Ministers also change over the course of their premiership. Heath started off being determined not to get involved in day-to-day matters, such as Wilson's practice in the 1960s of giving 'beer and sandwiches' in Number Ten to both sides in industrial relations disputes. Yet he soon found himself drawn into the details of policies on prices and incomes, Northern Ireland, and Europe. When asked why he had abandoned his original inclinations, he said:

> The simple fact was that in each case those with whom the Government was negotiating insisted on dealing personally and directly with me as Prime Minister.[1]

Wilson and Callaghan went through this same transition to becoming more 'hands-on'. Mrs Thatcher was a relentless intervener and would selectively involve herself in the details of a policy in which she was interested. Her energy and the exceptional length of time she was in office enabled her to affect a number of policy areas. John Major began in 1990 with a collegial approach to Cabinet. This style suited his nature but was also explained by his colleagues' reaction to Mrs Thatcher's 'bossiness' and by the fact that some of them were more experienced than he was himself. Later, as Cabinet itself became increasingly polarised, notably on Europe, and began to leak against him, Major became wary of his original consensual and open style of leading Cabinet. He became so secretive towards the end that even close ministers found it hard to read his mind.

All holders of the top post were suspicious to varying degrees either of the Treasury as an institution or of the Chancellor of the day as an individual and either clashed with, or overruled, him on key policies. Number Ten–Foreign Office was the other key axis. Mrs Thatcher's difficulties with Francis Pym (1982–83) and then Geoffrey Howe (1983–89) as Foreign Secretaries, however, were the exception in generally good Number Ten–Foreign Office relations. Heath's relations with Douglas-Home (1970–74) and Major's with Hurd (1990–95) were the high points of Number Ten–FCO harmony.

The speed with which the exit of a British Prime Minister and the installation of a new one are accomplished is remarkable. In contrast, an incoming US President has ten weeks between election and taking office.

Six of the ten men and one woman who have held office as Prime Minister since 1939 first assumed it at relatively short notice during the course of a Parliament (Churchill in 1940, Eden in 1955, Macmillan in 1957, Home in 1963, Callaghan in 1976 and Major in 1990). To be seen to be preparing for the succession, even if such an eventuality were foreseen, would run the risk of being accused of disloyalty to the Prime Minister. And an opposition leader, although a Prime Minister designate with considerable chances to prepare for power, wants to avoid a charge of hubris. Nevertheless, time for preparation may be an enormous boon for a Prime Minister, as Wilson found in 1964, Heath in 1970, Mrs Thatcher in 1979 and Blair in 1997.

Virtually all Prime Ministers claim to have learned lessons from the past. Every opposition leader from Clement Attlee down to Blair has been critical of the Prime Minister he or she succeeded and has promised to do things differently. Some lessons are learned from personal experience, others vicariously via a reading of history or anecdotes of past practice from colleagues. At best, the learning is based on a very selective reading of the past. In 1964 Wilson promised to be a decisive chairman, like Attlee, allegedly, and his claims that he would make his office a powerhouse and set strategy reflected his judgment on the performance of his immediate predecessor, Alec Douglas-Home. For his second term of office in 1974 Wilson opted to be less interventionist. The talk now was of being a 'sweeper' rather than a powerhouse, a reflection of the fact that his political authority and physical energy had both declined markedly compared with ten years earlier. Heath's interest in the machinery of government and strategy, and his hostility to what he called 'gimmicks', were reinforced by his perception of Wilson's performance during 1964–70. Mrs Thatcher thought the premierships of Wilson and Callaghan were weak and indecisive and she opted for a more authoritarian style. Major reacted and wanted something more consensual, and Blair something tougher and more focused. It is perhaps inevitable that a Prime Minister's learning from the past is often based on shallow evidence and an inadequate or ungenerous understanding of the constraints under which their predecessors operated.

Arrangements or commitments about future appointments and institutional changes are usually kept informal and confidential, although opposition leaders often have to be more specific about future policies, ironically, as they have more control over the former than the latter. A striking theme of our interviews was the way in which political appointments to Number Ten were rarely discussed before victory had been won. Some of Blair's staff commented, 'We didn't want to tempt fate', or, 'To talk about jobs in government would seem like taking the outcome for granted'.

Douglas Hurd recalls the day after the 1970 general election poll when it became clear that the Conservatives had won and Heath told him to go and inform Downing Street officials that the new Prime Minister would be arriving shortly. When Hurd queried his status for such a task, Heath replied: 'Tell them that you are my Political

Secretary'. It was the first that Hurd had heard of his new job. After a visit to the Palace, Heath sent for his pyjamas and toothbrush and began work in Downing Street.[2] This transition followed an exhausting and difficult election campaign. Heath, like other new Prime Ministers, immediately began the task of making over a hundred government appointments, tackling the in-tray of urgent foreign and economic problems and being briefed by the Cabinet Secretary. The rushed transition is typical, despite the incoming government having done so much to prepare for office beforehand.

Bernard Donoughue, an academic at the London School of Economics and a Labour activist, was giving informal election advice to Harold Wilson from late 1973. During the February 1974 general election campaign Wilson casually mentioned that there might be a task for him after the election if Labour formed a government. Nothing more. Labour was not expected to win. When Wilson became Prime Minister and asked Donoughue to head his Policy Unit, the latter had to negotiate a hurried leave of absence from his university.

Mrs Thatcher's first approach to John Hoskyns as Head of the Policy Unit was some weeks before the 1979 election: 'We want you to stay around after the general election. Go and talk to Victor Rothschild about Whitehall.'[3] One of Blair's staff admitted that he had some expectations that he would be offered something: 'I was part of Tony's team in Millbank. Future jobs were only talked about diffidently . . . Hubris and all that. If you were still there in the last few days and people were friendly and thought you were doing a good job, then you could feel confident that there would be something for you.' A few weeks before the 1997 election Blair held a heavily provisional discussion with him about the future. 'Tony felt he had to say something and was clearly uncomfortable. It was all phrased hypothetically, along the lines: "If we were to form a government . . .".'[4] Most of the discussions were conducted by Blair's Chief of Staff, Jonathan Powell.

In opposition the party leader may also wish to retain as free a hand as possible. Both Wilson and Callaghan were constrained by a strong and assertive extra-parliamentary party organisation which wished to tie them down over policy and appointments. Elevation to the premiership transforms the party leader's authority vis-à-vis colleagues and the party organisation. He now has patronage to dis-

Conclusion

pense and can ask people to make a commitment to work for him. There is, however, a downside to this caution over appointments. In 1970 the CPRS, so important to Heath's new style of government, took four months to have Rothschild in post as its head and several more months before it was fully operational in 1971. Donoughue did not know that there would be a Policy Unit until Prime Minister Wilson told him and then took weeks to recruit staff. It has thus often proved difficult for incoming Prime Ministers to 'hit the ground running' with all their staff fully in place.

Once in office, Prime Ministers have rarely found the time to give much attention to the machinery of government. The daily grind takes over: they have to cope with the flow of papers, meetings to attend and to prepare for, foreign trips, as well as reacting to the inevitable economic down-turns, difficult colleagues, a scandal, a factory closure, or a by-election defeat. To prepare in much detail in opposition looks over-ambitious and even foolish, because the leader usually also lacks hands-on experience. They therefore take largely what they find.

Describing the work of a small group of people who operate in such a confined area is an exercise in miniaturism. Individual chemistry often matters more than formal titles, flexibility more than standing on job remits, and collegiality is more evident than hierarchy. Number Ten echoes the politics more of a bustling and anarchic village than that of a settled bureaucracy. Staff, both official and political, are often acquainted with each other before they move into Number Ten. Business is frequently conducted in small meetings, over the telephone and in brief unscheduled chats; the private secretaries in their two open-plan rooms would rely on each other to pick things up; staff snatch moments with the Prime Minister between meetings or as he moves around the building. Christopher Meyer, Number Ten Press Secretary (1994–96), commented in mid-office upon the virtual impossibility for historians of ever being able to re-create the sequence of events or the interplay of relationships in the fast-moving and fluid Number Ten.[5] The small numbers and tight space, on the other hand, and the overlap in duties undoubtedly facilitate co-ordination (though occasionally they can foster rivalry). A premium is placed on interpersonal trust, pride in doing a highly professional job and remaining calm under pressure. Private secretaries living virtually cheek by jowl during their long working hours and accustomed to reading and listening to each others' business correspondence and phone conversations, have no secrets within the Private Office and few within Number Ten as a whole.

The senior Civil Service staff have been overwhelmingly male, as well as public/grammar school and Oxbridge educated and London-based. They are all on secondment from their departments, but will have had their working style and ethos honed by many years in the Civil Service before their joining Number Ten. The temporary political staff, who come and go with changes of premier, also exhibit the classic Civil Service skills of networking, drafting papers and anticipating or reflecting the thinking of their client, the Prime Minister. These qualities support their interests in practical policy ideas, links with the ruling political party and skills in speechwriting or communication. Where the temporary political staff do not acquire Whitehall 'know-how', as did Hoskyns (Head Policy Unit, 1979–82), their effectiveness is reduced.

Most of the official and political staff who work for a Prime Minister speak of the sense of community, comradeship and unique excitement that comes from being at the very centre of affairs. Many, for the remainder of their careers, will never recapture the same intense interest and prestige from being so close to the fount of power: some find their later careers and life an anticlimax, punctuated by the mixed blessing of periodic requests for 'interviews' arriving from students and other researchers. When still *in situ*, the morale of the political staff fluctuates depending on such ephemera as opinion polls, media comment and the Prime Minister's performance in the Commons. In this respect, the mood in Downing Street rises and falls like that in a Whitehall department, and even the official Private Office staff are not untouched by it.

Their shared commitment to the Prime Minister notwithstanding, different actors within Number Ten have different motives. Prime Ministers think of their place in history, while denying they ever do any such base thing. Political staff think of their next job. Civil servants want to be well regarded by colleagues, especially the Head of the Home Civil Service or the Permanent Secretary at the FCO, and are usually careful not to appear over-committed to the transitory incumbent who happens to be Prime Minister. But they share the sense of failure, as a Prime Minister departs for the last time. When Andrew Turnbull, Principal Private Secretary under Mrs Thatcher, received a CBE (in her resignation honours list) he took the Queen aback by commenting that it seemed odd to receive an honour for losing a Prime Minister. John Colville, Philip de Zulueta and Charles Powell were rare examples of over-identification, and resigned from the Civil Service on leaving Number Ten. All had FCO backgrounds. Apart from Tim Bligh (1959–64), outside our period, no 'home' civil servant similarly became too identified with the Prime Minister: most returned to mainstream Civil Service life on leaving Number Ten. Number Ten staff therefore mark their success individually and most, other than the Prime Minister, emerge with their career prospects enhanced.

The political staff know that the present phase of their careers will end with the resignation of the Prime Minister, but that civil servants have tenure. 'She was my life and I could see that she was in trouble,' said Robin Harris, a member of Mrs Thatcher's Policy Unit, 'there were too many bureaucrats and not enough political support in the building.' He was reacting to the fraught atmosphere in the building before her fall.[6] Even civil servants develop surprisingly close personal bonds with the Prime Minister, but they know their jobs are secure whatever happens: the political staff must find new employment.

The Prime Minister's staff provides many services. Those of policy adviser, speech writer, correspondent, trouble shooter, spokesperson, and buffer are well known. But a Prime Minister surrounded by ministerial colleagues, who are also rivals for his job, needs people to turn to for comfort and reassurance. He turns to those who are loyal to and dependent upon him, his aides. In contrast with Cabinet ministers, they are not elected. He is their constituency. With his closest helpers he can sound off, be indiscreet, float ideas, and speculate (sometimes about the plots and leaks of rivals and their sympathisers). Many are at first surprised to be party to such confidence. Heath, Wilson, Thatcher and Major could repair with them late at night to the flat upstairs at Number Ten and unwind over a glass of whisky. Except in the case of Heath, Cabinet ministers were rarely part of this group.

There is a cost to this intense, high pressured if exciting life. The punishing hours, typically twelve or so a day for the political staff and even more for the Private Office, take their toll. Mistakes are not tolerated easily. It is understandable why few official or even political staff last more than three years. One Political Secretary to a beleaguered Prime Minister remarked, 'People have to leave after a few years. The place sucks the life out of you.'[7] A sense of professionalism, adrenaline ('it kept us going all hours', said one), and a fierce loyalty to the Prime Minister are important in motivating staff to work at such intensity. Not uncommonly Private Secretaries may be up half the night finishing a speech or watching developments, or fly in overnight, having worked non-stop on the plane writing communiqués or redrafting notes of meetings: all have to be ready to go in at 8 am the next morning for a full and exhausting day's work in Downing Street. Not all cope: some break under the strain. Michael Halls (Principal Private Secretary 1966–70) died suddenly in April 1970, a death blamed by his widow on the stresses of the job.

A number of trends emerge in our study of the support system for Prime Ministers over the period 1970–2000 and some of them are marked under Blair.

There has been a marked increase in the size of the Number Ten staff from 71 in June 1970 at the beginning of Heath's premiership to nearly 200 in December 1998 in the early stages of Blair's. This trend continues the slow growth of the years before 1970 with a considerable increase under Blair. If these levels are, in comparison with the staff of other heads of state, not large, Number Ten is clearly ceasing to be a small office, although terms like 'family atmosphere' and 'small group, informal politics' are still appropriate.

The trend towards a collective premiership has continued steadily over the period 1970–2000. Faced with more pressures, the Prime Minister has had little choice but to rely more on the staff around him in Number Ten. He has no more hours in the day available than did Robert Walpole. The Prime Minister also needs time to relax, to think and to spend time with his or her family. No appointment of a Deputy Prime Minister, 'Cabinet Enforcer', or other such posts can disguise the fact that the Prime Minister's time is finite. Hence the need for a competent and loyal team of officials and political aides around the Prime Minister. With the establishment of the Political Office and the Policy Unit, there has been a move to a larger political element within Number Ten. Blair, in contrast, befitting for a man with three years as leader to prepare, already knew or had worked with all of the senior people he brought into Number Ten. The scale of Blair's importation and his familiarity with them resembles the way in which a new US President brings his own 'team' to the White House. Conservative political staff at Number Ten often had prior Whitehall experience as special or political advisers to ministers, and then left government service after finishing at Number Ten. Stephen Sherbourne, Norman Blackwell, Jonathan Hill and Howell James are the equivalents of the 'in and outers' in the USA.

The growth of 'para-political' careers as special advisers, lobbyists and researchers in parties and think tanks has provided an entrée for the politically interested become advisers and to move on to be an MP.[8] The post of Political Secretary has been a springboard for entry to the House of Commons for Douglas Hurd, Tom McNally, Richard Ryder, John Whittingdale and Judith Chaplin. The same is true of the Policy Unit; witness the careers of John Redwood, Oliver Letwin, Damien Green, Hartley Booth and David Willetts. Few of Blair's Unit have experience outside 'para-political' posts.

As the 'circles of influence' diagrams in Appendix II show, different Prime Ministers rely on different offices and sources of advice. The Private Office has remained the most consistently influential office of all those at the Prime Minister's disposal; premiers often arrive at Number Ten suspicious of officials and determined to rely more on political appointees and politicians than on officials but they usually leave with the position reversed. There is no time when a Private Office official, normally the Principal Private Secretary, is not a member of the inner ring. The Foreign Affairs Private Secretary has been the second most consistently influential official in the circles.

Most accounts of Number Ten underestimate the role of the Private Office and exaggerate that of political appointments. This is surely a consequence of the fact that many political actors write memoirs and books, and speak on the record, whereas civil servants rarely do any of the above. Yet Private Office staff often spend several hours each day with or near the Prime Minister. The influence of officials has often been less to change a Prime Minister's mind than to reinforce him or her in their instincts; thus Robert Armstrong helped Heath pave the way for entry into the European Community and Charles Powell reinforced Mrs Thatcher in a more Eurosceptical conversely direction in the mid and late 1980s.

In practice, despite the burgeoning in the number of political appointments, and attempts to rationalise Number Ten's structure, there remains an overlap of interests and responsibilities between the Political Office, Policy Unit and Press Office in matters such as election planning, policy launches, Prime Minister's speeches and government presentation. Overlaps present opportunities for 'turf' disputes as well as incentives co-ordination.

Rivalries are not necessarily only between political and official staff. Tensions on the political side reached a high point under Wilson with Joe Haines and Bernard Donoughue on one side and Marcia Williams on the other. Under Major, tensions between Sarah Hogg and Judith Chaplin also became uncomfortable. In the early Thatcher years there were strongly negative feelings between the political appointee Hoskyns and officials. Later in her premiership, rivalry reached a high point between Charles Powell and other officials. Blair has emphasised co-operation within Number Ten: it has yet to be shown whether he will be more successful in achieving it in the long term than many of his predecessors.[9]

Officials in Number Ten have become more comfortable with political appointees. Compared with the difficulties experienced by Marcia Williams in 1964 and John Hoskyns in 1979 the roles of the Political Office and Policy Unit are now secure and they have larger remits. Indeed, it is now inconceivable that a Prime Minister would operate without either or revert to the small scale units that they were when they were first set up. In some areas, for example the Cabinet Office servicing of and Private Office attendance at variously-named presentation and co-ordination committees, and at Number Ten seminars under Major and Blair, or staffing the Policy Unit, there have been extensions of the Civil Service input, and a blurring of rigid distinctions. The trend has continued under Blair, with more political penetration of official units, and with special advisers appointed to the Private Office, the Press Office, the Strategic Communications

Unit and the Performance and Innovation Unit. Before Blair, political appointees were largely confined to the Policy Unit and Political Office but now they are found in many units, often working alongside officials.

The main expansion has been in the Cabinet Office. The Cabinet Office has expanded in an ad hoc way, 'by convulsion and spasms', to quote one Cabinet Secretary.[10] It gained responsibilities following negotiations for entry to and membership of the EEC from 1973, the abolition of the Civil Service Department in 1981 and the CPRS in 1983, and the creation of the Efficiency Unit, the Citizen's Charter Unit and Heseltine's Deregulation Unit, to name but a few. This pattern of absorption has continued under Blair, with the Social Exclusion Unit and the Performance and Innovation Unit. Number Ten has been the beneficiary of the expanded Cabinet Office. But for the lack of space, some of the new units would have been located in Number Ten.

The Cabinet Secretariat was set up in 1916 to service Cabinet and its committees, and thus to work for the Cabinet as a whole, but in practice the primary political figure whose needs and wishes it has served has been the Prime Minister. Blair's creation of so many task forces with policy remits running across departments has added to pressure for greater co-ordination. Over the years, periodic calls were heard, as the realisation dawned of how hard it was for a small Number Ten to do more than react to events, for the Cabinet Office to play a greater role in planning ahead and helping the government to anticipate problems. Before Blair moved into Number Ten the Cabinet Office's official remit was '. . . to provide an effective, efficient and impartial service to the Cabinet Committees. The Secretariat has no executive powers beyond serving the Cabinet and Committees and co-ordinating Departmental contributions to the government's work'. Under Blair the remit has changed and now the Cabinet Office is expected: '. . . *to support efficient, timely and well informed collective determination of government policy and to drive forward the achievement of the government's agenda*' (emphasis in original). By the end of the century, the Cabinet Office was indeed expected to be more of a policy-oriented and a proactive co-ordinating body. It also has a Cabinet minister as a ministerial and enforcing head. The Cabinet Office must now be considered something of a corporate headquarters overseeing government strategy.

The Press Office has also expanded to take on a more proactive role and to cope with the rapidly growing demands since 1970 of an avaricious and subtle mass media – which provide continuous coverage of political and governmental affairs – and the greater number of press conferences, summits and policy launches involving the Prime Minister. The establishment of the Strategic Communications Unit (SCU) in 1998 and additions to the Press Office staff meant that the number of communicators in Number Ten (excluding the Policy Unit) virtually doubled in just twelve months after John Major left office. Blair's staff also believe in a more focused way than any of their predecessors that a successful policy requires good presentation and that effective government requires a clear and consistent 'message'.

The Policy Unit, created in 1974, has worn very different guises under different administrations. Staff largely share the values of the Prime Minister they work for. The tone of John Major's Unit was different from that of Mrs Thatcher's; some members of the former's staff would not have served the latter, and vice versa. Members of Conservative Policy Units have often had experience in industry and commerce, while Labour's have had experience in academe, media or the party. From 1985, members have had the right to attend Cabinet committee meetings dealing with issues in which they specialise. One insider has distinguished between Unit heads 'who shot with rifles' – for example, John Hoskyns concentrating on the economy and trade unions, Ferdinand Mount on social policy and Brian Griffiths on broadcasting and education – 'and those who shot with blunderbusses' – for example, Bernard Donoughue, Sarah Hogg and Norman Blackwell, all of whom ranged widely.[11] The Unit represents additional pairs of hands, eyes and ears for the Prime Minister, enabling him or her to keep in touch with what is happening in Whitehall departments, following up his policy interests, providing briefing for meetings with colleagues and outsiders and drafting political speeches. Since 1979, its head has increasingly taken a major role in overseeing election preparations and drafting the general election manifesto. The Policy Unit's staff now oversee virtually all departments, although they concentrate largely on domestic politics. In the Conservatives' Units (1979–97), a quarter of staff were civil servants, compared with only three members or just over 10 per cent of Labour Units (1974–79 and 1997–2000).

The Private Office has grown by four appointments in the past thirty years: in 1975 a second domestic Private Secretary was added and in 1994 an assistant Foreign Affairs Private Secretary was brought in to help with the growing foreign and Irish work, and in 1999 Blair added another two. He also appointed a Chief of Staff, based in the Private Office, and then in 1999 a Deputy Chief of Staff, Pat McFadden. The Treasury still supplies the Private Secretary for economic affairs and the Foreign Office both Private Secretaries for foreign affairs, so consolidating further their positions with Number Ten. Other staff deal with parliamentary affairs, social, and other domestic policy, the diary and there is also a Duty Clerk constantly at work. The workload is heavy and modern communications and technology demanding immediate responses have only added to the pressures. The fact that the private secretaries are drawn from and expect to return to their original departments means that they are able to network with the rest of Whitehall to a degree which is unknown in the offices of political leaders in other countries.[12] In the best Civil Service traditions of impartiality and flexibility, they are on 'loan' or secondment from Whitehall to Number Ten.

A recurring theme of reform, regardless of party, is the attempt to promote co-ordination to curb the centrifugal effects of departmentalism. Past attempts to enhance central control have included the setting up of an 'inner' Cabinet, 'giant' departments, 'overlords' and the CPRS. The 1970 White Paper on the *Reorganisation of Central Government* spoke of the need for the centre to take a synoptic view of government. The reasons advanced for changing the Whitehall status quo were twofold. One was the difficulty of tackling issues which crossed departmental boundaries; the second was the fact that a minister's departmental policies do not always support the government's overall objectives. The Prime Minister, freed from the responsibility of running a Whitehall department and supported by the Cabinet Secretary, appears well placed to form a clear overview of how departments interact. In the first two years, Blair's initiatives included the fifteen-month comprehensive spending review (CSR), the creation of the Social Exclusion Unit in the Cabinet Office, the establishment of some sixty task forces, the grafting of a Performance and Innovation Unit onto the Cabinet Office and the Treasury agreements with departments, following the allocations of public spending in 1998.

Prime Ministers have had little time for, or sustained interest in, intelligence and security matters. They dabbled, and liked to show off their knowledge of the world of John Le Carré, and they wanted to make the security services feel valued. But the intelligence and security world barely impinged on their time or thinking. Harold Wilson was the main exception, but his interest was regarded by many insiders as paranoid. Callaghan was more knowledgeable than most.

Flexibility and informality are the rule. Number Ten has remained a loose, unhierarchical office, in which political and official staff help out where the pressure is greatest. Job descriptions are a recent development and other procedures common in private sector organisations, such as staff appraisal, have only been implemented in the 1990s. The widescale use of computers only came in the 1990s, a good ten years after their introduction in the private sector. Information up until then would primarily come into Number Ten on paper or by telephone: security concerns were the main reason given for Number Ten being slow to come on line with the rest of Whitehall, or indeed with its own 'intranet'. Increasingly, communications within Number Ten are now conducted by e-mail. The Number Ten computer system has its own security firewalls. The 'I Love You' bug which damaged so many computers in May 2000 had hardly any effect on the Number Ten system.

None of the various elements that have gone to make up Number Ten have had a static influence during 1970–2000.

The influence of the Policy Unit since its creation in 1974 has fluctuated. Its first Head, Donoughue, in his book *Prime Minister*, has presented a long list of initiatives which failed to make progress under Callaghan, largely because of the lack of co-operation by departments or, by implication, the lack of prime ministerial commitment or authority.[13] The same is true of later Policy Units. Influence depends partly on the perceived quality of its advice and the degree of access to the Prime Minister, and partly on the Unit's ability to gain the respect and co-operation of key ministers and civil servants; the latter is likely to be shaped by the former. Blackwell's Unit (1995–97) suffered from some Cabinet ministers having little time or apparent respect for it. Perceived influence helps to create actual influence, getting inside what one former member, David Willetts (1987), called the 'virtuous' policy loop. Once the Unit has persuaded the Prime Minister to act, its ultimate impact depends on his authority over colleagues. But it simply does not have the resources to make policy, or to push a policy uphill if there is considerable resistance outside Number Ten. What it can do, on the Prime Minister's behalf, is to progress-chase, or question and modify what comes from departments, or suggest alternative lines to follow. Our impression is that Prime Ministers found it most useful in the periods 1974–76, 1984–85, 1990–93, and again since 1997.

The Principal Private Secretary in the Private Office has often – but, as we show, not always – been a commanding figure throughout the postwar period; some, like Leslie Rowan, John Colville, Tim Bligh, Robert Armstrong, Ken Stowe, Robin Butler, Andrew Turnbull and Alex Allan stand out in this respect. Mrs Thatcher's Private Office's influence as a whole grew, partly because of her own strong views on many policy issues, partly because of her disenchantment at times with the two key departments, the Foreign Office and the Treasury, and partly because of her growing personal interest in overseas affairs. The importance of the Private Office coincided in the 1980s with some reduction in the Cabinet Secretary's autonomy, as Robert Armstrong (1979–87) reacted against the Cabinet Office's accumulation of powers under his predecessor John Hunt (1973–79) and assumed additional and time-consuming responsibilities as sole Head of the Home Civil Service from 1983.

The Foreign Affairs Private Secretary is one particular post to have increased greatly in authority. Over the years from Tom Bridges (1971–74) to John Coles (1981–84) the post was influential but comparatively subordinate. The change came after Charles Powell's arrival in 1984, to a position almost akin to the National Security Adviser in the White House. The 'hot line' to the White House during Powell's tenure was placed on the Foreign Affairs Private Secretary's desk.

Subsequent tenants, Stephen Wall, Rod Lyne and John Holmes were all the beneficiaries of his tenure in the 1980s. All continued to communicate directly with the National Security Advisers and their equivalents in other countries. They were all key players in the prime ministerial initiatives in Northern Ireland under Major and Blair, and in the Prime Minister's relations with EU partners, not least when Britain held the Presidency.

There have been two main types of Cabinet Secretary. Burke Trend (1967–73) and Robin Butler (1988–97) were highly efficient co-ordinators of government business and had more detached relationships with the Prime Minister (though the former was closer to Wilson than to Heath and the latter closer to Thatcher than to Major). The other kind of Cabinet Secretary was more closely identified personally with the Prime Minister and with their policies. John Hunt (1973–79) was a leading figure in discussions on incomes policy and trade unions: Armstrong (1979–87) was involved with Mrs Thatcher's policies on GCHQ, the Anglo-Irish Agreement and 'Spycatcher', and Richard Wilson (1998–) is closely involved with Blair's project to modernise the civil service and improve policy delivery.

The Political Office, consisting of the Political Secretary, the Parliamentary Private Secretaries, a constituency secretary and (in 1997) two Assistant Political Secretaries, is perhaps the least integrated of all the Number Ten units. The role of the Political Secretary has combined acting as the Prime Minister's troubleshooter or 'fixer' with the party and being an adviser on policy and tactics. The success of the party role depends in large part on the Prime Minister's authority, although there was more scope for the Political Secretary under Wilson and Callaghan, given the fractious state of the Labour Party, than when the party has been more settled. Some Political Secretaries, such as Hurd, McNally, Sherbourne and Hill, have made a significant input into speechwriting, but others, such as Marcia Williams, Ryder, James and Sally Morgan, did little or none. As an adviser on strategy and day-to-day politics the Political Secretary was probably most important in the periods 1970–74, 1983–87 and 1992–97.

The Press Office has responded to media pressures and ministers' determination to set the media agenda. The Chief Press Secretaries under Mrs Thatcher and Tony Blair seem to have been the closest personally to the Prime Minister and their advice on the presentation of policies and appointments could not but help shade into substance. The two non-Civil Service appointments, Joe Haines and Alastair Campbell, both helped with speechwriting, and both were in the inner circle of advisers.

The continuing centrality of Civil Service influence emerges clearly from the preceding chapters. The Treasury and FCO, in particular, have maintained a heavy dominance over not just the Private Office but also the Cabinet Secretariat, which is likewise made up of those seconded by other departments. The Private Office has retained the closest physical proximity to the Prime Minister and the Cabinet Room, even after Tony Blair's shift of office into the inner Private Secretaries' room in 1998.

The 'new' offices in Number Ten have generally been less significant. The Political Office, created in 1964, rarely recovered the influence it had up to 1970 under its first head, Marcia Williams. The Central Policy Review Staff (1971–83) excited much attention among academics, but what little influence it had under its first head, Rothschild, had disappeared from the mid-1970s. The Policy Unit, set up in 1974, battled hard early on to establish its niche. It has been periodically influential in helping set the Prime Minister's agenda, mainly when the head was close to the Prime Minister. Whatever importance the 'new' offices may have had, it has rarely been at the expense of the Civil Service.

Number Ten has not for any protracted period since 1970 established itself as a strategic centre. High hopes of being able to command the agenda are common to those entering Number Ten. Within a few months, the pressure of events, the difficulty of finding an appropriate response and unrealistic expectations of prime ministerial power have usually combined to make Number Ten more of a reactive body. Prime ministerial authority varies greatly, even within the tenure of the same Prime Minister, and is clearly apparent only for short periods in our study. The ultimate conclusion of our study – the relative weakness of the Prime Minister since 1970 – cannot, with certainty, be laid at the door of Number Ten. Other factors are more likely to be responsible, though this fact did not stop the Blair team believing that a comparatively weak Number Ten impeded the effectiveness of central control before May 1997.

The nature of the Prime Minister's job – national leader, chief policy formulator, head of the executive, leader in Parliament and of the majority party, chief appointer – has altered little since the date at which our historical overview Chapter 2 began, namely 1868. But the complexity of the job has changed as has the balance between the different roles. The volume of communications bombarding Number Ten, the requests for meetings and media interviews, the demands of Europe, the burgeoning of interest groups and the need to make immediate decisions and responses, have all increased dramatically. The media is less respectful in its treatment of political authority and its focus on personality can add to the difficulties of a vulnerable leader. In negotiations with other heads of government in the European Union or with parties in Northern Ireland a Prime Minister is only one among equals.

It can hardly be claimed that the Prime Minister lacks information and the resources for analysis. He alone is served by the Policy Unit, the Private and the Political Offices, the Cabinet Office, business managers and, up to a point, the party organisation. He is the only minister to see, as of right, all the Cabinet and key committee papers and correspondence. Nobody else is as well placed to take an overview of the government's direction and drive it forward. But the availability of more resources for the Prime Minister to carry out political and governmental tasks and greater demands on and opportunities for him to intervene across the policy board should not be confused with an increase in power. Yet the aura of power surrounding the Prime Minister often dazzles not just the public, but also many in Whitehall and in the media into thinking the incumbent is far more powerful than he in fact is. 'It feels often like a very hostile world out there,' said one former Prime Minister to us, 'and the fact was I could do very little about it.' A Permanent Secretary under John Major agreed but added, 'The Prime Minister is still part of the game plan for a department. Clearing an initiative with the Policy Unit and getting the Prime Minister on side are golden rules for a permanent secretary.'

Although it is often difficult to point to the precise genesis of a policy, most derive not from Number Ten but from the parties' work in opposition or friendly 'think tanks', or from within the departments, which then go on to shape them and in so doing can change them beyond recognition. There are always cases of Prime Ministers having their own particular policy domain (e.g. Neville Chamberlain on foreign policy), or handing a minister his marching orders (as Churchill did in 1951 to Macmillan on housing and to Walter Monckton on industrial relations or Mrs Thatcher to Nigel Lawson on exchange rate policy), or prompting and suggesting (as Macmillan did to Selwyn Lloyd, his Chancellor of the Exchequer, over economic planning and incomes policies or Mrs Thatcher on many policies), or simply intervening in a more direct way.

Clear cases of strong prime ministerial interventions in the period of our study are:

Heath and pay policy, entry to the EC, and direct rule in Northern Ireland.

Wilson and pay policy in 1975.

Callaghan and the IMF negotiations in 1976 and the 'seminar' on monetary policy.

Thatcher and the 1981 Budget, ending trade union membership at GCHQ in 1984, vetoing British membership of the ERM between 1985 and 1990, reforms in education and health, and the poll tax.

Major and the Citizen's Charter and the Anglo-Irish Downing Street Declaration.

Blair and welfare reform and Northern Ireland.

Few postwar Prime Ministers, however, have left much of an intended and enduring legacy on public policy. The exceptions are Attlee and Mrs Thatcher, both of whose governments shaped the political agenda for years after they left office. But even they were inheritors of their predecessors' decisions before they were choosers when it came to the major government spending programmes.[14]

Most Prime Ministers have taken leave of Downing Street with their reputations lower than when they entered. In part they have suffered because of the relative postwar decline of Britain's economic and diplomatic strength, in part because of the electorate's sense of disappointment with their records. Macmillan's reputation was stymied by the failure of negotiations to enter the European Community and by the Profumo scandal. The standing of Wilson by 1970 had been marred by devaluation, the collapse of the National Plan and the failed reform of the trade unions. The concluding stages of the Heath government were dominated by industrial relations conflicts, the three-day working week and a 'crisis' general election, and of the Callaghan government by the winter of discontent and the crumbling of his government's authority. Little survived long on the statute book from the administrations of Heath, Wilson and Callaghan. Mrs Thatcher made herself the most unpopular Prime Minister since opinion surveys were conducted and she was the first Prime Minister to be forced out after a ballot of Conservative MPs. Major, after the collapse of Britain's membership of the ERM in September 1992, found his authority openly flouted by his party's MPs and by fellow ministers. Memoirs and 'insider' accounts by Number Ten people for much of the 1970s and 1980s, at least, describe an office often under siege.[15]

Prime Ministers rarely feel powerful and their so-called 'power grabs' are often a reaction to felt weakness, a frustration with the inability to pull effective levers. Compared with most departmental ministers, a Prime Minister has a tiny budget, a small staff and few formal powers. He has to work through Secretaries of State in whom statutory powers are vested. Viewed from Number Ten, Whitehall departments can look at times like a series of baronial fiefdoms, to which it can only react. Departmental ministers have large staffs, budgets, policy networks, information and expertise, and can draw up legislation in their areas of responsibility. At times a frustrated Prime Minister may 'ache to collar a department of his own', as one Number Ten adviser reflected. It is salutary to reflect that education and health, both priorities for Blair, are handled in Number Ten by only three members of the Policy Unit and two Private Secretaries, all of whom also oversee other policy areas. The two departments, on the other hand, have a combined total of nine special advisers and thousands of officials. So much for critics of a 'power grab' by Number Ten. A Political Secretary reflected on these limits:

It is difficult for Number Ten to step in and move things along.
A Prime Minister never really 'owns' a policy.[16]

The strength of most departments is such that it requires enormous
willpower, obstinacy, political authority and excellent briefing for the
Prime Minister to prevail on scores of senior civil servants (Grade III
and above). A Prime Minister does not give instructions to a minister;
this would be a step prior to or tantamount to dismissal. Instead,
discussions on policy lines are usually 'cloaked in collective decency',
to quote Ferdinand Mount, although Mrs Thatcher sometimes went
beyond this. Frequent assertions of Prime Minister's will, however,
entails costs in his or her political support and time. A minister who
resents interference may resign and damage the Prime Minister in the
process; Mrs Thatcher's authority was severely shaken each time by
the resignations of Heseltine, Lawson, and Howe. Concentrating on
one or two policy areas involves the neglect of many others. Mount
reflected that Margaret Thatcher's leadership style required 'remorse-
less nagging and repeated reshuffles'.[17] Few have her zeal and self-
confidence and even she felt frustrated at some departments' tardiness
in producing radical policies. Major's Number Ten complained that
departments were far too ready to drift along in their own direction
and resisted prods from Number Ten, such as over the Citizen's
Charter. 'Ministers have all gone native' (i.e. adopted their department's agenda) was a common cry in Major's time at Number Ten.
Changing a weak or recalcitrant minister is one answer, but to do it
more than once exposes the Prime Minister's position. Moreover,
some ministers are virtually unsackable for political reasons.

Faced with a policy crisis an activist Prime Minister, as we have
seen, is tempted to 'call the problem into Number Ten'. This was
understandable in the case of Kosovo and Northern Ireland. But Blair
has also taken personal responsibility for such complex issues as
welfare to work and, in 2000, reform of the NHS. But becoming
involved in day-to-day policy has its costs. Rod Rhodes, reviewing
the lengthy list of constraints and dependency relationships facing a
Prime Minister, believes that most interventions are in fact 'sporadic,
counter-productive or ineffective'.[18] Departments are a force for frag-
mentation and they are helped by their policy networks, their expertise,

by traditions of autonomy and by the political weight of the minister.[19]

Pulling issues into Number Ten may create overload and slow down decision making, as the departments wait for responses from Number Ten. The profusion of new units and practices, for example, the PIU and the SEU, greater role of the Cabinet Office, appointment of Tsars for problem areas, Treasury oversight of the public service agreements with departments and task forces – has added to confusion over responsibility. Professor Peter Hennessy, in evidence to the Public Administration Committee on 24 May 2000 commented on what he regarded as the resulting overlaps. He complained that Blair 'hops in and out all the time' and added: 'This is the most disjointed government I have ever observed.' A Prime Minister also has colleagues who are potential rivals for his job and he has to devote time to building and maintaining political support among them. British membership of the EU potentially empowers the Prime Minister's policy role *vis-à-vis* most of his colleagues because he has to speak for Britain at its gatherings. But in EU councils he is not even *primus inter pares*, only one of fifteen national political leaders. Greater media coverage of the Prime Minister, and the implication that he is responsible for government policy, may be an advantage when things go well, but it is an embarrassment when things go badly.

Claims that a British Prime Minister is dominant are often accompanied by the assertion (or complaint) that he is behaving in a presidential manner. In so far as the comparison is with the US President this fails to take account of the constitutional and political limits on the President's power. He has to bargain with Congress and depends on Senate's approval for some acts. But a Prime Minister, in contrast with the President has few staff, limited control over the Budget – which the Office of Management and Bureau provides for the President – and no White House Council of Economic Advisors. As Thatcher and Major found, the annual prospect each autumn or indeed actuality of a leadership challenge from colleagues was also a profound limitation. On the other hand, the President has no guaranteed party majority in the legislature and even if he does, he cannot rely on its supporting him. He depends on congressional approval for his key appointments. Richard Rose's judgment, 'The view from the top of British government, like that from any government, is remote. A Prime Minister presides over much that is done by others',[20] applies just as much to the US President.

Our study of prime ministerial power over the last thirty years reveals that prime ministerial passivity has been at least as frequent as prime ministerial power. Is a small Number Ten office to blame: might the Prime Ministers have done much better if they had had a personal staff numbering hundreds? The pressure on the centre has certainly encouraged some observers to blame the quality or range of advice at Number Ten and thus to advocate the creation of a larger Prime Minister's office or even something more institutionalised, like a Prime Minister's Department. Is the right diagnosis being made?

Complaints about a hole in the centre are sometimes linked to the performance of the Cabinet.[21] Criticisms of the Cabinet as an executive body are well known. It is too large to despatch business: including officials there are usually around thirty in attendance, and its size and composition are designed to take account of political and representational factors. Since the early 1970s it has met weekly as a rule (before then it met twice a week), has had few papers before it and often rubber-stamps recommendations from other committees. On many matters coming to Cabinet, ministers may be inadequately briefed (heightened since the abolition of the CPRS in 1983) and may not be particularly engaged on some items. Robin Butler in a 1999 lecture claimed that the Cabinet has 'reverted to something close to what it was in the late 18th and 19th centuries – a meeting of political friends and colleagues at which issues of the moment were informally reported or discussed'. Lawson, perhaps overstating, said that attending Cabinet was the most restful period of his life as a minister.[22] It is a reporting and reviewing body rather than a decision taker.[23] One Cabinet Secretary we interviewed suggested that, as a rule, issues did not go to Cabinet unless they were already largely agreed.[24]

Tony Blair has weakened Cabinet further. As a project-orientated Prime Minister he is more inclined to create teams and units than set up a Cabinet Committee. Cabinet Committees still handle policy, but more co-ordination is done outside the Cabinet system. 'He sees a problem and sets up a group to tackle it' said a civil servant.

Many ministers are departmentally minded; it is a fact of political life that they make their reputations as departmental ministers, fighting for their budgets and programmes. Prime Ministers and Chancellors often keep economic policy, certainly discussion of interest rates or monetary policy as well as the Budget or economic strategy, off the agenda for long periods. In 1964 Harold Wilson stifled Cabinet discussion of devaluation for many months, as Mrs Thatcher did over economic policy in 1979 and membership of the ERM after 1985. The economic policies of both governments were internally divisive, but crucial for many other policies. Blair's downplaying of Cabinet continues a trend towards it becoming, like the monarch before it, a 'dignified' rather than an efficient part of the constitution.

Policies are often decisively shaped in meetings between the Prime Minister and the relevant Secretary of State, what Lawson calls 'creeping bilateralism', or to a cynic, 'divide and rule'. Once the Prime Minister and minister have agreed a course of action it is difficult for other Cabinet ministers to overturn it, especially if Treasury funding has been secured. These shortcomings do not detract from the functions of the Cabinet as a sounding-board, occasional court of appeal, or reporting forum, all of which underpin the sense of collective responsibility. Nor should a Prime Minister ignore the reservations of senior colleagues, who may have their own followings in the Commons. In some circumstances, to do so can be fatal, as Mrs Thatcher found. But the decline of the Cabinet has been noted in other Westminster-type systems such as those of Canada, Australia and New Zealand.

The Cabinet Office has been another target for those who call for a stronger centre. Its remit is to co-ordinate the work of the Cabinet system and move decisions along. It does this by organising meetings, preparing agendas, writing minutes and forwarding papers to relevant ministers, officials and advisers. The Secretariat serves the Cabinet and its committees, and has sought to avoid being seen to have its own view. Ferdinand Mount, drawing on personal experience, complained that its briefs, with their studied balance of pros and cons about a course of action and advice on procedure, lack analytical bite. '. . . In general, the quality of the information is poor – and this includes the information provided to the Prime Minister.'[25] The commitment to neutrality and the greater resources on policy available to departments '. . . tends to prevent the Cabinet Office's work from providing the concrete and specific material which would underpin sensible and coherent decision-making'.[26] The approach can be frustrating for those, often political staff, who look for more initiative and greater co-ordination at the centre.

'Traditionalists', often civil servants, argue that these qualities, if required, should come from elsewhere. One Conservative official with experience of the party in power commented in the 1970s: 'It is no part of his [the Cabinet Secretary's] responsibilities to evaluate or provide an independent critique of the policies that are emerging as a result of the interaction between different Ministers (and their Departments).'[27] The same source approvingly quoted Lord Trend's private advice to him: 'You should have no truck with a Prime Minister's Department.' This has been a persistent Whitehall theme; it is the politicians and advisers who have been more likely to argue for a Prime Minister's Department. Some insiders regard the reforms announced in July 1998 as a Whitehall attempt to meet the problems and head off demands for a Prime Minister's Department. Blair has effectively built up a Prime Minister's department, but by not calling it such he has avoided some of the controversy that would accompany such a step.

Proposals for a stronger Prime Minister's office usually involve a revamping or an absorption of parts of the Cabinet Office – not least to avoid the creation of yet more, and overlapping, bodies. The staffing and organisational changes in Number Ten introduced by Blair, in connection with his operating style and the new capabilities of the Cabinet Office announced in July 1998, are the latest attempts to achieve more co-ordination. They are also perhaps the most explicit statement that the Office's role is to advance the government's policy objectives as defined by Number Ten.

The management reforms in Whitehall in the last decade, however, may have compounded the problems of departmentalism. More civil servants work in agencies, which are subject to framework agreements and work to meeting specific targets and performance indicators. What has been neglected has been the idea of 'working more corporately across the boundaries', as Richard Wilson, effectively speaking on behalf of the Prime Minister, told a gathering of senior civil servants in October 1998. The attempts to encourage joined-up policy making, focus on policy outcomes and encouragement of cooperation across departments are an answer to this.

Some have drawn on their personal experience of Number Ten to call for a stronger office. Kenneth Berrill (ex-CPRS) argues that a Prime Minister now needs his own Department.[28] Douglas Hurd (Political Secretary and twenty years later Foreign Secretary under Thatcher and Major) regards the centre as 'ill-equipped' and would increase the number of staff working for the Prime Minister.[29] Lord Hunt (Cabinet Secretary under Heath, Wilson, Callaghan and Thatcher) has concluded that the new responsibilities and demands on British government leave 'a hole at the heart of government' and that the Prime Minister required a stronger support system, an office of the Chief Executive.[30] Bernard Donoughue (Policy Unit under Wilson and Callaghan) reflects 'when you are in there, you don't feel you can do anything and I was more aware of the constraints on, than the massive impact of, prime ministerial power'.[31] A Private Secretary working for the most dominant of our Prime Ministers reported: 'Any idea that you have a powerhouse running things from Number Ten is entirely misplaced. I soon discovered that it was done with brown paper tied with string.'[32]

A second group point to failures in policy as evidence of weakness of the centre. Devaluation (1967), incomes policy (1972), the energy crisis (1973), IMF intervention (1976) and exit from the ERM (1992) are all examples of British governments being blown off course. Political aides have sometimes complained about the quality of Civil Service briefing and position papers for some of these episodes. Experiencing Whitehall's 'silence' after the collapse of the Heath government's policies on prices and incomes, and 'Bloody Sunday' in Northern Ireland, Hurd found it difficult from his Downing Street base to agree that the Civil Service ran the country.[33] But more often it has been political difficulties which have undermined the Prime Minister. One can look back to the periods 1965 to 1969, most of the 1970s, 1980 to 1982 and 1992 to 1997 when governments of the day were undermined by policy failures, bad opinion polls, by-election disasters, ministerial resignations, scandals over 'sleaze', negative media coverage, internal divisions or lack of a parliamentary majority. Day-to-day political pressure and demands (often from the media) for an 'instant' reaction, often make life in Downing Street short term and reactive, crowding out planning for the medium term. Macmillan acknowledged: 'Events, dear boy, events.'

The final group draws on comparisons with the resources available to political leaders abroad, most appropriately those operating with parliamentary Cabinet systems.[34] Patrick Weller points to the Privy Council Office and Prime Minister's Office in Canada, which support the Prime Minister in his two roles as head of government and party leader respectively. The former office is staffed entirely by civil servants and serves the Cabinet; the latter consists of party appointments (up to about one hundred). The first is like our Cabinet Secretariat, the second like a highly expanded Policy Unit cum Private Office. In Australia, there is a Department for the Prime Minister and Cabinet, which carries out similar functions. It has about five hundred staff (organised in divisions covering, for example, external relations, Parliament, trade and industry, correspondence, welfare and Prime Minister's correspondence). In both systems the bodies collectively do what the various units in Number Ten do.

At one time some of Blair's political staff expressed interest in the German Chancellory under Gerhard Schröder. The Chancellor's office has a staff of around 450 and many work in policy units which may mirror the policy field of a single ministry or deal with cross-departmental policies. Political appointees head the units and direct senior civil servants.[35] The mix of political and official staff has been slow to develop, although some change has occurred since 2 May 1997. Might the Prime Minister's hard-pressed Private Office and Policy Unit be reconfigured and reinforced in this direction to enable Number Ten to enable the Prime Minister to intervene in more areas and exercise strategic oversight? The combination of strong departments and a weak Cabinet increases the need for the Prime Minister to provide this.

Three qualifications need to be made about any scheme for creating a new body in Number Ten. It could be that this 'easy fix' solution fails to identify the real need. Organisational reform of its own will not improve things *unless* the Prime Minister has, at the least, a strong sense of political purpose, strategic direction, and determination, and communicates them to colleagues. It will also not fully compensate for divisions in the party, lack of an assured parliamentary majority, hostile media and public opinion, or a defective policy. The premiership records of Wilson and Heath, the two institutional reformers, remind one of the limited policy or political impact which such reform on its own will deliver. Some calls for reform are a form of scapegoating. A Prime Minister's Department or a stronger Number Ten would not have averted the 1967 devaluation, the three-day week in 1973, the soaring inflation in the mid-1970s, the poll tax or the ERM failure. These came from political decisions and/or pressures from outside Number Ten. An institutional 'fix' is not necessarily the answer to a policy or a political failing. In early 1993 the *Economist* reviewed various claims about why John Major's Number Ten was so weak, and concluded that the central failure was Major's lack of political authority.

Second, there is little point in drawing up a system which requires a superman as Prime Minister. A David Lloyd George or (war-time) Winston Churchill are exceptions. And to give a Prime Minister more responsibilities simply ignores the time constraints that already operate. As one Number Ten insider said: 'The bottleneck is the Prime Minister. Everyone wants to see Tony Blair. He has to see everything important. No-one can take decisions for him.' Proposed reforms should try and build on what is already available in Number Ten, help the Prime Minister to concentrate on his priorities, provide good advice on policy and facilitate effective delegation. There is no case at all for adding to the flow of paper the Prime Minister must read or the staff he must regularly meet with. Well-designed institutions and well-staffed institutions can be set up, but the Prime Minister must appreciate the need for them and understand how to use them. If not, they will not add value.

Third, a point frequently made in interviews by ministers, civil servants and political appointees at the centre, was that, in a phrase, structures and administrative arrangements matter less than people. They insisted that no rearrangement of institutions or duties would work unless there were good personal relations between the key players. 'There is no "right" way in organisational structure. It is very personal. Prime Ministers have to feel comfortable with people and arrangements,' says David Willetts, member of Margaret Thatcher's Policy Unit. 'Longstanding good personal relationships between Blair and Brown explain why they get on. Bad personal relationships between some of their staff explain why there are so many negative stories in the press. The tribes are causing the trouble.' confirms a member of Blair's Policy Unit. Charles Powell agrees, 'No mechanism could have stopped the row over Westland – a piddling little issue – it was a battle of egos between Thatcher and Heseltine. It was bound to end in tears.' Jonathan Hill, Political Secretary to John Major, commented: 'Creating a stronger Number Ten was irrelevant. John Major perhaps did not always realise the authority that exists in the office. That vacuum in turn allowed personal rivalries to flourish. I read medieval history at university and I understood the subject much better when I came to Downing Street. New institutions were no answer.' 'The problem is people not policy: ministers know what they are doing when leaking and behaving disloyally,' said one of John Major's Cabinet Ministers.

Our study of Prime Ministers in power since 1970 suggests that the initiative has only been held by Prime Ministers for eleven of the thirty years: 1970–71, 1982–86, 1987–88, 1990–92, 1997–2000. The key to whether or not they have held the initiative is the interplay of four factors: ideas (whether they were operating with the grain of the prevailing climate of opinion); circumstances (whether factors beyond the control of Number Ten were operating overall as a positive or negative force); interests (whether the prevailing financial, industrial, media sectional and other forces were running in favour of the government or not); and, finally, individuals (this relates primarily to the leadership quality and effectiveness of the Prime Minister, but more generally to the quality and cohesion of his/her senior ministerial team).

The table on the next page, inevitably impressionistic rather than scientifically rigorous, tries to assess the weighting of the above factors in determining each premier's fortunes, and gives pointers to each premier's fortunes. The table helps to explain why it has only been for roughly a third of the period that the Prime Minister has been in control of events. It shows that where the Prime Minister has not held

FACTORS INFLUENCING PRIME MINISTER'S FORTUNES

Prime Minister	Ideas	Circumstances	Interests	Individuals
Heath I (1970–71)	●	●	–	●
Heath II (1971–74)	X	X	X	—
Wilson (1974–76)	X	X	X	—
Callaghan (1976–79)	—	X	X	●
Thatcher I (1979–82)	●	X	X	●
Thatcher II (1982–88)	●	●	●	●
Thatcher III (1988–90)	●	—	X	—
Major I (1990–92)	X	●	●	●
Major II (1992–95)	—	X	—	—
Major III (1995–97)	X	X	X	X
Blair I (1997–2000)	●	●	●	—

KEY: ● = a positive influence
X = a negative influence
— = a neutral or mixed influence

the initiative (i.e. 1971–74, 1974–79, 1979–81/2, 1988–90, 1992–97) circumstances were far more powerful than the size and effectiveness of the Number Ten office that have been at play. If one accepts this analysis, then one should be cautious about laying too much store by seeing a bolstered Number Ten as the panacea for removing future prime ministerial problems.

The prospects for creating a Prime Minister's Department were probably at their highest under Heath in 1970, a time when managerial reform was the fashion. Heath was an advocate of such reform, created giant departments as well as the Central Policy Review Staff and inaugurated prime ministerial press conferences. In opposition, David Howell had already proposed that Heath create a Prime Minister's Department, on the lines of similar bodies in Germany, the USA, Canada, France and Italy, and staff returned to the idea when Heath was in office. But Heath refused to take the extra step and minor adjustments were made, as there was little enthusiasm from departments or senior civil servants. Callaghan in 1977 and Thatcher in 1982 also considered the idea, and some of Tony Blair's staff in opposition supported it.

The likely political and administrative costs of creating such a body have been canvassed at length by George Jones and others and their assessments are persuasive.[36] Over time, such a body may develop its own agenda or, in developing a prime ministerial line, may set Number Ten apart from the Cabinet or increase strife with a department. If the staff is large it may weaken the sense of collegial decision making or reduce the direct contact staff will have with the Prime Minister. At present the chain of command is short, aides have close proximity to the Prime Minister and they can get a response very quickly. If a Prime Minister wants to prevent the office from developing a line perhaps independent of himself – a tendency with some departments ('the departmental view') – he will be tempted to recruit extra staff to control it, and add to the problems of administration and lengthen lines of communication. Interestingly, a civil servant in private spoke strongly on this. 'Ministers share power with their civil servants. A Prime Minister does not, because he has no department. That is one way in which he differs from his colleagues. It also gives him an alibi. At present he can blame the department if something goes wrong.'[37]

In rivalling the other departments it may set up tensions and resentments among ministers and thus add to problems of political management. The spectacular resignations of George Brown (1968), Michael Heseltine (1986), Nigel Lawson (1989) and Geoffrey Howe (1990) involved complaints that the Prime Minister of the day was over-reaching his or her responsibilities and for relying excessively on unelected advisers. The behaviour of the Prime Minister of the day was condemned as 'presidential' and unconstitutional in seeking to put a Number Ten gloss on policy, purportedly at the cost of the responsible minister, or even by-passing the latter. Such incidents remind us that Cabinet (and collective responsibility) may provide some political protection for the Prime Minister in the way of blame-sharing if it has endorsed a policy which goes wrong.

It is not unusual for Number Ten staff or advisers, particularly if they are thought to be influential or become high profile, to be surrogate targets for critics of the Prime Minister. This was the fate of Horace Wilson under Chamberlain, Lord Cherwell under Churchill, Marcia Williams under Wilson, Ingham, Powell and Walters under Thatcher, and Sarah Hogg under Major. Similar attacks have been made on Alastair Campbell, Philip Gould and Peter Mandelson under Prime Minister Tony Blair. Fellow ministers have complained in diaries and memoirs about the access enjoyed and the influence allegedly exercised by an *'éminence grise'* or by such 'kitchen cabinets' over Harold Wilson and Margaret Thatcher in the latter stages of their premierships. Prime Ministers, however, have always had policy priorities or even, more ambitiously, agendas of their own, and have always intervened in departments from time to time. A Prime Minister's Department would not of itself create such tensions, although it would probably add to them. Gossip, scheming for preferment, rivalries and jealousies among ambitious politicians are a fact of life at the top.

Some of these difficulties, however, can be exaggerated. Widespread discussion among Cabinet Ministers did not remove the defects of the poll tax, and widespread endorsement did not protect Mrs Thatcher from the hostility which it attracted (it was still widely regarded as 'her tax'). Widespread support among the economic establishment and across the political spectrum for entry into the ERM in 1990 did not save John Major when the policy failed two years later. Notwithstanding the reservations expressed by Jones and others, parliamentary systems do cope with a Prime Minister's office. There are times when a Prime Minister has to stand alone, speaking in public for the government at Question Time in the Commons, at press conferences and in interviews, in meetings and at international summits. But it is the increase in the volume of demands on the Prime Minister from other governments, summits, the media and expectations from the public who require the Prime Minister to deal with them. He needs more help.

A Prime Minister's Department, constructed on the lines of what exists in Australia or New Zealand, would contain units or staff covering policy, party, media, diary and speechwriting matters, as well as

relations with government departments. What is interesting is that
staff dealing with these tasks are already in place in Number Ten.
Apart from administrative tidiness it is not immediately apparent that
consolidating them into one department would make a big improvement. The present arrangements have the advantage of flexibility, and
staff can be added and units created as desired. This is essentially
what has happened since 1916. Until the creation of the Cabinet Office
in that year, the Private Secretaries prepared the Cabinet agenda and
summoned Cabinet ministers to meetings. Until the late 1920s they
also handled party business and until the 1930s a Private Secretary
dealt with press relations. As the world outside became more complex,
so the Prime Minister's staff in Number Ten and the Cabinet Office
have responded by establishing specialised units, achieving 'requisite
variety', in management speak. They constitute an executive office in
all but name.[38]

Even if one accepts that many of the difficulties faced by Prime
Ministers stem from factors that have nothing to do with the size and
quality of their support staff, one could still make out a strong case
for expanding the Prime Minister's office. The transition could be
achieved by adding more political and official staff with policy expertise, providing more support for them, and probably locating the entire
operation in a new building.

Various interests in Whitehall have their own reasons for keeping
Number Ten at arm's length or enfeebled in staffing terms. It is
not clear, however, that such conditions help good government.[39] At
present the system 'works', thanks to the talent and stamina of too
small a group of people. The Private Office has long been so
undermanned, that some high fliers refuse an appointment there
because of the very long hours.[40]

A Prime Minister's office which mixes political and Civil Service
appointments, representing a fusion of political and Whitehall skills,
has much to recommend it. Civil servants and political advisers, to
be effective policy-makers, have to combine political sensitivity,
administrative know-how and subject expertise. It is foolish to draw
a rigid line between administration and politics, and similar systems
elsewhere do not do so. As George Jones notes: 'At the top of a
department administration is not an activity that is separate from

politics, nor is politics an activity separate from administration.'[41] All the staff are reporting to and are loyal to the Prime Minister. One senior civil servant who had worked in Number Ten nearly twenty years earlier warned that in practice it was impractical to insist on a rigid compartmentalisation between the Political and Private Offices:

> Number Ten is a seamless place. You have to take on board the divisions in the party if you are to give good advice to the PM. You can't be too prissy.[42]

Blair's much-vaunted modernisation of government should also encompass the Prime Minister's office facilities. Over the years, the extra staff have been squeezed into nooks and crannies and into the additional space which various conversions have made available. There are, however, limits to the extent and effectiveness of such conversions, particularly in a listed building. A golden opportunity for creating extra space was lost in the early 1960s, when an entirely re-built and re-designed Number Ten was on the agenda. The government decided to preserve rather than build afresh, and Raymond Erith, the architect commissioned to execute the work believed, 'the arrangement of the rooms which has evolved naturally over the years, is essentially right ... my aim is, therefore, to repair the building by working within its established framework.'[43] Was Erith right? Number Ten contains only a handful of rooms suitable for meetings; the expanded Policy Unit lacks such a room. Some staff are located in the equivalent of attic rooms. There is no facility to serve and eat meals and aides have been despatched to nearby shops to purchase sandwiches for Major and for Blair. After 1997, with the recruitment of additional staff, the problems were so pressing that benign neglect was no longer a suitable managerial response. The physical layout of the building was impacting adversely on working practices. A decision was taken to appoint an Executive Secretary and a Board of Management, drawing on all sections of staff to consider the efficiency of the building. The Board considers issues of personnel, administration and finances. One possibility to meet the need for more space is to expand Number Ten into parts of the Cabinet Office or Foreign Office, or even the Privy Council. All, especially the Foreign Office, originally built in the 1860s to house four separate departments of state, have ample space for Number Ten to expand into. The Foreign Office, which has its own Cabinet Room, would also impart a sense of grandeur and scale that the crowded Number Ten lacks. So far Blair has opted for refurbishing the present accommodation and converting space on the top floor to offices.

Another idea, welcomed by a number of staff, has been the suggestion that they move out of Number Ten completely. At the beginning of a new century, there is a strong case for accommodating the Prime Minister's office in a large designated building. The Millennium would be the ideal time for such a major commission. Number Ten would then become a dignified rather than efficient part of the British body politic, and could be transformed into a 'Museum of British Premiership'. It would make an ideal stopover for tourists following their visit to Buckingham Palace.

PRIME MINISTERS' STAFF 1945–99

Clement Attlee
1945–51

PRIVATE OFFICE

Principal Private Secretary

Leslie Rowan	1945–47
Laurence Helsby	1947–50
Denis Rickett	1950–51
David Pitblado	1951–

Private Secretary for Overseas Affairs

John Colville	1945
John Addis	1945–47
Lawrence Pumphrey	1947–50

Private Secretary for Economic Affairs

Laurence Helsby	1945–47

Private Secretary for Parliamentary Affairs

Edith Watson	1945–46

Other Private Secretaries

John Peck	1945–46
Joseph Burke	1945–46
Paul Beards	1945–48
Francis Graham-Harrison	1946–49
Paul Osmond	1948–51
Geoffrey Cass	1949–
David Hunt	1950–

Appointments Private Secretary	–1947
Appointments Secretary	(1947–)
Anthony Bevir	1945–51

PRESS OFFICE
Press Secretary
Francis Williams   1945–47
Philip Jordan   1947–51

POLITICAL STAFF
PPS
Geoffrey de Freitas   1945–46
Arthur Moyle   1946–51

ADVISERS
Economic Adviser
Douglas Jay   1945–46
William Gorrell-Barnes   1946–48

CABINET OFFICE
Cabinet Secretary
Edward Bridges   1945–47
Norman Brook   1947–51

Winston Churchill
1951–55

PRIVATE OFFICE
Principal Private Secretary (Joint)
David Pitblado   1951–55–57
John Colville   1951–55

Private Secretary for Overseas Affairs
David Hunt   1951–52
Anthony Montague Browne   1952–55

*Private Secretaries for Parliamentary
and for Home Affairs*
Peter Oates   1951–54
Geoffrey Cass   1951–52
Gwen Davies   1954

APPOINTMENTS SECRETARY
Anthony Bevir   1951–55

PRESS OFFICE
vacant
T Fife Clark   1951–55
('Adviser' on Public Relations to the PM)

POLITICAL STAFF
PPS
Christopher Soames   1953–55

CABINET OFFICE

Cabinet Secretary
Norman Brook   1951–55

Anthony Eden
1955–57

PRIVATE OFFICE
Principal Private Secretary
David Pitblado   1955–56
Freddie Bishop   1956–

Private Secretary for Overseas Affairs
Freddie Bishop   1955–56
Philip de Zulueta   1956–

Private Secretaries
Guy Millard   1955–
Neil Cairncross   1955–

PRESS OFFICE
Press Secretary
William Clark   1955–56

APPOINTMENTS SECRETARIES
Anthony Bevir   1955–56
David Stephens   1956–

POLITICAL STAFF
PPS
Robert Carr   1955–
Robert Allan   1955–57

CABINET OFFICE
Cabinet Secretary
Norman Brook   1955–57

Harold Macmillan
1957–63

PRIVATE OFFICE
Principal Private Secretary
Freddie Bishop   1957–59
Tim Bligh   1959–

Private Secretary for Overseas Affairs
Philip de Zulueta   1957–63

Private Secretaries
Caryl Ramsden   1957
Anthony Phelps   1958–61
Philip Woodfield   1961–

APPOINTMENTS SECRETARY
David Stephens   1957–61
John Hewitt   1961–

PRESS OFFICE
Press Secretary
Harold Evans   1957–63

POLITICAL STAFF
PPS
Robert Allan   1957–58
Anthony Barber   1958–59
Knox Cunningham   1959–63

POLITICAL AND PERSONAL PRIVATE SECRETARY
John Wyndham   1957–63

CABINET OFFICE
Cabinet Secretary
Norman Brook   1957
Burke Trend   1957–63

Alec Douglas-Home
1963–64

PRIVATE OFFICE
Principal Private Secretary
Tim Bligh   1963–64
Derek Mitchell   1964
Private Secretaries
Philip Woodfield   1963–
Oliver Wright   1963–
Malcolm Reid   1963–

PRESS OFFICE
Press Secretary
Harold Evans   1963–64

CABINET OFFICE
Cabinet Secretary
Burke Trend   1963–64

Harold Wilson
1964–70

PRIVATE OFFICE
Principal Private Secretary
Derek Mitchell   1964–66
Michael Halls   1966–70
Sandy Isserlis   1970

Private Secretary for Overseas Affairs
Oliver Wright   1964–66
Michael Palliser   1966–69
Edward Youde   1969–70
Peter Moon   1970–

*Private Secretary for Parliamentary
(and Home 1964–67) Affairs*
Philip Woodfield   1964–65
Peter Le Cheminant   1965–68
Peter Gregson   1968–

Private Secretary for Home (and General 1964–67) Affairs
Malcolm Reid	1964–66
Derek Andrews	1966–70
Roger Dawe	1966–69
Alan Simcock	1969–

APPOINTMENTS SECRETARY
John Hewitt	1964–

PRESS OFFICE
Press Secretary
Trevor Lloyd-Hughes	1964–69
Joe Haines	1969–70

Deputy Press Secretary
Henry James	1964–69
George Holt	1969–70

Senior Information Officer
Miss S. Jefferies	1965–67
Miss J. Price	1967–69
Janet Hewlett-Davies	1969–70

POLITICAL STAFF
PPS
Ernest Femyhough	1964–67
Peter Shore	1965–66
Harold Davies	1967–70
Eric Varley	1968–69

Personal Political Secretary
Marcia Williams	1964–70

IN CABINET OFFICE:
Cabinet Secretary
Burke Trend	1964–70

Scientific Adviser
Solly Zuckerman	1964–70

Adviser on Economic Affairs
Thomas Balogh	1964–68

Assistant Advisers
J.S. Allen	1964–65
Stuart Holland	1966–67
Michael Stewart	1964–67
Andrew Graham	1967–69

UNOFFICIAL FIGURES

Arnold Goodman   Legal adviser
Gerald Kaufman   Political office assistant

Edward Heath
1970–74

PRIVATE OFFICE

Principal Private Secretary
Robert Armstrong   1970–

Private Secretary for Overseas Affairs
Peter Moon   1970–72
(Lord) Tom Bridges   1972–

Private Secretary for Parliamentary
Affairs
Christopher Roberts   1970–72
Robin Butler   1972–

Private Secretary for Economic Affairs
Peter Gregson   1970–72
Christopher Roberts   1972–74
Nick Stuart   1973–

Private Secretary for Home Affairs
Alan Simcock   1970–72
Mark Forrester   1972–

APPOINTMENTS SECRETARY

John Hewitt   1970–73
Colin Peterson   1973–

PRESS OFFICE

Chief Press Secretary
Donald Maitland   1970–73
Robin Haydon   1974–74

Deputy Press Secretary (Title: Press
Secretary)
Henry James   1970–71
Tom McCaffrey   1971–72

Press Secretary (Press Relations)
H.R. Hayles   1972–74

Press Secretary (Co-ordination)
John Pestell   1972–74

Chief Press Officer
George Holt   1970–71

Principal Information Officer
Gerald Moggridge   1971–74

Senior Information Officer
Janet Hewlett-Davies   1970–72
Barbara Hosking   1970–72
Miss I.M. Lally   1972–74
Janet Whiting   1972–74

POLITICAL STAFF
PPS
Timothy Kitson   1970–74

Political Secretary
Douglas Hurd   1970–74
William Waldegrave   1974

Assistant Political Secretary
William Waldegrave   1973–74

IN CABINET OFFICE:
Cabinet Secretary
Burke Trend   1970–73
John Hunt   1973–74

Scientific Adviser
Solly Zuckerman   1970–71
Alan Cottrell   1971–74

Special Adviser (economics)
Brian Reading   1970–72

CENTRAL POLICY REVIEW STAFF
Head
Victor Rothschild   1971–74

Harold Wilson
1974–76

PRIVATE OFFICE
Principal Private Secretary
Robert Armstrong   1974–75
Kenneth Stowe   1975–

Private Secretary for Overseas Affairs
Tom Bridges   1974–75
Patrick Wright   1975–

**Private Secretary for Economic and
    Home Affairs**
Robin Butler   1974–75
Mark Forrester   1974–75
Nigel Wicks   1975–76
Philip Wood   1975–76

**Private Secretary for Parliamentary
    Affairs**
Nick Stuart   1974–76

SECRETARY FOR APPOINTMENTS
Colin Peterson   1974–76

PRESS OFFICE
Press Secretary
Joe Haines   1974–76

**Assistant Press Secretary (Press
    relations)**
Janet Hewlett-Davies   1974–76

**Assistant Press Secretary
    (Co-ordination)**
Charles Birdsall   1974–75
Gerald Moggridge   1975–76

POLITICAL STAFF
PPS
Willie Hamling   1974–75
Kenneth Marks   1975
John Tomlinson   1975–76

Personal and Political Secretary
Marcia Williams (Falkender)   1974–76

Political officer
Albert Murray   1974–76

POLICY UNIT
Head
Bernard Donoughue

CABINET OFFICE
Cabinet Secretary
John Hunt   1974–76

CENTRAL POLICY REVIEW STAFF
Head
Kenneth Berrill   1974–76

James Callaghan
1976–79

PRIVATE OFFICE
Principal Private Secretary
Kenneth Stowe   1976–

Private Secretary for Overseas Affairs
Patrick Wright   1976–77
Brian Cartledge   1977–79

Private Secretary for Parliamentary Affairs
Nick Stuart   1976
Philip Wood   1976–79
Nick Sanders   1979

Private Secretary for Economic Affairs
Nigel Wicks   1976–78
Tim Lankester   1978–79

Private Secretary for Home Affairs
John Meadway   1976–78
Nick Sanders   1978–79
Michael Pattison   1979

Diary Secretary
David Holt   1976–79

SECRETARY FOR APPOINTMENTS
Colin Peterson   1976–79

PRESS OFFICE
Press Secretary
Tom McCaffrey   1976–79

Deputy Press Secretary
Janet Hewlett-Davies   1976–77
John Woodrow   1979
Peter Brazier   1977–79

Assistant Press Secretary

M. Garrod	1976–77
John Woodrow	1977–79

POLITICAL STAFF

PPS

John Cunningham	1976
Roger Stott	1976–79

Political Secretary

Tom McNally	1976–79

Personal and Constituency Secretary

Mrs Ruth Sharpe	1976–79

POLICY UNIT

Head

Bernard Donoughue	1976–79

CABINET OFFICE

Cabinet Secretary

John Hunt	1976–79

CENTRAL POLICY REVIEW STAFF

Head

Kenneth Berrill	1976–79

Margaret Thatcher
1979–90

PRIVATE OFFICE

Chief of Staff

David Wolfson	1979–85

Principal Private Secretary

Ken Stowe	1979
Clive Whitmore	1979–82
Robin Butler	1982–85
Nigel Wicks	1985–88
Andrew Turnbull	1988–

Private Secretary for Overseas Affairs

Michael Alexander	1979–81
John Coles	1981–84
Charles Powell	1984–90

Private Secretary for Economic Affairs

Tim Lankester	1979–81
Michael Scholar	1981–83
Andrew Turnbull	1983–85
David Norgrove	1985–88
Paul Gray	1988–90

Private Secretary for Parliamentary Affairs

Nick Sanders	1979–81
Michael Pattison	1981–82
William Rickett	1981–83
Timothy Flesher	1983–86
Mark Addison	1986–88
Andrew Bearpark	1988–90
Dominic Morris	1990

Private Secretary for Home Affairs

Michael Pattison	1979–81
William Rickett	1981–82
Timothy Flesher	1982–83
David Barclay	1983–85
Mark Addison	1985–86
Andrew Bearpark	1986–88
Dominic Morris	1988–90
Caroline Slocock	1990

Assistant Secretary

John Vereker	1980–82

SECRETARY FOR APPOINTMENTS

Colin Peterson	1979–82
Robin Catford	1982–

PRESS OFFICE

Chief Press Secretary

Henry James	1979
Bernard Ingham	1979–90

Deputy Chief Press Secretary

Neville S. Gaffin	1979–83
Romola Christopherson	1983–84
Jean Caines	1984–86
Jim Coe	1986–87
Terry Perks	1987–90

POLITICAL STAFF
PPS
Ian Gow	1979–83
Michael Alison	1983–87
Archie Hamilton	1987–88
Peter Morrison	1988–90

Political Secretary
Richard Ryder	1979–82
Derek Howe	1982–83
Stephen Sherbourne	1983–88
John Whittingdale	1988–90

Personal Assistant and Diary Secretary
Caroline Stephens (Ryder)	1979–87
Tessa Gaisman	1987–89
Amanda Ponsonby	1989–90

POLICY UNIT
Head
John Hoskyns	1979–82
Ferdinand Mount	1982–83
John Redwood	1983–85
Brian Griffiths	1985–90

Staff
Norman Strauss	1979–82
Andrew Duguid	1979–82
John Vereker	1982–83
Christopher Monckton	1982–86
Peter Shipley	1982–84
Nicholas Owen	1983–86
Robert Young	1983–84
David Pascall	1983–84
Oliver Letwin	1983–86
John Redwood	1983
Peter Warry	1984–86
John Wybrew	1984–88
Hartley Booth	1984–88
David Hobson	1983–86
David Willetts	1984–86
Norman Blackwell	1986–87
Peter Stredder	1986–88

John O'Sullivan	1987–88
Howell Harris-Hughes	1990
George Guise	1986–90
Greg Bourne	1988–90
Carolyn Sinclair	1988–90
Ian Whitehead	1988–90
Andrew Dunlop	1988–90

ADVISERS
Economics
| Alan Walters | 1981–84 |
| Alan Walters | 1989 |

Efficiency
| Derek Rayner | 1980–83 |
| Robin Ibbs | 1983–88 |

Foreign Affairs
| Anthony Parsons | 1982–83 |
| Percy Cradock | 1984–92 |

Defence Affairs
| Roger Jackling | 1983 |

CABINET OFFICE
Cabinet Secretary
John Hunt	1979
Robert Armstrong	1979–88
Robin Butler	1988–

CENTRAL POLICY REVIEW STAFF
Head
Kenneth Berrill	1979–80
Robin Ibbs	1980–82
John Sparrow	1982–83

John Major
1990–97

PRIVATE OFFICE
Principal Private Secretary
| Andrew Turnbull | 1990–92 |
| Alex Allan | 1992–97 |

Private Secretary for Overseas Affairs
| Charles Powell | 1990–91 |
| Stephen Wall | 1991–93 |

Roderick Lyne   1993–96
John Holmes   1996–97

Private Secretary for Economic Affairs
Paul Gray   1990–91
Barry Potter   1991–92
Mary Francis   1992–95
Moira Wallace   1995–97

Private Secretary for Parliamentary Affairs
Dominic Morris   1990–92
William Chapman   1992–94
Mark Adams   1994–97

Private Secretary for Home Affairs and Diary
Caroline Slocock   1990–91
William Chapman   1991–92
Mark Adams   1992–94

Parliamentary Clerk
Roy Stone   1990–97

APPOINTMENTS SECRETARY
Robin Catford   1990–93
John Holroyd   1993–

PRESS OFFICE
Chief Press Secretary
Gus O'Donnell   1990–94
Christopher Meyer   1994–96
Jonathan Haslam   1996–97

Deputy Press Secretary
Terry Perks   1990–91
Jonathan Haslam   1991–95

POLITICAL STAFF
PPS
Graham Bright   1990–94
John Ward   1994–97
Lord McColl   1994–97
Gary Streeter   1997

Political Secretary
Judith Chaplin   1990–92
Jonathan Hill   1992–94
Howell James   1994–97

Assistant Political Secretary
George Bridges   1994–97

Diary Secretary
Arabella Warburton   1994–97

POLICY UNIT
Head
Sarah Hogg   1990–95
Norman Blackwell   1995–97

Deputy Head
Nick True   1992–95
Dominic Morris   1995–97

Staff
Carolyn Sinclair   1990–92
John Mills   1990–92
George Guise   1990–91
A. Dunlop   1990–92
Howell Harris-Hughes   1990–92
Nick True   1991–92
Jonathan Hill   1991–92
Alan Rosling   1992–95
Damian Green   1992–94
Tim Collins   1995
Simon Walker   1995–97
Carolyn Fairbairn   1995–97
David Soskin   1995–97
Sean Williams   1995–97
Katherine Ramsey   1994–97
Dominic Morris   1992–95
Lucy Neville-Rolfe   1992–94

ADVISERS
Foreign Affairs
Percy Cradock   1990–92
Rodric Braithwaite   1992–94

Efficiency
Angus Fraser   1990–92

CABINET OFFICE
Cabinet Secretary
Robin Butler   1990–97

Tony Blair
1997–

PRIVATE OFFICE
Chief of Staff
Jonathan Powell 1997–

Deputy Chief of Staff
Pat McFadden 1999–2000

Principal Private Secretary
Alex Allan 1997
John Holmes 1997–99
Jeremy Heywood 1999

Private Secretary for Overseas Affairs
John Holmes 1997
John Sawers 1999
Philip Barton (asst) 1997–
Michael Tatham (asst) 1999
Magi Cleavor (asst) 1999–
Anne Weschberg (asst) 2000–

Private Secretary for Economic Affairs
Moira Wallace 1997–
Jeremy Heywood 1997–99
Owen Barder 1999–2000
Simon Virley 2000–

Private Secretary for Parliamentary Affairs
Mark Adams 1997
Rob Read 1997–2000
Clare Sumner 1999–

Private Secretary for Home Affairs
Angus Lapsley 1997–99
Clare Hawley 1998–99
David North 1999

PARLIAMENTARY CLERK
Roy Stone 1997–

APPOINTMENTS SECRETARY
John Holroyd 1997–99
William Chapman 1999–

PRESS OFFICE

Chief Press Secretary

Alastair Campbell   1997–

Press Officers

Tim Allan   1997–
Hilary Coffman   1997–

Assistant Press Secretary

Lindsay Wilkinson   1997–

POLITICAL STAFF

PPS

Bruce Grocott   1997–
Ann Coffey   1997–

Political Secretary

Sally Morgan   1997–

Special Assistant for Presentation and Planning

Anji Hunter   1997–

Diary Secretary

Kate Garvey   1997–

POLICY UNIT

Head

David Miliband   1997–

Staff

Jim Gallagher   1999–2000
Robert Hill   1997–
Peter Hyman   1997–
Roger Liddle   1997–
Liz Lloyd   1997–
Pat McFadden   1997–99
Geoff Mulgan   1997–2000
Geoffrey Norris   1997–
Ed Richards   1999–
James Purnell   1997–
Derek Scott   1997–
Andrew Adonis   1998–
Brian Hackland   1999–
Jonathon Rees   ·1997–
Carey Oppenheim   2000–
Sharon White   1997–

CABINET OFFICE
Cabinet Secretary

Robin Butler	1997–98
Richard Wilson	1998

The 1977 Civil Service Year Book (information for Nov. 1976) was the first to list the PM's office separately. Previously it had been listed under the Treasury, with information duplicated under the Civil Service Department.

N.B. With especial thanks to Nick Sanders for his assistance with the tables.

APPENDIX II

CIRCLES OF INFLUENCE

HEATH I
1970–72

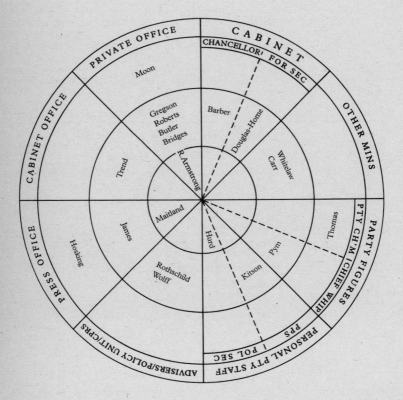

HEATH II
1972–74

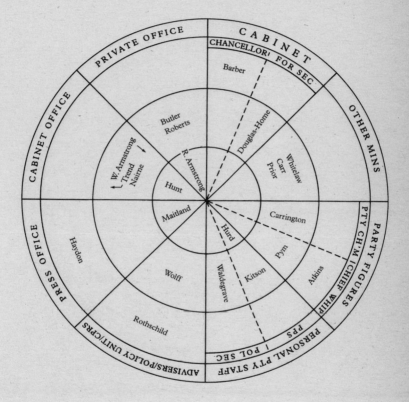

WILSON
1974–76

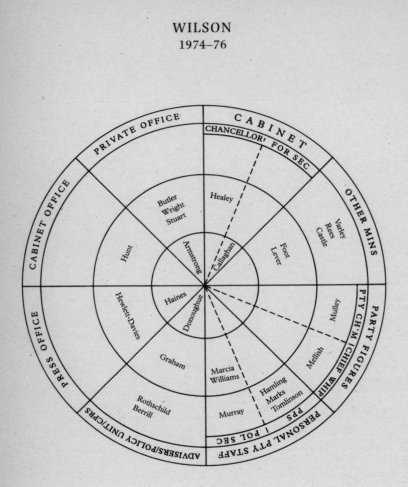

CABINET

PRIVATE OFFICE

CHANCELLOR, FOR SEC

CABINET OFFICE

OTHER MIN'S

PRESS OFFICE

PTY CH'M/CHEF

PARTY FIGURES

WHIP

PPS

POL SEC

PERSONAL PTY STAFF

ADVISERS/POLICY UNIT/CPRS

Healey

Butler
Wright
Stuart

Hunt

Armstrong

Callaghan

Foot
Lever

Varley
Rees
Castle

Haines

Donoughue

Nalley

Hewlett-Davies

Mellish

Graham

Marcia
Williams

Hamling
Marks
Tomlinson

Rothschild
Berrill

Murray

CALLAGHAN
1976–79

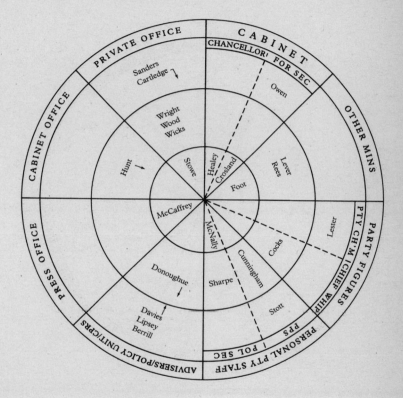

THATCHER I
1979–81/82

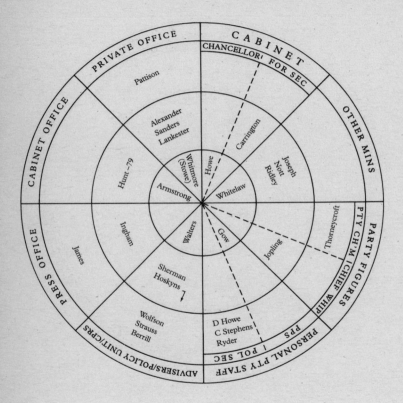

Diagram labels (clockwise from top):

CABINET

CHANCELLOR FOR SEC

PRIVATE OFFICE

Pattison

Alexander
Sanders
Lankester

CABINET OFFICE

Hunt –79

Armstrong

Whitmore
(Stowe)

Howe

Whitelaw

Carrington

Joseph
Nott
Ridley

OTHER MINS

PARTY FIGURES

Thorneycroft

PTY CH'M/CHIEF WHIP

Jopling

Gow

Walters

Ingham

James

PRESS OFFICE

Sherman
Hoskyns

Wolfson
Strauss
Berrill

ADVISERS/POLICY UNIT/CPRS

D Howe
C Stephens
Ryder

POL SEC

PPS

PERSONAL PTY STAFF

THATCHER II
1982–88

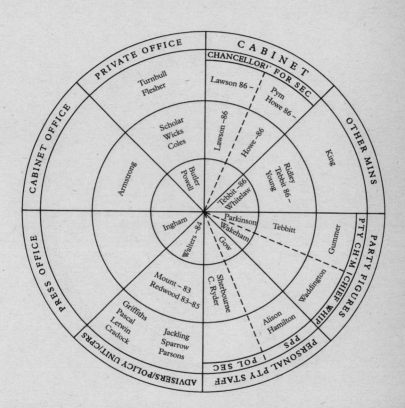

THATCHER III
1988–90

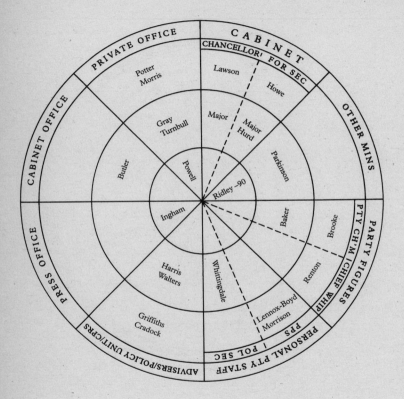

MAJOR I
1990–92 (Sept.)

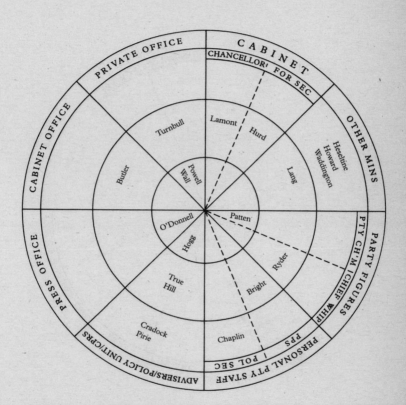

PRIVATE OFFICE

CABINET

CHANCELLOR; FOR SEC

CABINET OFFICE

OTHER MINS

PRESS OFFICE

PARTY FIGURES

PTY CH·M ;CHIEF WHIP

ADVISERS/POLICY UNIT/CPRS

PERSONAL PTY STAFF

PPS

POL SEC

Turnbull

Lamont

Hurd

Heseltine
Howard
Waddington

Butler

Powell
Wall

Lang

O'Donnell

Patten

Hogg

Ryder

True
Hill

Bright

Cradock
Pirie

Chaplin

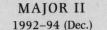
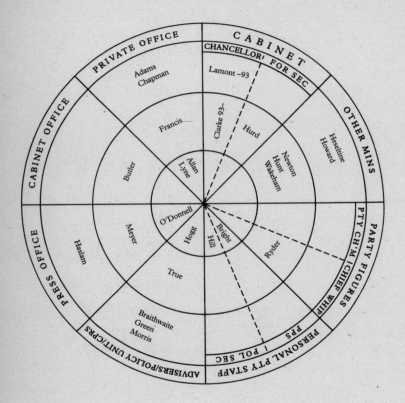

PRIVATE OFFICE

CABINET

CABINET OFFICE

PRESS OFFICE

ADVISERS/POLICY UNIT/CPRS

PERSONAL PTY STAFF

PARTY FIGURES

OTHER MINS

CHANCELLOR; FOR SEC

PTY CH'M | CHIEF WHIP

PPS | POL SEC

Adams
Chapman

Lamont –93

Clarke 93–

Hurd

Francis

Butler

Allan
Lyne

Newton
Hunt
Wakeham

Heseltine
Howard

O'Donnell

Meyer

Hogg

Bright
Hill

Ryder

Haslam

True

Braithwaite
Green
Morris

MAJOR III
1995–97

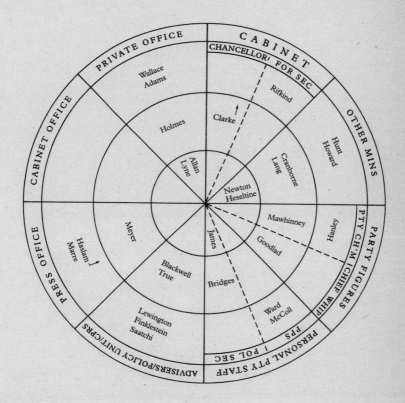

BLAIR I
1994–97

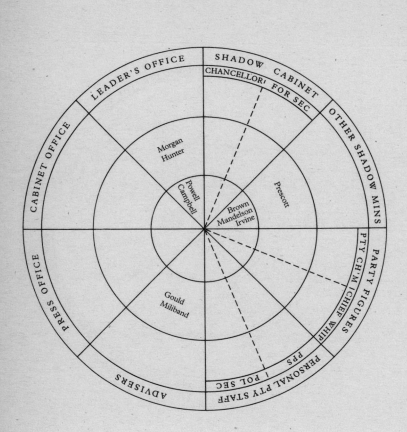

BLAIR II
1997–2000

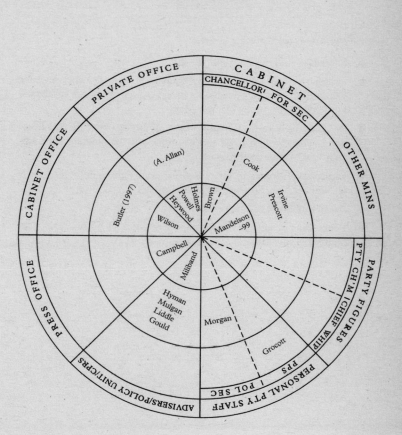

SOURCES

We have relied on the following sources:

- Interviews with over 150 individuals.

- Earlier interviews. We also drew extensively on earlier interviews for separate but relevant projects, for example, 550 interviews conducted for Seldon's biography of John Major.

- Press. Scans have been made over press articles over the last thirty years. They contain some useful profiles of the building and individuals who have worked within it.

- Parliamentary material. There is some useful data on different aspects of Number Ten, advising staffing numbers.

- Articles/monographs/memoirs.

- Public Record Office; Private papers of Michael Wolff and former Number Ten staff.

BIBLIOGRAPHY

Anderson, P., and Mann, N., *Safety First*. London, Granta, 1997.

Bahlman, D., ed., *The Diary of Sir Edward Walter Hamilton 1880–85*. Oxford, Oxford University Press, 1972.

Baker, A., *Prime Ministers: The Rule Book*, London, Politcos, 2000.

Baker, K., *The Turbulent Years. My Life in Politics*. London, Faber & Faber, 1993.

Barnett, J., *Inside the Treasury*. London, André Deutsch, 1982.

Berrill, K., 'Strength at the Centre:- The Case for a Prime Minister's Department', in King, A., ed., *The British Prime Minister*, 2nd ed. London, Macmillan, 1985.

Blackstone, T., and Plowden, W., *Inside the Thinktank: Advising the Cabinet, 1971–1983*. London, Heinemann, 1988.

Blake, R., *The Unknown Prime Minister*. London, Eyre & Spottiswoode, 1955.

Bogdanor, V., 'The Politics of Power', *The Guardian*, 4 June 1997.

Borthwick, R., 'Prime Minister and Parliament', in Shell, D., and Hodder-Williams, R., eds, *Churchill to Major. The British Prime Ministership since 1945*. London, Hurst, 1995.

Brooks, D., ed., *The Destruction of Lord Rosebery: From the Diary of Sir Edward Hamilton 1894–95*. London, Historians' Press, 1986.

Burch, M., and Holliday, I., *The British Cabinet System*. Hemel Hempstead, Prentice Hall/Harvester Wheatsheaf, 1996.

Burch, M., and Holliday, I., 'The Prime Minister's and Cabinet Offices: An executive office in all but name', *Parliamentary Affairs*, vol. 52, 1999.

Burnham, J., and Jones, G., *Institutional Development and Individual Choice: Advising the Prime Minister 1868–1998*. Paper to the ESRC Conference at Birmingham University, 17–19 December 1998.

Butler, D., Adonis, A., and Travers, T., *Failure in British Government*. Oxford, Oxford University Press, 1994.

Butler, D., and Kavanagh, D., *The British General Election of 1987*. London, Macmillan, 1987.

Butler, D., and Kavanagh, D., *The British General Election of 1997*. London, Macmillan, 1997.

Callaghan, J., *Time and Chance*. London, Collins, 1987.

Cameron, S., 'Tony be more civil to the servants' *The Times* 9 July 1999.

Campbell, C., *Governments Under Stress*. Toronto, University of Toronto Press, 1983.

Campbell, J., *Edward Heath*. London, Jonathan Cape, Weidenfeld, 1983.

Castle, B., *The Castle Diaries, 1974–76*. London, Weidenfeld, 1980.

Cecil, Lady Gwendolen, *Life of Robert, Marquis of Salisbury.* Vol. 3, 1880–86, London, Hodder & Stoughton, 1931.

Clark, W., *From Three Worlds.* London, Sidgwick & Jackson, 1986.

Cockerell, M., Hennessy, P., and Walker, D., *Sources Close to the Prime Minister.* London, Macmillan, 1984.

Cockett, R., *Thinking the Unthinkable: Think-Tanks and the Economic Counter-Revolution.* London, HarperCollins, 1994.

Colville, J., *Downing Street Diaries.* London, Hodder & Stoughton, 1985.

Colville, J., *Footprints in Time.* London, Collins, 1976.

Cradock, P., *In Pursuit of British Interests.* London, John Murray, 1997.

Crewe, Marquess of, *Lord Rosebery.* London, John Murray, 1931.

Davies, J., *The Prime Minister's Secretariat.* Newport, Monmouth, 1951.

Dell, E., *Hard Pounding.* Oxford, Oxford University Press, 1991.

Donoughue, B., *Prime Minister; The Conduct of Policy under Harold Wilson and James Callaghan.* London, Jonathan Cape, 1987.

Donoughue, B., and Jones, G., *Herbert Morrison, Portrait of a Politician.* London, Weidenfeld, 1973.

Dunleavy, P., *et al.*, 'Leaders, Politics and Institutional Change: The Decline of Prime Ministerial Accountability to the House of Commons, 1868–1990', in Rhodes, R., and Dunleavy, P., eds, *Prime Minister, Cabinet and Core Executive.* London, St Martin Press, 1995.

Dynes, M., and Walker, D., *The New British State.* London, Times Books, 1995.

Egremont, Lord (John Wyndham), *Wyndham and Children First.* London, Macmillan, 1968.

Egremont, Max, *Balfour.* London, Collins, 1980.

Evans, H., *Downing Street Diary.* London, Hodder & Stoughton, 1981.

Falkender, Lady, *Downing Street in Perspective.* London, Weidenfeld, 1982.

Foley, M., *The Rise of the British Presidency.* Manchester, Manchester University Press, 1993.

Gavin, N., and Sanders, D., 'The Economy and Voting', *Parliamentary Affairs,* vol. 50, 1997.

Gould, P., *The Unfinished Revolution.* London, Little Brown, 1998.

Gower, G.L., *Years of Content 1858–1886.* London, John Murray, 1940.

Haines, J., *The Politics of Power.* London, Jonathan Cape, 1977.

Hamilton, E., *Mr. Gladstone: A Monograph.* London, John Murray, 1898.

Harris, K., *Attlee.* London, Weidenfeld & Nicolson, 1982.

Harris, R., *Good and Faithful Servant: The Unauthorised Biography of Bernard Ingham.* London, Faber, 1990.

Healey, D., *The Time of My Life.* London, Michael Joseph, 1989.

Heffernan, R., and Stanyer, J., 'The Enhancement of Leadership Power: The Labour Party and the Impact of Political Communication', in Pattie, C., *et al.*, eds, *British Elections and Parties Yearbook,* vol. 7. London, Cassell, 1998.

Hennessy, P., *The Blair Centre: A Question of Command and Control.* London, Public Management Foundation, 1999.

Hennessy, P., 'The Blair Style of Government: an historical perspective and an interim audit', *Government and Opposition,* vol. 33, 1998

Hennessy, P., *Cabinet*. Oxford, Blackwell, 1986.

Hennessy, P., *Muddling Through*, London, Gollancz, 1996.

Hennessy, P., *The Prime Minister: The Office and Its Holders Since 1945*, London, Penguin, 2000.

Hennessy, P., *Whitehall*. London, Secker & Warburg, 1989.

Hennessy, P., Morrison, S., and Townsend, R., 'Routine Punctuated by Orgies: The Central Policy Review Staff 1970–83', *Strathclyde Papers on Government and Politics*, No. 31, Strathclyde University, 1985.

HM Treasury, 'Modern Public Services for Britain: investing in reform', Cm 4011, July 1998.

Hogg, S., and Hill, J., *Too Close to Call*. London, Little, Brown, 1995.

Horne, A., *Macmillan: 1957–86*. London, Macmillan, 1989.

Hoskyns, J., 'Conservatism is not enough', *Political Quarterly*, 1984.

Howe, Lord, *Conflict of Loyalty*. London, Macmillan, 1994.

Hunt, Lord, 'The United Kingdom', in Plowden, W., ed., *Advising the Rulers*. Oxford, Blackwell, 1987.

Hurd, D., *An End to Promises*. London, Collins, 1979.

Hutchinson, H., ed., *Private Diaries of Rt Hon. Sir Algernon West*. London, John Murray, 1922.

Hyde, H.M., *Neville Chamberlain*. London, Weidenfeld & Nicolson, 1976.

Ingram, B., *Kill the Messenger*. London, HarperCollins, 1991.

James, R.R., *Anthony Eden*. London, Weidenfeld & Nicolson, 1986.

James, R.R., *Rosebery*. London, Weidenfeld & Nicolson, 1963.

James, S., *British Cabinet Government*. London, Routledge, 1992.

James, S., 'Cabinet Government: A Commentary', *Contemporary Record*, vol. 8, 1994.

Jenkins, R., *Asquith*. London, William Collins, 1978.

Jenkins, R., *Baldwin*. London, Macmillan, 1995.

Jones, C., *No. 10 Downing Street: The Story of a House*. London, BBC, 1985.

Jones, G., 'Prime Minister's Department Really Create Problems: A Rejoinder to Patrick Weller', *Public Administration*, vol. 61, 1983.

Jones, G., 'The Prime Ministers' Secretaries', in Griffith, J.A.G., ed., *From Policy to Administration: Essays in Honour of William A. Robson*. London, George Allen & Unwin, 1976.

Jones, N., *Soundbites and Spin Doctors*. London, Indigo, 1996.

Jones, T., *Whitehall Diary*. Oxford, Oxford University Press, 1969.

Kandiah, M., ed., 'Witness Seminar, No 10 Policy Unit', *Contemporary British History*, vol. 10, 1996.

Kavanagh, D., 'The Fatal Choice: The calling of the February 1974 election', in Ball, S., and Seldon, A., eds, *The Heath Government 1970–74*. London, Longmans, 1996.

Kernell, S., *Going Public. New Strategies of Presidential Leadership*. Washington D.C., Congressional Quarterly Press, 1993.

King, A., ed., *The British Prime Ministers*, 2nd ed. London, Macmillan, 1985.

King, A., ed., *New Labour Triumphs: Britain at the Polls*. London, Chatham House, 1998.

Lamont, N., *Norman Lamont: In Office*, London, Little Brown, 1999.

Lawson, N., *The View From No. 11: Memoirs of a Tory Radical.* London, Bantam Press, 1992.

Lawson, Lord, and Armstrong, Lord, 'Cabinet Government in the Thatcher Years', *Contemporary Record,* vol. 8, 1994.

Lee, J.M., 'The Ethos of the Cabinet Office: a comment on the testimony of officials', *Public Administration,* vol. 68, 1990.

Lee, J.M., Jones G. and Burnham J. *At the Centre of Whitehall.* London, Macmillan, 1998.

Lipsey, D., *The Secret Treasury,* London, Viking, 2000.

Lloyd, J., 'The Politics of Debt', *New Statesman,* 1 January 1999.

MacDougall, G., 'The Prime Minister's Statistical Section', in Chester, D.N., ed., *Lessons of the British War Economy.* Cambridge, Cambridge University Press, 1951.

Macintyre, D., *Mandelson: The Biography.* London, HarperCollins, 1999.

Macleod, I., *Neville Chamberlain.* London, Frederick Muller, 1961.

Madgwick, P., *British Government: The Central Executive Territory.* Hemel Hempstead, Philip Allan, 1991.

Maitland, D., *Diverse Times, Sundry Places.* Brighton, Alpha Press, 1996.

Major, J., *John Major: An Autobiography,* London, HarperCollins, 1999.

Malcom, N., 'Margaret Thatcher, Housewife Superstar', *The Spectator,* 25 February 1989.

Mallaby, G., *From My Level.* London, Hutchinson, 1965.

Mandelson, P., and Liddle, R., *The Blair Revolution. Can Labour Deliver?* London, Faber, 1996.

Margach, J., *The Abuse of Power: The War Between Downing Street and the Media from Lloyd George to James Callaghan.* London, W.H. Allen, 1978.

Marquand, D., *Ramsay MacDonald.* London, Jonathan Cape, 1977.

Marr, A., *Ruling Brittania.* London, Michael Joseph, 1995.

Matthew, H.C.G., *Gladstone 1809–1874.* Oxford, Clarendon Press, 1985.

Matthew, H.C.G., *Gladstone 1875–1898.* Oxford, Clarendon Press, 1995.

McAlpine, A., *Memoirs of a Jolly Bagman.* London, Weidenfeld & Nicolson, 1997.

McKenzie, K., 'Hair Yesterday and Gone Today', *The Spectator,* 9 July 1997.

McSmith, A., *Faces of Labour.* London, Verso, 1996.

Middlemas, K. and Barnes, J., *Baldwin.* London, Weidenfeld & Nicolson, 1969.

Millar, R., *A View from the Wings.* London, Weidenfeld, 1993.

Milne, K., 'The Rule of Tony's Teeny-boppers', *New Statesman,* 24 July 1998.

Minney, R.J., *No. 10 Downing Street.* London, Cassell, 1963.

Moneypenny, W.F., and Buckle, G.E., *The Life of Benjamin Disraeli Earl of Beaconsfield.* London, John Murray, 1929.

Morgan, K., *James Callaghan.* Oxford, Oxford University Press, 1997.

Mount, F., *The British Constitution Now.* London, Heinemann, 1992.

Naylor, J., *A Man and an Institution.* Cambridge, Cambridge University Press, 1984.

Norris, P., *et al.*, *On Message: Communicating the Campaign.* London, Sage, 1999.

Norton, P., *Conservative Dissidents.* London, Temple Smith, 1978.

Norton, P., 'The Lady's Not For Turning: But What About the Rest?', *Parliamentary Affairs,* No. 43, 1990.

Norton, P., 'The New Barons? Senior Ministers in British Government'. Paper delivered at Conference at Birmingham University, December 1998.

Oborne, P., *Alastair Campbell,* London, Aurum Press, 1999.

Padgett, S., *Adenauer to Kohl:* London, Hurst & Co., 1994.

Parris, M., *Great Parliamentary Scandals.* London, Robson, 1995.

Petrie, Sir Charles, *The Powers Behind the Prime Ministers.* London, Macgibbon & Kee, 1958.

Pimlott, B., *Harold Wilson.* London, HarperCollins, 1992.

Pliatzky, L., *The Treasury under Mrs Thatcher.* Oxford, Blackwell, 1989.

Plowden, W., 'Providing Countervailing Analysis and Advice in Career-Dominated Bureaucratic Systems: The British experience, 1916–1988', in Campbell, C., and Wysomirski, eds, *Executive Leadership in Anglo American Systems.* Pittsburgh, University of Pittsburgh Press, 1991.

Plowden, W., ed., *Advising the Rulers.* Oxford, Blackwell, 1987.

Powell, C., 'Yes Prime Minister: You are the Master now', *Sunday Telegraph,* 11 May 1997.

Pryce, S., *Presidentialising the Premiership.* London, Macmillan, 1997.

Pym, F., *The Politics of Consent,* London, Hamish Hamilton, 1985.

Ranelagh, J., *Thatcher's People.* London, Fontana, 1992.

Rawnsley, A. *Servants of the People: The Inside Story of New Labour,* London, Penguin, 2000.

Rentoul, J., *Tony Blair.* London, Little Brown, 1995.

Rhodes, R., 'From Prime Ministerial Power to Core Executive', in Rhodes, R., and Dunleavy, P., eds, *Prime Minister, Cabinet and Core Executive.* London, St Martins Press, 1995.

Rhodes, R., 'Shackling the Leader? Coherence, Capacity and the Hollow Crown', in Weller, P., *et al,* eds, *The Hollow Crown.* London, Macmillan, 1997.

Rhodes James, R., *Memoirs of a Conservative.* London, Weidenfeld & Nicolson, 1969.

Richards, S., 'A Resolution for Tony Blair: Try not to Neglect the Cabinet', *The Independent,* 1 January 1999.

Riddell, P., *Honest Opportunism. 'The Rise of the Career Politician'.* London, Hamish Hamilton, 1993.

Riddell, P., 'President Blair Told: "You Have Lost Touch"', *The Times,* 16 March 1998.

Riddell, P., 'We're missing you, Mr Blair', *The Times,* 10 June 1998.

Riddell, P., 'You'll never walk alone, Mr Blair', *The Times,* 22 February 1999.

RIPA, *Top Jobs in Whitehall: Appointments and Promotions in the Senior Civil Service.* London, Royal Institute of Public Administration, 1987.

Rose, R., 'British Government: The Job at the Top', in Rose, R., and

Suleiman, E., eds, *Presidents and Prime Ministers*. London, American Enterprise Institute, 1980.

Rose, R., and Davies, P., *Inheritance and Public Policy: Change Without Choice in Britain*. New Haven, Yale University Press, 1995.

Rose, R. *The Paradox of Power: The Prime Minister and His Shrinking World*, Oxford, Polity, 2000.

Routledge, P., *Gordon Brown: The Biography*. London, Pocket Books, 1998.

Routledge, P., *Mandy: The Unauthorised Biography of Peter Mandelson*. London, Simon & Schuster, 1999.

Seldon, A., 'The Cabinet Office and Co-ordination 1978–89', *Public Administration*, vol. 68, 1990.

Seldon, A., *Churchill's Indian Summer*. London, Hodder & Stoughton, 1981.

Seldon, A., *Major. A Political Life*. London, Weidenfeld & Nicolson, 1997.

Seldon, A., *The Riddle of the Voucher*. London, Institute of Economic Affairs, 1986.

Seldon, A., *Number Ten Downing Street: An Illustrated History*. London, HarperCollins, 1999.

Seymour-Ure, C., 'Prime Minister and the Public: Managing Media Relations', in Shell, D., and Hodder-Williams, R., eds, *Churchill to Major: The British Prime Ministership since 1945*. London, Hurst, 1995.

Shell, D., and Hodder-Williams, R., eds, *Churchill to Major: The British Premiership since 1945*. London, Hurst, 1995.

Silvester, R., 'How Blair's "secret burden" is bringing Labour to a halt.' *Independent on Sunday* 18 July 1999.

Smith, M.J., *The Core Executive*. London, Macmillan, 1999.

Smith, M.J., 'Reconceptualizing the British State', *Public Administration*, vol. 76, 1998.

Sopel, J., *Tony Blair; The Moderniser*. London, Michael Joseph, 1995.

Stephens, P., *Politics and the Pound*. London, Macmillan, 1996.

Thatcher, M., *The Downing Street Years*. London, HarperCollins, 1993.

Theakston, K., 'The Heath Government, Whitehall and the Civil Service', in Ball, S., and Seldon, A., eds, *The Heath Government 1970–74. A Reappraisal*. London, Longman, 1996.

Theakston, K., *Leadership in Whitehall*. London, Macmillan, 1998.

Thompson, R., and Donoughue, B., 'On the Treadmill: Presidents and Prime Ministers at Work', Glasgow Studies in Public Policy, No. 169.

Thorpe, D.R., *Alec Douglas-Home*. London, Sinclair-Stevenson, 1996.

Turner, J., *Lloyd George's Secretariat*. Cambridge, Cambridge University Press, 1980.

Urban, G., *Diplomacy and Disillusion at the Court of Margaret Thatcher*. London, I.B. Taurus, 1996.

Wakeham, Lord, 'Cabinet Government', *Contemporary Record*, vol. 8, 1994.

Waterhouse, N., *Private and Official*. London, Jonathan Cape, 1940.

Watkins, A., *A Conservative Coup*, London, Duckworth, 1991.

Weintraub, S., *Disraeli: A Biography*. London, Hamish Hamilton, 1993 .

Weller, P., *First Among Equals; Prime Ministers in Westminster Systems*. Sydney, Allen & Unwin, 1985.

West, A., *Recollections 1832–1886*, 2 vols. London, Smith, Elder, 1908.

Wheeler-Bennett, J., ed., *Action This Day: Working with Churchill*. London, Macmillan, 1968.

Whitehead, P., 'The Labour Governments 1974–79', in Hennessy, P., and Seldon, A., eds, *Ruling Performance*. Oxford, Blackwell, 1987.

Willetts, D., 'The Role of the Prime Minister's Policy Unit', *Public Administration*, Vol. 65, 1987.

Williams, M., *Inside Number Ten*. London, Weidenfeld, 1972.

Williams, P., 'Changing Styles of Labour Leadership', in Kavanagh, D., ed., *The Politics of the Labour Party*. London, Allen & Unwin, 1982.

Wilson, H., *The Labour Government, 1964–1970*. London, Weidenfeld, 1971.

Wilson, Sir Richard, 'Modernising Central Government: the role of the senior civil servant'. London, 13 October 1998.

Wolff, M., 'The Power of the Prime Minister: Should He Pick up the Ball and Run With It?', *The Times*, 24 May 1976.

Young, H., 'Brown has not only lost his spindoctor, but also his untouchability', *The Guardian*, 5 January 1999.

Young, H., *One of Us*. London, Macmillan, 1989.

Ziegler, P., *The Authorized Life of Lord Wilson of Rievaulx*. London, Weidenfeld, 1993.

REFERENCE NOTES

Introduction

1. A literature is only now beginning to develop: see in particular Michael Lee, George Jones and June Burnham (1998) and Martin Burch and Ian Holliday (1999).
2. Ferdinand Mount (1992), p. 136.
3. Douglas Hurd (1979), p. 37.
4. Private interview.
5. Harold Wilson (1971).

1. The Geography of Influence

1. Private interview.
2. Ken Stowe (1975–79) was the main exception.
3. Michael Palliser (1975–82), Patrick Wright (1986–91).
4. Private interview.
5–8. Private interviews.
9. See Chapter 2.
10. Michael Lee, George Jones and June Burnham (1998), p. 37.
11. Bernard Donoughue (1987), p. 20.
12. Philip Williams (1982).
13. Simon James (1992), p. 88.
14. James Callaghan (1987), p. 403.
15. Anthony Seldon (1997), p. 814. Ronald Thompson and Bernard Donoughue (1989).
16. Andrew Marr (1995), p. 271. Also see Ferdinand Mount (1992).

2. The Development of the Prime Minister's Office 1868–1970

1. Charles Petrie (1958), p. 32.
2. Algernon West (1899), vol. 1, p. 340.
3. Algernon West (1899), vol. 1, pp. 341–42.
4. Algernon West (1899), vol. 1, p. 349.

5. Dudley Bahlman (1972), Introduction.
6. George Jones (1976), p. 19.
7. June Burnham and George Jones (1998), p. 6.
8. Stanley Weintraub (1993), p. 438.
9. Charles Petrie (1958), p. 16.
10. Although in the earlier stages of the Balkan crisis Corry was 'in nervous collapse from overwork'. Stanley Weintraub (1993), p. 587.
11. Charles Petrie (1958), p. 24.
12. Stanley Weintraub (1993), p. 625.
13. Stanley Weintraub (1993), p. 580. W.F. Moneypenny and G.E. Buckle (1929), p. 333.
14. George Jones (1985), pp 98, 100.
15. Letter, Lord Jenkins to authors, 16.2.99.
16. Gower (1940), p. 154.
17. George Jones (1976), pp 13–38.
18. Colin Matthew (1995), vol. 2, p. 231.
19. Colin Matthew (1995), p. 233.
20. Edward Hamilton (1898), p. 92.
21. June Burnham and George Jones (1998), p. 6.
22. Gwendolen Cecil (1931), pp. 168–196.
23. Gwendolen Cecil (1931), p. 168.
24. Thomas Jones (1976), p. 22.
25. June Burnham and George Jones (1998), p. 8.
26. Gwendolen Cecil (1931), p. 207.
27. Charles Petrie (1958), p. 44.
28. Hutchinson (1922).
29. Hutchinson (1922), pp. 45–46.
30. Letter, Lord Jenkins to authors, 16.2.99.
31. Hutchinson (1922), pp. 140–41.
32. The article is reproduced in Hutchinson (1922), pp. 128–35.
33. David Brooks (1986), p. 120.
34. David Brooks (1986), p. 170.
35. Crewe (1931), vol. 2, p. 654.

36. George Jones (1985), p. 97.
37. Lord Egremont (1980), p. 132.
38. Lord Egremont (1980), p. 132.
39. Harold Wilson (1973), p. 469.
40. Harold Wilson (1973), p. 469.
41. June Burnham and George Jones (1998), p. 9.
42. Roy Jenkins (1978), p. 8.
43. Charles Petrie (1958), pp 85–97.
44. Letter, Lord Jenkins to authors, 16.2.99.
45. Roy Jenkins (1978), pp. 184–85.
46. Letter, Kenneth Morgan to authors, 18.2.99.
47. John Naylor (1984), pp. 31–33.
48. John Naylor (1984), pp. 32–33.
49. John Turner (1980), pp. 140–41.
50. John Naylor (1984), p. 91.
51. John Turner (1980), *passim.*
52. John Turner (1980), p. 7.
53. John Turner (1980), p. 169. George Jones (1969), p. 39.
54. June Burnham and George Jones (1998), p. 10.
55. George Jones (1969), pp. 215–16.
56. Letter, Kenneth Morgan to authors, 18.2.99.
57. Robert Blake (1955), p. 501.
58. Robert Rhodes James (1969), p. 162.
59. Robert Blake (1955), p. 402.
60. It is perhaps safest to say, with Roy Jenkins (1995, p. 188), that 'there remains an impression of something slightly odd about Waterhouse'.
61. Keith Middlemas and John Barnes (1969), p. 497.
62. Roy Jenkins (1995), p. 65.
63. Roy Jenkins (1995), p. 65.
64. June Burnham and George Jones (1998), p. 11.
65. John Naylor (1984), pp. 156–57.
66. Keith Middlemas and John Barnes (1969), p. 499.
67. David Marquand (1977), p. 307.
68. David Marquand (1977), p. 308.
69. Charles Petrie (1958), pp. 149–50.
70. David Marquand (1977), p. 494.
71. Charles Petrie (1958), p. 141.
72. Charles Petrie (1958), p. 145.
73. Nourah Waterhouse (1940), pp. 306–7. James Margach (1978), p. 39.
74. David Marquand (1977), p. 494.
75. June Burnham and George Jones (1998), p. 13.
76. Michael Cockerell, Peter Hennessy and David Walker (1984), p. 37.
77. James Margach (1978), pp. 51–53.
78. Sir John Colville (1985), pp. 29–30.
79. Sir John Colville (1985), p. 39.
80. Sir John Colville (1985), p. 75.
81. Sir John Colville (1976), p. 72.
82. Letter, David Dilks to Anthony Seldon, 15.2.99.
83. Sir John Wheeler-Bennett (1968).
84. Sir John Colville (1985), pp. 294–95.
85. George Jones (1985), pp. 136–39. Sir John Colville (1985), pp 475–76.
86. Donald MacDougall (1951), pp. 58–68.
87. June Burnham and George Jones (1998), p. 14.
88. Francis Williams (1970), pp. 215–17.
89. Francis Williams (1970), pp. 215–17.
90. James Margach (1978), p. 90.
91. June Burnham and George Jones (1998), p. 14.
92. George Jones (1976), p. 33.
93. George Mallaby (1965), pp. 36–37.
94. Anthony Seldon (1981), pp. 28–35.
95. Anthony Seldon (1981), p. 33.
96. Harold Evans (1981), p. 45.
97. Sir John Colville (1985), pp. 668–70.
98. Anthony Seldon (1981), p. 116.
99. William Clark (1986), p. 156.
100. June Burnham and George Jones (1998), p. 15.
101. Robert Rhodes James (1986), p. 406.
102. Robert Rhodes James (1986), p. 411.
103. William Clark (1986), p. 147.
104. James Margach (1978), pp. 110–11.
105. William Clark (1986), p. 196.
106. Robert Rhodes James (1986), p. 412.
107. William Clark (1986), p. 208.
108. Harold Evans (1981), p. 13.
109. Harold Evans (1981)p. 22. It is reproduced in Lord Egremont (1968), p. 171.
110. George Jones (1973), p. 363.
111. Lord Egremont (1968).
112. Harold Evans (1981), p. 29.
113. June Burnham and George Jones (1998), p. 16.
114. Alistair Horne (1989), p. 160.
115. Michael Cockerell, Peter Hennessy and David Walker (1984), p. 66.
116. Michael Cockerell, Peter Hennessy and David Walker (1984), p. 68.

117. Harold Evans (1981), p. 63.
     Anthony Seldon (1997).
118. James Margach (1978), p. 118.
119. Harold Evans (1981), pp. 37–38.
120. Harold Evans (1981), p. 23.
121. George Jones (1985), pp. 153–54.
122. R.J. Minney (1963), Appendix.
123. Harold Evans (1981), p. 38.
124. Anthony Seldon (1981), p. 179.
125. D.R. Thorpe (1996), pp. 328–30.
126. PRO file PREM 13/816.
127. Ben Pimlott (1992), p. 338.
128. Marcia Williams (1972), pp. 21–22.
129. Marcia Williams (1972), pp. 29, 66.
130. George Jones (1973), p. 368.
131. Marcia Williams (1972), p. 46.
132. PRO file PREM 13/236.
133. PRO file PREM 13/236. This memo
     was produced in the *Sun* 23.2.77,
     although a copy that did not include
     Wilson's last comment and gave a
     misleading impression of his
     intentions.
134. James Margach (1978), pp. 143–44.
135. PRO file PREM 13/816.
136. PRO file PREM 13/816.
137. PRO file PREM 13/816.
138. Private interview.
139. Marcia Williams (1972), pp. 53–54.
     Joe Haines (1977), p. 7.
140. Private interview.

3. Edward Heath 1970–1974

This chapter is a substantially revised
version of Lewis Baston and Anthony
Seldon (1996).

1. Kevin Theakston in Stuart Ball and
   Anthony Seldon (1996).
2. Howell paper, CRD/3/14/4.
3. Schreiber memorandum 30 April
   1968, CRD/3/14/4.
4. Interview, Lord Hunt of Tanworth.
5. Interview, David Howell.
6. Heath describes some of this activity
   in his book on music.
7. Lady Falkender (1982), p. 104.
8. Lady Falkender (1982), pp. 104–7.
   John Campbell (1993), pp. 292–94.
9. Interview, Janet Hewlett-Davies.
10. Interview, Sir Donald Maitland.
11. *Evening Standard*, 25 May 1972,
    interview with Robert Carvel and
    Charles Wintour.
12. Interview, Lord Armstrong of
    Ilminster.
13. Interview, Lord Armstrong of
    Ilminster.
14. Interview, Geoffrey Tucker.
15. Dennis Kavanagh (1996).
16. Interview, Sir Donald Maitland.
17. Private interview.
18. Douglas Hurd (1979), p. 27.
19. Letter, Lord Bridges.
20. Douglas Hurd (1979), pp. 34–35.
21. Douglas Hurd (1979), p. 51.
22. Douglas Hurd (1979), p. 33.
23. Interview, Brendon Sewill.
24. Interview, William Waldegrave.
25. Interview, Sir Timothy Kitson.
26. Lady Falkender (1982), p. 105.
27. John Campbell (1993), p. 667. Philip
    Norton (1978).
28. Interview, Henry James.
29. Interview, Sir Donald Maitland.
30. Interview, Sir Donald Maitland.
31. Interview, Henry James.
32. Interview, Sir Donald Maitland.
33. Interview, Sir Donald Maitland.
    Interview, Henry James.
34. *Evening Standard*, 25 May 1972.
35. Interview, Sir Donald Maitland.
36. Interview, Barbara Hosking. Letter,
    Barbara Hosking.
37. Interview, Lord Bridges.
38. Interview, Henry James.
39. Wolff papers, 'Co-ordination of
    information' minutes 1972–74,
    esp. 28 Nov. 1973, 5 Dec. 1973.
40. Wolff papers, Box L5 'Press and
    media'.
41. Ibid.
42. Private interview.
43. James Margach (1978), p. 166.
44. Lord Hunt of Tanworth (1988),
    p. 44. Also Douglas Hurd (1979).
45. Letter, Lord Armstrong of Ilminster.
46. Private interview.
47. Letter, Joe Haines to authors,
    24.9.98.
48. Letter, Lord Armstrong of Ilminster.
49. Interview, Sir Edward Heath.
50. Interview, Lord Armstrong of
    Ilminster.
51. Interview, Lord Armstrong of
    Ilminster.

52. Interview, Lord Bridges.
53. Interview, Lord Bridges.
54. Douglas Hurd (1979), p. 34.
55. Letter, Lord Armstrong of Ilminster to Anthony Seldon, 24.9.98.
56. Interview, Lord Armstrong of Ilminster.
57. Interview, Janet Whiting.
58. Interview, Lord Bridges.
59. Interview, Lord Bridges.
60. Letter, Lord Armstrong of Ilminster to Anthony Seldon, 24.9.98.
61. Interview, Lord Bridges.
62. Letter, Lord Armstrong of Ilminster.
63. Interview, Janet Whiting.
64. Interview, Sir Edward Heath.
65. Interview, Lord Armstrong of Ilminster.
66. Interview, Lord Bridges.
67. Interview, Lord Hunt of Tanworth.
68. Interview, Lord Bridges.
69. Interview, Lord Hunt of Tanworth.
70. John Campbell (1993), p. 491.
71. Peter Hennessy (1989), pp. 238–41.
72. Interview, Sir John Chilcot.
73. Private interview.
74. Interview, David Howell.
75. Interview, Sir Edward Heath.
76. John Campbell (1993), pp 490–92.
77. 'Sir William Armstrong talking with David Wilcox', *The Listener*. 29 March 1974. See also Kevin Theakston (1988).
78. Tessa Blackstone and William Plowden (1988), pp. 53–54.
79. Wolff paper, minute M121/73, C1/18/CPRS.
80. Interview, William Waldegrave.
81. Private interview.
82. Interview, David Howell.
83. Interview, Sir Edward Heath. Interview, William Waldegrave. Tessa Blackstone and William Plowden (1988), p. 54.
84. Interview, William Waldegrave.
85. Interview, David Howell.
86. Interview, David Howell.
87. Interview, Sir Donald Maitland. Interview, Henry James.
88. Wolff papers, L4 'Address on Europe'.
89. Douglas Hurd (1979), p. 73.
90. Douglas Hurd (1979), p. 81.
91. Interview, James Douglas.
92. Interview, Sir Donald Maitland.
93. Interview, Barbara Hosking.
94. James Margach (1979), p. 54.
95. Interview, Sir Donald Maitland.
96. Interview, Douglas Hurd.
97. Peter Hennessy (1989), pp 382–87.
98. Interview, David Howell.
99. Andrew Graham in Michael Kandrah (1996).

4. Harold Wilson 1974–1976

1. But a letter from Joe Haines to the authors, 24.9.98, states that Wilson expected to win. Haines holds a letter from Marcia Williams making it clear that they were expecting victory.
2. Private information.
3. Interview, Lord Armstrong of Ilminster.
4. Private interview.
5. Anthony Seldon (1981).
6. Interview, Lord Armstrong of Ilminster.
7. Private interview.
8. Private interview.
9. Private interview.
10. Private letter.
11. Ben Pimlott (1992). Philip Ziegler (1992).
12. Phillip Whitehead in Peter Hennessy and Anthony Seldon (1987), p. 242.
13. Ben Pimlott (1992). Edmund Dell (1991), Chapter 5.
14. Phillip Whitehead (1987), p. 246.
15. Private interview.
16. Private interview.
17. This section draws heavily on the account in Robert Thompson and Bernard Donoughue (1989), pp. 16–19.
18. Private interviews.
19. Robert Thompson and Bernard Donoughue (1989), pp. 16–17.
20. Private interview.
21. Barbara Castle (1980), p. 227.
22. Robert Thompson and Bernard Donoughue (1989), p. 17.
23. Letter, Andrew Graham to authors, 25.9.98.
24. Robert Thompson and Bernard Donoughue (1989), p. 17 and private interviews.

25. Private interviews.
26. Robert Thompson and Bernard Donoughue (1989), p. 18.
27. Bernard Donoughue (1987), p. 19.
28. Private interview.
29. Private interview.
30. Private interview.
31. There were also two special London conferences, in November 1974 and April 1975.
32. Robert Thompson and Bernard Donoughue (1989), p. 19.
33. Robert Thompson and Bernard Donoughue (1989), p. 19.
34. Private interviews.
35. Private interview.
36. Private interview.
37. Private interviews.
38. Interview, Janet Hewlett-Davies.
39. Ben Pimlott (1992), pp. 622–23.
40. Interview, Lord Donoughue of Ashton.
41. Private interview.
42. Private interview.
43. Letter, Andrew Graham to authors, 25.9.98.
44. Interview, Joe Haines.
45. Interview, Lord Donoughue of Ashton.
46. Interview, Lord Wright of Richmond.
47. Kevin Theakston (1998), p. 202.
48. Private interview.
49. Interview, Lord Bridges.
50. Private interview.
51. Interview, Lord Armstrong of Ilminster.
52. Interview, Lord Armstrong of Ilminster.
53. Interview, Joe Haines.
54. Interview, Sir Kenneth Stowe.
55. Private interview.
56. Interview, Lord Wright of Richmond.
57. Private interview.
58. Private interview.
59. Interview, Sir Kenneth Stowe.
60. Private interview.
61. Private interview.
62. Ben Pimlott (1992), p. 683.
63. Private interview.
64. Interview, Lord Butler of Brockwell.
65. Private interview.
66. Private interview.
67. Private interview.
68. Ben Pimlott (1992), p. 620. Private information.
69. Letter, Joe Haines to authors, 24.9.98. Also see Joe Haines (1977).
70. Interview, Joe Haines.
71. Interview, Joe Haines.
72. Interview, Joe Haines.
73. Interview, Janet Hewlett-Davies.
74. Interview, Joe Haines.
75. Bernard Donoughue (1996), p. 119.
76. Other Whitehall innovations, notably the creation of independent public audit and inspection, rank highly.
77. Bernard Donoughue and George Jones (1973).
78. Bernard Donoughue (1987) and (1996), p. 115.
79. Private information.
80. Letter, Lord Donoughue of Ashton to authors, 25.9.98.
81. Andrew Graham ran the Unit after Balogh's departure in 1968 before Graham went to Oxford in 1969. Interview, Andrew Graham.
82. Andrew Graham in Michael Kandiah (1992), pp. 197 and 207 (where he lists the Balogh Unit members). See also Andrew Graham (1996), pp. 112–13.
83. Bernard Donoughue (1996), p. 115.
84. Interview, Lord Donoughue of Ashton.
85. Interview, Lord Donoughue of Ashton.
86. Bernard Donoughue (1987), p. 19.
87. Interview, David Piachaud. But the Treasury ministers disagree. See Edmund Dell (1991) and Denis Healey (1989).
88. Bernard Donoughue (1996), p. 116.
89. Interview, Andrew Graham.
90. Private interview.
91. Private interview.
92. Bernard Donoughue (1996), p. 115.
93. Private interview.
94. Interview, Lord Donoughue of Ashton.
95. Interview, Andrew Graham.
96. Interview, Andrew Graham.
97. Interview, David Piachaud.
98. Bernard Donoughue (1996), p. 118.

99. Bernard Donoughue (1996), p. 117.
100. Interview, David Piachaud.
101. Interviews, Andrew Graham, David Piachaud.
102. Private interview.
103. Bernard Donoughue (1987) and (1996), p. 116.
104. But this is challenged in Edmund Dell (1991), Chapter 15.
105. Bernard Donoughue (1996), p. 116.
106. Interviews, Lord Donoughue of Ashton, Joe Haines.
107. Interview, Lord Donoughue of Ashton.
108. Private interviews.
109. Interview, Lord Armstrong of Ilminster.
110. Private interview.
111. Private interview.
112. Private interviews.
113. Private interviews.
114. Interview, Joe Haines.
115. Matthew Parris (1995), pp. 191–200.
116. Edmund Dell (1991). Denis Healey (1989).

5. James Callaghan 1976–1979

1. Interview, Roger Stott.
2. Interview, Lord Donoughue of Ashton.
3. James Callaghan (1987), p. 397.
4. Private interview.
5. This section leans heavily on Robert Thompson and Bernard Donoughue (1987), pp. 16–19.
6. Interview, Lord McNally of Blackpool.
7. Interview, Roger Stott.
8. Private interview.
9. Interview, Sir Tim Lankester.
10. Interview, Lord McNally of Blackpool.
11. Robert Thompson and Bernard Donoughue (1989), p. 17.
12. Letter, Sir Tom McCaffrey to authors, 8.10.98.
13. Robert Thompson and Bernard Donoughue (1989), p. 17.
14. Private interview.
15. Kenneth Morgan (1997), pp. 508–9.
16. Kenneth Morgan (1997), p. 508.
17. Robert Thompson and Bernard Donoughue (1989), pp. 152–53.
18. Robert Thompson and Bernard Donoughue (1989), p. 18.
19. Letter, Sir Tom McCaffrey to authors, 8.10.98.
20. Robert Thompson and Bernard Donoughue (1989), p. 19.
21. Robert Thompson and Bernard Donoughue (1989), p. 19.
22. Interview, Lord Wright of Richmond.
23. Private interview.
24. Private information.
25. Bernard Donoughue (1989), p. 19.
26. Interview, Lord Donoughue of Ashton.
27. Private interviews.
28. Interview, Lord McNally of Blackpool.
29. Private interview.
30. Interview, Lord McNally of Blackpool.
31. Interview, Lord Donoughue of Ashton.
32. Interview, Lord McNally of Blackpool.
33. Private interviews. Kenneth Morgan (1997), p. 492(?).
34. Letter, Lord Donoughue of Ashton to authors, 25.9.98.
35. Private interview.
36. Private interviews.
37. Private interview.
38. Private interview. Kenneth Morgan (1997), p. 494.
39. Private interview.
40. See Tessa Blackstone and William Plowden (1988).
41. Kenneth Morgan (1997), p. 505.
42. Private interview.
43. Kenneth Morgan (1997), p. 496.
44. Letter, Lord McNally of Blackpool to authors, 25.9.98.
45. Interview, Roger Stott.
46. Private interview.
47. Interview, Lord McNally of Blackpool.
48. Interview, Sir Tom McCaffrey.
49. Interview, Sir Tom McCaffrey.
50. Interview, Sir Tom McCaffrey.
51. Kenneth Morgan (1997), p. 497.
52. Interview, Sir Tom McCaffrey.

53. Private letter.
54. Interview, Sir Tom McCaffrey.
55. Letter, Sir Tom McCaffrey to authors, 8.10.98.
56. Interview, Sir Tom McCaffrey.
57. Interview, Sir Tom McCaffrey.
58. Letter, Sir Tom McCaffrey to authors, 30.3.99.
59. Kenneth Morgan (1997), p. 490.
60. James Callaghan (1987), p. 406.
61. Private interviews.
62. Private interview.
63. Interview, Sir Tim Lankester.
64. Interview, Roger Stott.
65. Private interview.
66. Letter, Lord McNally of Blackpool to authors, 25.9.98.
67. Kenneth Morgan (1997), p. 489.
68. Private interviews.
69. Kenneth Morgan (1997), p. 500.
70. Private interview.
71. Interview, Lord McNally of Blackpool.
72. Private interview.
73. Letter, Lord McNally of Blackpool to authors, 25.9.98.
74. Kenneth Morgan (1997), p. 496.
75. Kenneth Morgan (1997), p. 640.
76. Private interview.

6. Margaret Thatcher
1979–1983

1. John Ranelagh (1991).
2. Private interview.
3. Private interview.
4. Private interview.
5. Private interview.
6. Interview, Sir Clive Whitmore.
7. Interview, Sir Timothy Lankester.
8. Interview, Lord Butler of Brockwell.
9. Private interview.
10. Private interview.
11. Private interview.
12. Private interview.
13. Private interview.
14. Peter Hennessy (1987), p. 629.
15. Margaret Thatcher (1993), p. 47.
16. Private interview.
17. Peter Hennessy (1987), pp. 592ff.
18. Interview, Lord Armstrong of Ilminster.
19. Kevin Theakston (1998), p. 206.

20. Ronald Millar (1993), p. 290.
21. Much of this section draws on interviews with John Hoskyns. Also see Ronald Millar (1993), pp. 289–90.
22. Geoffrey Howe (1994), p. 249.
23. Private interview.
24. Richard Cockett (1994), p. 312. Also interview with Norman Strauss.
25. Richard Cockett (1994), p. 315.
26. Interview, John Hoskyns. Also see Hoskyns (1984).
27. Interview, Ferdinand Mount.
28. Private papers.
29. See Arthur Seldon (1986).
30. Bernard Ingham (1991), p. 156.
31. Interview, David Wolfson.
32. Interview, David Wolfson.
33. Interview, David Wolfson.
34. Margaret Thatcher (1993), p. 394.
35. Private interview.
36. *The Times*, 30 March 1981.
37. Private interview.
38. Private interview.
39. Interview, Lord Butler of Brockwell.
40. Private interview.
41. Peter Hennessy (1989), pp 635–36. Hugo Young (1989).
42. Margaret Thatcher (1993), p. 30.
43. Private interview.
44. Margaret Thatcher (1993), p. 47.
45. Private interview.
46. Private interview.
47. Interview with Kenneth Harris, *The Observer*, 25 April 1979.
48. Geoffrey Howe (1994), p. 147.
49. Peter Hennessy (1986).
50. *Sunday Times*, 24 May 1981.
51. Private interview.
52. Margaret Thatcher (1993), pp. 567–68.
53. Quoted in Ronald Millar (1993), p. 281.
54. Interview, Sir Timothy Lankester.
55. Private interview.
56. Anthony King (1985), p. 137.

7. Margaret Thatcher
1983–1990

1. Private interview.
2. Private interview.
3. Private interview.

4. Hugo Young (1989), p. 356.
   Interview, Lord Howe of Aberavon.
5. Private interview.
6. Interview, Lord Armstrong of Ilminster.
7. Interview, Lord Armstrong of Ilminster.
8. Ferdinand Mount, (1992), p. 138.
9. Private interview.
10. Kevin Theakston (1998), p. 212.
11. Private interview.
12. Private interview.
13. Private interview.
14. Private interview.
15. Private interview.
16. Interview, Sir Andrew Turnbull.
17. Interview, Sir Charles Powell.
18. Private interview.
19. Geoffrey Howe (1994), p. 538.
20. Private interview.
21. Private interview.
22. Private interview.
23. Private interview.
24. Margaret Thatcher (1993), p. 512.
25. Private interview.
26. Interview, Sir Charles Powell.
27. Percy Cradock (1997), p. 44.
28. Interview, Lord Howe of Aberavon.
29. Private interview.
30. Interview, Stephen Sherbourne.
31. Interview, Stephen Sherbourne.
32. Interview, Stephen Sherbourne.
33. Interview, John Whittingdale.
34. Noel Malcom (1989), pp 8–10.
35. Nigel Lawson (1992), p. 467.
36. Interview, Sir Charles Powell.
37. Interview, David Willetts.
38. Interview, Ferdinand Mount.
39. David Willetts (1987).
40. Private interview.
41. Interview, Robin Harris.
42. Private interview.
43. Margaret Thatcher (1993), pp 489–90.
44. Margaret Thatcher (1993), p. 713.
45. Margaret Thatcher (1993), pp 715–17.
46. Anthony Seldon (1997), p. 112
47. George Urban (1996).
48. Percy Cradock (1997), p. 207 and pp 111–12.
49. Alan Watkins (1991).
50. Interviews, Lord Wakeham, John Whittingdale.
51. Interview, Lord Wakeham.
52. Interview, Stephen Sherbourne, 30 June 1987.
53. Margaret Thatcher (1993), p. 565.
54. Interview, Stephen Sherbourne.
55. Interview, Robin Harris.
56. Nigel Lawson (1992), pp 488ff.
57. Private interview.
58. Private interview.
59. Nigel Lawson (1992), p. 937.
60. Margaret Thatcher (1993), pp 709–13. Interview, Sir Charles Powell.
61. Geoffrey Howe (1994), p. 395.
62. Private interview.
63. Interview, Lord Wakeham.
64. David Butler, Andrew Adonis and Tony Travers (1994).
65. Interview, Ferdinand Mount.
66. Interview, David Willetts.
67. Private interview.
68. Robert Armstrong (1994).
69. Private interview.
70. Kenneth Baker (1993), p. 320.
    Geoffrey Howe (1994), p. 473. Nigel Lawson (1992), pp 389 and 680.
71. Alistair McAlpine (1997), p. 261.
72. Alistair McAlpine (1997), p. 262.
73. Geoffrey Howe (1994), p. 473.
74. Francis Pym (1985), p. 34.
75. Nigel Lawson (1992), p. 680.
76. Private interview.
77. Interview, William Waldegrave.
78. Private interview.
79. Private interview.

8. John Major 1990–1997

1. Margaret Thatcher (1993), p. 717.
2. Private interview.
3. Dennis Kavanagh in Dennis Kavanagh and Anthony Seldon (1994).
4. Anthony Seldon (1997), p. 195.
5. Interview, John Major.
6. Interview, Jonathan Hill.
7. Private interview.
8. Anthony Seldon (1997), p. 197.
9. Anthony Seldon (1997), p. 814.
10. Interview, David Willetts.
11. Interview, William Waldegrave.
12. Sarah Hogg and Jonathan Hill (1995), p. 136.
13. Private interview.

14. Interview, Sir Rodric Braithwaite.
15. Anthony Seldon (1997), pp. 198–99.
16. On Major and the tabloids, see Kelvin McKenzie (1997).
17. Private interview.
18. Anthony Seldon (1997), p. 202.
19. Anthony Seldon (1997), p. 599.
20. Interview, Howell James.
21. Interview, Chris Patten.
22. Anthony Seldon (1997), p. 140.
23. Sarah Hogg and Jonathan Hill (1995), p. 85.
24. Sarah Hogg (1995).
25. Anthony Seldon (1997), p. 257.
26. David Butler and Dennis Kavanagh (1997), p. 41.
27. Interview, Norman Blackwell.
28. Private interview.
29. Private interview.
30. Interview, Sir Robin Butler.
31. Private interview.
32. N. Lamont (1999).
33. Interview, Jonathan Hill.
34. David Butler and Dennis Kavanagh (1997).
35. Private interview.
36. Anthony Seldon (1997), p. 381.
37. Anthony Seldon (1997), p. 171.
38. Private interview.
39. See Philip Stephens (1995).
40. Private interview.
41. Private interview.
42. Private interview.
43. See Neil Gavin and David Sanders (1997).
44. Anthony Seldon (1997), pp. 192, 193.
45. 'The Matrix of Power', Radio 4, 3 September 1998.
46. Philip Stephens (1995), p. 305.
47. Private interview.
48. Private interview.

9. Tony Blair – Preparations

1. On the 1997 general election, see David Butler and Dennis Kavanagh (1997), and Anthony King (1998).
2. For early biographies of Tony Blair, see John Sopel (1995), and John Rentoul (1995).
3. Richard Heffernan and Jeffrey Stanyer (1998). On Blair's associates, see Paul Anderson and Nita Mann (1997), Andy McSmith (1996) and John Rentoul (1996).
4. Private interview.
5. On Gordon Brown, see Paul Routledge (1997). On the debt, see John Lloyd (1999).
6. On Mandelson, see Paul Routledge (1999) and Donald MacIntyre (1999).
7. Philip Gould has written about his work under Kinnock and Blair in his *The Unfinished Revolution* (1998).
8. On this, see Nick Jones (1996).
9. Philip Gould (1998), p. 294.
10. David Butler and Dennis Kavanagh (1997), p. 63.
11. Richard Heffernan and Jeffrey Stanyer (1998), p. 173.

10. Tony Blair 1997–May 1999

1. Private interview, Blair adviser.
2. Private interview, Blair adviser.
3. Peter Mandelson and Roger Liddle (1996).
4. Report of the Working Group on the Government Information Service. Cabinet Office, November 1997.
5. Private interview, Number Ten official.
6. Private interview, Blair adviser.
7. Lord Cranborne, who as Conservative Leader in the Lords was negotiating with Labour over reform of the upper house, recalled a conversation with Blair about a proposal: 'I must ask Alastair, to see whether he approves and I can't really say yes or no until I've talked to him.' *Inside the Lords*, BBC2, 17 January, 1999. Blair has subsequently denied this interpretation placed on the remark. Private information.
8. Private interview, Number Ten official.
9. Kirsty Milne (1998).
10. Private interview, Blair adviser.
11. Private interview.
12. Private interview. Also see Richard Wilson (1998)
13. Paul Routledge (1998).

14. Nigel Lawson (1994), p. 273.
15. See Philip Norton (1998).
16. Samuel Kernell (1986) and Michael Foley (1993).
17. Peter Riddell (1998a) and (1998b).
18. Patrick Dunleavy *et al* (1995), Robert Borthwick (1995) and Richard Rose (1980).
19. Private interview, Blair adviser.
20. Private interview, Number Ten official.
21. Private interview.
22. Private interview.
23. Sarah Hogg and Jonathan Hill (1995).
24. Martin Burch (1999), p. 44.
25. Vernon Bogdanor (1997), Charles Powell (1997), and Ferdinand Mount (1992).
26. See below, Chapter 11.
27. Private interview.
28. Interview.
29. Interview.
30. Private interview.
31. Anthony King (1991).
32. For example, Peter Riddell (1999), Steve Richards (1999) and Hugo Young (1999).
33. Sue Cameron. 'Tony, be civil to the servants' *The Times* 9 July 1999.
34. Rachel Silvester 'How Blair's "secret burden" is bringing Labour to a halt'. *Independent on Sunday* 18 July 1999.
35. Peter Hennessy (1999).

11. Conclusion

1. Michael Wolff (1976).
2. Interview, Douglas Hurd, and Douglas Hurd (1976), p. 26.
3. Interview, John Hoskyns.
4. Private interview.
5. Private interview.
6. Private interview. Harris went on to work in Lady Thatcher's office and co-ordinate the writing of her memoirs.
7. Private interview.
8. Peter Riddell (1993).
9. But one account reports rivalry. See

'Bitter feuding among Labour's leading ladies gives Downing Street a headache', *The Sunday Telegraph*, 27 September 1998.
10. Private interview.
11. Private interview.
12. John Campbell (1983).
13. Bernard Donoughue (1987), Chapter 5.
14. Richard Rose and Philip Davies (1994).
15. Douglas Hurd (1979), Bernard Donoughue (1987), Joel Barnett (1982), Anthony Seldon (1997).
16. Interview, Stephen Sherbourne.
17. Ferdinand Mount (1992), p. 145.
18. Roderick Rhodes (1995), pp 5–6.
19. Roderick Rhodes (1997), p. 201.
20. Richard Rose (1980), p. 49.
21. *The Economist*, 3 December 1993.
22. Nigel Lawson (1992), p. 125, and (1994).
23. Lord Wakeham (1994).
24. Private interview.
25. Ferdinand Mount (1992), p. 138.
26. Ferdinand Mount (1992), p. 139. Also in Michael Dynes and David Walker (1996).
27. James Douglas, *Preparation for Government*, 29 November 1976.
28. Kenneth Berrill (1985).
29. Interview, Douglas Hurd, 5 April 1995.
30. Lord Hunt (1983).
31. Peter Hennessy (1996), p. 119.
32. Peter Jenkins (1987), p. 185.
33. Douglas Hurd (1979).
34. Patrick Weller (1983), (1987), Richard Rose and Ezra Suleiman (1980).
35. F. Muller-Rommel in Stephen Padgett (1994).
36. George Jones (1983).
37. Private interview.
38. Martin Burch and Ian Holliday (1999).
39. Charles Powell (1997).
40. 'Gentleman and Players', editorial, *The Times*, 27 November 1998.
41. George Jones (1976), p. 13.
42. Private interview.
43. Anthony Seldon (1999) pp. 30–33.

INDEX